Personal Financial Planning

Theory and Practice

Debbie Harrison

 **Prentice Hall**
FINANCIAL TIMES

An imprint of **Pearson Education**
Harlow, England • London • New York • Boston • San Francisco • Toronto • Sydney • Singapore • Hong Kong
Tokyo • Seoul • Taipei • New Delhi • Cape Town • Madrid • Mexico City • Amsterdam • Munich • Paris • Milan

Pearson Education Limited
Edinburgh Gate
Harlow
Essex CM20 2JE
England

and Associated Companies throughout the world

Visit us on the world wide web at:
www.pearsoned.co.uk

First published 2005

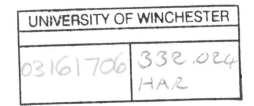

ISBN 978-0-273-68101-4

British Library Cataloguing-in-Publication Data
A catalogue record for this book is available from the British Library

Library of Congress Cataloging-in-Publication Data
A catalogue record for this book is available from the Library of Congress

10 9 8 7 6 5 4 3 2
09 08

Typeset in 10/13pt Sabon by 25
Printed by Ashford Colour Press Ltd, Gosport

Personal Financial Planning

Visit the *Personal Financial Planning* Companion
Website at **www.booksites.net/harrison_pfp** to find
valuable **student** learning material including:

- Learning objectives for each chapter
- Multiple choice questions to help test your learning
- Guide to preparing a financial plan
- Links to relevant sites on the web
- An online glossary to explain key terms

We work with leading authors to develop the strongest
educational materials in finance, bringing cutting-edge
thinking and best learning practice to a global market.

Under a range of well-known imprints, including
Financial Times Prentice Hall, we craft high-quality print
and electronic publications which help readers to
understand and apply their content, whether studying
or at work.

To find out more about the complete range of our
publishing, please visit us on the world wide web at:
www.pearsoned.co.uk

Contents

Preface   xv

How to use this book   xix

Acknowledgements   xxi

Part One: The social, economic and regulatory framework for financial planning   1

1 The principles of modern financial planning   3

What is personal financial planning?   4
Scope of study   5
Sources of information for research   5
Financial planning and financial advice   5
Financial planning as a multi-disciplinary profession   8
The individual's risk profile   8
Exhibit 1.1 A risk assessment kit   10
The financial plan   11
The client agreement   13
Exhibit 1.2 Summary of the key elements of a financial plan   13
Exhibit 1.3 Assessment of recommendations including timing,
implementation and reviews   14
Exhibit 1.4 A simple net worth statement   14
Exhibit 1.5 Crisis planning   15
Activity 1.1   16
Activity 1.2   16
Activity 1.3   16

2 The economic and regulatory environment   21

The historical context for personal financial planning   22
Background to the regulatory regime for financial services   26
The current regulatory regime   26
The Financial Ombudsman Service (FOS)   28

The Financial Services Compensation Scheme 29
Mis-selling 29
Exhibit 2.1 Financial fraud and boiler room share scams 31
Illegal activities 33
Consumer education 34
Activity 2.1 34

3 Market fundamentals 39
How bubbles burst and markets crash 40
Market cycles 41
How to read economic information 42
Economic indicators 44
Impact of the economy on companies and share prices 46
Activity 3.1 47
Activity 3.2 47

4 Asset classes and investment styles 49
Securities 50
The correlation coefficient 50
The FTSE International Indices 52
Alternative Investment Market 53
Companies ineligible for the All-Share 53
Shareholder activism 53
The main asset classes 54
Comparing equities, bonds and cash (deposits) 60
Investment styles 62
Activity 4.1 64

5 Asset allocation in portfolio construction 67
Coherent allocation at total portfolio level 68
Asset allocation studies 68
Asset class characteristics 69
Diversification overseas 69
Capital asset pricing model (CAPM) 70
Systematic and non-systematic risk 70
The deployment of active management fees 71
Efficient markets 71
'Star' managers 71
Reweighting a portfolio 72
Private investor indices 73
Activity 5.1 75

6 Performance measurement and monitoring   77

Measurements for performance   78
Portfolio measurement   78
Collective funds   79
Periods of measurement   80
Guide to reading the financial pages   81
Activity 6.1   87

Part Two: Putting the theory into practice   89

7 Protection insurance   91

Life assurance   92
Income protection   95
Critical illness   97
Waiver of premium for pension plans   97
Private medical insurance   97
Long-term care   100
Activity 7.1   102
Case study   103

8 Banking and debt   105

Banking   106
Debt   107
The annual percentage rate (APR)   110
Consumer protection   111
Debt consolidation   112
Consumer help organisations   112
Activity 8.1   113

9 Savings   115

Taxation   116
Deposit accounts   116
National Savings & Investments (NS&I)   117
Tax-exempt special savings accounts (TESSAs)   120
Cash individual savings accounts (ISAs)   121
Gilts and bonds   121
Index linked gilts   121
Guaranteed income bonds (GIBs)   122
Permanent income bearing shares (PIBs)   123

Stepped preference shares of split capital investment trusts 123
Purchased life annuities 123
Case study 125

10 Gilts and bonds 127

Bonds defined 128
Standard & Poor's credit ratings 128
Exhibit 10.1 What the credit letter ratings mean 129
Price fluctuations in traded gilts and bonds 130
Gilts 130
How to assess gilt and bond income 131
Exhibit 10.2 How gilt prices are shown in the *FT* 132
Index linked gilts 132
Corporate bonds 134
Activity 10.1 135

11 Equities 137

How shares are grouped 138
The FTSE UK Index Series 138
Classification by sector 139
Shareholder perks 140
New issues 140
What information will a company provide? 140
How to value shares 140
Key indicators in practice 141
Dividend cover 142
The price/earnings (P/E) ratio 142
Net asset value 142
Financial gearing 143
The acid test 143
Asset backing 143
The pre-tax profit margin 143
The return on capital 144
Making comparisons 144
Buying and selling 144
Higher risk investor strategies 144
Company share schemes 146
Activity 11.1 147
Activity 11.2 147

12 Collective funds 1 — 149

The four basic structures — 150
The costs — 150
Unit trusts and open-ended investment companies (OEICs) — 150
Investment trusts — 151
Taxation of unit and investment trusts — 153
Life insurance investment bonds — 153
Friendly society policies — 156
Offshore funds — 156
Selecting collective funds — 157
Open architecture — 157
Activity 12.1 — 158

13 Collective funds 2 — 161

With profits funds — 162
Exhibit 13.1 Key points on with profits — 164
Exhibit 13.2 The guaranteed annuity rate: an exercise in poor actuarial analysis — 165
Traded endowment policies (TEPs) — 166
Protected and 'guaranteed' funds — 168
Diversification and funds of funds — 170
Alternative investments — 170
Activity 13.1 — 174

14 Tax-efficient wrappers and administration platforms — 177

Tax-efficient wrappers — 178
Personal equity plans (PEPs) — 178
Individual savings accounts (ISAs) — 178
Wrap accounts — 181
Fund supermarkets — 181
Activity 14.1 — 181

15 Ethical investments, pensions and banking — 185

What does ethical investment involve? — 186
Ethical Investment Research Service (EIRIS) — 186
Exhibit 15.1 Defining an ethical policy — 187
Pension schemes — 188
Banks — 188
Islamic finance — 189

The impact of ethical screening on performance 189
Alternative investments 190
FTSE4Good 190
Activity 15.1 192

16 Tangible (alternative) assets 195

The regulation of tangible assets 196
Forestry 196
Wine 197
Theatre 199
Film financing 200
Gemstones 201
Antiques and fine art 201

17 Property 203

Buying the main family residence 204
Second homes 211
Residential homes overseas 212
Buy-to-let 212
Commercial property 214
Equity release 214
Activity 17.1 217
Activity 17.2 218
Case study 219

18 Lloyd's of London 221

Developments in the market 222
How Lloyd's works 222
Reform 223
Changes to the market 224
Investment opportunities 225

19 Taxation 229

Keep it legal 230
Personal tax allowances and exemptions 230
Income tax personal allowance 231
Capital gains tax 232
Inheritance tax planning 234
Domicile and residence 236
Charitable giving 237

Making a will   237
Self-assessment   239
Exhibit 19.1 Key self-assessment dates for the calendar year   241
Taxation and investing for children   241
Activity 19.1   242
Case study   244

20 Education fee planning   247

The importance of education fee planning   248
State school admissions   248
What does private education cost?   248
How to meet the costs   249
Entry requirements   250
Tertiary education   250
Changes for university students from 2004 to 2005   252
Exhibit 20.1 Department for Education and Skills timetable for
university fees application   253
Activity 20.1   253
Case study   255

21 State pensions   257

The framework for state pensions   258
Equal pension ages   258
National insurance contribution record   258
The 'married woman's stamp'   259
Eligibility for the basic state pension   259
Married couple's pension   260
The pension credit   260
BSP and occupational pension schemes   260
Additional pension (SERPS)   261
The State second pension (S2P)   262
Pension forecasts   262
Appeals   262

22 Defined benefit occupational pension schemes   265

The occupational pension scheme 'crisis'   266
The Pensions Act 2004   268
Pension tax 'simplification' in April 2006   269
Introduction to company pension schemes   270
Defined benefit (DB) explained   271

Contributions to company schemes pre-April 2006 272
The position of higher earners pre- and post-April 2006 277
Separate occupational schemes for executives 279
Special schemes for small family companies 279
Pensions and divorce 280
Activity 22.1 280
Case study 282

23 Defined contribution (DC) schemes and plans 285

DC explained 286
Contracted in money purchase schemes (CIMPS) 287
Stakeholder schemes 287
Contributions to stakeholders and personal pensions 288
Retirement annuities 289
Pensions for children and spouses 289
Contracting out of the state scheme 290
How to choose a personal pension 290
Options at retirement 291
Charges and terms for DC arrangements 291
Checklist for DC 292
The DC 'default' option 292
Exhibit 23.1 The automated asset allocation strategy for DC 294
Family protection benefits 294
Pension statements 294
Self-invested personal pensions (SIPPs) 295
New investment opportunities for DC from April 2006 296
Exhibit 23.2 Key features of tax simplification for DC 297
Activity 23.1 297
Activity 23.2 297

24 DC funds and the retirement income 299

Market developments 300
Basic retirement income objectives 300
Conventional annuities 301
Options for DC investors at retirement 302
Summary of DC choices at retirement 303
How conventional annuities work 304
A higher income for those with shorter life expectancy 306
Investment-linked annuities 308
Flexible annuities 310

Drawdown and phased retirement   310
Activity 24.1   313

25 Working and retiring abroad   315
Overseas assignments   316
Exhibit 25.1 Checklist for a successful overseas assignment 317
Retiring abroad   318

Appendices
Appendix 1: Glossary of terms   325
Appendix 2: A–Z of websites   347
Appendix 3: How to prepare a financial plan   351
Appendix 4: Financial planning case study   357

Bibliography   379

Index   381

Companion Website resources
Visit the Companion Website at **www.booksites.net/harrison_pfp**

For students
- Learning objectives for each chapter
- Multiple choice questions to help test your learning
- Guide to preparing a financial plan
- Links to relevant sites on the web
- An online glossary to explain key terms

For lecturers
- Complete, downloadable Instructor's Manual
- PowerPoint slides that can be downloaded and used as OHTs

Also: This website has a Syllabus and Profile Manager, online help, search functions, and email results functions.

Preface

Personal Financial Planning: Theory and Practice is the first dedicated discursive textbook for undergraduate students studying this important subject. It is quite distinct from the product-based UK regulatory guidebooks for practitioners and from the consumer guides to personal finance.

What sets this text apart is the interdisciplinary approach it takes to a subject that is regarded as an essential financial, social, and economic objective for the UK in the 21st century; namely that each individual should achieve financial independence and security throughout their working life, and should save sufficient funds to achieve financial independence and security throughout retirement.

If we were to identify two points in modern economic history when a seismic shift occurred in the balance between state, occupational and private provision of financial services and benefits we would select the late 1970s and the late 1990s. Since the late 1970s successive governments have sought to shift the burden of financial welfare from the state to the private sector. In the late 1990s serious faultlines began to appear in what had hitherto been regarded as rock solid employer-sponsored pension schemes. From this point onwards there was a marked trend away from the apparent security of Defined benefit (DB) pension schemes to Defined contribution (DC) schemes, and the consequential transfer of investment risk from the employer to the individual scheme member.

By the year 2000 the 'personal' in personal finance no longer relegated this field to a position secondary to state and occupational welfare provision. With the withdrawal of the state as the predominant provider of benefits, and the reduction in the security and value of occupational benefits, personal finance is positioned as one of the most important foundation stones for modern society and for social welfare as a whole.

The aim of the book is to help students achieve greater breadth and depth in their understanding of all aspects of personal finance, both from an academic and a practical perspective. With this in mind it combines technical detail with an analysis of the economic, social and regulatory environment in which financial planning, as a blend of services and products, is delivered in the first decade of the 21st century.

The discursive approach is important. Students should learn to question all source material for accuracy and partiality – whether this is from the media, policymakers, independent 'experts' or the websites of financial providers. While a great deal of the material in this book is derived from such sources, nevertheless it is recognised and acknowledged that each party has its own corner to fight and therefore will lend its particular bias to any arguments and conclusions offered. This is also true of government agencies, such as the Treasury, the Inland Revenue and the Department for Work and Pensions, which are not always united in their purposes and do not always achieve coherence in the way they draw up policy.

Against this background, the study of personal finance is far more than an exercise in learning tax rules, product descriptions and the contents of financial services legislation. Rather, the objective of this book is to help students develop an understanding of the changing needs of individuals within modern society, to identify trends and to develop a questioning outlook.

Following international corporate scandals such as Enron, WorldCom and Parmalat, we can no longer rely on major companies to provide a reliable return to shareholders, or to support the debt they issue. In the UK we can no longer rely on highly distinguished institutions to thrive simply because they are household names. When the Italian dairy foods group Parmalat collapsed in December 2003, it left creditors holding Euro 12.5bn in debt. In the UK Equitable Life – one of the world's oldest and most respected mutuals – stands as an example to policyholders as to what may happen when financial strength fails and when 'with profits' becomes 'with losses'.

The vulnerability of those relying on private sector pension schemes cannot be overstated. Before the Pension Protection Fund (PPF) was firmly in place (April 2005) – and it has proved its mettle – there was little to protect DB occupational pension scheme members where an employer becomes insolvent and the pension scheme is underfunded. As the members of the former steelworkers' pension scheme at Allied Steel and Wire (ASW) know to their cost, it is possible to pay into a pension scheme for 30 years and to end up with less than half of the promised benefits.

These types of problems are far ranging and complex. While there are no single solutions that meet the needs of individual beneficiaries, employers, the welfare system, the taxpayer and the shareholder, nevertheless students should be prepared to engage with these issues and be able to construct articulate arguments that suggest how a repetition of such events can be avoided in future. I hope this book, with its research-based approach to further learning, and the accompanying website will help students as they develop an understanding of the causes and the impact of financial crises and gain confidence in their ability to construct persuasive arguments, whether these support or oppose the status quo.

In particular the following groups will find this book and its approach to personal finance of interest and support in their studies:

- Undergraduate students aged 18–24 who are majoring in finance or incorporating a personal finance planning and investment module in their curriculum. These students need to develop an understanding of both the theory and practice set out in the book, and to expand their own sources of information, starting with the research recommendations provided here.
- Part-time undergraduates, aged 18+, some of whom will have experience in the financial services industry but who may lack awareness of current theory and practice and who may also benefit from a more discursive approach to modern financial planning.

- The academic course planner and lecturer, who may find this text and the supporting website at **www.booksites.net/harrison_pfp** a useful teaching aid.
- Postgraduates studying financial theory, who may also find that this book provides a useful summary of key issues and is a timely reference tool, particularly when used in conjunction with the source material and research recommendations.
- Those who work in financial services, who may benefit from stepping back from the day-to-day aspects of their work to reconsider the role of the financial planner in a more objective light.
- Policymakers, regulators and independent researchers, who may find that this book presents the most advanced approach to financial planning available at present, with its blend of academic discipline and practical knowledge.

It is hoped that students, lecturers, practitioners and policymakers will find that the interactive format, the comparatively relaxed style and the blend of academic and practical analysis combine to make this book a readily accessible resource. The purpose is to construct and maintain a clear vision of the contemporary role of financial planning, which is to help the individual to achieve life goals through the adoption of a pragmatic financial strategy.

In conclusion, I hope that by using this book the reader will gain a thorough grounding in financial planning and its role in modern society, and will enjoy the theory every bit as much as the practice.

Debbie Harrison

How to use this book

Financial planning is a highly integrated subject and therefore any attempt to separate and classify topics inevitably is subjective and at times artificial. Nevertheless, for the student it is helpful to take a thematic approach to help assimilate information in a logical way. The book, therefore, follows what I hope is a logical sequence. Part One starts with an examination of the meanings of personal financial planning, progresses through the economic, fiscal and regulatory environment, and provides an analysis of investment theory. Part Two examines practical subjects, such as protection insurance, savings and investment, property purchase and retirement planning.

Students who follow the sequence of the book and attempt the activities and review questions will find that this will support their course and also help develop transferable research and analytical skills. At the outset I would encourage the student to read Part One before progressing to the specific insurance and investment subjects examined in Part Two. This will ensure a good grounding in the fundamental issues and should help avoid the natural frustration that arises when we encounter a term or concept that has been discussed earlier. Having said that, if there are specific subjects on which the reader needs to focus immediately, then the style and format of the book should make it easy to dip in and out of the text, using the glossary as a guide to terminology and the index for cross-referencing.

It is difficult to find a style that will suit all readers at all levels, so I assume genuine interest but no formal qualifications in finance. Jargon is unavoidable for those who want to engage with financial planning theory but we explain terms clearly within the text as they arise, where they are highlighted, at the end of each chapter, and again in the glossary.

Integrated assessment material

Throughout the book there is a range of features designed to help students assimilate material and to prompt a questioning and critical approach. The roots of our financial services market can be traced back as far as the 17th and 18th centuries and anyone who has worked in the sector or who has been closely connected with it, no doubt will have observed that while tradition can have an important stabilising effect, yet it also goes hand-in-hand with a somewhat reactionary approach to change.

If students were hoping to pass a regulatory examination then it would be enough to learn facts and to be able to crunch numbers. The academic requirements of a university course demand much more than this and it is important to be able to articulate with confidence your own views on issues such as sales commissions vs. fees, the regulation of products vs. advice, the accountability of the management of companies that fall foul of mis-selling rules, consumer education and responsibility, to give just a few examples.

The Activities are designed to test your approach to different problems and to encourage private research, particularly using the Internet. Case study responses to these scenarios are not required but rather some reflection and group discussion on what issues you might address in a particular situation. This will help you in three important ways:

- To build up your knowledge within a structured framework.
- To enable you to discuss issues with confidence within the lecture and seminar groups.
- To act as revision prompts.

In addition there are detailed exercises, which are set out in several chapters. These will require a more thorough reading and the assimilation of information, and so should not be attempted in the early weeks of the course. Case study material and exam-style questions from a wide and varied range of sources is provided here. Lecturers should direct students to the most appropriate exercises for their course.

End-of-chapter assessment material

At the end of each chapter there are Review questions. These can be used to help you build up your own narrative response to verbal questions and as the subject of a debate. The aim of these questions is to help you consolidate and recall the important factual material you have just studied and to evaluate the key issues critically.

Companion Website material

Consult the **Companion Website** at **www.booksites.net/harrison_pfp** for multiple choice quizzes relating to each chapter. You will also find links to relevant websites of interest, and an online version of the glossary.

Throughout students are encouraged to engage with a wide range of material that will help them increase their knowledge and to develop a clear and critical approach to personal financial planning. I strongly recommend that all students read the *Financial Times* as a matter of course, as well as a selection of the personal finance pages in the weekend press. This will help you apply your growing theoretical knowledge to practical issues and current events, and will encourage a critical analysis of press coverage.

Acknowledgements

The publishers and the author would like to thank the university lecturers who reviewed the synopsis and draft manuscript. They would also like to thank the professional institutions and financial organisations that provided technical assistance and recommendations to ensure that the subject matter and methodology of the text reflects the best in current thinking and practice. These include the Association of British Insurers, Association of Private Client Investment Managers and Stockbrokers, Barclays Capital, Bloomsbury Financial Planning, The Bureaux, the Chartered Institute of Banking, the Chartered Insurance Institute (CII), the Debt Management Office, Deloitte & Touche, Distribution Technology Ltd, the Ethical Investment Research Service (EIRS), the Financial Services Authority, the *Financial Times*, FTSE International, Independent Research Services, the Institute of Chartered Accountants, the Institute of Financial Planning (IFP), the Institute of Financial Services (IFS), the Investment Management Association, the Law Society, Lloyd's of London, London International Financial Futures and Options Exchange (LIFFE), The London Stock Exchange (LSE), Mercer Human Resources, *Moneyfacts*, *Money Management*, the National Association of Pension Funds (NAPF), ProShare, Standard & Poor's, William Burrows Annuities and the WM Company.

Dictionary definitions are either compiled by the author or drawn from *Lamont's Glossary*, which is available as a book and online and is a valuable resource for all students of financial planning (**www.lamonts-glossary.co.uk**).

Publisher's acknowledgements

The publishers would like to express their gratitude to the following academics, as well as additional anonymous reviewers, who provided invaluable feedback on this book in the early stages of its development:

Bob Davidson, Glasgow Caledonian University
Rob Jones, University of Newcastle upon Tyne
James Mallon, Napier University
Gareth Myles, University of Exeter

We are grateful to the following for permission to reproduce copyright material:

Exhibits 1.2–1.4, Appendices 3 and 4 from Institute of Financial Planning's *Certified Planner Licence Syllabus and Tuition Manual*, 4th edition; Figures 3.1, 4.1 and

Tables 4.1 and 4.2 from *Barclays Capital Equity Gilt Study, 2004*; Table 5.1, 6.1 and 15.1 from the FTSE group, various sources; Figures 6.1, 6.2, 6.3, 6.4, 10.1 Cut-outs from share services page, © *Financial Times*, 2 April 2004; Case Studies 7.1, 9.1, 17.1, 19.1, 20.1, 22.1 from Financial Planner of the Year Awards 2003, FT Business, *Money Management*; Displayed calculation in Chapter 10 from *Gilts Market – Private Investor's Guide*, UK DMO; Figures 22.1–22.3 from the NAPF *Annual Survey Commentary*, www.napf.co.uk, National Association of Pension Funds.

The author would like to thank the following for kindly allowing her to refer to their material: Distribution Technology, for reference to the Dynamic Planner, a web-based financial tool, on the Bloomsbury Financial Planning website; Independent Research Services for material from the IRS *Alternative Investments Lesson* in Chapters 16 and 18; Lane Clark & Peacock for details about its DCisive 'lifestyle' model for DC schemes; Simon Philips for the section on intestacy in Chapter 19, from *The Deloitte & Touche Financial Planning for the Individual* (Gee Publishing, 2002).

Part One

The social, economic and regulatory framework for financial planning

Chapter 1 ●●●●

The principles of modern financial planning

Introduction

The logical starting point for a book about personal financial planning is an examination of the material and issues with which this discipline engages. This chapter, therefore, explores the functions of personal financial planning, considers how a financial plan might be constructed, and critically assesses what the plan sets out to achieve and how effective it is in meeting its objectives.

Objectives

When you have completed this chapter you should be able to:

- Provide a clear definition of the objectives of personal financial planning.
- Describe the objectives of the plan itself.
- Explain why planning should not be a transaction-driven process.
- Outline the information that is required for the plan.
- List the key individual assets and liabilities the plan should assimilate.

●●●● What is personal financial planning?

A simple definition of financial planning is as follows:

Financial planning is a service that helps individuals and families to achieve their personal objectives through the construction of an appropriate financial plan. The financial plan represents a journey from the point of departure – that is, where the individual is at present – to the desired goal.

The Institute of Financial Planning (IFP), which issues the annual Certified Financial Planner (CFP™) licence in the UK and overseas, provides a more detailed definition. For the IFP and its members, financial planning is the process that determines whether and how an individual can meet financial objectives through proper management of financial resources. The process would typically include, but is not limited to, the following six elements:

● Data gathering.
● Goal/objective setting.
● Identification of financial issues.
● Preparation of alternatives and recommendations.
● Implementation of decisions selected from the alternatives.
● Revision of the plan.

In practice a financial plan must always start with a thorough assessment of the individual's current circumstances before it can map out the steps that need to be taken to reach the desired targets or goals. Each goal has its own time horizon. For example a couple might make financial security in retirement their ultimate goal but along the journey they may also want to save for education fees for their children, and to pay off their mortgage and any other major debts.

Financial plans must be flexible because the overall objective is to meet the individual's *personal* objectives. Only after these are known can the individual's *financial* goals be set. This means that the goals should be drawn up to match personal ambitions, and not vice versa. So, 'I want to retire at age 60 and climb mountains' is a goal. 'I want to pay more into my pension plan' is not, although it may become one of the recommendations a planner makes in order to help the individual achieve their personal ambition.

Financial planning based on the model described is a very tough discipline and requires expertise and experience in equal measure. Personal information must be extrapolated together with realistic economic assumptions – for example about future earnings, investment growth and inflation. Given that leading lights in the fields of economics and econometrics constantly get these factors wrong, it is no mean feat for a financial planner to construct a pragmatic and workable plan that takes into account the vagaries of the economic climate and world stock markets, as well as the idiosyncratic demands of the individual.

Scope of study

Students of personal financial planning will need to study all the traditional financial subjects such as insurance, investment, taxation, trusts, mortgages, pension planning, the interaction between state and private benefits, and estate planning, among others. While engaging with theory and practice we must not abandon common sense, and so I do not recommend investing for investment's sake, insurance 'just to be on the safe side', or setting up trusts to avoid tax where the trust is more expensive than the tax saved. It is also important to keep in mind the need for flexibility. Higher earners, for example, may have tremendous scope to improve their pension arrangements but in certain cases the individual may prefer to invest a significant proportion of retirement capital outside of a tax-favoured Inland Revenue-approved scheme or plan, in order to avoid the restrictive rules on how approved pension funds can be used at retirement.

Sources of information for research

It is imperative to keep abreast of the rapid changes in the financial services market. In this book the student will encounter a wide range of sources for information and further research. We should always strive to develop a questioning approach to source material and be aware of any biases or limitations in books, journals, newspapers, and other areas of the media, such as television and the Internet. The media and the Internet can be both informative and misleading. Professional journalists can and do make mistakes, and it is impossible to tell from the printed page or screen whether the author is an expert or a jack of all trades who has been asked to provide a feature on a topic that fits between two advertisements for the products discussed. This is not intended to be cynical but rather to highlight the fact that journalism is a job like any other, and that media organisations have shareholders like any other commercial operation. A keen, critical approach to published material, therefore, is an essential weapon in the student's armoury.

Financial planning and financial advice

Before examining the component parts of financial planning in more detail, it is helpful to consider how personal financial services are delivered in the UK. This section provides a brief overview of financial planning and explains why it is different from traditional financial 'advice'. Chapter 2 explores the economic environment and the regulatory framework for financial planning services and products.

The term used to describe the very disparate range of sales staff, multi-tied advisers and independent advisers who sell financial services and products is **intermediaries**, that is, people and organisations that mediate between the providers of financial products and services, and the consumers who make the purchases. For our purposes the term 'intermediary' is not sufficiently specific and so it is important to understand the fundamental difference between the traditional approach to providing financial advice in the UK and financial planning. To stress this point it is helpful to take a rather simplistic approach, provided we understand that in practice these roles tend to blur. Most financial advisers sell insurance and investment products. Some do this very well. The big firms with sophisticated websites search out the best terms and prices in the market and use their negotiating power and economies of scale to the consumer's advantage. **Discount brokers** – advisers of this type who offer access to a vast range of **mutual (collective) funds** – are a good example. Financial planners frequently use these advisers where they have identified a financial product that will help implement a plan, and where they cannot compete on price and speed of service.

Certain firms of financial advisers are specialists, for example in the field of retirement annuities, disability insurance and long-term care. Again, planners that do not specialise in these areas may refer clients to a specialist to ensure they receive appropriate advice and make an informed choice, based on the full range of products and providers. Most firms of planners also use an external investment manager for clients who want to invest directly in equities.

The traditional adviser is not a specialist, however. The adviser you might find in the local high street is likely to cover the whole retail market for savings, investment, mortgages, health insurance and retirement planning, among other services. This breed of adviser is in decline and ultimately may become scarce – rather like the corner shop. For the modern 'general practitioner' of the financial world to survive it is necessary to concentrate on a core service and to form strategic alliances with specialists in order to provide a full service.

Remuneration

Remuneration is an important and thorny issue for financial services, and it is important for students to understand how the market works in order to appreciate why the basis for the adviser's remuneration *may* affect the range and quality of advice. Traditionally, most adviser remuneration has been transaction-based and therefore dependent on the sales commission from the product providers, rather than a direct fee from the client. This is still the most common method of remuneration. Where an individual invests a lump sum in a unit trust, for example, there would be an up-front or **initial commission**. On top of this there is an annual or **trail commission** paid from the first anniversary of the sale onwards until the investment is cashed in or transferred elsewhere. Commission is expressed as a percentage of the fund and herein lies an important aspect of the controversy, because this means that the level of remuneration is not linked to the time spent on a case but to the value of the transaction. It might take the same time to identify an appropriate fund for an individual with £50,000 to invest as it does for the individual with £5,000, yet the commission of, say, 5% of the transaction, will yield £2,500 in the former case and £250 in the latter.

Commission rates vary depending on the size of investment or insurance premium but they also depend on the term (number of years of duration) of the contract, where applicable. An investment in a unit trust or open-ended investment company (OEIC) has no predetermined term, whereas a pension contract may be linked to an assumed retirement date that will set the maximum term the contract is expected to be in force. Inevitably, these definitions are somewhat arbitrary as some unit trusts assume an investment period of at least five years and impose penalties if the capital is withdrawn earlier. Certain insurance company investments – insurance bonds, for example – also have a fixed period, as do many of the protected and structured products that base the return on the movement of one or more indices, or basket of shares over a specific term. While there may be legal or regulatory reasons for some product terms, in many of these cases the minimum term is dictated by the provider's desire to recoup costs and to make a profit before allowing the investor to withdraw without penalty.

As a rough guide, on a **single premium** or one-off payment to a pension or life assurance investment plan the sales commission will be 4%–6% of the capital paid. Traditionally insurance companies paid the bulk of the commission upfront and in this case for a 25-year **regular premium** plan, where the individual agrees to pay a certain amount each month, the commission could be worth about 70% of the value of the first year's contributions. In recent years, however, providers have moved to a single premium commission basis, so that each contribution attracts a smaller commission deduction. This avoids high early-termination penalties where an individual pulls out of a contract long before maturity.

Most financial planners charge a fee for their advice. It makes no difference to the fee-based planner if individuals buy 10 financial products or none at all, provided individuals are well placed to implement the plan and to achieve their goals. Where the provider of a product automatically incorporates a commission into the pricing (and many do), the commission can be offset against the fees. With investment products, wherever possible, planners tend to look for **commission-free** structures, as these are inherently 'cleaner' than products where there is an element of commission deduction built into the pricing. Where commission is built in they may ask for this to be reinvested in the plan.

The fee vs. commission debate is complex and the subject of heated debate. The 'old school' argues that life assurance and savings products in the mass market must be 'sold' because otherwise people would not buy these essential items. The same school of thought argues that individuals will not pay for advice, and therefore the cost of the sale has to be deducted from the investments or premiums. Opinion is changing as individuals recognise the need for financial security and the value of professional help. However, it has to be said that while fee-based advice sounds logical, at present the structure of retail investment funds and protection products is still designed for a commission-based distribution network and there seems little chance that we will move to a fee-basis in the mass market, certainly not in the short to medium term.

It is not the intention of this book to argue categorically that the only way to advise is on a fee basis. The important point, however, is that financial planning should separate the financial advice from the purchase of any products. This means that we construct the plan and only then examine which products, if any, may be required to implement it. Today's planner will operate on a time/cost platform so that all charges are set out clearly, whether these are met by fees, commission payments, or a mixture of the two.

Financial planning as a multi-disciplinary profession

The delivery of financial planning can be seen as multi-disciplinary – that is, it draws on a range of disciplines to create an appropriate approach to satisfying the individual's requirements. It is also practical. So, for example, where the planner realises that an individual will not be able to retire early based on the current pension and investments forecasts, the planner will explain this to the client and where it is not possible to increase pension contributions will suggest that the client continues to work on a part-time consultancy basis for a few years or moves to a cheaper house, for example.

Planners come from a wide variety of backgrounds. Those who hold the CFP™ licence, for example, can be found in accountancy, actuarial firms, banking, investment and the law, among other professions. In addition there are several trade associations and professional bodies for advisers that examine to a very high standard, including the Institute of Financial Services (the official brand name for the Chartered Institute of Banking), the Chartered Insurance Institute (CII) and the Pensions Management Institute (PMI). The professions are very active in financial planning; for example many chartered accountants and solicitors have a planning department and are authorised to offer investment advice and sell collective funds. Some offer full portfolio management, a service traditionally the preserve of the private client stockbroker. Private client stockbrokers and 'private wealth managers' – the contemporary term many firms prefer – also tend to offer a full financial planning service, so we can see how the boundaries between the different professions are blurring. Very large firms, for example the wealth management departments within major consultancies, would employ a full range of professionals, with the possible exception of stockbrokers.

The individual's risk profile

This section looks briefly at individual risk in relation to savings and investment. This will provide an introduction to the more detailed examination of these subjects in later chapters.

The technical definition of **risk**, in financial terms, is 'the standard deviation of the (arithmetic) average return'. For the private investor, however, risk has a range of less technical meanings and can be very subjective. Conventional theory suggests that the two chief risks for private investors are capital loss and inflation. These are certainly very valid but a more holistic financial planning approach considers risk in the context of not achieving an objective. For example the annual return of a private pension fund could be measured against an index, such as the FTSE All Share, and against similar funds, but first and foremost it should be measured against the return needed to achieve the desired retirement objective.

The reward for individuals who take investment risks is the **total return**, which is usually expressed as a percentage increase of the original investment taking account of both the income (yield) reinvested plus any capital growth (the rise in the market price). This may seem an obvious point but some of the more recent financial scandals have involved the sale of **structured products** that achieve the stated income *or* growth target but where the total return has been far less than the amount invested (see Chapter 13).

Inflation risk

Savings and investments that often expose the investor to inflation risk usually fall into the 'safe' category. For example, private investors tend to think of building society deposit accounts as risk free. If the intention is to avoid the loss of the original capital then, provided we stick with the well-regulated UK building societies and other deposit takers (including Internet accounts), money on deposit should certainly be safe from capital loss. The capital will not diminish but nor will it grow unless interest is reinvested. However, the growth will be modest and the **real return** (adjusted for inflation) may even be negative, depending on the relationship between prevailing rates of interest and inflation. This does not mean individuals should ignore deposit accounts. In practice they play a very important part in providing an easy access home for emergency funds and for short-term savings where capital security is the primary goal (see Chapter 9). Generally, however, over the medium to long term, deposit accounts are often synonymous with capital erosion.

Bonds, which are issued mainly by the government (**gilts**) and companies (**corporate bonds**), can offer the prospect of higher returns than a deposit account but with **corporate bond funds** there is a risk that the borrower may dip into the investor's capital in order to maintain the flow of income. Also, like deposits, conventional bonds do not offer any guaranteed protection against increases in inflation.

Capital risk

Historically, if we wanted to match or beat inflation over the long term we would have had to invest in equities. However, with equities, unless a fund offers a guarantee (and these can be costly – see Chapter 13), the individual's capital certainly is at risk.

Exhibit 1.1 A risk assessment kit

Chapter 5 looks at diversification within a portfolio in order to reduce risk at the total portfolio level. However, it is also important to be able to recognise the level of risk inherent in a financial product and this is not always apparent. Most of the major mis-selling scandals in the financial services markets are a result of naivety and misunderstanding on the part of investors, and the disingenuous desire to mislead on the part of providers and advisers.

The following benchmarks take a very broad-brush approach to investment, which provides a useful starting point to the assessment of an asset class, product or scheme. It does not matter whether we are examining deposit accounts, collective funds, direct equity and bond investments or higher risk investments such as venture capital trusts, which invest in the shares of unquoted trading companies – measuring risk against certain benchmarks helps to keep a good overall perspective.

The benchmarks will also help students to focus on the important fundamentals as opposed to the 'bells and whistles', which are used so successfully in marketing literature to make products and services look more attractive, safer, tax efficient or ethical than they really are.

- **Aims**: What are the stated aims and benefits of the investment? Do these fit in with the individual's aims and objectives?

- **Returns**: Compare the potential net returns of the investment with after-tax returns on very low-risk products such as high-interest deposit accounts, short-term conventional gilts and National Savings & Investment low-risk products. Is the potential out-performance of the investment really worth the additional risk?

- **Alternatives**: Which other investments share similar characteristics? Are they simpler, cheaper or less risky?

- **Investment period**: For how long can the individual genuinely afford to invest the money? Compare this with the stated **investment term** and then check how the charges undermine returns in the early years. Check for any exit penalties and remember that a 'loyalty bonus' on an insurance product usually acts as a penalty in disguise if the individual does not continue the investment for the required period.

- **Risk**: What is the risk that the investment will not achieve either its own stated aims or the individual's private objectives? What is the most he or she could lose? Is the capital and/or income stream at risk? What is the likely effect of inflation? How is the investment regulated? What happens if the firm/investment manager defaults?

- **Cost**: Look at the establishment costs and ongoing charges. Remember that high annual management charges on collective funds, particularly for long-term investments, will seriously undermine the return. With direct equity portfolios watch out for the high transaction charges and turnover costs associated with 'portfolio churning' (unnecessary and excessive buying and selling to increase transaction charges).

- **Tax:** The way the fund and the investor are taxed is important because it will affect the ultimate return. Check for income and capital gains tax implications and consider how these might change over the investment period; for example if the individual retires and moves from a higher to a basic rate of taxation. As a general rule never invest purely for the sake of obtaining tax relief; investments must be appropriate for the individual's circumstances and must be attractive with or without the tax breaks.

●●●● The financial plan

In Appendix 3 we provide the guidelines for a financial plan as set out by the Institute of Financial Planning (IFP), together with an examination-length case study in Appendix 4. This section considers the purpose of the plan and how this is constructed.

- Broadly speaking, a financial plan aims to consolidate in one place the individual's personal goals and aspirations and the ways in which these are to be financed.
- Its implementation should make the most effective use of the existing resources and should identify alternative ways to achieve the stated goals to provide the individual with choices and flexibility.
- It will consider personal objectives and ambitions, assess priorities and take into account the taxation implications of insurance, investment, pensions, inheritances and trusts.
- Key issues will include an examination of the best ways to build and protect the individual's capital and income to achieve the stated objectives.
- Equally important, the planning process will identify goals that are simply not achievable. This will alert the individual to the fact that it is necessary to adjust personal goals to a more appropriate level.

The task includes the following steps, which are covered in more detail in later chapters:

- A full fact find about the individual's financial circumstances, problems (health issues, elderly dependents, for example) and objectives.
- An assessment of individuals' risk profile; that is, how much investment risk they can comfortably tolerate over different periods of time. Note that there is usually a gap between individuals' apparent risk tolerance, based on personal circumstances and their private views.
- A financial statement analysis. Essentially this involves drawing up an individual balance sheet to set out clearly existing assets vs. liabilities (see below). The process can include the use of appropriate software to construct cash flow analysis and personal budgeting.
- The use of appropriate financial data to make realistic assumptions about inflation, future earnings, investment growth and mortality, among other factors, to develop the plan.
- The production of a written plan. This has two key functions. First it identifies the individual's objectives, priorities and, where applicable, time frames; and second it sets out how to implement the plan, making the most effective use of existing financial resources and new arrangements.
- A schedule for regular reviews of the plan plus additional reviews to meet the needs of lifestyle and lifecycle events; for example where one partner stops work to raise a family, where education fees commence and cease and where retirement is on the agenda.

'Assets' in the broadest sense may include any of the following:

- Earnings, less taxation. Some planners would place this elsewhere but where employment is stable, earnings can be seen to resemble a bondlike stream of income.
- Savings and investments.
- Property equity including the main home, second home(s), and property purchased and let to tenants ('buy-to-let'). The equity value of a property is defined as 'market value less mortgage'.
- Company share schemes.
- Occupational and private pensions.
- Tangible assets; for example works of art, antiques and classic cars. However, these should only be included in the balance sheet where the owner is prepared to part with them.

Liabilities cover a wide range of outgoings, including the following:

- Living expenses.
- Mortgages and other loans.
- Credit card debts.
- Education fees.
- Charitable giving.
- Any other items that require insurance and/or maintenance.

The plan will consider the best way to achieve the stated goals and will cover the following areas:

- Income from earnings, investments and regular gifts.
- **Cash flow planning**, with projections of net cash flow on an annual basis.
- **Debt management**, including mortgages.
- Taxation of the whole family.
- Investments, including a current and recommended asset allocation, and consideration of liquidity requirements (for example where there is a known capital sum required on a specific date in the future, or regular outgoings such as education fees).
- **Risk management** (insurances), covering **mortality** (life assurance) and **morbidity** (health-related insurances, including income protection).
- Retirement planning.
- Education fee planning.
- Special needs, including provision for a disabled child, the individual's parents' or own long-term care.
- Disposal of a business, where relevant.
- Estate planning, including wills and trusts.

The client agreement

Where the planner is a practitioner then a clearly worded client agreement provides a benchmark against which the individual can judge the planner's services. This should cover:

- The regulation of the planner under the Financial Services and Markets Act 2000.
- Which services this entitles the planner to carry out and the services it is not authorised to undertake; for example it may not be able to hold client money.
- Permission for the planner to act on the client's behalf to negotiate mortgages, loans, and overdrafts.
- The period of agreement and period of notice on both sides (usually a minimum of 30 days).
- The client's responsibility to provide the information the planner needs (for example to give appropriate advice the adviser needs information on existing investments and insurances).
- Access to the individual's other advisers; for example the accountant and solicitor.
- The client's right to veto any recommendations.
- A confidentiality clause.
- Details of how documents will be stored.
- Fee rates per hour and details of any due dates for regular fees.
- Details of VAT likely to be charged.
- Treatment of commissions if the planner acts on a fee basis; for example whether the firm reinvests this money or offsets it against fees.
- Treatment of complaints and disputes.

Exhibit 1.2 Summary of the key elements of a financial plan

The plan must include or take into account the following:

- It is based on 'hard' facts, such as age, earnings, health, investments; and 'soft' data such as attitudes, beliefs and values.

- The plan must be a clearly written, logical document that uses language appropriate to the individual.

- It must summarise the individual's needs, objectives and concerns including attitude to investment risk.

- It sets out a statement of the individual's goals and objectives.

- It identifies additional problems and issues, which must be identified and addressed.

- Any assumptions made must be stated and justified, including price inflation, earnings inflation, deposit interest rate, equity growth rates over 5–15 and 15+ years, annuity rates.

- Consideration must be given to the individual's assets and debts and this will be set out as a **net worth statement** (a personal balance sheet). This should include all assets with the ownership basis identified. Debt must be apportioned accurately.

- The inclusion of income tax calculations and review of tax position.

- Gross and net income and expenditure analysis, for example, as a cash flow or budget summary. Careful identification of shortfall or surplus income over expenditure. Liquidity and a cash reserve should be established.

- It should conclude with recommendations including timing, implementation and reviews.

Source: Based on the Institute of Financial Planning's *Certified Financial Planner™ Licence Syllabus and Tuition Manual, 4th edition*.

Exhibit 1.3 Assessment of recommendations including timing, implementation and reviews

On construction of a plan we must consider the following questions:

- Are recommendations made for each of the problems/concerns? Is each goal and objective identified?

- Are there clear explanations of how the proposed solution solves the problem? For example does an income replacement policy actually meet the income requirements?

- Is there a clear statement of required action, timing and responsibilities?

- Are review periods, updates, and actions stated?

- Do the solutions match the individual's investment risk profile?

- Is the ownership and method of arranging policies and assets clearly explained?

Source: Based on the Institute of Financial Planning's *Certified Financial Planner™ Licence Syllabus and Tuition Manual, 4th edition*.

Exhibit 1.4 A simple net worth statement

Readily realisable assets	**(£)**	
Bank account	8,000	
Building society account	160,000	
Other assets		
House	225,000	
Personal effects	25,000	
Quoted shares	7,500	
Liabilities	0	
Total readily realisable assets	168,000	(39%)
Total other assets	257,500	(61%)
Liabilities	0	
Total Net Assets	**425,500**	

Source: Based on the Institute of Financial Planning's *Certified Financial Planner™ Licence Syllabus and Tuition Manual, 4th edition*.

Exhibit 1.5 Crisis planning

Many investors pride themselves on planning well for the known events in life but, as Robert Burns tells us, 'the best laid schemes of mice and men gang aft agley'. If they do the individual will be in a state of shock and very vulnerable. At such times they may be too exhausted coping with a bereavement, an unexpected redundancy, an injury, or forced early retirement, for example, to be able to deal effectively with silver-tongued financial salespeople.

Life crises tend to trigger either total inactivity or ill-advised over-activity. The latter is potentially very dangerous, particularly as the individual may be anxious to hear comforting words and sympathetic advice. Despite the best endeavours of the chief regulator, the Financial Services Authority (FSA), there are still far too many advisers who can spot an inheritance, a redundancy cheque, or an insurance payment at 1,000 paces and who will try to get the vulnerable to invest it in unsuitable long-term products before you can say 'sales commission'. The regulators often catch up with such activities but it can take a long time to secure compensation. In 2004, for example, the Financial Services Compensation Scheme declared R.J. Temple in default, leaving the way open for hundreds of investors to make a claim for the mis-selling of pensions, 'precipice' bonds, and split capital investment trusts. The adviser – one of Britain's biggest firms – specialised in 'counselling' women who had suffered bereavement and who would therefore be in receipt of a life assurance lump sum.

When we face a crisis our thinking is clouded. But there is an even better reason for not investing: *good financial planning for the long term can only be achieved where both the current situation and future financial goals are known. At times of crisis only the current financial position can be assessed and therefore long-term planning should be avoided at this stage.* The planner, therefore, will focus on the immediate needs and revisit the case at regular intervals.

In cases of redundancy, for example, we must check the value of the company redundancy package and any other investments held and assess liquidity by dividing them into cash, easy access, notice accounts and so on. At this stage we would urge the individual to avoid drawing on long-term investments where there may be a penalty for early termination or where the value depends on stock market movement and timing. We can complete the current picture by calculating the level of net income the family requires. Once we have the full picture we might suggest a holding position for at least 6 to 12 months, find the best deposit rates and, where appropriate, take advantage of annually limited tax and investment allowances such as Individual savings accounts (ISAs). We would warn against splashing out on a world cruise, an expensive car and other 'feel good' spends.

Pension choices for the redundant are surprisingly simple: do nothing in the short term unless it is absolutely necessary. Under normal circumstances the individual should not transfer to a personal pension plan because it will cost money and will involve the loss of valuable guarantees. Depending on age, the individual should line up the next career move or retirement plans before making any decisions.

In another example, where a husband dies and the wife has not kept a close eye on the family's finances, the planner must make sure the widow receives all of her entitlements. With a letter of authority from the widow the planner can check through all the insurance policies. Any lump sums can be placed on deposit for the time being until she has decided on her new objectives. Immediate cash flow and liquidity are of particular importance. We must check the widow's financial commitments – for example if there are any education fees that must be met out of income and capital. While making provision for these bills we should also recommend that she rewrite her will and that she should take out appropriate insurance, if necessary, to ensure that the children's needs are covered. We would suggest to her that she avoids making any big financial decisions for at least six months and preferably a year.

10-point crisis plan

- Stick to short-term financial planning and put any lump sums on deposit.

- Avoid any big decisions like moving house or starting a new business.

- Check state and company benefits – particularly if any new ones apply due to long-term sickness or unemployment, for example.

- Check all insurance policies to see if any will pay out in the circumstances.

- Make any necessary adjustments to the family protection policies.

- Check to see if it is necessary to rewrite a will.

- In the case of redundancy, leave the pension with the former employer if possible – at least until a decision is made on the next job move or early retirement.

- Take stock of all savings and investments plans but don't be pressured into making premature investment decisions with any new lump sums.

- Ensure adequate liquidity for any unforeseen events.

- Make sure there is a sufficient amount in an easy access account to cover important existing outgoings such as education fees, the mortgage and so on.

Activity 1.1

Buy a range of national weekend newspapers (broadsheet and tabloid) and draw up a list of topics covered. Determine which features relate to an event in the preceding week – for example a rise in base rates, the closure of a major firm of advisers, the publication of a consultation document that affects financial services. Consider the following questions:

- How do different papers approach the subject and make it relevant to their readers?

- Can you detect bias or imbalance in the arguments? Discuss.

- How helpful would you say the articles are in informing readers of important events and their rights? How would you improve coverage?

Activity 1.2

Anna Brown is 50 and has just lost her husband Dennis, who used to look after the family's finances. What would be your initial concerns and how would you help Anna construct an appropriate financial plan?

Activity 1.3

Alan Brandon is 45 and has just been made redundant. What would be your initial concerns? Alan has a substantial company pension benefit with a major plc. He says he wants to transfer this fund to a private pension plan, where he would be able to run the investments himself. What do you think of this idea?

Summary

This chapter covered a lot of ground. It considered the objectives of financial planning and how these must take account of the individual's own goals and circumstances. Briefly it also looked at risk, as the understanding of personal risk and the management of this risk is central to financial planning.

Key terms

- Cash flow planning p. 12
- Commission: initial and trail p. 6
- Commission-free p. 7
- Corporate bonds p. 9
- Corporate bond funds p. 9
- Debt management p. 6
- Discount broker p. 6
- Gilts p. 9
- Intermediary p. 5
- Investment term p. 10
- Morbidity p. 12

- Mortality p. 12
- Mutual (collective) funds p. 6
- Net worth statement p. 13
- Real return p. 9
- Regular premium p. 7
- Risk, inflation risk, capital risk p. 8
- Risk management p. 12
- Single premium p. 7
- Structured products p. 9
- Total return p. 9

Review questions

1 Why is financial planning different from the traditional approach to selling insurance and investment?

2 Give an example to show the difference between a personal goal and a financial goal and explain why the personal goal must come first.

3 List some of the key personal assets and liabilities.

4 List three hard facts and three soft data that you would accommodate in the plan.

5 Explain what we mean by risk.

6 How does a life crisis, like bereavement or redundancy, change the nature of a financial plan?

Go to the Companion Website at **www.booksites.net/harrison_pfp** for a multiple-choice quiz to test your understanding of this chapter.

Further information

Appendix 3 has a sample questionnaire that forms part of the Institute of Financial Planning's *Certified Financial Planner™ Licence Syllabus and Tuition Manual, 4th edition.* An increasing number of financial planners and advisers are setting up online fact finds, which allow you to crunch numbers for yourself to help you spot areas that need attention. A good example of this is the Dynamic Planner at Bloomsbury Financial Planning: **www.bloomsburyfp.co.uk**. The Dynamic Planner is designed by Distribution Technology Ltd (**www.distribution-technology.com**).

Below are the main websites for information about financial planning:

Regulation

The Financial Services Authority (FSA) explains how the regulation of advice works and provides links to useful websites: **www.fsa.gov.uk**.

Examining bodies

The Chartered Insurance Institute is one of the main examining bodies in the financial services market. Associateship (ACII) is its highest qualification: **www.cii.co.uk**.

The Institute of Financial Planning (IFP) is the training and examining body for the Certified Financial Planner Licence (CFP™) in the UK. Its highest qualification is Fellow (FIFP): **www.financialplanning.org.uk**.

The Institute of Financial Services is the brand of the Chartered Institute of Banking (CIB) and is a major examiner in this sector: **www.ifslearning.com**.

The Society of Financial Advisers is the financial services arm of the Chartered Insurance Institute. Its highest level is Fellow (FSFA): **www.sofa.org**.

The UK Society of Investment Professionals oversees the Investment Management Certificate, which is the benchmark examination for individuals engaged in discretionary or advisory investment management: **www.uksip.org**.

Professional bodies

The Chartered Institute of Banking: **www.ifslearning.com**

The Institute of Actuaries: **www.actuaries.org.uk**

The Institute of Chartered Accountants for England and Wales: **www.icaew.co.uk**

The Law Society: **www.solicitors-online.com**

The Pensions Management Institute: **www.pensions-pmi.org.uk**

Trade and professional associations

There is a wide range of trade organisations that promote their members' interests. Students should visit these websites to gain a perspective on the complexity of the distribution of financial advice in the UK and also to form opinions on the vested interests at work:

The Association of British Insurers: **www.abi.org.uk**

The Association of Consulting Actuaries: **www.aca.org.uk**

The Association of Pension Lawyers: **www.apl.org.uk**

The Association of Private Client Investment Managers and Stockbrokers: **www.apcims.co.uk**

The Association of Solicitor Investment Managers: **www.asim.org.uk**

The National Association of Pension Funds (NAPF): **www.napf.co.uk**

Solicitors for Independent Financial Advice: **www.solicitor-ifa.co.uk**

Financial adviser websites

IFA Promotions runs a website for fee- and commission-based advisers. It is a non-profit organisation sponsored by a wide number of product providers: **www.unbiased.co.uk**.

The Association of Independent Financial Advisers (AIFA) is the independent advisers' trade body: **www.aifa.net**.

Chapter 2 ●●●●

The economic and regulatory environment

Introduction

This chapter provides an introduction to the economic and regulatory environment in which financial planning is delivered today, beginning with an overview of historical trends in welfare and the changes in the balance between state, occupational and private provision; this is followed by an analysis of the current regulation of financial services.

Objectives

When you have completed this chapter you should be able to:

- Refer to important demographic changes that indicate why it is crucial that individuals take responsibility for their own financial well-being.
- Provide examples of how the political and social environment has changed to discourage dependency on state benefits and encourage private provision.
- Explain how financial advice is regulated under the 'depolarisation' regime introduced in 2004.
- Describe the role of the Financial Services Authority.
- Explain how the Financial Ombudsman Service and the Financial Services Compensation Scheme work and interrelate.

●●●● The historical context for personal financial planning

To understand the critical importance of personal financial planning we need to consider briefly the historical, social and political context in which the discipline developed in the second half of the 20th century. The most relevant starting point is the establishment of a formal structure for the delivery of state welfare in the early 1940s under the Beveridge system, which was introduced in response to welfare problems highlighted by the post-World War II period. From that time to the present day, demographic and economic trends have led to significant changes in the accumulation of taxes and **National insurance contributions (NICs)**, and the distribution of social security benefits.

The post-war climate was one of social and industrial reconstruction in which the new welfare state, based on the Beveridge Plan of 1942, provided a vehicle for the delivery of what were perceived as essential benefits. Until the mid-1970s, welfare provision as a state-run collectivist regime progressed along a near-linear trajectory. However, in 1976 the then Labour prime minister, James Callaghan, made an historic speech in which he told the Labour Party Conference that governments could no longer be expected to spend their way out of recession and that welfare must respect government budgets.

The resulting retreat from the so-called 'cradle-to-grave' welfare state was continued in a vigorous fashion by the long Conservative and largely Thatcher-dominated government from 1979 to 1997, which sought to reverse the role of the state in welfare distribution and drive provision into the private sector. This trend has continued through the more recent Labour government of 1997 to the time of writing, and has embraced private funding for further education as part of the shift away from state provision. It is interesting, therefore, to consider the extent to which Conservative and Labour Party ideology converges on key social welfare policy.

Welfare and National Insurance myths

There are many myths and misconceptions about the early welfare state, the most significant being that it provided for an individual's needs from cradle to grave. While citizens may have viewed the welfare state in this way at the time, we should avoid an anachronistic interpretation of public opinion from the period 1940–1970. Since then our definitions of 'essential' have changed significantly. In the 1940s the essential benefits represented what today we would regard as little more than a subsistence level of income. This was designed to protect the chief (usually the only) breadwinner – who was assumed to be male – and his family in the event of the cessation of earned income. While able to work the breadwinner would pay National insurance contributions (NICs), which would entitle him and his family to claim benefits in the event of his illness, retirement or death. It was a comparatively simple model but nevertheless remains highly relevant as the starting point for financial planning today.

The second myth is that there is a 'National Insurance Fund' that builds up a reserve out of which all future payments can be met, irrespective of the balance between the number of people in the labour market and the number drawing benefits. In practice, state benefits in the UK – as in most developed and many developing countries – are delivered on a **pay-as-you-go (PAYG)** basis, whereby the NICs of those in employment are used to pay the benefits for those who are not. It has been many years since NICs covered the entire social security bill in full and in practice the government relies on a subsidy from the Treasury (ie taxes) to support the state's liabilities to claimants. It is also fair to argue that the bill for benefits is far less than potential claims would indicate due to low take-up of **means-tested benefits** (see Figure 2.1 and Table 2.1). Certainly, whatever the government's intention, the use of means testing reduces the benefits bill compared to what it would be if we had a system of **universal benefits**, which were in part reclaimed through the taxation system.

Sadly, the group that suffers most under the means-testing system are the over-70s, since many in this thrifty generation regard benefits as a form of charity rather than a right and will not put themselves in the role of supplicant. The sheer complexity of the claims mechanism is also thought to deter potential beneficiaries of all ages. Evidence for this argument is available from independent sources. For example in 2002 the charity Age Concern said that over £1bn in means-tested benefits went unclaimed because the system was too complicated.

Labour market and demographic statistics

The post-war model for welfare was launched on a platform of near-full employ-ment and comparatively low life expectancy. In the UK boys and girls born in 2002 could expect to live to 76 and 81 years of age respectively. This contrasts with the turn of the last century where boys born in 1901 could expect to live to 45, while girls could

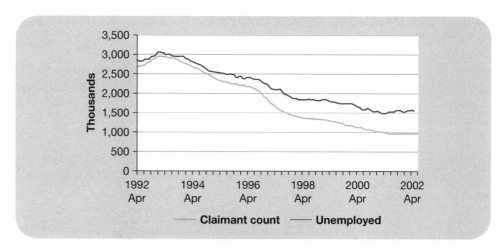

Figure 2.1 The unemployment and the claimant count
Source: Office for National Statistics.

Table 2.1 How well do means-tested benefits deliver?

In February 2004 the Department for Work and Pensions (DWP) issued the following figures, based on the 2001–2002 tax year:

- Income support: 350,000 people missing out on up to £880m.
- Minimum income guarantee*: 870,000 missing out on up to £1.26bn.
- Housing benefit: 680,000 missing out on up to £1.23bn.
- Council tax benefit: 2.43m missing out on up to £1.06bn.
- Jobseeker's allowance: 600,000 missing out on up to £1.44bn.

Note: The minimum income guarantee has been replaced with the pensions tax credit.
Source: *Financial Times*, 27 February 2004.

expect to live to 49. Over more recent years, the increase in life expectancy among older adults has been particularly dramatic. Between 1970 and 2002 in England and Wales, life expectancy at age 65 increased by 4 years for men and 3 years for women. By 2002, men who were aged 65 could expect to live to the age of 81, while women could expect to live to the age of 84. The latest (2002-based) projections from the Office for National Statistics suggest that these expectations will increase by a further 3 years by 2021 (see Figure 2.2). Despite these substantial increases in longevity, the age of retirement has generally fallen – adding considerably to the imbalance between workers and pensioners. At the turn of the century just over 50% of men aged 55–64 were active in the labour market. This figure from the Organisation of Economic Cooperation and Development Labour Force Statistics (OECD) will not include those in receipt of undeclared income.

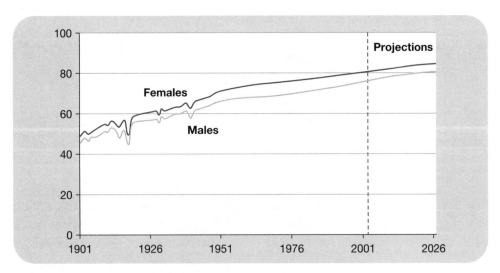

Figure 2.2 Life expectancy from 1900 to the present day
Source: Government Actuary's Department.

Table 2.2 Changing demographic patterns

Age structure (65 or older, %)

	1960	2000
Italy	9.0	17.1
Japan	5.7	17.3
Germany	10.8	17.2
France	11.6	16.1
UK	11.7	15.6
US	9.2	12.6
Canada	7.6	12.5

Source: OECD/*Financial Times*.

Even allowing for discrepancies in the assessment of the numbers in work, we can see that the UK, like most of the developed economies, has an ageing population – that is, the number of people in retirement is rising more rapidly than the number of people in employment (see Table 2.2). As a result, one of the most pressing issues for the government and for society as a whole is how to achieve individual financial security through private investments and insurances, and to reduce the reliance on state benefits, which can no longer be delivered in full through the NI and taxation system.

Retirement and disability pensions

It is helpful to consider a few examples of how the state benefit system can be manipulated to reduce the welfare bill. In April 1995 the government changed the definition of qualifying disability for long-term sickness from 'can't do own job' to 'can't do *any* job' – an extremely effective way of reducing the bill for short- and long-term sickness benefits.

With regard to the state pension, while the government has taken steps to ensure a minimum guaranteed income through the basic state pension and means tested top-ups, the right to an earnings related pension has been eroded with the closure of the **State earnings related pension scheme (SERPS)** in April 2002. Even before SERPS was replaced with the less valuable **State second pension** (S2P) its value had been reduced from a maximum of 25% of the best 20 years' earnings to 20% of earnings averaged over the entire working life. Widows' benefits have also been cut. In October 2002 the government cut the maximum amount of SERPS that a widow or widower could inherit from 100% to 50%.

Education is still delivered through the state system and is funded by taxation. This makes primary and secondary education free at the point of delivery, although an increasing number of parents are choosing to send their children to private schools. Tertiary education, however, has become much more expensive in recent years for every family. The withdrawal of university grants in the 1998–1999 academic year resulted in saddling most students with at least £10,000 of debt after a three-year course. Top-up fees, if introduced, will increase this debt substantially.

This is a brief highlight of important changes that will be examined in more detail in the relevant chapters, but which in aggregate demonstrate why individual private protection insurances, education fee planning and retirement planning, among other elements, are so important.

Background to the regulatory regime for financial services

Personal financial planning cannot be studied in isolation. Rather it is part of a dynamic process that is closely involved with the regulation and distribution of services and products within the UK. It is inevitable, therefore, that the study of financial planning will take a commercial tilt.

Historical perspective

As students of financial planning we should apply a clear and critical approach to any discussion of regulation. Investor protection is a vital platform for a well-regulated private sector financial services market but its success depends on a proficient and proactive regulatory regime. The system in the UK is far from perfect, as can be seen by the major mis-selling scandals that have riddled the system since it was introduced in the mid-1980s: personal pensions, home income plans, endowment mortgages, split capital investment trusts and precipice bonds have cost the industry billions of pounds in investigations and compensation.

The original Financial Services Act (1986), from which the current system stems, established a series of **self-regulatory organisations (SROs)** for different types of financial institutions and firms under the overall supervision of the Securities and Investments Board (SIB). **Self-regulation**, where the industry was responsible for regulating its own, was always open to criticism. When investors and the government realised that the major perpetrators of mis-selling personal pensions, for example, were the most powerful and influential institutions under the self-regulatory system, it became apparent that it was irreparably compromised.

Self-regulation was replaced in 1997 with statutory independent regulation and in 1998 the government merged banking supervision (previously the remit of the Bank of England) and investment services regulation under the SIB. The SIB formally changed its name to the Financial Services Authority (FSA) in October 1997. More recently the FSA has taken over responsibility for Lloyd's Insurance Market and the supervision of deposit takers, general insurance, and mortgages, among other activities.

The current regulatory regime

The FSA is an independent non-governmental body that was granted statutory power by the Financial Services and Markets Act 2000. When the Act came into force in December 2001, the FSA became the single regulator for financial services in the UK. The FSA board, appointed by the Treasury, consists of a chairman, a chief executive officer, two managing directors, and 11 non-executive directors, including the deputy chairman. The board sets overall policy, but day-to-day decisions and management of staff fall within the remit of the executive. There is also a Consumer Panel that includes representatives of consumer organisations.

The FSA's Investment Firms Division regulates about 7,000 investment organisations ranging from global operations, investment banks, major UK stockbrokers and networks of financial advisers to individual financial advisers. It also directly regulates many professional firms, such as lawyers and accountants, where the firms offer mainstream investment business. Other professional firms that do not provide specific investment advice may be regulated by their **Designated professional body**; for example the Law Society for solicitors and the Institute of Actuaries for actuarial consultants. The FSA is also responsible for supervising exchanges, such as The London Stock Exchange, Lloyd's Insurance Market, recognised overseas investment exchanges, and market infrastructure providers, such as Recognised clearing houses.

Polarisation and depolarisation

Before **depolarisation**, which was expected to come into force in the last quarter of 2004, there were more than 27,000 independent financial advisers (IFAs) in the UK, several thousand more professional advisers (accountants and solicitors who give investment advice, for example) and a further 70,000 company representatives who worked for financial institutions. Under the Financial Services and Markets Act 2000 it is a criminal offence to give investment advice without being authorised.

Not everything sold as an investment has to be authorised. Most regulated investments are **non-tangible assets** like shares, gilts, bonds and collective funds. Physical or **tangible** assets sold directly rather than through a collective fund – gold coins, rare stamps, antiques, vintage cars and wines, for example – are not covered by the Act or the compensation scheme.

Under the FSA rules, advisers must demonstrate a minimum level of competence (the **Financial Planning Certificate** is considered as equivalent to an AS level) and that they are financially sound and honest. Until late in 2004 the system of regulation demanded that advisers were either **tied**, in that they would only sell the products of one company, or **independent**, where they would be in a position to choose products from across the entire market. This system was known as polarisation. Frankly, it was never well understood by consumers, many of whom would still regard their local bank branch as a source of independent advice, long after the bank had become a representative of an insurance company for insurance and investment products. Whether people will understand depolarisation is a moot point.

Under depolarisation advisers are able to become multi-tied and offer products from a range of providers. Adviser, in this context, includes the banks and building societies. Firms that want to call themselves independent must be able to advise across the whole market and must allow clients to pay for advice through fees, where this is required.

The overriding objective of depolarisation, according to the FSA, is to help individuals understand what they are paying for and how much it costs.

At the time of writing it was too early to gauge the impact of depolarisation but we can expect to see an increasing concentration of the mass-market product distribution in the hands of a few major banks, building societies and networks of advisers, squeezing out the smaller independent firms. The major fund supermarkets and discount brokers are likely to survive while they can maintain a substantial market share of business and competitive prices. **Execution-only** on-line services are likely to flourish but these do not offer any advice. At the top end of the market a smaller number of financial planners and specialist wealth managers will cater to the fee-paying wealthier consumer.

The Financial Ombudsman Service (FOS)

The Financial Ombudsman Service (FOS) is the body that resolves disputes between consumers and regulated companies. It cannot intervene if the firm against which the complaint is brought is not authorised. The service is free to consumers and does not preclude the consumer from taking the case to court. However, if the consumer accepts the decision it is binding on both the individual and the firm. The remit of the FOS covers:

- Banking services.
- Credit cards.
- Financial and investment advice.
- Insurance policies.
- Life assurance.
- Mortgages.
- Personal pension plans.
- Savings plans and accounts.
- Stocks and shares.
- Unit trusts.

Making a complaint to the FOS

Where an individual believes they were mis-sold a financial product covered by the Financial Services Authority it is important in the first instance to approach the firm or company that sold the product. If the company has gone out of business then the individual can go to the Financial Services Compensation Scheme (see below).

All regulated companies are required to have in place a complaints procedure and to tell you how to use it. If the response is unsatisfactory then the individual should go to the Financial Ombudsman Service. Time limits apply and generally you have to complain to the ombudsman within six months of receiving the final response from the firm to which you have complained. The FSA publishes a useful guide to making a complaint, available on its website. For occupational pension schemes the service to

approach is the Pensions Advisory Service. In difficult cases the service may refer cases
to the Pensions Ombudsman.

The Financial Services Compensation Scheme

Among other points, the FSA insists that advisers have **professional indemnity
insurance (PI)**, which covers compensation claims against the firm. However, if a firm
has gone into liquidation or is in financial difficulties and cannot meet a claim, the
Financial Services Compensation Scheme (FSCS) can investigate and pay compensation.
As with the FOS, the FCSC only covers business carried out by firms regulated by the
Financial Services Authority. The scheme covers deposits, investments and insurance.
However, there may be monetary limits on the compensation depending on the type of
organisation in default. These distinctions can be confusing – for example a with profits
endowment policy is classed as long-term insurance because it has an element of life
assurance. In this case there is no maximum ceiling on compensation, whereas there is a
ceiling on pure investments such as unit trusts. Examples of compensation available are:

- Deposits takers: maximum of £31,700 per person (based on the formula 100% of
  the first £2,000 and 90% of the next £33,000).
- Investment firms: maximum of £48,000 per person (based on the formula 100%
  of the first £30,000 and 90% of the next £20,000).
- Insurance firms: the first £2,000 of the insurance claim or the insurance policy is
  covered in full. After this the scheme will pay 90% of the balance. Compulsory
  insurance is covered in full. Annuitants would receive 90% of the value of their
  guaranteed income, although for investment-linked annuities, for example, an
  actuarial valuation would be necessary to determine the amount.

The FSCS has a default database on its website, where consumers can see if a firm
they have dealt with has been declared in **default** – that is, not able to pay claims,
usually because it has stopped trading or is insolvent.

Mis-selling

Surprisingly, the term **mis-selling** does not appear in the FSA's rulebook but it is used
to refer to an advised sale that does not meet the FSA's standards. This is a regulatory
offence and the FSA has statutory powers to investigate and impose fines. To date the
most common problem has been where a product involved a much higher level of risk
than the consumer realised, or where the product was sold with reassurances and
guarantees that it was not designed to meet. Classic examples include:

- **Endowment mortgages:** These are combined life assurance and investment
  products that aim to provide a capital sum to repay the loan by the end of the
  mortgage term or on the death of the borrower (see page 162). The 'with profits'

endowment dominated the mortgage repayment market during the 1980s and 1990s, with some 10 million policies sold during this period. One of the big selling features of endowments in the 1970s and early 1980s was life assurance premium relief (LAPR). This was abolished for new endowments taken out after March 1984. By 2004 the insurance trade body the Association of British Insurers (ABI) estimated that 70% of these policies would fail to meet their target, forcing millions of homeowners to find other sources of capital to repay their mortgages in full. At the time of writing over £1bn had been paid in compensation. The point we must remember about endowments is that they are not guaranteed products; that is, they have no mechanism to guarantee that the investment will repay a specific sum by a specific date. A common problem in the 1990s was where advisers selling endowments looked at past performance figures from the equity bull market and assumed similar returns would continue in the future. Instead, the end of the 20th century and the first years of the 21st were marked by a long bear market and considerable market volatility.

- **Split capital investment trusts**: These were widely sold in the 1980s and 1990s as very low risk investments. The 'split' refers to the fact that this special type of investment trust has different types of shares – typically two: one providing income, and one providing a predetermined sum after a specific period (see p. 152). Collusion between the so-called 'magic circle' of split capital investment trust managers led to inter-company trading and holdings, maintaining an artificially high price and an incestuous asset allocation. In many cases these trusts were highly geared – that is, they had a high proportion of debt to equity. At the turn of the century the bubble burst when markets fell and trusts were unable to service the high level of bank debt. They were forced to cut dividends and as share prices collapsed it had a knock-on effect for all trusts in the magic circle. At the time of writing 23 trusts out of 140 in the split cap sector had collapsed, resulting in heavy losses to private investors.

- **Personal pensions**: In the late 1980s and early 1990s thousands of employees were persuaded to transfer out of occupational pension schemes, where the pension was linked to salary, to personal pensions, where the pension was linked to stockmarket returns. At the time of writing the bill for compensation for personal pensions and 'top-up' plans, known as free-standing voluntary contributions, was about £14bn.

Other products that have caused concern include:

- **Income drawdown**: Instead of buying an annuity at retirement it is possible to leave the personal pension fund invested and to draw an income directly. For the wealthy with several sources of retirement income this can be beneficial, particularly from the point of view of estate planning. However, losses can be heavy and investors can face a greatly reduced retirement income as a result.

- **Precipice bonds**: These offered apparently high returns but in practice **downside gearing** meant that where the indices on which performance was based fell below a certain level investors lost most of their original capital.

- **Equity release mortgages**: These offer the elderly the opportunity to sell a part share of their home in return for a regular income or lump sum. However, many older people may not have understood the complexity of the arrangement.
- **Corporate bond funds**: Income seekers have been tempted by bond funds with high yields and have not understood the high risks associated with sub-investment grade debt.

The response to mis-selling: regulated products

Compensation claims for mis-selling has wreaked havoc in the adviser market, forcing some companies out of business and others to close voluntarily as the cost of professional indemnity (PI) insurance rocketed.

The classic hallmarks of mis-selling are complex product structures that are sold on misleading or insufficient advice for the individual to make an informed choice. The government and the regulators are keen to move towards the greater regulation of products rather than the traditional system of regulation, which focuses on policing advice. In particular the government is looking to extend the range of products like stakeholder pensions and **CAT-marked Individual savings accounts (ISAs)**. These products must offer fair Charges, flexible Access, and reasonable Terms – hence the acronym 'CAT'. In particular they must accept comparatively low monthly premiums, have a maximum annual management charge and must not impose exit penalties, allowing for free switching between providers.

The next generation of 'Sandler' products following stakeholder pension schemes and ISAs takes its name from Ron Sandler, the former Lloyd's of London chief executive, who carried out a government-commissioned review of the savings market in 2002. His idea was that there should be a range of low cost, simple and regulated products for short-, medium- and long-term investors. Typically the terms would include a maximum annual charge, no exit penalties and clear risk warnings. The idea behind such products is that they will not need to be 'sold' but that the FSA can provide a 'guided self-help' decision process to enable people to find out if the product is suitable for their needs.

By eliminating advice the FSA, rightly or wrongly, believes it can keep costs down and avoid mis-selling scandals. In practice it is not the product design that is the problem but the marketing. Ideally, if the FSA wishes to introduce what will in effect be execution-only products it might consider close supervision of the marketing material and marketing campaigns. Alternatively it could insist that providers distribute impartial FSA guides to products together with any marketing material, to ensure the prospective investor fully understands the risks.

Exhibit 2.1 Financial fraud and boiler room share scams

Financial **fraud** is a serious problem for the UK at present and this section looks at the most significant fraud of this type – boiler room share operations. Indeed, you would have to look as far back as the 1980s to find a period when these share scams were as common as they are today.

Fraud is both a **criminal** and **civil offence**, which means that if found guilty the perpetrators can be fined and/or sent to prison. With a civil offence, victims can sue and recoup damages. As the financial market's regulation has improved, financial fraud has become increasingly international and moves from one overseas jurisdiction to another, targeting UK investors from the outside.

Financial fraud is regarded as theft by deception in the UK but it is defined and treated differently in other jurisdictions. Whereas here it is both a criminal and civil offence, elsewhere it might be a civil offence or just a breach of financial regulations.

The term **boiler room** is used to describe the high-pressure call centres from which fraudsters target their victims to sell unattractive, often non-existent shares. The origins of the phrase date back to 1930s America, when con artists set up 'investment' operations in the basements of office buildings. All they needed was a couple of phones and a smart address in the financial area of the city and investors would assume they were dealing with respectable organisations.

A good example of financial fraud is the high-tech stocks issued by American companies in the wake of 9/11 (the bombing of the World Trade Center in 2001). Typically these are start-up companies that claim to be developing new security systems such as eyeball recognition devices. The companies have little or no track record. Some barely exist. If you buy these shares the chances are that the price will plummet and you will never be able to sell them again. In these cases the stockbroker might appear to be based in Britain and even have a British telephone number but in practice the number is likely to be rerouted to a call centre in Spain, Switzerland, Budapest, America, or Canada, for example. Given the lucrative nature of the business, serial fraudsters can afford to live the high life in luxurious locations where they benefit from a combination of loopholes in local law, lax financial regulation, and an overworked police force. Their business is scams, not shares, and the anti-fraud websites point out that the same names crop up again and again, whether they are trying to persuade you to invest in technology companies, fine wines or diamonds.

The Department of Trade and Industry (DTI) and the FSA issue warnings about boiler rooms on their websites and provide useful tips on how to avoid the scams. The Crimes of Persuasion website – an independent anti-fraud information service – notes a particularly cunning approach whereby the broker demonstrates the company's research skills by giving the target the name of a share that will go up in price. When it does, the broker phones to tell the target the name of a share that will go down in price. When that proves correct the target may feel inclined to hand over their money. 'What you have no way of knowing is that the scammer began with a calling list of 200 people,' Crimes of Persuasion warns. 'In the first call he told 100 people that the price would go up and the other 100 that it would go down. When it went up he made a second call to the 100 who had been given the "correct forecast". Of these, 50 were told the next price move would be up and 50 were told that it would be down.' The net result is a potential target of 50 'convinced' victims out of just 200 contacted.

Planners should be particularly alert to the dangers of dealing with English-language share salespeople in Barcelona – the current hot spot for financial fraudsters targeting British investors. Under Spanish law, provided a firm is only offering advice and is not actually selling shares, it does not have to be regulated by the CNMV – the Spanish equivalent of the FSA. So, the adviser talks up the sale and when the target says they want to buy, the adviser explains that a colleague will call to arrange the details. A separate company – often in a separate jurisdiction – then phones the target and takes what is in effect an execution-only order for the shares. The victim will probably be asked to send the cheque to a third location. Given this type of complex network the regulators find it very difficult to decide who has committed the fraud, whose rules have been broken, and where the deception actually took place.

It is hard to be exact about the number of share scam operations currently operating. Unlike respectable regulated businesses, they rarely advertise their wares but prefer to cold call, frequently the same people they have previously conned into buying wine, fine art or precious gems. Unless a fraudulent company is closed down and the perpetrators jailed, we may never hear about it. Financial regulators have limited scope to protect consumers in these cases, as these are national organisations established to protect the indigenous population from its native con artists. Fraud, by comparison, is international in scope and is no respecter of boundaries.

Indeed, the serial fraudsters make good use of the gaps between different regulatory jurisdictions. These highly efficient, versatile people establish a boiler room in one location and if it is discovered – as is usually the case after a period of time and a sufficient number of complaints – they simply pack their bags, and change their name and address, often targeting investors in a different country. At this point the regulator that exposed the original scam loses interest because the people it is designed to protect are no longer threatened and responsibility is passed to the regulator of the new jurisdiction.

Life would be much more difficult for the career con artist if the national regulators and fraud squads automatically swapped information. The more proactive regulators and police operations do this to an extent but the system is far from perfect. The Regulatory Intelligence Agency (RIA) and several other anti-fraud websites are unusual in that they provide international intelligence, but these are independent information services and have no legal powers. All they can do is warn individual and institutional investors and try to prevent crime by helping regulators identify the offenders who move in on their patch.

10 tips to avoid the fraudsters

- Always suspect cold calls.

- Tangibles like gemstones and wine are likely to be a con.

- Never invest in start-up companies directly.

- Check the firm's authorisation with the FSA.

- Beware of unusual guarantees and 'risk-free' investments.

- Don't assume a UK address means the firm is based here.

- Check the FSA's list of unauthorised overseas firms targeting the UK.

- If the individual is told the information is confidential, we should assume it is a con.

- Don't be pushed into making a quick decision.

- Never give any bank or credit card details.

Illegal activities

There are many activities that are classed as illegal but the two most relevant are:
Money laundering: This is where money from illegal sources is made to appear legal – for example by 'washing' it through legitimate bank accounts, or investing it and then withdrawing the capital. Following the bombing of the World Trade Center in September 2001, the UK government, like many others, cracked down on money laundering to try to prevent money reaching terrorist organisations.

Insider dealing/trading: This is where an individual or company trades in shares when it is in possession of price-sensitive information that is not known in the market at large.

●●●● Consumer education

To avoid future mis-selling would require a dramatic improvement in the way products are sold, and a corresponding improvement in the level of consumer understanding. The Personal Finance Education Group (pfeg – the acronym is lower case) is a charity established to harness resources from the private sector to help schools teach basic finance in the classroom. 'Financial capability' now forms part of the national curriculum and falls under the aegis of 'Personal, social and health education' (PSHE). Pfeg brings together teachers, government departments, consumer bodies, the FSA and financial institutions in a bid to ensure teachers have suitable guidance and materials for teaching finance. The group screens material offered by private sector institutions and awards a quality mark where the information is instructive and unbiased.

The FSA has also pledged to improve consumer understanding and in 2004 allocated £10m a year to this end. In practice it is doubtful if such a sum will achieve much in a financial services market worth £1.8bn a year, and given that according to the FSA's own research one-quarter of the UK's population cannot work out percentages, while almost the same number cannot use the Yellow Pages.

Arguably, while consumer education is a laudable aim, it is likely that the FSA will be more effective at preventing future scandals if it vets products more carefully and engages in a dialogue with financial institutions about their intended target market before the products hit the streets. At the time of writing there was considerable interest among product providers in obtaining an FSA seal of approval. This would look at inherent risk, such as complexity, volatility, and liquidity; control risk, such as commission payments creating product bias; and consumer impact, which would assess whether the products were suitable for the intended target. Where products carry appropriate and very visible financial health warnings, fewer investors could complain that they did not understand the risks.

Activity 2.1

Trace the history of a major mis-selling scandal and draw up a list of features that led to the scandal. Find out which resources at your college and at libraries to which you have access provide historical news searches. To what extent was the problem:

1 Poor product design per se.

2 An inappropriate product for the intended market.

3 Sold on the basis of insufficient or confusing advice.

How could this problem have been prevented?

Summary

This chapter examined economic history and the development of the framework for financial planning in the UK, with reference to the broader picture and also to the role of the key organisations. It also looked back at the recent history of mis-selling, which helped us to gain an awareness of why and how this particular aspect of financial services history has a tendency to repeat itself. Fraud is on the increase and it is important that we are aware of just how plausible and sophisticated financial fraud can be.

Key terms

- Boiler room p. 32
- CAT-marked products p. 31
- Civil offence p. 32
- Corporate bond funds p. 31
- Criminal offence p. 32
- Default p. 29
- Depolarisation p. 27
- Designated professional body p. 27
- Downside gearing p. 30
- Endowment mortgages p. 29
- Equity release mortgages p. 31
- Execution-only p. 28
- Financial planning certificate p. 27
- Fraud p. 31
- Income drawdown p. 30
- Independent financial adviser p. 27
- Insider dealing/trading p. 34
- Means-tested benefit p. 23
- Mis-selling p. 29
- Money laundering p. 33
- National insurance contributions (NICs) p. 22
- Pay-as-you-go (PAYG) p. 23
- Personal pensions p. 30
- Precipice bonds p. 30
- Professional indemnity insurance p. 29
- State earnings related pension scheme (SERPS) and S2P p. 25
- Self-regulation p. 26
- Self-regulatory organisation p. 26
- Split capital investment trusts p. 30
- Tangible and non-tangible assets p. 27
- Tied agent p. 27
- Universal benefit p. 23

Review questions

1 Consider in what ways Conservative and Labour ideology converges on key social policy.

2 Provide two examples of how the bill for state welfare and education has been reduced in recent years.

3 Explain the difference and provide three examples for tangible and non-tangible assets.

4 Describe how the Financial Services Compensation Scheme distinguishes between different financial products and why this can affect the maximum compensation available.

5 What are the classic hallmarks of mis-selling? Describe what went wrong in three examples.

6 Why is the international nature of fraud such a problem for regulators?

Go to the Companion Website at **www.booksites.net/harrison_pfp** for a multiple-choice quiz to test your understanding of this chapter.

Further information

Political parties and government or national offices

The Conservative Party: **www.tory.org.uk**

The Labour Party: **www.labour.org.uk**

The Liberal Democrat Party: **www.libdems.org.uk**

The Department for Work and Pensions: **www.dwp.gov.uk**

The Government Actuary's Department: **www.gad.gov.uk**

HMSO (for Hansard Debates among a wealth of other material): **www.parliament.the-stationery-office.co.uk**

The Inland Revenue: **www.inlandrevenue.gov.uk**

The National Audit Office: **www.nao.gov.uk**

National Statistics Online: **www.statistics.gov.uk**

The Treasury: **www.hm-treasury.gov.uk**

The regulators

The Financial Ombudsman Service: **www.financial-ombudsman.org.uk**

The Financial Services Authority (FSA): **www.fsa.gov.uk**

The Financial Services Compensation Scheme: **www.fscs.org.uk**

The Pensions Advisory Service: **www.opas.org.uk**

The Pensions Ombudsman: **www.pensions-ombudsman.org.uk**

Fraud websites

The Financial Services Authority (FSA): **www.fsa.gov.uk/consumer/consumer_help/ consumers/mn_boiler.html** (this includes a list of unauthorised foreign firms known to be targeting the UK).

The Department of Trade and Industry (DTI): **www.dti.gov.uk/ccp/scams/page9.htm**

Independent fraud websites (several of these have a US-slant but nevertheless provide very useful advice): **www.the-ria.com; www.quatloos.com; www.worldwidescam.com; www. investdrinks.org; www.crimes-of-persuasion.com**

Other useful economics and social policy websites

Centre for Economic Policy Research: **www.cepr.org**

Economic and Social Research Council: **www.esrc.ac.uk**

Institute for Economic Affairs: **www.iea.org.uk**

The Institute of Fiscal Studies: **www.ifs.co.uk**

National Institute for Economic and Social Research: **www.niesr.ac.uk**

Policy Studies Institute: **www.psi.org.uk**

Resources for Economists on the Internet: **www.netec.mcc.ac.uk**

Chapter 3

Market fundamentals

Introduction

This chapter and the two that follow take a closer look at stock markets and the economic factors that drive market direction.

One of the most worrying aspects of stock market investment is the tendency of professional and private investor alike to behave like lemmings under certain economic conditions. An economic slump can trigger a bear market; mass hysteria can trigger a stock market crash. In practice, however, crashes are few and far between. Of more concern – and a much more likely scenario – is that slow slide into a long bear market such as the one experienced in the UK from 1999 to 2002. At the risk of over-simplification, a **bear market** is where share prices are falling, while a **bull market** is where shares are rising. A 'bearish' investor believes share prices are due to take a tumble, while the bullish investor believes the opposite is true.

Objectives

After reading this chapter you will be able to:

- Describe what happens when there is a market crash.
- Explain the **equity-risk premium** and why the traditional view may be flawed.
- Describe the key **economic indicators**.
- Explain why the **Consumer prices index** was introduced and the differences between this and retail prices.

How bubbles burst and markets crash

The best source on any historical index values is **www.ftse.com**. The website has a students' section which provides historical index values for the All-Share and the FT 100 indices, among others. The information is set out on a spreadsheet. By following the timeline it is possible to identify specific dates when there was a sudden change in the index level. Tracing the timeline enables you to find the pre-crash or bear market value and to follow it forward to determine when the index regained its position.

To understand the lemming-like activity associated with a market crash (or burst **bubble**, as in 'South Sea' and 'Mississippi' – see below) it is useful to consider the period leading up to these events to spot the common denominators. This is not a particularly technical exercise. As we learned from the **TMT** bubble (technology, media and telecom shares) in the late 1990s, the most obvious features of the pre-crash market mentality are those well-known human characteristics, greed and fear. In a wise little volume called *Bluff Your Way in Economics* (Ravette Publishing, 1996, p. 40), Stuart Trow describes bubble mentality:

> A speculative bubble occurs when people become obsessed with a particular investment. Fear plays a large part in the bubble's build-up, with investors desperate not to miss the boat and willing to buy at any price, completely disregarding logic.

History provides some examples that are both illuminating and, due to the passage of time, quaintly amusing. Take the Mississippi Bubble. In the early 18th century, the Mississippi Company held a monopoly on all French territories in North America. The King of France and the French government were enthralled by the prospect of untold riches promised from the New World to the extent that they allowed the Royal Bank to issue banknotes backed, not by gold or silver as was common at the time, but by shares in the Mississippi Company. Trow explains:

> When the company crashed in 1720, the entire French monetary system was wiped out. Even people who had not invested in the company lost out as the bank notes became worthless. (Ibid.)

British investors suffered when the South Sea Bubble burst after the collapse of the extraordinarily speculative South Sea Company in the 18th century. This followed a period of extreme stock market activity, and so the sudden loss of confidence in one major company appeared to trigger a loss of confidence in the entire market.

From these examples we can see that market crashes are devastatingly indiscriminate. For tumbling together with the bubble company share prices are those of some of the most respected companies in the economy. Nor do markets recover quickly – hence the need to take a long-term view with equities. The Wall Street Crash of 1929, for example, saw US stocks lose almost 90% of their value. They did not regain their pre-crash levels until the mid-1950s. Turning to more recent history, in October 1987 the UK stock market crashed with a vengeance. Although pundits still argue about the precise cause, the essential point is that once again greed and an unbridled speculative frenzy had overtaken logic. Investors continued to buy shares because they failed to see that the prices could not go on rising indefinitely.

The bubble mentality does not just apply to shares. Other assets are equally vulnerable. A similar frenzy was characteristic of the UK housing boom in the late 1980s when people paid excessive prices only to find themselves in the negative equity trap once the housing bubble had burst. (**Negative equity** is where the value of an asset is exceeded by the loans secured against it.) Investors today are as vulnerable as they were in 1987. Some would argue more so, due to the increased number of **leveraged investors** – those who take out a loan in order to invest in the stock market. Leveraging may sound a high-risk strategy but in practice this is precisely what homeowners do when they arrange an interest-only mortgage backed by an endowment or Individual savings account (ISA), for example. For this arrangement to succeed the rates of return must be sufficient to service the loan *and* make a profit.

Market cycles

Chapter 4 looks at how shares are categorised into different sectors. As a general rule the companies in a sector share certain characteristics, which make them respond in a certain way to changes in the market cycles. This is why it is important, although not essential, to build a portfolio which spans all the major sectors. This helps to spread risk and avoids your portfolio crashing in a nasty way as the economy enters or emerges from a recession. (Economic cycles are discussed later in this chapter.) Remember though, that many of the blue chip companies which form the FTSE 100 index have considerable exposure overseas and so are not only affected by economic cycles in the UK.

Surviving market volatility

To survive and, indeed, thrive during volatile market cycles the individual needs a clear strategy. Fortunately, private investors are less constrained than the professional institutional investment managers because there are no clients waiting for their next quarterly figures and there is no pressure to compete with other asset managers.

A simple approach to portfolio management is to purchase shares for the long term income and gains and to recognise that it is inefficient, time consuming, and costly to change or churn a portfolio on a regular basis. In theory at least, if we invest in the right type of shares – even if it is apparently at the wrong time – our portfolio should be able to ride market cycles. If, after careful research, we considered that a company was worth investing in two months ago, its shares will still be worth holding today, even if the market direction has changed. In most cases the company will still pay out dividends, even if there has been a sudden switch from a bull to a bear market. Provided we chose wisely in the first place, in most cases the capital growth will return. But there is no guarantee when that might be.

This logic is fairly sound when applied to **blue chips** because these businesses are themselves well diversified and represent a spread of risk across markets (and often continents too) within just one shareholding. However, the logic does not necessarily extend to smaller, more speculative companies. In the run up to October 1987, for example, some companies came to the stock market which were very speculative and considerably overpriced. They did not recover. In this case investors got the worst of all worlds. They paid dearly for their shares, prices fell, and they never recovered capital value. Moreover, they did not even benefit from a decent run of dividends.

Remember also that certain market sectors are cyclical. Shares in engineering or construction companies, for example, usually do well when the general economy is flourishing, while shares in consumer goods companies and retailers will do well while consumer spending is expected to rise.

The following explanation attempts to demystify some of the economic jargon of market fundamentals but do bear in mind that these are generalisations only. If we buy a tinpot company in the first place, no amount of economic alchemy is going to turn it into a crock of gold.

How to read economic information

For the student of financial planning it is helpful to be aware that the economics reports in newspapers rely on just a few key phrases. Yet with these the economists manage to mystify most of the people most of the time. We should regard the jargon as no more than a form of shorthand and remember that it is one thing to understand the theory, but entirely another to interpret economic events correctly. Economics is a very imprecise science (rather like investment) and the experts frequently get it wrong but nevertheless are paid a great deal for their views.

The equity risk premium (ERP)

This is a phrase frequently used to describe the relative value of equities in comparison with lower risk assets. Investors need to take a decision as to what excess return they should demand from equities relative to risk-free government bonds (gilts). Rather confusingly the term is used to describe the excess return investors might expect to receive (the *ex ante* premium) and also the return they did receive (the *ex post* premium), as was pointed out in a paper by Robert Arnott and Peter Bernstein, 'What Risk Premium is Normal?'(*Financial Analysts Journal*, March/April 2002). See Figure 3.1.

The equity risk premium for the 10 years from 2002 was expected to be 3.75%, according to Barclays Capital. However, some economists suggest that this is too high. A study by Elroy Dimson, Paul Marsh, and Mike Staunton of the London Business School, for example, challenges several aspects of the traditional approach to assessing the ERP:

● Survivorship bias. Equity indices compiled retrospectively tend to be based on only those companies that have survived and prospered. This does not take account of the risk of investing in companies that fail.

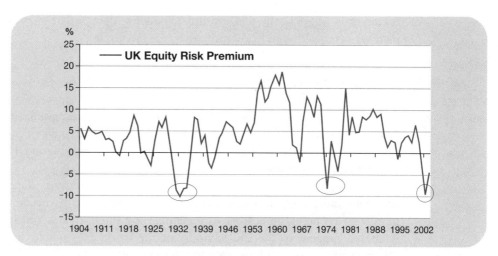

Figure 3.1 UK Equity risk premium: excess return of equities relative to gilts (five year annualised returns)

Source: Barclays Capital.

- Choice of market. Studies tend to concentrate on the US and UK markets. These are not sufficiently representative of world markets and exclude important emerging markets like Brazil, Russia, India, and China, for example.
- Time period. The majority of research focuses on the second half of the 20th century, when equity performance was high by historical standards.

The research concluded that equities are not guaranteed to outperform bonds over the medium term, defined here as anything up to 20 years. Taking the above factors into account, for the UK the ERP might be closer to 2.3%, while the World Index ERP is closer to 2.9%. However, this might be a rather pessimistic view. The point for students to appreciate is that for every economic and investment indicator, there is a counter-argument. In particular it is always relevant to question the criteria on which an opinion is based.

The ERP in practice

While it is important for students of financial planning to understand the theory surrounding the equity risk premium, it is equally important to keep a clear eye on practical considerations such as the investor's personal level of debt. This is particularly relevant for those with credit card debt, which tends to charge a very high rate of interest compared with mortgages, for example. Investing in debt (bonds and gilts) is only sensible if the individual can secure a return higher than the rate at which they are servicing personal debt. For example investing £1,000 in a high interest tax-free Individual savings account (ISA) offering 3.75% pa would produce a net return of £37.50. If you use the same £1,000 to reduce a credit card balance at a typical rate of 12% you would reduce the interest by £120. As the interest on the credit card account is paid from net income the effective gross return on that £1,000 for a basic rate taxpayer is 15.58%. In this example, reducing debt rather than investing would increase net wealth by £82.50 more than the ISA route.

Economic indicators

This section looks at the principles behind the key economic indicators, while Chapter 11 considers how this information can be applied to direct equity investment. The best source of information about economic indicators is National Statistics Online (**www.statistics.gov.uk**).

The economy is the financial state of the nation. Certain statistics, known as **economic indicators,** show the state of the economy at a particular time. The most important economic indicators to remember are **interest rates** and **inflation** because whatever happens to the UK economy or the world as a whole, it usually ends up affecting one or both of these rates and this in turn has an effect on government lending policy and companies' performance, which in turn affect private investments.

Interest rates

Interest rates are important because they may affect directly the amount a company is charged for borrowing, although the extent will depend on the structure of the debt. The Bank of England is responsible for setting short-term interest rates and uses them to curb or encourage spending. If we are all spending far too much ('we' being both individuals and companies) then the Bank will increase interest rates to stop us borrowing to spend. Likewise, if we are saving too much and not spending enough, the Bank might lower interest rates to encourage more borrowing and spending.

Retail Prices Index

The Retail prices index (RPI) is published by the Office for National Statistics every month and until 2003 was the most common measure for inflation. At the time of writing RPI was low at 2.5%, with wages inflation 1% higher at 3.5%. The RPI is calculated by constructing a so-called 'basket' of goods and services used by the typical household (based on a sample survey of about 7,000 households throughout the country). The basket includes housing and household expenditure, personal expenditure, travel and leisure, food and catering, alcohol and tobacco. The most recent base date was January 1987, which had a value of 100.

You may come across other types of inflation. For example **underlying inflation** is the unofficial term given to the inflation rate in an economy measured by Retail prices index minus mortgage interest payments (RPIX). **Headline inflation** is the full RPI, including mortgage interest costs.

Consumer Prices Index

In his Pre-Budget Report statement in December 2003, the chancellor confirmed that the UK inflation target would be based in future on the Harmonised index of consumer prices (HICP), better known as the Consumer prices index (CPI). The initial level of the new CPI inflation target was set at 2% and applied from 10 December 2003. From this date the CPI has been regarded as the main UK domestic measure of inflation for the purposes of econometrics (the application of mathematical and statistical techniques to economic theories). At the time of writing the CPI was 1.4%, just over one percentage point below RPI at 2.5% (April 2004).

HICPs were developed in the EU first to assess whether prospective members of the European Monetary Union would pass the inflation convergence criterion, and secondly to act as the measure of inflation used by the European Central Bank to assess price stability in the Euro area. The main requirement therefore was for a measure that could be used to make reliable comparisons of inflation rates across EU member states. Such comparisons are not possible using national consumer price indices due to differences in index coverage and construction. The HICP was developed by Eurostat – the EU statistical office – in conjunction with member states.

The RPI and indices based on it, such as RPIX, continue to be published alongside the CPI. Pensions, benefits and index-linked gilts continue to be calculated on exactly the same basis as previously, that is, with reference to the all-items Retail prices index (RPI) or its derivatives.

Table 3.1 Changes to the RPI and CPI baskets in March 2004

CPI division	RPI group	New item	Items removed
Food and non-alcoholic beverages	Food	Lamb mince Fresh turkey steaks Regional cheese	Frozen turkey Cheese slices
Alcoholic beverages and tobacco	Alcohol (off sales)		Gin
Clothing and footwear	Clothing and footwear	Men's sport sweatshirt	Child's fleece jacket
Furniture, household equipment and maintenance	Household goods	Electric heater Shower unit Fabric conditioner Dishwasher tablets Kitchen roll	Toaster Wine glass Washing machine liquid Dishwasher powder
Recreation and culture	Leisure goods	Digital camera CDs purchased over the internet Acoustic guitar Infant's activity toy Fishing rod Men's football boots	Mini-disc player PC printer Exercise bike Local newspaper
Restaurants and hotels	Alcohol (on sales)	Mineral water	
Miscellaneous goods and services	Personal services Household services	Basic manicure Bank charges	

Source: Office for National Statistics.

The difference between the CPI and RPI

The RPIX annual rate generally exceeds the CPI by 1%. In terms of commodity coverage, the CPI excludes a number of items that are included in RPIX, mainly related to housing – for example council tax and a range of owner-occupier housing costs such as mortgage interest payments, house depreciation, buildings insurance, estate agents' and conveyancing fees. The CPI covers all private households, whereas RPIX excludes the top 4% by income and pensioner households who derive at least three quarters of their income from state benefits. The CPI also includes the residents of institutional households such as student hostels, and also foreign visitors to the UK. This means that it covers some items that are not in the RPI, such as unit trust and stockbrokers' fees, university accommodation fees and foreign students' university tuition fees.

The RPI and CPI baskets change periodically. The most recent changes at the time of writing are shown in Table 3.1.

●●●● Impact of the economy on companies and share prices

This section now considers how all this comes together to affect a portfolio, whether this belongs to a private investor or a major pension fund. Rising interest rates increase the cost of borrowing for the companies in which we invest. The profits of a company that is highly geared (that is, it has a high ratio of borrowing to assets) naturally will suffer if the cost of servicing its debts increases. This cost will be passed on to shareholders because it will lower the profits out of which it pays dividends.

At the same time the dividends available from equities will start to look uncompetitive to income investors who will find better sources of income elsewhere if interest rates are high. Moreover, high interest rates may damage a company's growth prospects because they might encourage a company to keep its spare cash in deposits rather than to take a risk and invest it in expanding the business.

Low interest rates have the opposite effect and can be good for companies because the cost of borrowing comes down, and the share value rises. So, although a fall in interest rates sounds gloomy because it follows news of high unemployment or a slowdown in the economic growth (usually expressed as the gross domestic product or GDP – see below), for equity investors it can be good news.

Gilts react to fluctuations in inflation. A rise in inflation usually forces gilt prices down and therefore yields go up. This is because there is less demand for fixed interest securities at these times. An improvement in gilt yields in turn can have a detrimental effect on the stock market because gilts become more attractive relative to equities.

The **public sector borrowing requirement (PSBR)** also has an impact on the gilt market. The PSBR is the public sector deficit, that is the amount by which government spending (including local authorities and nationalised industries) exceeds the income from taxation, rates, and other revenues. One of the main methods the government uses to finance this debt is to sell gilts. If the PSBR is higher than expected, the price of gilts may fall, as there will be a greater supply.

The budget deficit is similar to the PSBR but also includes income from occasional 'extraordinary revenue' – for example from privatisations of public sector companies. So, a cut in the budget deficit or PSBR will be good news for gilts because supply is more limited and so prices rise. However, if the government has achieved the cut by increasing corporate taxation, this will generally be bad news for shares.

Other factors to affect a portfolio include the health or otherwise of retail sales, which obviously largely affects the retail stores and supermarkets, and housing starts (the number of new homes being built), which is generally viewed as a leading indicator of a future pick-up in the economy.

Diversification to deal with market cycles

No combination of investments will be absolutely suited to a particular phase of the market and even if we plan ahead, we will find that each successive market cycle displays different characteristics from its counterpart in the previous cycle. Nevertheless, as the following chapters show, a diversified portfolio is more likely to hold its value or at least limit the damage, compared with a portfolio that is weighted towards just one or two sectors.

Activity 3.1

Using information provided in this chapter, discuss how you would research the market crash of October 1987 and the long bear market that began in 2000. How can you judge when the index returns to the pre-crash or bear market values?

Activity 3.2

Professional investors read economic indicators in order to predict the way the economy is moving. Where would you find current and historic information about key indicators and what might they tell us about the economy?

Select two or three indicators and track changes. See how these changes are discussed in the press coverage; for example in the *Financial Times* and on national television news.

Summary

This chapter considered the key economic drivers of markets, the market cycles, and the language used to describe the state of the economy – the economic indicators. For those students who wish or need to find out more about the economic environment, the websites listed below will provide a useful starting point. Students for whom economics is less important should nevertheless remember how valuable it is to consider the factors that affect share prices and investment decisions in the wider context. This way we can avoid the dangerous bubble mentality that can lead to serious losses.

Key terms

- Bear and bull markets p. 39
- Blue chip p. 42
- Bubble p. 40
- Consumer Prices Index (CPI) p. 39
- Economic indicators p. 39
- Equity risk premium (ERP) p. 39
- Headline inflation p. 44
- Inflation p. 44
- Interest rates p. 44
- Leveraged investing p. 41
- Negative equity p. 41
- Retail Prices Index (RPI) p. 44
- Public sector borrowing requirement (PSBR) p. 46
- Technology, media and telecom shares (TMT) p. 40
- Underlying inflation p. 44

Review questions

1 Explain what factors can lead to a market crash.

2 What is the difference between a crash and a bear market?

3 What is the equity risk premium and why might this traditional method of calculation be misleading?

4 Describe the two main types of inflation and why they differ.

5 What are the other measures of inflation?

Go to the Companion Website at **www.booksites.net/harrison_pfp** for a multiple-choice quiz to test your understanding of this chapter.

Further information

The Bank of England: **www.bankofengland.co.uk**

The London Stock Exchange: **www.londonstockex.co.uk**

Office for National Statistics (National Statistics Online): **www.statistics.gov.uk**

Chapter 4 ●●●○

Asset classes and investment styles

Introduction

This chapter explains investment terminology with the focus on asset classes, which represent the building blocks of any portfolio whether this is for the private investor or a multi-million pound pension fund. Once you have read this chapter you may wish to use it as a storehouse to which you can return when you encounter unfamiliar terms and concepts later on. The following chapter applies information on asset classes to portfolio construction.

Objectives

After reading this chapter you should be able to:

- Describe the main asset classes.
- Explain the terms **correlation**, **negative (inverse) correlation**, and **non-correlation** with reference to different asset classes.
- Explain what is meant by the terms **value** and **growth**.

●●●● Securities

Investment literature uses a lot of confusing jargon. Commonly used (and misused) terms include 'securities', 'stocks' and 'shares'. **Securities** is the general name for all **stocks** and **shares**. What we call shares today were originally known as stocks because they represented part ownership in the joint stock companies – the precursors to today's public limited companies (plcs). So to some extent the terms stocks and shares are interchangeable, and we still use the terms *stock* markets and *stock*brokers.

Broadly speaking, stocks are fixed interest securities with a redemption date, while shares are securities with no fixed 'coupon' or redemption date. The four main types of securities listed and traded on The London Stock Exchange are:

- **UK (domestic) equities:** ordinary shares issued by over 2,000 UK companies.
- **Overseas equities:** ordinary shares issued by non-UK companies. (The term 'international' denotes both domestic and non-domestic.)
- **Gilts:** bonds issued by the British government to raise money to fund any shortfall in public expenditure.
- **Bonds:** fixed interest stocks issued by companies and local authorities, among others.

If a company wants to raise finance it has two main options. It can sell part of the ownership of the company by issuing ordinary shares (equities), or it can borrow money by issuing bonds. Shares and bonds are bought and sold on the stock market.

●●●● The correlation coefficient

For non-statisticians it is easier to think of **correlation** in its literal meaning – that is a co-relationship, or a relationship that corresponds or is linked to something. In statistical terms correlation refers to the extent of this correspondence between the pattern or the behaviour demonstrated by two variables. The **correlation coefficient** is a statistical measure of the extent to which these two (or more) variables – asset class price indices, for example – follow the same path or direction. The coefficient usually lies between the numbers minus one and plus one (–1 and +1, both known as 'unity').

The three terms we tend to come across are **positive correlation**, **negative (inverse) correlation** and **non-correlation**. A coefficient of +1 means that the variables are positively correlated – that is, one variable increases linearly as the other increases. A coefficient of 0 indicates that there is no linear relationship and so the variables are not related. A coefficient of –1 indicates the variables have a negative correlation and so as one increases linearly, the other decreases by the same amount. The closer the coefficient to zero the weaker the relationship, whereas the closer the coefficient to unity, the stronger the relationship. See Figures 4.1 and 4.2.

We must be careful when we consider how different asset classes are correlated. Equities and bonds are regarded as correlated but whether this is negative or positive

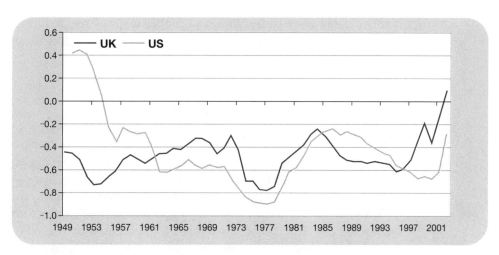

Figure 4.1 Rolling correlation between equity real total returns and RPI
Source: Barclays Capital.

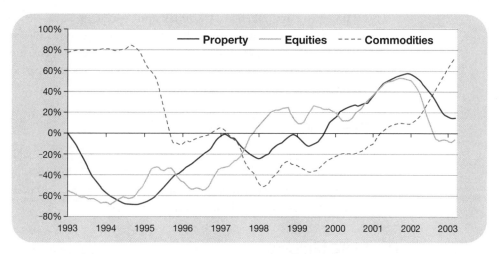

Figure 4.2 Rolling correlation of real annual total returns and inflation
Source: IPD, GSCI, Datastream, Barclays Capital.

depends on what we are comparing – the price or the yield/earnings. As explained later in this chapter, when bond prices rise, bond yields fall relative to the asset price. To add to the complication, if we were to look at equity and bond yields, for example, then generally we would say that they are positively correlated, but at the time of writing they were negatively correlated.

For the purposes of the financial planner the most important point is to understand the difference between assets classes that are correlated – equities and bonds, for example – and asset classes that are non-correlated – equities/bonds and commercial property, for example, and equities/bonds and hedge funds. In theory, by introducing non-correlated asset classes into a portfolio, we may see considerable volatility at specific asset class level but the overall effect will be to reduce volatility at the total portfolio level.

The FTSE International Indices

The FTSE International Indices are arithmetically weighted by market capitalisation so that the larger the company, the greater the effect its share price movement will have on the index. **Market capitalisation** is the stock market valuation of the company, which is calculated by multiplying the number of shares in issue by their market price. To find out current total market capitalisations for each index visit the website at **www.ftse.com**. The easiest way to absorb information on the indices is to read this and related sections of the book with a copy of the *FT* to hand.

The FTSE All-Share

This is the most comprehensive UK index and represents 98%–99% of the UK stock market capitalisation. Within the All-Share, companies are allocated to over 30 different categories of shares according to industrial sector. (The number of sectors changes from time to time but was 35 in April 2004.) There are also sub-indices, of which the main three are:

The FTSE 100

This index consists of the 100 largest UK companies by market capitalisation and is the standard reference point for defining Britain's 'blue chip' companies (blue chip being the highest value chip in a game of poker). The FTSE 100 companies together represent about 80% of the UK stock market capitalisation.

The FTSE Mid-250

This index consists of the next 250 companies below the FTSE 100 and can include or exclude investment trusts. Together, these companies represent about 14% of the UK stock market capitalisation including investment trusts with a few exceptions (for example open-ended investment companies, split capital investment companies, currency funds and split capital investment trusts).

The FTSE SmallCap

This index does not have a fixed number of constituent companies but instead it comprises all the remaining companies in the All-Share which are too small to qualify for the top 350 (about 420 at the time of writing). Together they account for about 4% of the total UK capitalisation.

The FTSE Fledgling

The Fledgling market covers all of the companies that are too small at present to be in the All-Share index but otherwise are eligible to join the Exchange. Together the SmallCap and Fledgling indices are known as the All-Small index.

Alternative Investment Market

For companies too small to join the main market there is the Alternative Investment Market (AIM). AIM replaced the Unlisted Securities Market (USM) in 1995. It allows small and relatively new companies that are growing quickly to go public without having to go through the expensive and time-consuming full listing procedures required for a Stock Exchange main listing. Private investors should note that AIM companies are not regulated as strictly as fully listed companies. Once a company has been listed on AIM for two years, normally it will have the opportunity to seek admittance to the main market by using a special expedited process.

Companies ineligible for the All-Share

Some companies are not eligible to join the All-Share or the Fledgling market. This is not usually a question of size but of some other characteristic. For example the following are ineligible:

- Foreign companies (which would also be listed on their home country stock market), for example 'Americans', 'Canadians' and 'South Africans', which are listed after the AIM countries in the *FT Companies and Markets* section.
- Subsidiaries of companies already in the All-Share.
- Companies with less than 25% of shares in 'free float' (that is, over 75% is held by the family or directors).
- Companies whose shares were not traded for a minimum number of days in the previous year.
- Split capital investment trusts.

Shareholder activism

It is important to remember that directors of publicly. owned companies are not owners but managers. In practice they often behave like owners, which partly accounts for the increasing interest in shareholder activism. The best example of this activity is where institutional investors use their voting power in very sensitive areas such as executive pay and boardroom appointments. The key investor lobbies are the Association of British Insurers (ABI members own about one-fifth of the UK stock market), the National Association of Pension Funds (NAPF) and the Investment Management Association (IMA).

●●●● The main asset classes

UK equities

UK equities are the quoted shares of companies in the UK and tend to dominate most private investors' portfolios, whether they are held directly or through collective (mutual) funds such as unit and investment trusts and life assurance funds. The return achieved by UK equities, when measured over the long term, has exceeded both price and earnings inflation but starting in 2000 we entered a prolonged equity bear market and therefore short-term negative returns have dominated recent analysis. For certain periods both equity prices and bond yields have fallen, so the assumption that these two asset classes are inversely correlated can only be regarded as a theoretical explanation of asset characteristics. Broadly speaking, the equity investor's objective is to buy the shares of companies that will generate a satisfactory total return (growth and income) in exchange for an acceptable level of risk.

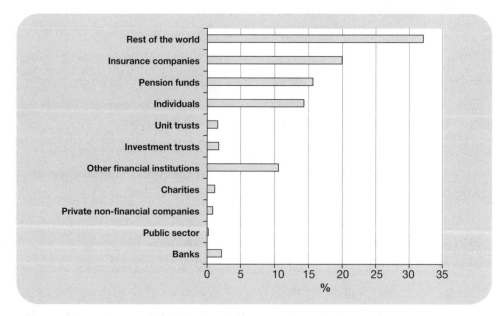

Figure 4.3 Share ownership 2002: a 26% fall in the markets

Note: Between 1 January 2002 and 31 December 2002 the market value of the stock market fell by £400bn to £1,154.6bn, representing a fall of 26%. Headline findings of the 2002 Share Ownership Survey show that institutional shareholders accounted for 49.4% of UK ordinary shares at 31 December 2001, with a combined value of £571.1bn. Of this, the largest components were insurance companies with £230.1bn and pension funds with £180.1bn.

Source: Office for National Statistics.

Companies 'go public' when they are quoted on The London Stock Exchange or Alternative Investment Market. In this way a company can raise the money it needs to expand by issuing shares. A share or equity literally entitles the owner to a specified share in the profits of the company and, if the company is wound up, to a specified share of its assets. The owner of shares is entitled to the dividends – the six-monthly distribution (less frequent with many smaller companies) to shareholders of part of the company's profits. The **dividend yield** on equities is the dividend paid by a company divided by that company's share price.

There is no set redemption date for an equity, when the company is obliged to return the original investment. If, as a shareholder, you want to convert your investment into cash ('to realise its value') you must sell your shares through a stockbroker. The price will vary from day to day – even from hour to hour – so the timing of the purchase and sale of shares is critical.

Share classes

There are different classes of shares. Most investors buy **'ordinary' shares**, which give the holder the right to vote on the constitution of the company's board of directors. Since this is the most common type of share, the term 'ordinary' is usually dropped unless it is to distinguish the shares from a different category. Voting rights may not be of interest to a private investor but institutions that own a significant holding in a company can and do influence the board's decisions by voting at annual and extraordinary general meetings – for example on appointments and dismissals (see activism above).

Preference shares carry no voting rights but have a fixed dividend payment, so can be attractive to those seeking a regular income. These shares have preference over ordinary shareholders if the company is wound up – hence the name.

There are several sub-classes of equities and equity-related investments, as follows.

● *Convertibles and warrants*

Convertibles and warrants are special types of shares with characteristics that make them attractive in certain circumstances. Convertibles are more akin to bonds (see below), in that they pay a regular income and have a fixed redemption date. However, a convertible confers the right to *convert* to an ordinary share or preference share at a future date. This can be an attractive proposition if the current price is attractive relative to the purchase price on the convertible date.

For private investors the main instrument is covered warrants, the listed derivatives launched by The London Stock Exchange in 2002. These confer a right but not an obligation on the holder to purchase (call warrants) or sell (put warrants) a quantity of a financial asset on a predetermined date at a predetermined price (the 'strike' or 'excise' price). We generally think of warrants in terms of shares but the asset (the 'underlying' security) may also be a basket of stocks, an index, a currency or a commodity like oil. The value of the warrant is determined by the difference, or premium, of the share price over the conversion price of the warrant. The warrant pays out cash if the price of the underlying security is above (for call warrants) or below (for put warrants) the excise price of the warrant. The payout is based on the difference between the price of the underlying security at the expiry date and the exercise price of the warrant. Covered warrants, therefore, are a type of option (see below) except that the downside is limited to the original investment. There is a good guide to this complex subject at **www.warrants.com**.

● *Derivatives*

Derivatives, as the name suggests, *derive* their value from the price of an underlying security. This is the generic term given to futures contracts and options, both of which can be used to reduce risk in an institutional fund or, in the case of options, even in a large private portfolio. Derivatives are also used in certain types of mutual funds to provide protection against a fall in the relevant index.

Futures

A future is an agreement (obligation) to buy or sell a given quantity of a particular asset, at a specified future date, at a pre-agreed price. The price is fixed at the time the contract is taken out. Futures contracts can be used by institutional funds to control risk because they allow the manager to increase or reduce swiftly the fund's exposure to an existing asset class. Futures have also proved popular as a cost-cutting mechanism, particularly in index tracking funds and other funds where there are rapid changes of large asset allocations.

These contracts can be based on any number of underlying assets. In addition to offering futures and options based on individual shares and stockmarket indices, the London International Financial Futures and Options Exchange (LIFFE) also offers futures and options based on bonds, interest rates, and agricultural commodities. Futures on equities allow you to gain exposure to specific shares, whereas FTSE 100 Index Futures allow you to gain exposure to the FTSE 100 index, which tracks the performance of the UK top 100 blue chip companies.

Options

An option simply gives the holder the right, but not the obligation, to buy or sell a specified underlying asset at a pre-agreed price on or before a given date. There are two types of options – calls and puts:

● The buyer of a **call option** acquires the right, but not the obligation, to buy the underlying asset at a fixed price. Call options generally rise in value if the price of the underlying asset rises.
● The buyer of a **put option** acquires the right, but not the obligation, to sell the underlying asset at a fixed price. Put options generally rise in value if the price of the underlying asset falls.

The buying of options involves limited risk – that is to say you cannot lose any more than the premium paid at outset. It is also possible to write (sell) options. The writing of call options, although having a wide range of uses, is a potentially high-risk strategy requiring a high degree of product knowledge. Since exercise of the option can involve the writer in a substantial financial commitment, option writers are required to deposit a margin with the broker to ensure the obligation of the contract can be met in full if required.

Overseas equities

These are similar in principle to UK equities but there are differences in shareholder rights. Investment overseas provides exposure to the growth in foreign markets including younger, faster growing economies, for example China, India, Russia and Argentina. However, these shares also expose the investor to currency fluctuations and, in the case of developing economies, to political risk and hyperinflation. The taxation of foreign shares can be less favourable than UK equities. In particular, some or all of the withholding tax on dividends deducted by the foreign country may not be recoverable.

UK Bonds

UK bonds are issued by borrowers. In the case of the UK government, the bonds are known as gilt edged securities or just gilts. Where the borrower is a company we refer to the instruments as corporate bonds. Bonds are also issued by local authorities, overseas governments and overseas companies, among others.

In return for the loan of your money, the borrower agrees to pay a fixed rate of interest (known as the coupon) for the agreed period and to repay your original capital sum on a specified date, known as the maturity or redemption date. Bonds are frequently referred to as 'fixed interest' assets because the coupon is fixed. However, the actual yield will depend on the price of the bond if it is traded.

UK domestic bonds are either secured on the company's underlying assets, for example the company's property, or they are unsecured, in which case there is no physical asset backing the bond's guarantee to pay interest and to repay the capital at maturity. Secured bonds are known as debentures and unsecured bonds are known as loan stocks. Since the security offered by debentures is greater than for loan stocks, the former tend to pay a lower rate of interest.

The point to remember about fixed interest securities is that the investment return is determined more by the prevailing interest rate than the issuing company's profitability. This is because bonds compete with other interest-paying assets. In particular the yield on bonds will generally exceed the yield on cash (deposits) in order to justify the additional risk. Provided the issuer remains sufficiently secure to honour the future coupon payments (the regular interest) and redemption payment (the return of the original capital) the investor will know exactly what the return will be, *provided* the bond is held to maturity.

Gilts offer the highest degree of security because they are issued by the British government. Private investors can access government instruments via a stockbroker. The best source of information on gilts is the Debt Management Office (DMO), which is part of the Treasury and has been responsible for issuing gilts since April 1998 (previously they were issued by the Bank of England).

Corporate bonds tend to pay a higher yield than gilts because of the perceived additional layer of risk. These bonds are classified by rating agencies (Standard & Poor's, and Moody's, for example) as investment grade (BBB⁻ and higher) or sub-investment grade, depending on the financial stability of the borrower. As shown in Chapter 10, sub-investment grade bonds can provide very attractive yields but these bonds are much more risky than investment grade debt and the skill of the bond fund manager is paramount if the fund is to avoid a run of defaults.

Traded bonds

When an individual investor or a fund manager buys a bond before its maturity date the value of the future coupon and redemption payments will depend on the prevailing interest rates at the time of purchase. If interest rates are rising, then the value of the fixed interest security will fall. This is because for the same amount of capital invested, it would be possible to get a better return elsewhere. Conversely, if interest rates are falling, then the value of the fixed interest security will be higher because it provides a greater stream of income than would be available from alternative sources with a comparable risk level. Significant fluctuations in the relative value of the coupon are more apparent with fixed interest securities that have a long period to run to maturity since they are more likely to be traded before redemption date.

To summarise, as a general rule equities are considered more risky and volatile than investment grade bonds because their relative value is influenced by a wide range of factors. With bonds, provided the company or government backing the contract is financially secure, the return on a bond *held to maturity* is predictable. However, it is not predictable if the investor sells before maturity, nor is it reliable in the case of sub-investment grade debt.

Eurobonds

UK companies can raise money outside the UK market by issuing 'Eurosterling' bonds – that is, bonds denominated in sterling but issued on the Eurobond market. Contrary to its name, the Euromarkets are not confined to Europe but are international markets where borrowers and lenders are matched.

The main advantage of Eurosterling bonds, from the borrower's point of view, is that they can reach a much wider range of potential lenders. However, generally this is not considered as a market for direct investment by private investors in the UK due to the size of transactions.

Index linked gilts

Index linked gilts are bonds issued by the UK government that guarantee to provide interest payments (the coupon) and a redemption value that increase in line with annual inflation. For this reason they are one of the lowest risk assets for income seekers investing for the long term, where inflation is an important issue – for example in retirement. In practice, index linked gilts are not always competitive when compared with other income-generating alternatives, so the investor must decide on the importance of the extremely low risk rating.

The return on index linked gilts in excess of retail price inflation varies but usually it is possible to buy these securities in the market at a price which guarantees a real rate of return to the holder, assuming that the stock is held to maturity.

Cash

Cash usually refers to deposits and money market accounts. Deposits have the advantage that the value in monetary terms is known and is certain at all times, provided the deposit taker is secure. What is not known is the level of interest, which will fluctuate unless this is a fixed income account that guarantees the rate for a pre-determined period. The relation between the interest rate for cash and the level of price inflation is critical as this determines whether the return on capital is positive or negative in real (after inflation) terms.

Commercial property

Property is a useful diversifier because it is not correlated with the equity and bond markets. In investment terms, property usually refers to the ownership of commercial land and buildings, although it can also refer to agricultural land. In the case of commercial property the owner receives income from the rent charged to the tenant and, over time, this rent is expected broadly to keep pace with inflation. The dominant factor in the value of a property is the desirability or otherwise of its location.

For the private investor, property is considered a good diversifier for an equity and bond portfolio. However, there are several problems with property. First, it is often sold in large blocks that cannot be easily split for investment purposes. As a result, only the larger institutional funds can afford (or are wise) to own property directly. Second, property is a very illiquid asset and it can take several years for the right selling conditions to arise. For the private investor, therefore, it is sensible to invest via collective funds, which provide access to a spread of properties and where units can be bought and sold easily.

An alternative way to invest in property is through a buy-to-let arrangement, where the individual takes out a mortgage for a residential property that can be let to private tenants. The merits and drawbacks of buy-to-let are discussed in Chapter 17.

Alternative investments

During the equity bear market, which began in 2000, an increasing number of private investors started to look to different asset classes to improve their returns and to avoid relying solely on traditional equity funds for capital growth. The two main 'alternative' asset classes are hedge funds and private equity. There are others that are

used mainly by institutional investors – currencies and sub-investment grade debt, for example. 'Alternative' refers to investments that are not correlated to the two major asset classes, equities and bonds.

As shown on page 50, non-correlation does not just mean that these assets behave in different ways from equities and bonds. Asset classes that are not correlated demonstrate no common pattern. They neither follow the same trajectory, nor do they follow an inverse trajectory. In theory if you hold a range of non-correlated assets this should improve returns and reduce volatility over the long term at total portfolio level. However, individual asset classes might be quite volatile, so you need to get the right balance.

Students will also come across **absolute return funds**, where the aim is to achieve a positive return throughout the market cycles and irrespective of movements in the equity and bond markets. In particular this type of fund aims to provide positive returns even when equity markets are falling. The most common alternative investment that is run as an absolute return fund is the fund of hedge funds.

It is important to remember that 'alternative' assets only attract this label because of what they are not; that is, they are *not* conventional equity and bond investment strategies. However, the alternatives markets are not homogenous. Even among hedge funds, for example, there is a wide range of investment strategies; some are speculative and some hedge risk.

Private equity

The British Venture Capital Association (BVCA) defines private equity as the equity financing of unquoted companies at many stages in their life from start-up to the expansion of companies of a substantial size; for example through management buy-outs and buy-ins. Private equity represents medium- to long-term investments in companies with growth potential. The investment capital is eventually released through trade sales or flotation on the public markets.

The investable universe is vast. The BVCA says that private equity investors have holdings in some 11,000 UK companies that employ almost 3m people. This represents about 18% of the private sector workforce. By comparison, there are only about 2,200 quoted companies on The London Stock Exchange, so you can see that the scope among private companies is impressive. Private equity funds returned 11.4% per annum over the five years to 31 December 2002, a better performance than most other asset classes.

Of course investing directly in an unquoted company is a very high-risk strategy, as are the specialist venture capital trusts (VCTs), which are only suitable for the very wealthy investor who can commit for the long term. The success of the VCT will depend heavily on the skills of the management company.

Comparing equities, bonds and cash (deposits)

It is common practice to compare returns on equities with bonds, and both asset classes with cash (deposits). However, as Barclays Capital points out in its annual

Equity-Gilts Study, it is important to view equities over the long term. Over a period of just a few years the returns can be volatile and even negative – as happened in 2000 when the total return from equities was −8.6% after adjusting for inflation. By contrast gilts returned +6.1% in real terms. Investors keen to keep up with the comparative movements of gilts and equities should refer to the *Financial Times*, which publishes the **gilt-equity yield ratio**. This tracks the yield on gilts divided by the yield on shares. The normal range is between 2 and 2.5, so if it dips or soars well out of this range it may indicate that shares are very expensive or that gilts are very cheap. Market analysts use this as one of the signals to indicate that a bull (lower figure) or bear (higher figure) market is imminent.

It is also important to keep in mind the relationship between inflation and returns. The Barclays Capital guide points out that inflation is a key determinant of investment returns. Stock markets may not be prepared for an **inflation shock** (a sudden and unexpected change) but they adjust over time and provide a long-term hedge against price rises. Gilts and cash are not suitable inflation hedges.

Period of investment

Historical statistics that show the long-term returns on equities, gilts, and cash should be viewed with some caution and certainly should not be treated as a guide to the future. While history indicates that equities generally have provided a better return than bonds over the *medium to long term*, individuals who invest in the stock markets for shorter periods can experience considerable volatility because the markets take a tumble just before they want to get out or because the fixed costs associated with investing undermine the return over the short term.

Dividend reinvestment

The reinvestment of dividends is an important factor in the overall return. The Barclays study states, 'Dividends account for nearly two-thirds of total returns to equities over long periods of time.' The value of equities, therefore, is directly linked to the value of the dividend flow. The interest on gilts may look attractive compared with the yield on equities but since gilt income is fixed, the flow of income from the gilt cannot rise over time in the same way as equity dividends (unless the gilt is index linked – but here the initial income would be quite low). See Tables 4.1 and 4.2.

Table 4.1 Real investment returns by asset class (% pa)

Asset class	2003	Last 10 yrs	Last 20 yrs
Equities	16.9	3.2	8.0
Gilts	−1.2	4.6	6.1
Corp. bonds	6.7	6.7	–
Index-linked	3.9	3.7	3.9
Cash	0.9	3.1	4.4

Source: Barclays Capital Equity Gilt Study 2004.

Table 4.2 Annualised returns (%) on asset classes 2000–2002

Asset class	% pa
15 yr corp. bonds	6.2
Cash	2.9
Equities	−19.3
Gilts	3.6
Building soc.	2.2

Source: Barclays Capital Equity Gilt Study 2004

Investment styles

Stock selection refers to the process where the investment manager or private investor chooses individual securities. The decisions that drive private investors are different from those of an institutional fund manager. This is not just because the objectives are different. The large pension funds can be worth millions, even billions of pounds. This means they can make a profit on minor price changes due to the sheer volume of their transactions. Moreover, compared with a private client, institutional funds benefit from very low dealing costs and, in the case of pension and charity funds, operate in a tax-favoured environment. This means that what might trigger a buy or sell transaction in the institutional market should often be interpreted as a much more cautious 'hold' position by the private investor.

Active management

Active investment managers aim to increase a fund's value by deviating from a specific benchmark – for example a stockmarket index. There are two basic techniques used in active stock selection. The starting point for active managers who adopt a **bottom up** approach is the company in which the manager may invest. The manager will look at in-house and external research on the company's history and potential future prospects. This will include an examination of the strength of the balance sheet, the company's trading history, the management's business strategy and the **price/earnings ratio** (**P/E** – the market price of a share divided by the company's earnings/profits per share in its latest 12 month trading period). From the company analysis the manager will proceed to look at the general performance and prospects for that sector (for example oil, retailers), any relevant factors that affect the market, and then take into consideration what national and international economic factors.

The **top down** manager works in reverse, looking first at the international and national economic factors that might affect economic growth in a country, a geographic area (for example the 'Tiger' economies of South-East Asia) or an economic category (emerging markets, for example) and gradually work down to the individual companies.

Among private investors, the fundamental analyst focuses almost exclusively on individual companies and would tend to disregard the economic climate and market conditions. The technical analyst, also known as a chartist, concentrates on historical price movements and uses these charts as a way of reading future movements in share prices.

In theory, active managers ought to be able to outperform their benchmark index after fees. In practice, this does not happen as frequently as it should, particularly in the well-researched markets.

Passive management

Passive managers aim to track or replicate an index; hence the reason it is also called index tracking. Here the manager aims to emulate the performance of a particular index by buying all or a wide sample of the constituent shares.

The passive manager does not consider the merits of each stock, of different sectors, and economic cycles. If it is in the index then it must be represented in the fund. To date index tracking funds have done well compared with actively managed funds, largely because the passive manager's charges are very low in comparison with the active manager. It does have flaws, however; for example the manager must include companies that are unethical or overpriced.

Some managers describe their style as enhanced passive. This is where they make small deviations from the index – for example excluding stocks they consider poor value – in order to generate a slightly higher return with very little additional risk.

Passive management becomes very complex when the process tries to outstrip the index returns by deviation based on mathematical and statistical formulae. This is known as quantitative management.

A comparatively new vehicle for institutional managers and sophisticated private investors is the **exchange-traded fund** (**ETF**). An ETF is a basket of stocks that is used to track an index or a particular industry sector. ETFs are extremely cheap – about half the cost of traditional index tracker funds – and can be traded more easily.

Large cap

'Cap' is shorthand for market capitalisation, which is the total value of the company's shares in issue in terms of its market price per share multiplied by the number of shares issued. In the UK the companies in the FTSE 100 index are classed as large cap. In the US the term is used to describe companies with a market capitalisation of over $5bn. The point about large cap companies is that they tend to be more reliable – in terms of dividend yield, for example – but they are well researched. This means that institutional investors ensure the market price reflects inherent value accurately and therefore it can be difficult for a private investor to spot pricing anomalies.

Mid cap

As the term suggests this refers to companies with a mid-ranking market capitalisation. In the UK this usually refers to companies in the FTSE Mid 250 index. In the

US it is used for companies capitalised at between $1–5bn. To state the obvious, these companies are less well researched than large cap but better researched than small cap.

Small cap

The definition of 'small' is somewhat arbitrary but in the UK we generally use this term for companies below the FTSE 350 (100 and 250 indices), which fall into the FTSE Small Cap index. It is in this market – and in the Alternative Investments Market – that institutional and private investors tend to find inefficiencies in share pricing; that is, share prices that do not reflect a company's inherent value, but also greater risk.

Value

Value investors aim to identify shares that are underpriced by the market, so they would look at the P/E ratio and dividend yield, for example, but would analyse the skills of the management team, among other factors. A high P/E ratio might indicate that a company is expensive but it could also indicate that it is about to increase its earnings per share – and vice versa.

Growth

Growth investors are looking for companies that they expect to achieve above average earnings growth. As mentioned above, growth stocks tend to have a high P/E ratio compared to the market, as investors anticipate that earnings will increase in the future.

Activity 4.1

Examine recent press coverage of investor activism, either in a newspaper search or on the websites of the main institutional investor organisations provided below. For example you might consider the press coverage of executive pay and investigate why there is a movement to prevent public companies from rewarding failure. Either as an individual exercise or a group debate, consider the extent to which institutional investors should influence board decisions. What are the arguments in favour and against?

Given the remuneration packages top fund managers themselves receive, do you think that such intervention is hypocritical or is it merely an attempt to act on behalf of the investors whose money an institution looks after? The fact that executive share options and pension arrangements are visible in the annual accounts makes it far easier for investors and researchers to see exactly what price a company is paying for its top brass. Get a range of annual reports covering different sectors in the All-Share. You can download these or request them via the *Financial Times* annual reports service. Details are provided on the London Share Service pages and the website is **http://ft.ar.wilink.com**.

Summary

This chapter examined the main asset classes and showed how to distinguish between them. It also considered briefly how shares are classified on The London Stock Exchange. Finally it looked at different investment styles and considered what factors drive these investors when they select companies in which to invest.

Key terms

- Absolute return funds p. 60
- Alternative investment market p. 53
- Bond p. 50
- Bottom up p. 62
- Call option p. 56
- Convertibles and warrants p. 55
- Correlation p. 50
- Correlation coefficient p. 50
- Derivatives p. 56
- Dividend yield p. 55
- Equity p. 50
- Exchange-traded fund (ETF) p. 63
- Futures p. 56
- Inflation shock p. 61
- Gilt-equity yield ratio p. 61
- Gilts p. 50
- Growth investing p. 64
- Market capitalisation p. 52
- Negative (inverse) correlation p. 50
- Non-correlation p. 50
- Ordinary shares p. 55
- Positive correlation p. 50
- Preference shares p. 55
- Price/earnings ratio p. 62
- Put option p. 56
- Securities p. 50
- Shares p. 50
- Shareholder activism p. 53
- Small, mid and large cap p. 63/4
- Stocks p. 50
- Top down p. 62
- Value investing p. 64

Review questions

1 Explain why shareholder activism has become more prevalent in recent years and where institutional investors may attempt to make changes.

2 Explain what is meant by the dividend yield?

3 Describe two types of derivatives and explain why they might be used by institutional investors and private investors.

4 How does a value investor differ from a growth investor?

Go to the Companion Website at **www.booksites.net/harrison_pfp** for a multiple-choice quiz to test your understanding of this chapter.

Further information

The Debt Management Office: **www.dmo.gov.uk**

FTSE International: **www.ftse.com**

The London International Futures and Options Exchange (LIFFE): **www.liffe.com**

Standard & Poor's: **www.standardandpoors.com**

The Stock Exchange: **www.londonstockex.co.uk**

Chapter 5 ● ● ● ●

Asset allocation in portfolio construction

Introduction

This chapter examines asset allocation in the context of the individual investor's portfolio, with reference to asset class studies and the key aim of diversification at total portfolio level.

Objectives

After reading this chapter you should be able to:

- Explain why asset allocation is so important as a starting point for building a portfolio.
- Describe **systematic** and **non-systematic risk**.
- Explain what is meant by **capital asset pricing model (CAPM)**.

●●●● Coherent allocation at total portfolio level

It is important that each individual makes fund and stock selections based on sound financial principles and considers asset allocation across their entire range of investments. This means maintaining a coherent allocation at total investment level, rather than regarding assets held in tax-efficient wrappers such as pension plans and Individual savings accounts (ISAs) as separate entities. A portfolio of funds and, where appropriate, individual equities, should reflect the individual's current financial position (and that of their family), the individual's current and future investment objectives, and tax status. It may also reflect ethical views (see Chapter 15).

Investing in collective funds helps to spread the risk that individual companies will go bust. This is particularly relevant in the smaller company market. The planner's task is to quantify the level of risk the individual can and is prepared to take (these may be quite different).

●●●● Asset allocation studies

Economic studies show that asset allocation accounts for over 90% of the outcome for institutional pension funds. The original study, 'Determinants of Portfolio Performance', was published by Gary Brinson, L. Randolf Hood, and Gilbert Beebower in the July/August 1986 issue of *Financial Analysts Journal*. This demonstrated that on average 91.5% of the variation in quarterly pension fund returns was due to investment policy and set as an optimal mix the 80/20 model for the passive/active management mix.

In June 2003 the research was revisited and revised by David Blake of the Pensions Institute, which is attached to the Cass Business School in London. *Financial System Requirements for Successful Pension Reform* (available at **www.pensions-institute.org**) argues that 99.47% of the total return for pension funds is determined by the strategic asset allocation set by the actuarial asset/liability model. The point of both papers is to stress the comparatively minor impact of active asset management in the overall return, which suggests that active management should be used sparingly and only where it can make a positive contribution after fees.

This type of research can be misinterpreted. Asset allocation will be a strong determinant in the outcome but it does not of itself determine a high return; rather, it sets the return parameters. A risk-averse asset allocation might provide an expected annualised return of 2% above gilt yields, for example, where a more adventurous asset allocation would provide 3%.

The objective of the planner is to ensure that the range of asset classes and the allocation to each of these is appropriate for the individual's objectives and risk profile. Institutional investors, such as pension funds, use **stochastic modelling** to estimate the probability of certain events occurring and to assess the impact on the portfolio and returns. It does this by simulating many different events that could impact on the investor and the portfolio. The result is a **mean expected outcome** and a **statistical**

distribution of outcomes. Stochastic modelling and similar processes such as Monte Carlo modelling do not predict with total accuracy but they produce parameters for possible outcomes.

Asset allocation is our first priority after the individual circumstances, objectives, and risk assessment analysis. It makes sense to use relevant tax efficient product wrappers only where they can enhance the return of the individual's preferred investments.

Assuming that an investor is looking for a combination of growth and income over the long term, then diversification across a broad range of asset classes and investment styles helps to reduce risk and volatility at the overall portfolio level yet still maintain the potential for outperformance (performance in excess of the relevant index and/or peer group). Of course in practice the markets never behave quite as they do in textbooks. Nevertheless, if we understand the way different asset classes generally behave we are less likely to be taken in by the 'flavour of the month' approach adopted by many ISA managers and financial advisers, for example, which often turns out to be flavour of last month or last year, and well past its sell-by date.

Asset class characteristics

The best way to understand this subject is to think in terms of the function asset classes perform as part of a portfolio. As seen in Chapter 4, assets are grouped into broad categories or classes according to how they respond to different economic conditions. Some provide a safe haven at times of crisis – cash and good quality bonds, for example – but the return they offer in terms of the yield or interest is relatively low compared with more dynamic asset classes *over the long term.*

Certain asset classes offer the prospect of an income stream – bonds again, which pay interest (the yield), but also commercial property, for example, where the yield is provided by the rental income. Yet others offer the potential for capital growth, where the return is achieved by an increase in the asset price, although the yield can also be a significant element in the total return.

Growth assets usually refer to the various equity markets (developed, emerging, and private equity). In turn, equity markets are subdivided into different sectors (for example banks, chemicals and transport) and also into large and small capitalisation. In the UK the FTSE SmallCap index refers to companies below the FTSE 350 in the All-Share.

Finally there is the far from homogenous class of alternative investments, which are not correlated with, and therefore offer diversification from, the traditional asset classes. Some of these are absolute return funds, which aim to provide positive returns throughout all market conditions.

Diversification overseas

Once we have built up a core UK equity portfolio it is a good idea to diversify overseas. However, it is important to do this in a way that achieves genuine diversification.

Contrary to received wisdom, continental European and US equity markets tend to move in a similar direction to the UK stock market and so, while these are very important markets, they do not necessarily act as efficient diversifiers. A more effective alternative would be to invest a modest amount in emerging markets and Japan, for example. Having said that, it is important to be able to identify specialist fund managers who really understand how these riskier capital markets work and where the inefficiencies lie. For example they need to take account of the structure of the local index, its concentration in specific companies, and any taxation barriers to active management, all of which help determine the available risk-return trade-offs.

Capital asset pricing model (CAPM)

This is relevant when considering positively correlated, negatively (inversely) correlated, and non-correlated assets (see page 50). A capital asset pricing model is an economic model for valuing assets that assumes that the expected excess return of a security over a risk-free asset will be in proportion to its beta. Beta is defined as a statistical measure of volatility that indicates the sensitivity of a security or portfolio to movements in the market index. For example a security with a beta of 1 is expected to give the same return as the index, and so it is considered to be highly correlated with the relevant index. Higher beta stocks or portfolios are expected to outperform in rising markets but will fall as market direction takes a downturn. Alpha is defined as outperformance created by the manager's skill.

Systematic and non-systematic risk

Investors are exposed to a range of sources of risk that include the following:

- A fall in the income derived from dividends or interest.
- Interest rates, which will affect the price of bonds, for example.
- Inflation risk, which will undermine real returns.
- Default risk; that is, where a borrower is unable to meet interest payments and/or cannot return the original capital (principal).
- Liquidity; that is, the inability to find a buyer or seller.
- Fiscal risk; for example a change to the tax on investments.
- Exchange rates, which can devalue an overseas investment.
- Economic risk; that is, the impact of economic cycles.
- Political risk; for example where a company is nationalised.

Analysts divide total risk into **systematic** and **non-systematic**. Non-systematic refers to factors that only affect that specific investment. Systematic (market risk) refers to general market influences and movements that affect all or most investments. It is possible to reduce non-systematic risk through diversification but this is not possible with systematic risk.

The deployment of active management fees

Once an individual has decided the proportion of investments to allocate to equities, bonds, property, alternatives, and cash – and to the different sub-sectors and styles within these asset classes – it is timely to consider how best to deploy active management fees. The cost of asset management is always relevant but this is particularly so in a period of prolonged low inflation and comparatively low returns, when paying an annual management charge (AMC) significantly in excess of 1% makes little sense if we can achieve the same result, after fees, with an index tracker. Average returns in any given asset class tend to relate to market efficiency – that is, the level of information and company research available to managers and the corresponding scope for identifying opportunities.

Efficient markets

A market is described as 'efficient' where there is a large amount of analysis available to potential investors and where new information is reflected quickly in the share prices. Generally it is considered more difficult to outperform in efficient markets. Students will also come across the term **efficient frontier**. This is a graphical representation of the relationship between risk and reward, which aims to show the greatest expected return for a given level of risk.

In the efficient markets less than 15% of UK and US domestic bond managers outperform the relevant index. Even in the semi-efficient UK and US equity markets, only 30% of managers achieve this distinction. By contrast, in the inefficient markets, such as emerging market equities and Japanese equities, the percentage of managers outperforming the index are much higher at about 45% and 60% respectively. This would suggest that the more efficient the market, the less the opportunity for skill-based outperformance and the more compelling the argument in favour of passive management.

While there is a wide range of passive equity funds, indexed bond funds are a rare breed in the UK and only available to the larger investor. However, exchange-traded funds (ETFs), which offer a similar profile to tracker unit trusts, are available for Euro and US bonds and are shortly expected to cover UK bonds, so the opportunities for index-style bond funds will increase.

'Star' managers

There is considerable debate about the merits of star managers – those who provide consistently good results over the medium to long term. The big discount brokers offer profiles of top managers and suggest that provided an investor buys within a low cost supermarket, it is cheap and simple to follow a star when they defect to a rival organisation. We should be cautious about accepting this logic without investigation.

While an individual manager may be the key driver behind a fund's performance, it is equally important to consider the environment in which that performance was achieved. When a manager moves we need to take a close look at the supporting analyst and research functions in the new environment. We should also consider carefully any change in the manager's responsibilities and level of involvement in the fund. On promotion a talented individual might become a manager of people rather than a manager of money and this could undermine future performance.

Reweighting a portfolio

In practice few individuals start taking interest in their investments from the very beginning. Most gain an interest over time and after they have already built up what may be a rather incoherent portfolio. This means that a reweighting of asset allocation will be the planner's first step after all the preliminary fact find. Here it will be necessary to sell certain shares because they are inappropriate for the individual's investment aims or because they represent too large a proportion of the portfolio and therefore create a concentration of risk. Consider, for example, the type of portfolio an individual may have if they responded to privatisation offers, received free 'windfall' shares from a demutualised building society or life assurance company, and applied for shares through the employer's share option scheme. This type of portfolio may have done quite well in the past but it will not be representative of the FTSE All-Share. Instead it is likely to consist of utilities (privatisation issues), financials (windfalls), and the sector into which the employer falls. Such a portfolio could lack representation in important sectors like foods, pharmaceuticals, and retailers, among others.

It is also important to remember that if an individual intends to invest a large sum – for example an inheritance, or the proceeds from a pension or endowment plan – there is no need to complete the process in a matter of days. Timing is critical to successful investments and in practice it could take 6 to 12 months to construct or rebalance a portfolio.

Where major reweighting is necessary it will be important to consider the individual's tax position, particularly the capital gains tax (CGT) implications of selling large chunks of shares. Tax may become more complicated if an individual is retired or close to retirement. At this point in addition to income tax and CGT considerations it will be necessary to give careful thought to inheritance tax (IHT) planning. Taxation is examined in Chapter 19.

Collective funds will play an important role even if the individual has significant capital to invest. It makes sense to use collectives to gain exposure to certain markets – smaller UK companies and overseas markets, for example. It can be risky or impractical to invest in one or two smaller companies (there are more than 400 in the SmallCap index) – unless, of course, the investor is really convinced of a company's merits.

Overseas markets can be more expensive to enter and individual share prices much larger than they are in the UK, where companies split shares when they become unwieldy. Swiss companies, for example, commonly have a share price of £5,000 each, so if you have £100,000 to invest in total overseas it is not sensible to have, say, two shares in one Swiss company. Rather, you should have £10,000 in units in a collective Swiss blue chip fund if you are keen on Switzerland – or possibly £20,000 in a European blue chip fund, which would invest in a selection of leading European companies.

Private investor indices

While asset allocation must be an individual decision, it is helpful to see how the experts approach the task of asset allocation for private investors. A good source of independent research is the private investor indices constructed by FTSE International in conjunction with the Association of Private Client Investment Managers and Stockbrokers (APCIMS). These are published in the 'Money FT' section of the *Financial Times* at weekends.

Typical model portfolios are based on three broad objectives: income, growth and balanced (see Table 5.1). The asset allocation of each model portfolio is based on research from a wide range of private client fund managers and stockbrokers. The weightings are amended on a regular basis, so the following figures will not necessarily be up to date, but nevertheless they serve to highlight the different strategies used to achieve the three most common investment goals. (See page 81 for a discussion on how these models can be used for performance measurement benchmarks.)

The difference in the UK equity weighting is not as great as we might expect, but the individual shares would be selected with different priorities in mind. Growth would be achieved by taking a slightly more aggressive approach and while you would expect a fair number of blue chips, there would also be some small- and medium-sized companies to boost growth prospects. By contrast the income portfolio would focus on higher yielding shares. Some investors might have a preference for the larger

Table 5.1 Private investor indices' asset allocation

	Income portfolio %	Growth portfolio %	Balanced portfolio %	Representative index
UK shares	50	60	55	FTSE All-Share
International shares	5	25	20	FTSE World Ex-UK index calculated in sterling
Bonds	40	10	20	FTSE Gilts All Stocks index
Cash	5	5	5	7-Day LIBOR –1% (London Interbank offer rate)
Total	100	100	100	

Note: The latest values of the indices can be found on the FTSE website (**www.ftse.com**).
Source: FTSE International/APCIMS (asset allocation March 2004).

companies (for example the FTSE 100 companies), which tend to have a steadier track record on dividends payments than some smaller companies. The point to bear in mind here is that size and risk do not go hand in hand but represent two different decisions for income seekers. Some smaller, higher risk companies can provide a high yield but might not be appropriate for a retired income seeker. However, many retired investors are looking not just for short-term income but also for income over 10 to 20 years. Over this period the bond and cash element would provide a stable guaranteed income but equities are needed to provide an element of capital growth to maintain the real value of the portfolio.

We should not assume that a client approaching retirement should automatically switch part of the portfolio out of equities and into gilts, bonds and cash. Many investors who retire early cannot or do not want to draw their pension immediately – either because it will not be paid until the employer's official pension age of 65 or because the pension would be substantially reduced. In this case the individual might be looking for an immediate and high income from the portfolio rather than long-term income and growth.

International equities play an important part in the growth portfolio in order to gain access to different economies, both developed and developing. Having said that, if an investor is interested in certain sectors – car manufacturing for example – the choice of UK shares is very limited and therefore we may suggest US shares, for example, to obtain the level of exposure and diversification.

Overseas investment is important but bear in mind the points mentioned above about where to find genuine diversification. Also, foreign investment exposes the portfolio to currency fluctuations and, in some countries, exchange control issues. Political instability and hyperinflation may be features of emerging economies.

Finally, the weighting of bonds and cash is probably the clearest indication of the portfolio's aim. In this case the income portfolio has 45% of its assets in these classes, while the growth portfolio has only 15%. A younger investor with a robust attitude to risk might not even bother with this amount but go wholly for UK and foreign equities.

For most investors, whether looking for income, growth, or a balance of the two, at least half of the portfolio will be invested in UK shares. Although there is a tendency to regard the FTSE 100 companies as somehow 'safer' than medium and small companies, it is not true to say that big is synonymous with secure. Exposure to the FTSE 250 (the 250 largest companies by market capitalisation after the top 100) and in particular to the SmallCap (the remaining 470 or so shares in the All-Share) can be achieved through collective funds, or direct, depending on the individual's attitude to risk and ability to research less well-known companies adequately.

The FTSE All-Share, which covers 98%–99% of the companies that are listed on The London Stock Exchange, has 35 sectors. Some include a large number of companies representing a broad spectrum of industry – Engineering & Machinery, for example. Others are designed to categorise just a few important companies in a very specific market.

Activity 5.1

Diane Evans has just inherited £100,000 on the death of her father. She is married with two young children and, as a university lecturer, her earnings are not high, although the University Superannuation Scheme provides an excellent pension. Consider how best Diane might deploy this capital. With the amount you decide to invest, provide a breakdown of the asset allocation and the rationale for this.

Comment: To answer this question you need to draw up a mini financial plan that sets out personal assets and liabilities. Your decision should take account of any debts (a mortgage, for example) and any future anticipated expenses.

Summary

This chapter considered some of the important factors that we should take into consideration when building a portfolio. Asset allocation is critical, as this will dictate the risk/reward profile. Model portfolios are a useful tool and provide benchmark allocations for investors seeking income, growth or a balance of the two.

Key terms

- Alpha p. 70
- Beta p. 70
- Capital asset pricing model (CAPM) p. 70
- Efficient frontier p. 71
- Mean expected outcome p. 68
- Statistical distribution of outcomes p. 68
- Stochastic modelling p. 68
- Systematic and non-systematic risk p. 70

Review questions

1 Explain why asset allocation is so important in the construction of a private investor's portfolio.

2 Describe alpha and beta with relation to performance.

3 What is the difference between systematic and non-systematic risk? Which of these can be reduced through diversification?

4 Describe how weightings to the main asset classes would vary in a portfolio that aims for income, compared with a portfolio that aims for growth.

Go to the Companion Website at **www.booksites.net/harrison_pfp** for a multiple-choice quiz to test your understanding of this chapter.

Further information

Details about the FTSE International/APCIMS Private Investor Indices can be found at the FTSE International website at **www.ftse.com** where a service called 'On Target' will allow you to analyse the performance of the portfolios free of charge. Alternatively, the indices are available on the APCIMS site at **www.apcims.co.uk,** and are reported in the *Financial Times* and other financial newspapers and publications.

The Pensions Institute: **www.pensions-institute.org**

The Pensions Policy Institute: **www.pensionspolicyinstitute.org.uk**

Chapter 6 ●●●●

Performance measurement and monitoring

Introduction

This chapter provides a basic guide for students who want to read and understand the financial pages, particularly as they appear in the *Financial Times*. This will provide the basic information required to monitor and measure the progress of individual shares and collective funds.

Objectives

After reading this chapter you will be able to:

- Explain why it is necessary to measure performance in absolute and relative terms.
- Discuss how shares and funds are classified by sector.
- Explain how to value shares.
- Describe bonds yield calculations.

Measurements for performance

To assess the performance of a portfolio we need to compare it first with the individual's objectives, and secondly, with a range of suitable independent benchmarks.

Compare with inflation

The simplest measurement also has the most serious drawbacks. To measure **absolute performance** we take inflation as the benchmark. Let's say, for example, that retail price inflation is 2.5% and an individual's portfolio, which is designed to achieve a balance of income and growth, returns 5% over the year. Considered in isolation we might be quite satisfied that the portfolio has grown by 2.5% in real terms – that is, 2.5% above the rate of inflation. However, we might be less satisfied if we discover that the FTSE All-Share had risen by 7%, or that model private investor portfolios with similar aims had achieved 8%.

The point to note is that when markets are rising most professional and private investors can achieve what appear to be reasonable results. The real skill is in achieving above-average returns throughout the market cycles, when compared with a suitable benchmark.

Compare with an index or peer group

To measure **relative performance** we need a benchmark relative to an index or a peer group. The most relevant index for a portfolio of UK shares is the FTSE All-Share, which is regarded as the main yardstick for the UK stock market as a whole. No matter how specialised a portfolio, it is always worth checking progress against a broad benchmark like the All-Share to help assess whether the deviation from this index is worth the risks. However, where a portfolio has a bias towards medium sized or smaller companies we might also measure against a more specific index such as the FTSE 250 or the SmallCap.

Portfolio measurement

Two independent services aim to provide a benchmark against which it is possible to measure private investors' portfolios. The first is the Private Investor Indices from FTSE International and the stockbrokers' association, APCIMS, and the second is from The WM Company, one of the leading performance measurers in the institutional market. However, the latter is only available to investment managers on a subscription basis, whereas the FTSE/APCIMS service is free (but less detailed). It appears on the website and also in the *Money FT* section of the weekend *Financial Times*, on the 'Databank' page. We refer to the FTSE/APCIMS model portfolios in Chapter 5 where we examined asset allocation (see page 73).

We can use the FTSE International indices (income, growth and balanced), which are published in the *Financial Times*, in several ways:

- To make a direct comparison with a portfolio.
- To use as the basis for a review of the asset allocation and structure of a portfolio with the investment adviser.
- As a benchmark against which we can compare and assess the performance of discretionary stockbrokers.

The FTSE/APCIMS indices show what happens to a portfolio which is run like a collection of index tracking funds – each element representing the appropriate index for UK equities, various overseas equity indices, cash and so on. Clearly, the asset allocation of any 'model' portfolio is to some extent arbitrary but given the expertise of the providers, this is as good a benchmark as any and will show whether the way that an individual's portfolio deviates from the indices actually improved returns or undermined performance.

WM's service is quite different as it is based on actual asset mix information from a wide range of managers, combined with the returns on the appropriate investment indices over the quarter measured.

Both services are very useful but remember that benchmarks are only intended to provide guidelines and should not be regarded as an absolute measure of performance. The FTSE/APCIMS indices, for example, are designed to relate to the average UK-based investor with a sterling denominated pool of savings. We must also remember that investors may have potential capital gains tax liabilities that must be taken into account, as must any advisory fees.

●●●● Collective funds

For fund comparisons it is important to measure against other funds with a similar asset allocation and ideally a similar management style, although this can be difficult. The trade associations for the three different types of funds are as follows and the websites are given at the end of the chapter (see also Chapters 12 and 13, which examine the structure of investment trust companies, unit trust funds and life office unit linked funds):

- Life assurance funds: the Association of British Insurers (ABI).
- Unit trusts and open ended investment companies (OEICs): the Investment Management Association (IMA).
- Investment trusts: the Association of Investment Trust Companies (AITC).

These organisations are responsible for setting the criteria for each of the investment categories, so that private and institutional investors can compare like with like. However, the categories are largely based on minimum and maximum asset allocation parameters and so the variation can be significant and can contain a wide range of risk profiles, particularly in the 'managed fund' sector for life assurance and pension funds, for example. Also, it is important to remember that the categories do not take into account investment style or approach to risk. This means that certain managers might have achieved an outstanding performance only because they took bigger risks than is typical for the fund sector as a whole.

We should check fund performance on a **discrete** rather than **cumulative** basis. Discrete results show year-on-year performance. A good cumulative result over five years might hide an outstanding (possibly lucky) short-term performance followed by several years of mediocrity. Standard & Poor's Fund Research is a useful resource here. Its fund ratings are based on quantitative data (performance screening and attribution, for example) and qualitative information (the manager's investment process and philosophy, the personnel and technical support, and the risk profile, structure and size of the fund itself, for example).

For individual funds, a good place to start with research is the managers' monthly reports, which are available on their websites. Citywire is a commercial service that measures the individual manager's performance and this can provide an interesting perspective. Many financial advisers have favourite fund managers and provide profiles on their own websites. Be careful with advisers, however, as they may be influenced by the level of commission they can secure from a particular fund manager.

For investment trusts a useful source of performance data is the monthly information sheet (MIS) from the AITC, which shows the results of £100 invested in each investment trust share and the performance of the underlying net assets. The latter is considered a far better measure of the company's investment expertise because it disregards the impact of market forces on the company's share price.

Periods of measurement

The costs of buying shares, whether direct or through a unit or investment trust, combined with the short-term volatility of markets, indicates that it is most relevant to measure performance over the medium to long term – typically over a minimum period of five years. However, regular monitoring is also important if we want to pick up on changes in fund management style or personnel, for example.

With equity investments clearly past performance is an imperfect guide to the future – whether we hold these directly or through collective funds. However, performance can give a good indication of a company's prospects where it is examined in conjunction with other essential data about the company and its investment processes.

Once we have identified the funds that are appropriate in terms of asset class and allocation it is important to assess different managers' investment style. For example was the performance achieved through a consistent ability to pick the right stocks or did the total returns rely on occasional periods of out-performance based on a high risk/reward strategy?

It is also important to keep track of the management team responsible for the performance. Individual managers and often whole investment teams have an annoying habit of defecting to rival companies. If this happens in an investment house where star managers rule the roost, we might consider a similar move, although we should first find out if the manager will have the same hands-on role in the new company and that the analyst support is of a similar standard.

Guide to reading the financial pages

The FTSE International website provides daily updates of the values of the indices (see Table 6.1).

The sections below on 'How to read the figures' were drawn from *The Financial Times Guide to Using the Financial Pages*, R. Vaitilingam, Financial Times Prentice Hall, London, 2001, and from details provided in the 'Guide to The London Share Service', which is published at the end of the share prices in the *Financial Times Companies & Markets* section.

Financial Times services

The *FT*'s London Share Service and the Managed Funds Service, published daily, include various investor services indicated by a symbol after the company name. A club symbol, for example, indicates we can obtain the current annual or interim report free of charge. Up-to-the-second share and fund prices are available from the *FT* Cityline service at **www.ftcityline.com** or phone 020 7873 4378.

Share prices information

Share prices, including investment trusts, are quoted on weekdays in the *FT Companies & Markets* section, and in the *FT Money & Business* section at the weekend. This includes companies in the All-Share, the Alternative Investment Market (the market

Table 6.1 FTSE APCIMS Private Investor Index Series Values

Last Updated: 31/03/2004 Index name	Index value	Total return index value	% Change 1 day	% Change 1 month	% Change 3 month	% Change 1 year	% Change 5 year
Growth portfolio	2491.4	1331.28	−0.33	−1.07	−0.13	21.09	−18.31
Balanced portfolio	2253.87	1354.01	−0.28	−0.94	−0.10	18.09	−16.73
Income portfolio	1875.59	1400.16	−0.18	−0.80	−0.08	12.42	−14.36
FTSE All-Share	2196.97		−0.50	−2.07	−0.47	26.57	−24.11
FTSE World (Ex UK) index	235.41		−0.21	0.47	0.33	22.73	−17.26
FTSE Gilts All-Stocks index	152		0.18	0.50	0.25	−3.49	−8.23
Cash on deposit	117.87		0.01	0.18	0.47	1.63	13.80
RPI	183.8		0.00	0.38	0.60	3.14	12.28

Source: FTSE.

for new smaller companies), and foreign companies. Students should also consult FTfm, which appears as a supplement each Monday. This includes FT Fund Ratings.

Daily guide to London Share Services pages: Figure 6.1

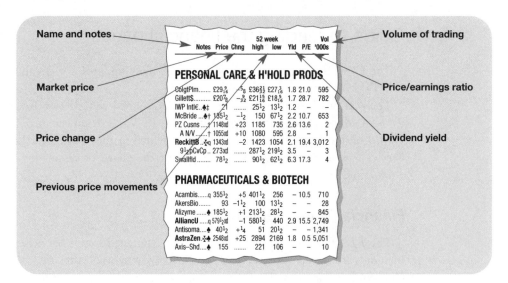

Figure 6.1

Source: Financial Times, 2nd April 2004.

How to read the figures

The column headings used in the *Financial Times* are shown in brackets.

Name and notes (Notes): The first column lists the company name or its abbreviation. The various symbols represent particular features of its shares. For example a diamond indicates that a merger, bid or reorganisation is in process, while a club indicates that there is a free annual or interim report available. A heart symbol indicates an overseas incorporated company listed on an approved exchange. Many shares of overseas mining companies fall into this category. A spade symbol indicates an unregulated collective investment scheme.

Market price (Price): The second column shows the average (or mid-price) of the best buying and selling prices in pence quoted by market makers (the financial institutions that actually buy and sell shares) at the 4.30pm close of the market on the previous trading day. If trading in a share has been suspended, perhaps because the company in question is involved in a take-over, the figure shown is the price at suspension and this is indicated by a hash symbol (#). The letters 'xd' following a price mean ex-dividend and indicate that a dividend has been announced recently but new buyers will not be entitled to receive it.

Price change (Chng): The third column gives the change in the closing price compared with the end of the previous trading day.

Previous price movements (52 week high/low): Columns four and five show the highest and lowest prices recorded for the stock for the past 12 months. At the weekend this figure shows the high and low for the calendar year.

Dividend yield (Yld): Column six shows the percentage return on the share. It is calculated by dividing the gross dividend by the current share price.

Price/earnings ratio (P/E): The seventh column is the market price of the share divided by the company's earnings (profits) per share in its latest 12-month trading period. In effect this is a measure of investor confidence since it compares the price of a stock with the amount the company is earning in profits. Generally the higher the figure the higher the confidence but you should only measure against companies in the same sector.

Yields and P/E ratios move in opposite directions. If the share price rises, since the gross dividend remains the same, the dividend yield falls. Also, if the share price rises, since the earnings per share are constant, the P/E ratio increases. Expect a big change in these figures when important company announcements are made on earnings and dividends.

Volume of trading (Vol '000s): The final column shows the number of shares traded the previous day rounded to the nearest 1,000. Dashes indicate that no trade has taken place or that there is no data available.

Weekly summary each Monday: Figure 6.2

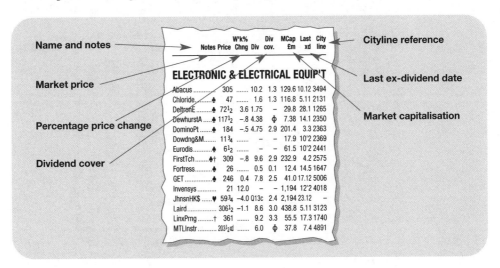

Figure 6.2

Source: Financial Times, 19th April 2004.

On Mondays the *FT* provides information on the following:

Market price (Price): As before.

Percentage price change (W'k % Chng): The weekly percentage change.

Dividend cover (Div cov.): This shows the number of times the dividend could have been paid out of net profits. The figure is a ratio of profits to dividends, calculated by dividing the earnings per share by the gross dividend per share. Analysts regard this as an important figure in assessing the security of the company and its ability to maintain the level of future dividend payments.

Market capitalisation (MCap £m): This is an indication of the stock market value of the company in millions of pounds sterling. It is calculated by multiplying the number of shares in issue by their market price. In order to calculate the number of shares in issue from the figures listed you can divide the market capitalisation figure by the market price. However, if there were other classes of share capital in issue, their value would also need to be added in order to calculate the company's total market capitalisation.

Last ex-dividend date (Last xd): The last date the share went ex-dividend.

Cityline reference (City line): This is the reference number if you want up-to-the-minute information from Cityline.

Managed funds service: Figure 6.3

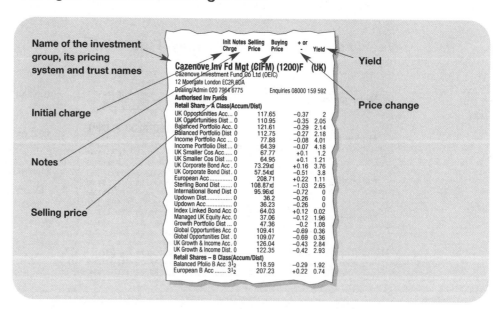

Figure 6.3

Source: Financial Times, 2nd April 2004.

Unit trust, open-ended investment company (OEIC), and insurance company fund prices appear under 'Managed Funds Service'. These are funds authorised by the Financial Services Authority and therefore can be marketed direct to the public. Unauthorised trusts are not sold to the public but are used as internal funds by the financial institutions.

Unit trust and OEIC management groups are obliged to provide certain information to unit holders and the accepted practice is to publish unit prices, together with other important information in the *Financial Times* and other national newspapers. The funds are grouped by fund manager and shown in alphabetical sequence.

Name of the investment group, its pricing system and trust names: This is shown as, for example, 'Artemis Fund Managers Ltd (1200)F (UK), followed by the company's address and telephone number for dealing or enquiries. The figure in brackets in the heading is the basis of the company's pricing system. The figure refers to the time at which the price was measured (using a 24-hour clock) and the basis of calculation. 'F' refers to forward pricing, which means orders are taken from investors and the price of units is determined by the next valuation. All larger groups have a valuation point each day, often at noon. So, if an investor phones through their order at 10am, the price will be struck at noon that same day. An investor who phones at 1pm will have to wait for a price until the following midday valuation. Some groups still deal on an historic price basis, indicated by 'H'. This means they buy and sell using the price agreed at the last valuation point.

Initial charge (Init chrge): Column two indicates the percentage charge deducted.

Notes: The symbols and letters in column 3 indicate particular features of a unit trust. For example 'E' indicates there is an exit charge when the investor sells units, 'C' indicates that the manager's annual charge is deducted from capital, not income. A full list of notes, some of which may appear against figures in other columns, can be found at the end of the Managed Funds Service section.

Selling price: This is also called the **bid price** and is the price at which investors sell units *back* to the manager.

Buying price: This is also called the **offer price** and is the price at which investors buy units.

Price change (+ or –): The sixth column compares the mid-point between the bid and offer prices with the previous day's quotation.

Yield (Yield): The last column shows the income paid by the unit trust as a percentage of the offer price. The quoted yield reflects income earned by the fund during the previous 12 months and therefore relates only to past performance.

Investment trust prices: Figure 6.4

Notes	Price	Chng	52 week high	low	Yld	NAV	Dis or Pm(-)
MerLyEnTc..♣	24^1_4	$+^1_2$	26^1_4	13^1_2	–	27.1	19.5
MerLyWld...♣	205^1_2xd	$+3^3_4$	227	115^1_2	0.8	227.0	9.5
Wts...........	12^1_2	$+1^1_4$	13^1_4	10^1_2	–	–	–
Mid Wynd...♣	561^1_2xd	....	564	400	1.6	675.6	16.9
Mithras.....♣z	61^1_2xd	....	62^1_2	35^1_2	6.2	75.4	18.4
Monks.......♣	173	$+2^1_4$	179	119^3_4	0.6	207.7	16.7
Mont UK....♣	134^1_2	$+^1_2$	136^1_4	95^1_2	1.9	174.7	23.0
Mor Abs......t	15xd	....	22^1_2	12^1_2	24.8	6.8	–121.6
ZDP..........	88	....	88	20	–	114.6	23.2
MurEmer....♣	19^1_2	....	22^1_2	3	15.7	28.1	30.6
Uts	295	....	295	145	3.1	342.0	13.7
ZDP..........	124^1_2	....	126	74^1_2	–	128.9	3.4
MurExtRt...♣	0^1_4	....	1^3_4	0^1_4	–	0.8	62.8
Inc...........t	19^1_2	....	24^1_4	15	35.9	–	–
ZDP..........	137^3_4	....	138^1_2	97	–	152.1	9.5
MurGlobl....♣	16^1_2xd	....	22^1_4	9	42.4	24.4	32.5
Uts ....t	154xd	....	164	93^1_4	4.9	171.8	10.4
ZDP..........	136^1_2	....	141^1_2	82^1_2	–	147.4	7.4
Mur Inc ....♣	420^1_4xd	....	449	363^1_2	4.2	480.8	12.6
Mur Int ....♣K	390	+2	397^3_4	306	4.2	424.5	8.1
B	335	....	335	272^1_2	–	424.5	21.1
MurVCT......s	23^1_2	....	40	23^1_2	12.1	34.6	32.1
MurVCT 2....s	28^1_2	....	45	25	3.5	43.6	34.6
MurVCT 3....s	29^1_2	....	45	27	5.4	58.5	49.6
MurVCT 4	50^1_2	....	60	42^1_2	4.0	77.6	34.9
New Fulc...♣t	16xd	....	17^1_2	4^1_2	42.5	22.0	27.2
ZDP..........	137^1_2	$+^3_4$	138^3_4	85^1_2	–	147.4	6.7
New Opps Inv	73^1_2	....	79^1_2	16^1_2	–	99.2	25.9

Discount or premium

Net asset value

Figure 6.4

Source: Financial Times, 2nd April 2004.

Investment trusts are quoted in the London Share Service section. Most of the information is the same as for other companies, with the exception of the last two columns.

Net asset value (NAV): This is the approximate value of the underlying assets owned by the company. The NAV is shown in pence per share.

Discount or premium (Dis or PM(–)): If the value of the underlying assets is higher than the share price, then the trust is said to be at a **discount**. In other words, assuming there is nothing untoward about the trust, the shares are likely to be good value because their underlying value is worth more than the price you pay. If the NAV is lower than the share price the shares are at a **premium** and this is shown as a negative figure.

FTfm Funds Ratings

This appears in the FTfm supplement on Mondays. The rankings are not intended as a recommendation (for further details go to **www.ft.com/fundratings**). There are three ratings for each fund, where applicable:

Risk (R) is measured by volatility. 1 is very low risk and 5 is very high.

Charges (C). 1 is very low risk and 5, very high.

Past performance (P) is measured relative to a fund's risk profile and adjusted for risk. 1 indicates very low performance and 5, very high.

Activity 6.1

Construct a portfolio of funds selected from the IMA listings and build up a detailed record of performance fluctuations by monitoring your fund's price changes (this would not show the impact of dividend reinvestment). Go to the websites for the funds selected and consult the monthly bulletins. For frequent updates check unit prices in the 'Managed Funds Service' in the *Financial Times*. On Saturdays the information appears in the *Money FT* section, while on weekdays you will find these figures in the *Companies and Markets* section. Compare percentage price changes with changes for an appropriate benchmark, with reference to this chapter. So, for example, you might only need the FTSE All-Share UK equity based unit trusts but may need others as well for more specialist or overseas funds.

If you find reading the pink pages rather daunting, a basic description of the column headings is provided in the FT itself but a more detailed source is the *Financial Times Guide to Using the Financial Pages*.

Summary

This chapter covered the main sources of performance information for individual shares and for funds. It analysed the share and fund service pages in the *Financial Times* to show how to interpret the very condensed information on prices, price movements, and yields, among other features.

Key terms

- Absolute and relative returns p. 78
- Bid and offer price p. 85
- Discrete and cumulative performance p. 80
- Dividend cover p. 84
- Dividend yield p. 83
- Discount and premium p. 86
- Net asset value p. 86
- Relative performance p. 78

Review questions

1 Describe three different benchmarks against which you can measure performance.

2 Explain the difference between absolute and relative performance.

3 Explain the difference between discrete and cumulative performance and why the former is preferable as a measure.

4 What do we mean when we say that an investment trust price is at a discount or premium?

Go to the Companion Website at **www.booksites.net/harrison_pfp** for a multiple-choice quiz to test your understanding of this chapter.

Further information

The Association of British Insurers: **www.abi.org.uk**

The Association of Investment Trust Companies: **www.aitc.org.uk**

The Association of Private Client Investment Managers and Stockbrokers: **www.apcims.co.uk**

Citywire: **www.citywire.co.uk**

The Financial Times: **www.ft.com**

FTfm Fund Ratings: **www.ft.com/fundratings.com**

FTSE International: **www.ftse.com**

Fund Management Rating **www.funds-sp.com**

The Investment Management Association: **www.investmentuk.org**

Standard & Poor's website for fund management: **www.standardandpoors-funds-com**

The WM Company: **www.wmcompany.com**

Further reading

Apart from the ever-growing online resources, there are several useful print sources. For shares read the *Financial Times* and *Investors' Chronicle*. The *FT* also covers collective funds but there are several additional sources of reference; for example the useful articles, surveys and statistics which appear in specialist publications such as *Money Management*, *Bloomberg Money* and *Moneywise* – all of which are available from newsagents. The Consumers' Association has developed a strong financial interest – see *Which?* magazine.

See also *The Financial Times Guide to Using the Financial Pages*, R. Vaitilingam, Financial Times Prentice Hall, 2001.

For a free sample copy of the AITC Monthly Information Service go to **www.aitc.org.uk**.

Part Two

Putting the theory into practice

Chapter 7 ●●●●

Protection insurance

Introduction

Protection insurance is a priority and must be addressed before any cash is allocated to savings and investments. The state provides limited benefits and many of these are means-tested. Employers often provide valuable insurance and it is important to know how these policies work and precisely what they cover.

Objectives

After reading this chapter you will be able to:

● Describe the different types of life assurance.
● Explain how income protection works.
● Outline the difference between income protection and critical illness insurance.
● Highlight the benefits and pitfalls of private medical insurance.
● Understand why long-term care is such a complex product.

●　●　●　● **Life assurance**

Life assurance is one of the few comparatively simple products discussed in this book. It is also cheap, assuming the individual is in average health.

Anyone with dependants or who shares with others the financial responsibility for the household should take out an appropriate level of life assurance. The 'sum assured' – that is, the amount of cover provided in return for the regular premiums – should do two things:

- It should repay any outstanding loans, including the mortgage.
- It should allow the family to maintain its standard of living by replacing the insured's income in full or by topping up any other benefits they may receive.

We need to give careful consideration to the period for which the life assurance is required. A sound approach is to cover the period during which any borrowing remains outstanding and until the children have ceased to be dependant – up to age 21 at least, if they are likely to go on to college or university. Bear in mind that both parents of young children should have insurance. Where the partner who is at home looking after the children dies, the cost of a full time nanny could easily run to £10,000 a year.

The basic calculation then is 'income requirement plus debt minus any existing cover'. Existing cover may be provided by a company pension scheme and/or other private insurances. Where an individual is covered by a company scheme they must replace this on changing jobs and also make sure there are no gaps in cover if there is a gap between jobs. Personal pension plans provide life cover. However, in this case the value will not be linked to salary but instead will depend on how much is in the fund. Where the individual only recently started a pension plan this could be very little so it will be necessary to pay for extra life assurance while the fund is building up in value. It is possible to do this with part of the pension contribution.

Which type of policy?

Once you identify the shortfall in provision you can use one of the methods listed below to fill the gap. The two simplest products are level term assurance and family income benefit. The term assurance lump sum can be invested to provide an annual income and/or used to pay off debt, while family income benefit can directly replace the shortfall in annual income.

Most life assurance policies work on the 'you drop dead, we pay up' principle. However, some companies offer 'whole of life' plans which combine insurance and investment by deducting the cost of life cover from your savings plan.

The following descriptions explain the basic options.

Level term assurance

This provides a tax-free cash lump sum if you die within the period insured. However, if you die the day after the term expires you get nothing. Unless the policy is assigned to cover a specific liability – for example a mortgage – it is sensible to write it under trust so that the lump sum does not form part of the individual's estate if they die. In this way the policy proceeds could be passed on to the children, for example, without having to wait for probate to be granted to the individual's executors.

Life assurance can be written on a **single** or **joint life basis**. A joint life policy covers more than one person – typically a husband and wife. It may be written to pay out if just one of the spouses dies ('joint life first death') or only when both have died ('joint life second death'). Joint policies can be useful in inheritance planning. Here the sum assured covers the bill for inheritance tax that the children might otherwise have to pay when the second parent dies.

Term assurance comes in other forms:

- **Convertible renewable term assurance** gives the person insured the right to extend the insurance period without further medical underwriting or, in some cases, to convert to an investment linked plan. The former can be useful if it is necessary to increase life cover when the individual is older. Without this facility, many older people would be asked to undergo a medical and could pay much higher premiums if they are not in good health.
- **Decreasing term assurance** reduces at regular intervals and can be used to protect a debt that reduces in a similar way, for example, where the outstanding debt decreases over the loan period at regular intervals. However, repayment mortgage protection insurance is structured in a slightly different way to accommodate the specific pattern of the capital debt reduction.

  Decreasing term assurance can also be used as a means of covering an inheritance tax (IHT) liability where the individual has transferred assets to someone other than the spouse (known as a 'potentially exempt transfer') and where there would be a reducing IHT liability if the donor died during the seven years following the transfer. Remember, the insurance need only cover the potential tax liability – that is, a maximum of 40% of the asset value in excess of the IHT threshold, not the whole of the gift (see Chapter 19).
- **Increasing term assurance** automatically increases the level of cover in line with retail price inflation or by a fixed amount per annum without further medical underwriting. With this type of insurance the annual premiums also increase.
- **Personal pension term assurance** is the same as standard life assurance but here the premiums are paid by the pension fund.

Family income benefit

Family income benefit (FIB) provides a level or increasing income from the date of death until the end of the insurance period. Tax treatment is favourable because although the proceeds are paid in the form of a regular monthly income, they are treated as capital and so there is no income tax to pay.

Whole of life plans

As the name suggests, whole of life plans pay a benefit whenever you die, so there is no specific term. Given the certainty that the policy must pay out at some point, naturally the premiums tend to be higher than for term assurance. Whole of life policies combine insurance and investment. The monthly premiums are invested and from this fund the insurance company deducts the amounts necessary to provide the life cover. When you die you get the fund value or the sum assured, whichever is greater. Some policies require you to pay premiums up to the time of your death, while others make them 'paid up' at a certain age, after which you no longer need to pay premiums. One common use for this type of policy is to provide a lump sum to cover an inheritance tax liability.

The application

The premiums for life assurance will depend on the individual's age, sex and state of health, among other factors. If the individual is overweight or smokes, premiums may be 'loaded' – in other words the individual pays more because there is a greater chance of an early death. Certain dangerous sports will also raise eyebrows in the under-writing department and in turn may raise premiums. In some cases a policy may not cover certain activities. However, if you omit or misrepresent any relevant information then the contract could be declared void by the insurance company.

'Lifestyle' questions

The proposal form will ask if the individual has ever been tested for HIV (AIDS). Where the answer is yes and the insurer refuses cover it may be worth consulting a planner or adviser who specialises in this area. The Institute of Financial Planning and IFA Promotion allow you to search for specialists in different areas.

The medical examination

Individuals who want to take out a large amount of cover should expect to be asked to undergo a medical examination. Despite the aversion most people have to this, it does actually work in their favour. Where life assurance is not fully underwritten (and this is usually the case with policies sold by direct mail or through off-the-page advertising) the underwriters assume there will be a greater incidence of claims so the premiums may be much higher than a medically underwritten contract, particularly where the target market is over 60.

Shop around for a competitive rate

Life assurance is a very competitive market and a financial planner needs access to a comprehensive database that will enable them to select the right features and the best rates available at any given time.

Check the premium rate is guaranteed

The cheapest rates may be offered by companies that reserve the right to 'review' premiums at any time. With reviewable premiums you are effectively writing the insurance company a blank cheque.

Pay by direct debit

Direct debit is the safest method of payment because the premiums are paid automatically. If by mistake the individual overlooks a reminder for the annual cheque the cover may lapse and if it is necessary to reapply they may find that rates have increased due to increased age or a change in health.

Income protection

Life assurance protects the individual's family if he or she dies but it is equally important to insure against loss of income through long-term illness or disability. Despite the plethora of product names there are essentially two types of insurance policy – one that pays a replacement income (income protection is also known as permanent health insurance or PHI) and a second that pays a lump sum (critical illness).

Buying income protection ought to be an easy exercise but some of these products are very complicated and riddled with small print. This can be very worrying, as the last thing we want is to find out too late that certain exclusions render the policy worthless.

State benefits

Employees have very little statutory protection when it comes to long-term sickness. The only requirement for an employer is to pay statutory sick pay from day 4 of an employee's illness to week 28. Statutory sick pay is about £65 per week, while the state long-term incapacity benefit is about £70, although there are various supplements for dependents. You can claim the state incapacity benefit while you are in receipt of your income replacement benefits.

The chances of qualifying for the state incapacity benefit are slim. In April 1995 the government changed the definition of qualifying disability from 'can't do *own* job' to 'can't do *any* job'. This means that even though your medical condition prevents you from continuing your profession, if you can sweep the streets you will be classed as fit for work and you will not qualify for the state long-term incapacity benefit.

The employer's scheme

Some employers provide good income protection insurance through group schemes at work. The company's policy should be set out in the individual's contract of employment. For example the contract might say that if an employee is ill the company will pay the full salary for a specified period after which the amount will depend on the terms and conditions of the group disability scheme. The self-employed and those whose employer does not provide insurance need a private policy.

Under a group income protection scheme the insurer pays the benefit to the employer who then deducts PAYE, National insurance and pension contributions in the usual way before paying the employee. This means that the individual is able to

remain an active member of the company pension scheme and maintain eligibility to state benefits.

Income protection only replaces income during working years, so once the individual reaches the employer's normal pension age the benefit stops and the employer's pension scheme starts to pay a retirement income.

Of course in most cases the employee would expect to return to work after a full recovery. At this point the benefit stops and the normal salary resumes. If an employee only partially recovers from an accident and is unable to resume the former occupation, a good income protection scheme will provide assistance with rehabilitation.

An increasing number of employers offer income protection at a below-market rate even though they do not make a contribution towards premiums. This type of 'voluntary' benefit can offer good value but employers are under no obligation to arrange competitive terms, so caveat emptor – buyer beware – applies just as much as any private purchase.

Private income protection insurance

Through a private income protection policy it is usually possible to insure up to two-thirds of the individual's salary (depending on how much they are prepared to pay in premiums) less any state benefits. Women pay higher premiums than men because of the higher claims experience.

It is possible to cut premiums if the individual is prepared to opt for a waiting period between the date of illness and the date of the first benefit payment. The minimum waiting period is four weeks but premiums reduce significantly after three, six or, in particular, a twelve month deferment period. Where the individual does opt for a long deferment then it is important to ensure there are adequate savings to cover outgoings during this period. Policies with a 'reviewable' premium may be cheaper but it is important to understand the risks. As with life assurance, 'reviewable' means you have no control over future rate increases, so frankly it is a gamble.

It is important to link the insured income to retail price inflation, both during the insurance period and during the payment period. This will cost extra but without it the purchasing power of the income would be eroded rapidly.

The definition of disability

The way that the insurance company defines disability is a key issue, as this will determine whether or not it pays the benefit. The best definition is 'unable to follow *own* occupation' with the possible addition of the phrase 'or an occupation suitable by training, education, experience and status'. The worst definition – and one to avoid at all costs – is 'unable to follow *any* occupation'. This type of policy will be cheaper but the individual must be totally incapacitated in order to claim – as is the case with the state scheme.

Critical illness

Critical illness insurance is quite different from income protection. This pays the owner of the policy a tax-free lump sum on the diagnosis of a range of illnesses or accidents. The lump sum is extremely useful if the individual becomes disabled or frail and needs to move to special accommodation or needs to make alterations to the house.

Most policies use six standard definitions but these do change as medical advances create a more positive prognosis for what in the past were considered life-threatening conditions. The main conditions include:

- Cancer.
- Heart attack.
- Stroke.
- Coronary artery bypass surgery.
- Kidney failure.
- Major organ transplant.

The most common criticism of this type of insurance is that if your illness or disability is not on the list of qualifying conditions you won't get a penny, even though you are unable to work. Some policies include 'permanent total disability' and this is a valuable addition.

Waiver of premium for pension plans

This is another restricted version of income protection. Waiver of premium insurance guarantees that the individual's pension premiums are credited until they are well enough to return to work or, if necessary, up to the date of retirement, when the pension itself can be drawn.

Private medical insurance

The waiting list for many operations under the National Health Service is still over a year for one in twenty patients and over six months for one in four. This does not include the lengthy period between GP referral and seeing a specialist. Regional variations in the provision of care can also make a huge difference to treatment times.

If you want to jump the queue you have to pay. While an increasing number of people are choosing to draw on savings, a more realistic option is to take out private medical insurance (PMI). About 11% of the population has some form of private cover at a cost of over £1.5bn in annual premiums.

What the state provides

The National Health Service aims to provide a full range of medical services for all residents regardless of their income. These services are financed mainly out of general taxation. Most forms of treatment, including hospital care, are provided free of charge 'at the point of delivery', to use the jargon, but you may have to wait a considerable time before being treated and this waiting period varies from area to area.

Employment-based policies

Many employers offer group PMI as part of the employee benefits package but the level of cover varies considerably. Due to the sharp rise in PMI premiums some employers have increased the number of exclusions – for example stress-related conditions are likely to be excluded since these can be very complicated and expensive. Employers often ask employees to pay an 'excess' – that is, the first £100 or so of any treatment. Alternatively an employer may cover the employee but not family members. Premiums paid by an employer are treated as a benefit in kind and are therefore taxable.

Those in a group scheme should find out what happens when they leave and want to continue the insurance on an individual basis. This is particularly important for those coming up to retirement, where age and the past medical treatment could result in very high individual premiums. Some insurers offer a discount when an individual moves from a group scheme to a private plan.

How PMI works

PMI is a complex product and contract conditions can be lengthy. Price is important but so is good service and prompt settlement.

It is important to understand what conditions private medical insurance does and, in particular, does *not* cover. PMI pays for private treatment for *acute curable conditions* – that is, cases where an operation or a short-term course of treatment can put things right permanently. It does not pay for emergency treatment. Nor does it usually pay for chronic illness.

This can lead to confusion. For example under a policy an individual may qualify for private treatment to have a condition investigated and diagnosed, but if it is a long-term illness rather than an acute curable condition they could be back with the NHS.

The premiums for PMI will depend on the level of cover required, the individual's age, and medical history. It will also depend on the type of hospital preferred. Most insurers group hospitals into three bands – London teaching (the most expensive), national, and provincial.

Different types of PMI

It can be difficult to compare PMI policies because they all seem to offer something slightly different. However, most fall into three broad categories:

- Standard.
- Budget.
- Over-60s.

Standard cover should pay for virtually everything but if the individual wants private alternative medicine, GP and dental treatment, for example, these features might only be offered in a deluxe version.

Budget plans limit the insurer's risk by imposing restrictions. For example a plan might restrict the treatment to a 'menu' of the most common operations. If your condition qualifies, then you receive prompt treatment. If it doesn't, you don't receive private treatment. A second method of reducing the insurers' costs is to set a monetary limit either per annum or per treatment. PMI companies claim these limits are usually generous enough to cover most major operations but there is always the concern that the budget might run out halfway through a course of treatment, particularly if complications set in.

An alternative budget concept is the 'six week' plan that provides standard levels of cover but only if the individual cannot be treated under the NHS within six weeks of the consultant's diagnosis. A six-week wait may not sound too onerous but do bear in mind that there may be a long delay between the GP's referral and actually seeing a consultant – unless of course you pay for a private consultation, which is unlikely to be covered by this type of policy.

Finally, as with employers' schemes, some individual plans contain costs by asking the policyholder to agree to pay an excess – that is, the first £100 or so of every claim. This is probably the most acceptable method of cutting premiums, although the reductions achieved are not so dramatic as under the other budget plans.

Managed care

With a managed care process the insurer monitors the claim from the outset, before treatment has started and before the first penny has been spent. This means the individual has to check the insurer will pay before you actually start treatment (this is known as pre-authorisation). It may also be necessary to use certain groups of hospitals where the insurer has negotiated special rates.

Medical history

In most cases the PMI insurer will exclude pre-existing conditions. This will be done in one of two ways. Where the contract is fully underwritten the individual discloses a full medical history and the insurer may impose exclusions as a result. If there is a **moratorium clause** you would not need to disclose your medical history, but all pre-existing conditions would be excluded for a period of time – typically two years – after which they would also be covered. Some pre-existing conditions – heart disease and psychiatric illness, for example – may be excluded permanently.

● ● ● ● Long-term care

Long-term care (LTC) refers to care in the individual's own home or a care home (residential or nursing) for chronic, usually permanent, conditions, and generally those associated with old age. The average nursing home in England costs £20,400 a year, rising to £25,000 in the South East. Residential home fees are slightly lower.

Under the NHS and Community Care Act 1993, the responsibility for assessing need and the payment of nursing home fees shifted from what was then the Department of Social Security (now known as the Department for Work and Pensions) to the already financially overstretched local authorities. The rules were revised in April 2001 and again in October 2003. Age Concern is one of several charities that maintain very detailed fact sheets on this subject, which are updated regularly. These also explain the interaction between care home benefits and other state benefits. Contact details are at the end of the chapter. Remember that the rules for Scotland are very different and there are separate leaflets from the DWP and charities to cover this.

If an individual has assets and investments worth over £20,000 they must pay the care bill in full. Where the assets fall below this level but are above £12,250 then the individual must pay a proportion of the fees. Below £12,250 the individual should not have to pay anything. Having said that, if the elderly person is in a private home, where the fees are higher than local authority homes, then they would have to make up the difference or move.

Since 1 April 2003 the NHS in England has been responsible for meeting part of the cost of care provided by registered nurses to all residents in homes that provide nursing care, whether self-funded or local authority assisted. At the time of writing the benefit was worth £40–£125 per week, depending on the assessment.

The value of the individual's house is not included initially in the means test but after three months this will be taken into account unless there is a spouse or other dependant relative still living at home. As a result many single people have to sell their homes in order to pay the fees.

Pre-funded LTC insurance

LTC is not easy to underwrite and the insurance products are complicated. There are several different models, so it is important to select the most appropriate for the individual's concerns. Expertise is essential here. IFACare is a voluntary association for independent advisers who agree to adhere to a high standard of ethics and a strict code of practice to ensure best advice is given on LTC.

Individuals acting on behalf of elderly parents must have **enduring power of attorney** in order to appoint a professional adviser to help manage their relative's affairs.

Rules exist to prevent individuals from giving away all their worldly goods in order to qualify for full financial support under the social services means test. If you make a substantial gift within six months of entering care your local authority may be able to claw back the assets. Where the gap is longer the authority could take you to court.

There are two ways to insure the cost of long-term care. With a 'pre-funded' plan the individual pays regular premiums or a lump sum ahead of the time when it may be necessary to claim. In the case of an elderly person who is not insured, it might be worth considering an annuity. This would guarantee a regular income to pay the nursing home fees but it might require a substantial investment (see below).

At the time of writing only half a dozen insurance companies offered pre-funded plans. The policies pay the benefit to the nursing home or, in some cases, to the carer. Individuals may also qualify for help towards the cost of home alterations where this would enable them to stay put. Annual benefit, which is tax-free, is usually limited to about £25,000. However, most people can insure for much less than this if they have other sources of income from pensions and investments.

To qualify for benefit the elderly person must fail two or three 'activities of daily living' (ADLs). ADL tests – also used by social services for those who qualify for state help – include washing, dressing, feeding, continence and mobility. Cognitive impairment should also be on the list, given the rapid increase in the number of sufferers of Alzheimer's disease and similar conditions.

As with income protection insurance it is possible to reduce premiums where individuals opt for a long 'deferment period' before receiving the first payment. This can be anything from four weeks to two years. It is also possible to reduce premiums if you restrict cover to a limited payment period – for example two to three years. However, whether an elderly person would enjoy peace of mind with this type of policy is questionable. Certainly, conditions that involve cognitive impairment can result in a lengthy stay in care.

Annuities

If an elderly person wants to be sure there will be an income for the rest of their life to pay the bills it might be worth considering a 'purchased life' (as distinct from a pension) annuity, although to fund this it may be necessary to sell the family home. Where the elderly person could stay at home, provided certain care was available and alterations were carried out, a home income plan might be more appropriate (see Chapter 17).

Annuities are examined in Chapters 9 and 24 but briefly this type of insurance contract provides a regular income for life in return for a lump sum investment. Elderly people with disabilities would qualify for special rates, as they would have a short life expectancy. Unlike pre-funded plans, the annuity payments are not tax-free. Part of the income is treated as a return of capital so this is not taxed. The interest element is taxed but this reduces with age.

LTC investment alternatives

Long-term care is an insurance product, not an investment. Insurance relies on the pooling of risk so the benefits of those who need to claim are paid for by the premiums of those who do not. This may be a price worth paying for peace of mind but some investors regard it as money down the drain.

There is an alternative that combines investment and insurance, but only a handful of companies offer this type of product. Under an LTC investment plan, you pay a lump sum into a fund from which the insurance company deducts monthly premiums to cover the LTC risk. If you need to claim, initially you draw your agreed annual benefit from your fund and when this is exhausted the insurer picks up the tab for as long as you remain in care. In some cases, for an extra cost, you may be able to protect part or all of your fund so that the insurance covers the benefit payments from the outset. However, if you remain healthy to the end and do not make a claim, you can pass your investment on to your dependants.

Activity 7.1

The funding of long-term care is a controversial issue. Individually or in a group, critically evaluate the current rules that apply in England and comment on whether or not you think they are fair.

Comment: Why might the eligibility rules be demeaning for a frail elderly person? Do you think that the state and local authorities should fund all care home fees to a basic level or do you think that it is fair to force the sale of an individual's home to cover the costs? What are the implications here for inheritances? Age Concern in particular provides excellent literature on this subject, which you should use in compiling the facts.

Summary

This chapter examined the main types of personal protection insurance that provide financial support to the family when an individual dies or is too ill to work. It also looked at private medical insurance, which can be used to speed up medical treatment for acute conditions.

Key terms

- Definition of disability p. 96
- Enduring power of attorney p. 100
- Moratorium clause p. 99
- Single and joint life policy p. 93

Review questions

1 Explain the purpose of life assurance, assuming an individual has dependants or shares with others financial responsibility for the household.

2 What is the basic calculation to determine the amount of life assurance required?

3 Explain the differences between income protection and critical illness insurance. If the individual can only afford one policy, which would you recommend and why?

4 Describe two ways in which it is possible to reduce private medical insurance premiums. Which do you think is the best option and why?

5 Explain the means tested rules for eligibility to state help towards care home fees.

Go to the Companion Website at **www.booksites.net/harrison_pfp** for a multiple-choice quiz to test your understanding of this chapter.

Further information

A list of independent firms of advisers who abide by the IFACare Code of Conduct is available from: **www.ifacare.co.uk**. Other useful organisations, most of which provide fact sheets, include The Association of Independent Care Advisers (**www.aica.org.uk**) and the charities Age Concern (**www.ageconcern.org.uk**), Help the Aged (**www.helptheaged.org.uk**) and Care and Repair (**www.careandrepair-england.org.uk**). See page 314 for annuity specialists.

Case study 7.1

Background

Edna Cane, 40 and a smoker, has just given birth to a daughter, Daisy. Edna's husband, Tom, died three months ago in a car accident. Tom's life assurance paid off the mortgage on their house. He had no other protection policies. Edna has income of £3,500 in total over the next three months whilst on maternity leave. Edna is relying on both financial and moral support from her mother who lives nearby. Edna's monthly outgoings exceed her net incomings by £4,000 pa. She intends to return full time to her job as a dentist's receptionist on a salary of £21,000 pa. She has £2,000 cash reserve for emergencies.

Problem

Edna regrets not looking into having more protection cover in the event of the death of either Tom or herself. She has a 20-year level term assurance for £50,000, paying £50 per month. Edna would like to ensure that if she became incapacitated or died, Daisy would receive proper care. Edna's sister, Marjorie, lives in Australia and would bring Daisy up as her

Case study 7.1 *(continued)*

own if the worst happened to Edna. Edna would like Daisy to have as many opportunities as money could buy if she died; eg private schooling, round the world trips, music and dancing lessons, should Daisy so wish.

Edna would like Daisy to attend a day nursery costing £120 per week when she returns to work. The dentist's practice has no income protection scheme if Edna fell ill or died. If she became ill, Edna would like to receive private medical assistance and both herself and Daisy to be cared for in their own home.

Advice

Edna needs help to establish what, if any, benefits she is entitled to since the death of Tom and the birth of Daisy. Edna does not intend either to move house or to obtain another mortgage and so would like to explore options for protection of her income stream and any capital requirements should she become ill or die. She feels that she has sufficient retirement funding. Edna will have up to £150 per month to meet her objectives when she returns to work.

Source: *Money Management*, Financial Planner of the Year Awards 2003, *FT Business*.

A full solution to this case study is available to lecturers via the password-protected area of the Companion Website at **www.booksites.net/harrison_pfp**.

Chapter 8 ●●●●

Banking and debt

Introduction

Banking is an essential component of financial planning and lies at the heart of the family's and the individual's cash flow system, yet it is often overlooked, at least in part because there is an understandable suspicion that all banks are the same and that current accounts are a necessary evil. This chapter considers current accounts, while deposit accounts for savings purposes are examined in the chapter that follows.

We also consider the problems associated with debt. This is an important issue for the consumer market and a key area where the cavaliers have taken advantage of the naive to quite an extraordinary extent. Given the rise in levels of student debt, readers may find that this chapter and Chapter 20 will have a particular resonance. Those interested in ethical banking or banks that cater for different religious groups should also read Chapter 15.

Objectives

After reading this chapter you will be able to:

● List the main criteria for selecting a bank.
● Explain how the main debit and credit cards work.
● Point out the dangers of debt consolidation agencies and suggest an appropriate alternative.

●●●● Banking

It has taken a long time for competitive banking to make a dent in the undeserved profits of the main high street banks but the market is changing and consumers are finally voting with their feet. In particular disgruntled account holders are turning to Internet banks, which provide 24-hour access and allow account holders to move money online, including the payment of bills. For busy people with work, family and other commitments this in itself can lead to better management of cash flow because it may be easier to find time in the evening and at the weekend to monitor accounts. Being able to access bank details via a PC also makes it easier to shift money to higher-interest accounts, so this should help in the general control of short-term savings.

Criteria for selection

Current account details change so frequently that it is worth mentioning only a few generic points here; the rest is down to shopping around. *Moneyfacts* is a good source of information and for those who do not have access to the website, the personal finance pages in the weekend press reproduce useful 'best buy' tables from *Moneyfacts* for comparison. A good generic website on the subject is the British Bankers' Association. Both websites are given at the end of the chapter.

Features to consider when choosing an account include:

- The rates of interest and any qualifying criteria – for example you may need to keep a minimum balance in the account.
- Overdraft charges. Consider how often you are likely to need an overdraft to decide how important low charges are to you.
- Moving money. Check you can pay bills and shift money into a high-interest account if necessary.
- Standing orders and direct debits. Find out how easy it is to change these details online.

The most important feature will be reliability. Internet banks tend to offer good value and better rates of interest than their high street competitors but if the provider's site is frequently unavailable due to technical problems this can be very frustrating.

With any current account it is important to ensure we are paying for the right types of services. Many people assume their bank makes no charges provided they are in credit. Of course the very fact they are in credit means that the bank is able to lend money overnight and on short-term loans in the institutional market and secure a good return – which is not passed on to the bank's customers.

Those who tend to have a high balance in their account should consider banks that pay a better rate of interest than the paltry amount generally offered by the main high street banks. Some of these higher interest accounts demand a very high balance or make an annual charge, which undermines their attractions significantly. Where they make a charge they try to justify it by providing often unwanted insurance and other services. It is far better to keep a closer eye on the account and siphon off any surplus to a high interest deposit account. Again the Internet providers tend to be very competitive and it is easy to move money between accounts online.

Most account holders find it useful to have a prearranged overdraft in case they accidentally overdraw or need to do so for a short period. Unauthorised borrowing usually results in a fine – typically £25.

Account aggregation

Account aggregation provides information across a range of online accounts from the various providers on one website – for example this might include a current account, a savings account, mortgage, credit cards, personal loans and reward schemes (air miles, for example). This can be very convenient but it does involve handing over details of personal identity numbers (PINs) so that the aggregation service can take information from the various websites. In some cases this could break the terms of agreements with online accounts. The FSA does not regulate account aggregation and so it is vital to ensure the provider has rigorous security processes and offers a clear-cut approach to any problems following a security failure.

Debt

Debt is a significant problem in the UK with total unsecured lending through personal loans, credit cards and overdrafts estimated at £170bn at the end of 2003 – a figure that is rising rapidly. Credit card debt alone rose by 59% between 1999 and 2004, according to the independent research agency Datamonitor. **Unsecured lending** is where the borrower does not have to assign an asset to which the lender has access in the event of default. (The most obvious example of secured lending is the mortgage, which gives the lender the right to repossess if the borrower cannot keep up interest payments.)

The Office of Fair Trading (OFT) is responsible for regulating this sector until 2005, at which point the Financial Services Authority takes over. This is part of the major overhaul of the 1974 Consumer Credit Act that followed a critical report from the Commons Treasury Select Committee in December 2003, which attacked the misleading advertising and terms for credit and store cards and laid part of the blame at the OFT's door. The Consumers' Association has been particularly vocal on unfavourable credit card terms.

While careful financial planning should avoid unnecessary debts, nevertheless the planner needs to know where an individual can look for help if they get into difficulties. The organisations and websites mentioned at the end of this chapter provide a range of useful fact sheets and guides and, importantly, spell out the individual's rights. **Debt consolidation** is an attractive concept but in practice it can be an expensive move and can extend the period of debt.

A recent development in the credit market is risk-based interest rates. This is where the lender checks the borrower's credit rating through a credit reference company and adjusts its interest rate upwards or downwards to reflect how promptly the individual has met repayments in the past. Everyone who considers taking out credit or a loan should bear in mind that if they owe money the creditor is entitled to try to get it back. However, the lender must not put a borrower under undue pressure – for example by contacting an employer or harassing the borrower in their home.

Interest free credit

The Consumer Credit Counselling Service (CCCS) warns that certain interest free credit agreements are not what they appear to be and that the interest free period lasts for only part of the repayment term, after which a rate of interest is charged.

Hire purchase

The difference between hire purchase and other forms of borrowing is that with the former, buyers do not become the legal owners of their goods until they have completed payments. In the case of default the supplier has a legal right to repossess the goods where the individual has paid less than one third of the value – or take the individual to court to claim the balance. As a general rule, hire purchase is to be avoided.

Credit and debit cards

Credit card issuers command a market estimated to be worth £60bn. The National Association of Citizens' Advice Bureaux deals with some three quarters of a million people with debt-related problems each year and half of these are to do with credit cards, store cards or other consumer credit arrangements.

There is a lot of confusion about plastic cards – which is not surprising given the number on the market (up from two or three to about twenty in the past few years) and the different functions they perform. One card will allow you to make virtually any purchase on credit, while others will do the same thing but donate a few pence to a trade union or a charity for every purchase you make. Yet others will allow you to buy goods on credit from certain stores.

Unlike banking cards, credit cards are not linked to a current account. Although they go by different names, broadly speaking there are two different types of card – a charge card and a credit card. Bear in mind that nobody is obliged to give credit and if an individual is turned down the company may have consulted a credit reference agency that keeps records of people who do not pay their debts. Credit reference agencies also make mistakes, so it is important to challenge any records that do not appear accurate.

Debit card

A debit card is in effect an 'electronic cheque'. The amount of the purchase is debited to (deducted from) the individual's account, usually two or three days later. The statement entry will often show the name of the supplier from which you bought the goods. Retailers, such as supermarkets, often allow shoppers to draw cash as well as pay for goods.

Credit card

A credit card allows us to pay for goods immediately but defer actual payment until later. The credit company will assess creditworthiness by considering an individual's income and regular commitments. It will then set a maximum limit per month, which the cardholder can spend to pay for goods and services. At the end of each month the credit card provider sends a statement, which itemises all purchases and any payments received. Users can repay the entire debt or just part of it. In fact, provided they meet the minimum payments they can stay in debt as long as they like and pay an often substantial rate of interest on the balance. Credit card companies – even the more respectable – are little more than loan companies in disguise.

The card selected should be suitable for the individual's spending habits. If they intend to pay in full every month and use the card just for convenience then the annual percentage rate of interest charged (APR) is pretty irrelevant. In this case it makes sense to look for a card that has no annual charge and that offers as long as possible to pay the bill. Some of the new entrants from the US appear to offer good value in this respect.

Charge card

A charge card works in a similar way to a credit card but it is necessary to repay the balance every month.

Affinity or donation card

Several leading charities, including Amnesty International, Comic Relief, Oxfam, Save the Children, and Unicef, among others, offer their own credit card. Most will make an initial donation of £5 or £10 to the relevant charity or affinity group as soon as you join. After that they donate anything between 0.25% to 0.5% of all purchases made with the card.

Whether or not individuals should opt for this type of card is very much a personal choice. However, from the planning point of view it is important to make sure that the card is no more expensive than those from mainstream issuers. If it is it would be better to use a standard card and make a modest monthly donation by standing order to a favourite charity. Where this is formalised through a deed of covenant the charity can also claim back the tax the individual has paid, which makes this a very efficient way of giving (see page 19).

Cheque guarantee card

This type of card provides a guarantee for a payment by cheque up to a specified amount – for example £200. Most issuers combine cheque guarantee with a debit card.

Cash withdrawal card

Cash withdrawal cards are available with many instant savings accounts through cash dispensing or 'automated teller' machines (ATMs). The user has a personal identity number (PIN). Again, this feature is usually combined in one debit card.

Store cards

Most major stores or high street chains offer a credit card, which works just like any other except you can only use it to purchase from that particular store or range of stores. It is debatable whether such cards are of any real value – much depends on the added convenience the card provides. For example, it may offer a discount on purchases and provide early access to sale items. The obvious drawback is that users will tend to spend more than they might otherwise have done – a point that hasn't gone unnoticed by the retailers.

Perks

Due to the increased competition, most cards offer some sorts of perks – for example travel accident insurance and insurance against loss or damage of items you purchase with the card. Others offer points you can trade for store vouchers or goods, or allow you to redeem points for money off your gas bill, TV licence and phone bills.

The annual percentage rate (APR)

The OFT explains that one of the main themes of the Consumer Credit Act 1974 is that there should be 'truth in lending', particularly in advertisements for credit and written agreements or other documentation. The Total Charge for Credit Regulations, made under section 20 of the Act, define a **total charge for credit (TCC)**, which includes interest and other charges that affect the real cost of borrowing – even if they are not payable under the credit agreement itself.

Simply knowing the amount of the credit charges is not usually enough for a borrower to compare one credit deal with another. The time at which the credit and charges have to be repaid affects the *rate* of the charges being made and how valuable or costly the deal is to the borrower.

Lenders use a number of different ways of charging interest and these can treat the time of payment in different ways. So, in addition to leaving out other charges, lenders' interest rates will not generally provide a useful comparison. The Total Charge for Credit Regulations also set down how to calculate an **annual percentage rate** of charge (**APR**), which expresses the TCC as a standard measure borrowers can use to compare the credit charges under one deal with another, whatever rate or method of charging is used. The APR should take into account the size, number and frequency of the payments and any other built-in charges. However, the calculation of the APR is extremely complicated and there are many variables. For example some credit card issuers charge interest from the day the purchase is noted on the individual's account. Others charge from the date it appears on the statement, which clearly is cheaper and may make an apparently less favourable APR more competitive.

The official technical guide to the APR is the Office of Fair Trading report 'Consumer Credit Act 1974 Credit Charges and APR', which can be downloaded from the OFT website (go to **www.oft.gov.uk** and look for publications, and then business leaflets). This leaflet describes the Regulations' rules on:

● The charges included in the total charge for credit (TCC) and those excluded.
● The mathematical equation used to calculate the APR.
● The assumptions which must be made in certain circumstances.
● The rules on showing APRs in advertisements and agreements.

The OFT leaflet includes example calculations and annexes that explain the concept behind the method of calculating APR and the mathematical and computer methods which can be used to carry out the calculation.

The APR is not the only factor the borrower needs to consider when choosing credit. For example the goods might be cheaper from another store, making that a better deal even though the credit charges are higher.

In addition to helping borrowers shop around for credit, the TCC and APR have other uses under the Act. The TCC is used in the calculation of rebates on early settlement (details of these provisions are given in the OFT's leaflet 'Matters arising during the lifetime of an agreement') and to determine the charges which a credit broker cannot make, or must return, if they do not obtain a loan for a borrower within a specified period. The APR must also be shown in advertisements for most mortgages, even though these are outside many of the Act's other controls (see Chapter 17).

Finally, the APR may also be an important factor when a court is asked to consider whether an agreement is an extortionate credit bargain (details of this are available in the OFT's leaflet 'Extortionate credit').

Consumer protection

Confusion over the terms of a loan and a lack of awareness of the consequences are considered to be largely responsible for the over-borrowing among consumers. There are certain pitfalls about which everyone should be aware before making a commitment:

● Early settlement fees: in many cases there is a penalty for repaying a loan early.
● APR calculations: there is still confusion between credit and store cards.
● Payment protection insurance (PPI): The Consumers' Association has shown that there is widespread mis-selling of PPI, which claims to protect individuals if they are unable to meet credit repayment because they are unable to work. This is a limited version of income protection and is generally considered to be expensive

and overly restrictive. It is important in particular to watch out for loan agreements that include the cost of PPI in the terms of the loan. In January 2005 the Financial Services Authority (FSA) takes over responsibility for regulating PPI.

Debt consolidation

Debt consolidation is where an individual takes out a loan or other credit agreement in order to pay off two or more existing debts. This process has received very negative publicity in recent years, with licensed credit brokers earning up to £1,000 in commission per case and the so-called 'loan sharks' even more. The cost of this sales commission is added to the borrower's repayment terms. Of particular concern is the pressure debt consolidators impose on applicants to restructure the debt as a secured loan using the individual's home as collateral. This puts the individual's home at risk.

The OFT has been active in raising consumer awareness and pressing lenders to provide clear, relevant information to make debt consolidation fairer and more transparent. It says that a variety of credit products can be used, including the following:

- An unsecured loan.
- An advance from an existing mortgage provider secured against property but which leaves the original mortgage intact.
- A second charge mortgage, which is a loan secured on a property from a lender other than the existing mortgage provider, and which leaves the first mortgage in place.
- A remortgage, where a new loan replaces and adds to the original.
- The transfer of balances to a credit card, including the use of credit card cheques to pay off non-credit card debts.

According to the OFT, in 2002 £32bn of unsecured lending and £8.8bn of secured personal lending were used for debt consolidation. This compares with an estimated £18.4bn of unsecured lending and £2.4bn of secured personal lending in 1999, so we can see a dramatic rise in this activity. In March 2004 the OFT submitted a report to the government on debt consolidation in which it observed that most borrowers do not shop around for credit for this purpose and that two-thirds of borrowers took whatever deal was offered by a single source. Borrowers in financial distress do not in general seek help, either from independent agencies or from the organisations to which they owe money.

Consumer help organisations

The OFT offers a budget planner and a loan ready-reckoner on its website, which allows individuals to work out the cost of taking out credit. The Citizens' Advice Bureau, the Consumer Credit Counselling Service (CCCS), and National Debtline are among several impartial organisations that host very helpful websites. The National

Debtline and CCCS sites include standard forms and letters that can be used to negotiate with creditors. Those who have been in debt may find it difficult to arrange
credit. In this case it is worth contacting the major credit referencing organisations
such as Experian, Call Credit and Equifax.

Activity 8.1

A common problem for borrowers arises when they misunderstand the impact on their
repayments of a dual rate loan, where there is a low APR for an introductory period, after
which the lender reverts to its standard variable rate. Find an example of this type of offer in
the press or on the Internet and consider how the APR is calculated in such cases.
Comment on whether this system is fair to the consumer. You may find it helpful to consult
the OFT report 'Consumer Credit Act 1974: Credit Charges and APR', which can be found
on the OFT website under publications/business leaflets. Part Three of this report includes a
section on this issue.

Summary

This chapter considered the issues that affect the choice of bank and addressed a
very important social issue; namely the risk of unmanageable debt that lies behind
some of the tempting offers from credit card and loan providers. While credit is a
useful financial tool, it should be taken very seriously indeed.

Key terms

- Account aggregation p. 107
- Annual percentage rate (APR) p. 110
- Debt consolidation p. 112
- Total charge for credit (TCC) p. 110
- Unsecured lending p. 107

Review questions

1 Explain the difference between a debit card, a credit card and a store card.

2 Do you think that cards linked to a charity or affinity group represent a good way to make
   a charitable donation? What is the alternative?

3 What is the annual percentage rate (APR) and how is this calculated? How does the APR
   differ from the total charge for credit (TCC)?

4 What are the dangers associated with debt consolidation? If an individual is concerned
   about his or her level of debt what might be a sensible way to restructure?

Go to the Companion Website at **www.booksites.net/harrison_pfp** for a multiple-choice quiz to test your understanding of this chapter.

Further information

A helpful website with a range of links is the Consumer Gateway, run by the Department for Trade and Industry (DTI). Go to **www.consumer.gov.uk/consumer_web/index_v4.htm** and click on the money section.

The Association for Payment Clearing Services: **www.apacs.org.uk**

The Association of British Insurers (ABI): **www.abi.org.uk**

The British Bankers' Association (BBA): **www.bba.org.uk**

The Building Societies Association: **www.bsa.org.uk**

The Consumers' Association: **www.which.co.uk**

Credit reference agencies: the three main companies at the time of writing were Callcredit (**www.callcredit.co.uk**), Equifax (**www.equifax.co.uk**) and Experian (**www.experian.co.uk**).

The Financial Services Authority: **www.fsa.gov.uk**

The Financial Services Ombudsman: **www.financial-ombudsman.org.uk**

Moneyfacts, a leading monthly directory of credit, debt and banking arrangements, as well as insurance and investment products: **www.moneyfacts.co.uk**

The Office of Fair Trading (OFT): **www.oft.gov.uk**

Chapter 9 ●●●●

Savings

Introduction

This chapter examines the products that are aimed primarily at investors with simple savings needs and also those looking for sources of income with full capital protection provided in a transparent and straightforward manner.

Following the volatility of recent markets, many investors are seeking safe havens. They are also beginning to recognise the value of inflation proofing for long-term savings. The 2004 Barclays Capital Equity Gilt Study of investment returns stated that inflation had 'nowhere to go but up' after two years in which central bankers had shown a new resolve to fight off deflation. (**Deflation** is a measure of the decrease in prices in an economy over a period of time, typically based on a basket of household goods and expenditure.)

Objectives

After reading this chapter you will be able to:

- Explain why it is important to align the tax treatment of the product with the tax status of the individual, and the interest rate offered.
- Describe the main savings products and point out key differences.

Taxation

Given the modest income or yield on savings products, taxation is a key issue in determining which might be most suitable for an individual's circumstances. As a general rule non-taxpayers should not invest in products where any tax deducted within the fund cannot be reclaimed. Having said that we must also take account of the interest rate offered. For example the income from National Savings & Investments' Pensioners' Bonds is paid gross but the income from insurance company guaranteed bonds effectively is paid net of basic rate tax and this cannot be reclaimed. In theory this should make the NS&I bonds a clear winner for non-taxpayers, but the slightly higher income available on the insurance bonds can offset this tax advantage. Depending on rates at the time, non-taxpayers should consider both products.

When the government reduces the maximum annual investment in Individual savings accounts (ISAs) from £7,000 to £5,000 in April 2006 savers will have to look elsewhere to replace this facility. As a result, National Savings & Investments (NS&I) index-linked saving certificates, for example, are expected to become even more popular than they are at present, particularly among older income seekers. It is worthy of note that the interest on these savings certificates is linked to the **Retail prices index (RPI)**, despite the fact that in December 2003 the government switched to the **Consumer prices index (CPI)** as the official measure of inflation. The RPI, which includes mortgage interest repayments, is significantly higher than the CPI, which excludes this item (see page 44).

Deposit accounts

All investors need an immediate access emergency fund to pay for unforeseen events such as sudden repairs to the house and car. However, this is not a role for equity-based investments. If an investor has to pull out of an equity fund in a hurry they could lose money, particularly in the early years when the investment is 'working off' the effect of initial charges or when the investment manager may impose an exit charge. Timing is an important aspect when it comes to selling equities due to the volatility of markets.

The traditional home for cash is the building society but a growing number of oganisations, including retailers, offer deposit accounts and there are an increasing number of attractive Internet accounts. Students should note that whereas in the past it was possible to gain a higher rate of interest by committing money for a number of months, or even years, these days some of the Internet accounts that offer immediate access are as competitive as the older-style postal accounts. Convenience of access is important for an emergency cash fund but this does not mean you have to stick to financial institutions that have a local outlet. The Post Office acts as a high street presence for several Internet and non-Internet providers, while the banks and building societies usually offer the facility for non-customers to withdraw funds using the ATM.

The size of an individual's emergency fund should be determined by monthly expenditure, liabilities, and the level of padding they feel is appropriate for peace of mind. As a very rough guide we might suggest it is worth keeping three times the family's or individual's monthly outgoings in an instant access account. If it is possible to find a higher-interest notice account this might be suitable to hold cash for known future capital expenditure – for example a holiday or school fees. Careful management of cash flow should ensure that money is in the right place at the right time.

The savings market changes rapidly as new products are launched and old ones are withdrawn, while rates of interest also fluctuate. For students who want to see an up to date list of relevant rates and information for savings products, an excellent source is the monthly *Moneyfacts* guide to mortgage and savings rates, which covers savings accounts, children's accounts, cheque accounts, credit cards, store cards, bonds, gilts, mortgages, National Savings & Investments and loans. *Moneyfacts* also publishes a separate monthly guide to life assurance and pension products. Details are provided at the end of this chapter.

You can also find useful information on the best rates for a variety of savings accounts in the personal finance pages of the weekend newspapers. Most newspapers publish useful summaries of best buys for different types of products and accounts (many of which are provided by *Moneyfacts*).

Check terms and conditions

Before we lock in to a fixed income product we must remember that if interest rates rise we will be committed to a low rate of return. Of course if the reverse happens and we lock in before rates plummet we will congratulate ourselves on making the right decision. Students should beware of taking too big a gamble on fixed rate products. If the economists consistently make errors in their predictions of interest rate trends, the chances of financial planners getting it right are, frankly, slim.

For most people, some form of inflation proofing is an essential element in their income-generating portfolio of investments. The purchasing power of £100 will be worth just £64 after 15 years of inflation at 3% and £48 if the inflation rate is 5%.

National Savings & Investments (NS&I)

National Savings & Investments was originally launched by the Palmerston government in 1861 as the Post Office Savings Bank, a simple savings scheme to encourage ordinary wage earners 'to provide for themselves against adversity and ill health'. The success of the scheme allowed the then chancellor, Gladstone, to borrow public money for public spending. Today NS&I is backed by the Treasury, which guarantees customers' deposits. The link with the Post Office is limited to distribution. The service offers a wide range of accounts and bonds designed to appeal to savers of different ages and tax status. NS&I changes its interest rates less frequently than building societies.

Premium Bonds

Premium Bonds are UK government securities issued in units of £1 under the National Loans Act 1968. Individuals can invest up to £30,000, in total, buying in multiples of 10, with the minimum investment set at £100. These bonds protect the original capital and offer the chance of monthly prizes ranging from £50 to £1m. As at March 2004 the total fund was worth £45.7m. The odds work out at about 30,000 : 1 for each £1 bond in each monthly draw. Based on these odds an individual who invests the full £30,000 could expect on average to receive 12 tax-free prizes per annum. Prizes do not have to be declared on the annual tax return.

To buy Premium Bonds you have to be over 16 but you can also buy on behalf of a child if you are the parent, guardian, grandparent or great grandparent. Bonds cannot be held jointly and are not transferable.

Cash Mini Individual Savings Account

This is an account that pays interest tax-free. Normally a taxpayer would be liable to income tax at 20% or 40% depending on the applicable marginal rate. The NS&I Cash ISA is very flexible, permitting deposits of as little as £10 and immediate access without penalty. As with any cash ISA, the maximum investment is £3,000 per annum until the 2005–2006 tax year, after which this reduces to £1,000. Anyone aged 16 or over can open an account provided they are resident in the UK for tax purposes.

Fixed Interest Savings Certificates

This is a lump sum investment with the interest rate fixed for the chosen term (usually two and five years). Individuals can invest from £1,000 up to £10,000 in each issue and the returns are free of CGT and income tax. It is not necessary to declare the interest on the tax return. For a basic rate taxpayer, a tax-free return of 3.6% is the same as a taxable return of 4.5% gross. For a higher rate taxpayer the return would be worth 6% gross. Anyone aged seven or more can invest either individually or jointly. Certificates can also be bought on behalf of a child under age seven and by trustees. At maturity you can cash in the investment, reinvest in a new issue, or in another NS&I product.

Index-linked Savings Certificates

These are lump sum investments where the original capital rises in line with RPI. These certificates also earn extra interest at rates that increase in line with RPI every year over the term (two and five years). They are free of income tax and CGT. One way to secure a safe inflation-linked annual income would be to take out a series of certificates over a period of years. If you withdraw your investment in the first year you get no interest. Anyone aged seven or over can invest, and it is also possible to invest on behalf of a child under seven. These certificates can be purchased by trustees.

The same terms apply on maturity as with a Fixed Interest Savings Certificate. Investors can deposit between £100 and £10,000 in each issue.

Income Bonds

Income bonds pay a monthly income; they have a three-month notice period for withdrawals, and must be held for a minimum period of one year. Investors who fail to give the required notice will lose 90 days' interest. The rate of interest is higher for investments of £25,000 or more. Anyone aged seven or above can invest from £500 to £1m, either individually or jointly. These bonds can also be bought by trustees for up to two personal beneficiaries.

Children's Bonus Bonds

These bonds are issued periodically and each issue has its rate of return. You can invest from £25 to £1,000 in each issue in units of £25. For five years a fixed rate of interest is added and on the anniversary of the launch there is a bonus that was fixed and guaranteed at the outset. Children's Bonus Bonds are owned by the child but held by the parent or guardian until the child is aged 16. There is no tax liability for the parent or guardian. To qualify for the full amount of interest and bonus these bonds must be held for five years or until the child is 21. No interest is earned where a bond is cashed in during its first year.

Pensioners' Guaranteed Income Bonds

These bonds can be bought by anyone aged 60 or over, and offer a monthly tax-free income guaranteed for different terms; for example one, two, and five. Although the interest is taxable NS&I does not deduct the tax, so for non-taxpayers there is no need to complete an Inland Revenue form to receive interest gross. Taxpayers need to declare interest on the annual return. The minimum and maximum investments are £500 and £1m. If you want access to your capital you must give 60 days' notice and there will be no interest paid during this period. Bonds encashed without notice suffer a penalty of 90 days' interest.

Fixed Rate Savings Bonds

This is a lump sum investment that earns guaranteed rates of interest, which can be reinvested or drawn as income. Where the income option is selected, this will be paid directly into the individual's bank or building society. Typically terms offered are for one, three and five years. The interest is taxable at the savings rate (20% at the time of writing). Non-taxpayers and those who pay tax at the lower rate of 10% can claim the excess back. Since tax is deducted at source, non-taxpayers are likely to find a gross interest investment more suitable. You can invest from £500 up to £1m.

Capital Bonds

Capital Bonds are available in series, each of which has its own guaranteed rate of return. You can invest from £100 to £1m. Each year interest is added at a fixed rate and reinvested. It is credited gross, so this type of bond is suitable for non-taxpayers. Anyone aged seven or over can invest either jointly or individually. Bonds can also be bought for children under seven and trustees can invest for up to two personal beneficiaries. Taxpayers need to declare the interest on the annual return.

Investment account

This is a traditional passbook savings account with tiered rates of interest. Interest is paid gross. The maximum investment is £100,000. Anyone aged seven or over can invest either individually or jointly with one other person. Accounts can also be set up for children under seven and can be held in trust for up to two personal beneficiaries of any age. People who live outside the UK can hold one of these accounts provided local regulations permit this. Where the individual gives one month's notice, withdrawals are penalty free. Withdrawals without notice suffer a penalty equal to the previous 30 days' interest. Interest is taxable but is credited gross. Taxpayers should include details on the annual tax return.

Easy access savings account

A saver can open this type of account with just £100, after which it is possible to pay in and make withdrawals freely provided there is a minimum £100 balance. Interest rates are tiered and variable. The maximum holding is £2m (£4m for joint accounts). A cash card is used to make withdrawals from cash points up to £300. Anyone aged 11 or over can open an account either individually or jointly with one other person. Interest is paid gross, so taxpayers must declare this on the tax return.

●●●● Tax-exempt special savings accounts (TESSAs)

TESSAs were launched in 1991 and withdrawn for new investment after 5 April 1999, so this section is for reference only. As this was a five-year account the last investments – a maximum of £9,000 – would have gone in by April 5 1999, which means the last maturity date was April 5 2004. The original capital, minus the interest, could be rolled over into a cash ISA (see below) or into a TESSA-only ISA (TOISA), which is limited to people with a maturing TESSA fund and can take the full £9,000. The amount transferred does not count towards the annual ISA allowance.

There are two types of TOISA. The first is a standard deposit account TOISA available from most high street banks and building societies, often with a choice of fixed or variable rate of interest. The alternative is an equity bond TOISA, which has to provide a 100% capital return at the end of the term. The interest is linked to stock market performance, via a link to an index or to a basket of shares. (For further details on guaranteed equity bonds, see page 169.)

Cash individual savings accounts (ISAs)

ISAs are discussed in more detail in Chapter 14, which also explains the tax position, but briefly, up to £3,000 of the £7,000 annual subscription can be paid into a deposit account, reducing to £1,000 from April 2006 (when overall maximum falls to £5,000). You can hold this in a cash-only or mini-ISA but if the individual takes out one of these they can't invest the rest of the annual subscription in a separate equity ISA.

Interest rates can be attractive on the top ISAs (see *Moneyfacts* for the best rates) but planners must keep an eye on providers that offer a special rate for just a few months and then drop back to a much more mundane level of interest.

Some ISA providers penalise those who want to transfer to a more competitive account. CAT-marked ISAs must offer instant access, among other features. CAT stands for charges, access and terms.

Gilts and bonds

Gilt-edged stocks are bonds issued by the UK government via the UK Debt Management Office (DMO), an executive agency of the Treasury. If you buy gilts you are lending the government money in return for a tradable bond that promises to pay a fixed regular income for a specified period, at the end of which the government repays the original capital. Investors can buy and sell gilts throughout the lifetime of the issue.

Gilts play an important part in a defensive or income-producing portfolio although investors might also look at corporate bonds to improve their yields and bond funds that include debt issued by stable governments – for example US Treasury Bonds and German Bunds. For more information on gilts and bonds, see Chapter 10.

Index linked gilts

These bonds are issued by the government and guarantee to increase both the six-monthly interest payments and the 'nominal' or original capital investment that is returned to you on the redemption date. The capital increases in line with the retail prices index (RPI).

Since the starting RPI figure used is eight months before the date of issue, the final value of the investment can be calculated precisely seven months before redemption (RPI figures are published one month in arrears). However, as discussed in Chapter 10, guarantees offered by gilts and corporate bonds only apply if you hold the bonds to maturity. Like conventional gilts, the index linked variety is traded actively, so the price and real value can fluctuate significantly between the issue and redemption dates.

Investors seeking absolute guarantees from their income-yielding portfolios might consider a balance between conventional gilts, which offer a comparatively high fixed income but no index linking of the capital value, and index linked gilts, which offer a low initial income but protect both the income and capital from rising inflation. (Gilts are examined in more detail in Chapter 10.)

Guaranteed income bonds (GIBs)

Guaranteed income bonds offer a fixed rate of interest over a specific term. Most investors go for three years or less. As a general rule, therefore, we can consider GIBs as comparatively short-term investments and look to corporate bond funds for the medium to long term. It is possible to invest anything from about £5,000 in a GIB and at maturity the borrower returns the original capital plus interest, unless the investor elects to have interest paid out during the term of the bond. Unlike a corporate bond fund, with a GIB both the capital and income are guaranteed.

In addition to the one to five year bonds, a limited number of providers offer 'odd-term' or 'made to measure' GIBs for wealthy investors who need to fix for a specific period. With such a variety of terms available, the made to measure bonds are considered ideal for two very different types of investor: risk-averse older people who need a regular income from savings, and wealthier individuals who want a first class cash management system. The odd-term bonds are often used to hold cash set aside to pay large income and capital gains tax bills each year on 31 January.

The taxation of life assurance funds is complicated but broadly, for the higher rate taxpayer, a deposit account rate of 5% gross will actually yield £3 for every £100 invested, whereas the GIB will yield £3.28. GIB providers are required to quote their rates net of basic rate tax, whereas the banks and building societies quote gross rates. To compare like with like, a higher rate taxpayer will need to deduct 40% from the building society rate and only 18% from the GIB rate.

GIBs pay interest net of basic rate tax and the non-taxpayer cannot reclaim this. For this reason GIBs are generally considered unsuitable for non-taxpayers. However, since these bonds usually pay slightly higher rates of income than the tax-free NS&I products it is worth considering both options.

A higher rate taxpayer who owns a GIB can defer any additional liability until the end of the investment term. Furthermore, once a bond matures, if the individual wants to reinvest the capital it is possible to defer the tax liability. In this case the insurance company will issue a formal offer to reinvest the entire proceeds in a new bond.

Given the fluctuating yields on the underlying assets, GIB rates change frequently so it is important to consider the timing of the investment. Interestingly, most GIB providers will only sell through independent financial advisers and the rates usually assume a commission payment. A fee-based planner can arrange for this to be reinvested, and in this way boost the level of income.

Permanent income bearing shares (PIBs)

An alternative to gilts and corporate bonds is permanent income bearing shares or PIBs. These form part of the permanent capital of a building society but have no repayment date and are more like an irredeemable loan than ordinary equities.

The point to remember about PIBs is that they are not on offer directly from building societies but are quoted on The Stock Exchange and must be bought through a stockbroker. Their prices are similar to gilts but they offer slightly higher yields because they do not have the same high level of security as the government. Nevertheless PIBs offer a useful income-bearing investment at competitive rates.

Stepped preference shares of split capital investment trusts

These offer an income that is expected to rise each year at a fixed rate, plus a fixed redemption price for the shares when the trust is wound up. Each trust offers a different yield and annual increase, depending on the nature of the underlying assets. However, following the split capital investment trust scandal (see page 30) there is justifiable concern about the ability of many investment trusts to meet their guarantees. The factors to consider are the risk profile, the current dividend yield, and the gross redemption yield – that is, the total return expressed as an annual percentage, assuming the share is bought at the present price and held to maturity.

The best source of general information on all types of investment trusts is the Association of Investment Trust Companies (AITC), which publishes useful fact sheets and the *Monthly Information Service*, which provides a breakdown of all the member trusts and performance statistics.

Purchased life annuities

Annuities, sold by insurance companies, guarantee to pay a regular income for life in return for a lump sum investment. The annuity 'rate' – or the level of regular income secured – will depend on several important factors including the individual's life expectancy and prevailing interest rates. Women tend to live longer than men, so usually receive a lower income in return for the same level of investment. Those in ill health may be able to get a higher income if the insurance company assumes that life expectancy is less than the average for the individual's age. The main point to remember with annuities is that unless the individual pays extra for a capital guarantee, once they hand over the money it is gone for good, even if the annuitant dies the following day. Annuity rates are interest rate sensitive and fluctuate considerably. This subject is explored in more detail in Chapter 24.

Summary

This chapter examined the range of savings products that provide a safe haven for longer-term income seekers and for those seeking a home for cash over the short to medium term. It considered the importance of aligning the tax treatment of the product with the tax status of the individual but noted the merits of taking the comparative interests rates into the equation.

Key terms

- Consumer Prices Index (CPI) p. 116
- Deflation p. 115
- Retail Prices Index (RPI) p. 116

Review questions

1 Explain why the taxation of savings products is so important. Give an example that shows why a mismatch between the product and the taxpayer can have adverse consequences.

2 Describe how three different products from National Savings & Investments work.

3 Explain the difference between a guaranteed income bond (GIB) and a corporate bond fund. How might you use both products within a portfolio?

Go to the Companion Website at **www.booksites.net/harrison_pfp** for a multiple-choice quiz to test your understanding of this chapter.

Further information

The Association of Investment Trust Companies: **www.aitc.org.uk**

Barclays Capital Equity Gilt Study: **www.equitygiltstudy.com**

Debt Management Office **www.dmo.gov.uk**. The site includes an online version of the informative 'Private Investors' Guide to British Government Stock'.

Moneyfacts: **www.moneyfacts.co.uk**

National Savings & Investments: **www.nsandi.com**

Case study 9.1

Background

Philip, 72, and Karen, 68, Fairfax are both non-smokers, in good health and live comfortably within their means. Recently their daughter Sarah and her husband Richard Seymour have been struggling to make ends meet. Philip and Karen know how important it is to save for future events but due to a long-standing medical problem with Richard, he can now only work part time. As a result, Sarah and Richard can pay the immediate bills but cannot save for the future. Philip and Karen wish to help them out by saving on behalf of their two grandchildren, Rachel (4) and Colin (13). Philip and Karen are very cautious investors and have the following assets available to meet their objectives:

- National Savings series 10 capital bond taken out in Karen's name on 23/02/03 bought for £8,000.
- Building society savings in joint names paying 3% net interest, value = £4,000.
- Premium Bonds taken out by Philip and Karen on 01/02/80, value = £7,500 each.

Both Philip and Karen are basic rate taxpayers.

Problem

Philip and Karen wish to save for three events:

1 Cash deposit each for Rachel and Colin to buy their own homes when they reach 21. Deposit required = £10,000 each in today's terms.
2 To pay for Rachel's tap dancing lessons costing £2,000 pa in today's terms between the ages of seven and 11 (ie starting in three years' time).
3 Cash deposit for Colin to buy a car when he reaches 17. Deposit required = £4,000 in today's terms.

The couple have sufficient assets and disposable income left over to meet their own requirements. They would like to ensure that these objectives can be met if either or both were to die beforehand.

Advice

Philip and Karen seek your advice to help them meet their objectives with minimal disruption to the existing assets set aside for this purpose. They would like you to comment on the suitability of these assets when recommending the best course of action to take. They have asked you to take account of their attitude to risk (very cautious) as they have very little investment knowledge and will only take up your recommendations if they are easy to understand and implement. They would like you to explain exactly how your recommendations will ensure that their wishes are achieved.

Source: *Money Management*, Financial Planner of the Year Awards 2003, *FT Business*.

A full solution to this case study is available to lecturers via the password-protected area of the Companion Website at **www.booksites.net/harrison_pfp**.

Chapter 10 ●●●●

Gilts and bonds

Introduction

This chapter examines government bonds (gilts) and corporate bonds, both of which are listed on The London Stock Exchange. These assets can be purchased individually but private investors generally buy them in collective funds. Collective funds, such as corporate bond unit trusts, can be held in an Individual savings account (ISA).

Objectives

After reading this chapter you will be able to:

- Describe how gilts and bonds work.
- Explain why for most private investors it is preferable to buy funds rather than individual bonds.
- Understand what determines the yield on a traded bond or gilt.
- Explain why certain corporate bond funds put the original capital at risk.
- Understand the difference between a bond's gross redemption yield and running yield.

Bonds defined

As described in Chapter 4, a bond is a debt instrument issued by a borrower, which promises to repay the loan (the **nominal** sum) in full at a fixed date in the future (at **maturity** or the **redemption date**). With conventional gilts and bonds the borrower pays interest, known as the **coupon**, usually twice a year at a fixed rate. As a general rule, the longer the term the higher the income – but also the greater the drop in the real value of the original capital at maturity. The two main categories of bonds are **investment grade** and **sub-investment** grade (the latter is also known as **high yield** or **junk bond**). Credit rating agencies such as Standard & Poor's provide ratings according to the issuer's financial strength (see below).

Gilts and qualifying bonds are free of capital gains tax on any profits because the 'return' or yield is classed as income. However, this means that you cannot offset a loss on bonds against capital gains.

Gilts are guaranteed by the government and are considered ultra secure. Corporate debt is guaranteed by companies. The company's ability to service the debt and repay the original capital is reflected in the company's credit rating. A very low credit stock can have a very high yield. However, the potential for capital loss is equally high (see below.)

Standard & Poor's credit ratings

Credit rating is an important subject. There are several rating agencies, including Standard & Poor's and Moody's. The following information is based on the Standard & Poor's fact sheet 'Understanding Credit Rating', which can be found on its website.

A credit rating is the rating agency's opinion of the general creditworthiness of a borrower, or the creditworthiness of a borrower with respect to a particular debt security or other financial obligation. Over the years credit ratings have achieved wide investor acceptance as convenient tools for differentiating credit quality.

S&P's ratings are based on information provided by the issuer together with other information the agency considers reliable. Ratings may be changed, suspended or withdrawn because of changes in or unavailability of information. Standard & Poor's assigns both local and foreign currency credit ratings reflecting an issuer's ability to meet financial obligations denominated in the issuer's domestic currency or in external currencies.

Bond and money fund managers use Standard & Poor's fund ratings to differentiate their bond and money funds from those of their competitors. The ratings provide investors with information on the credit quality and volatility of a fund.

What ratings mean

A Standard & Poor's long-term rating reflects a borrower's capacity to meet its financial commitments on a timely basis. Long-term ratings range from the highest category, 'AAA', to the lowest, 'D'. Ratings from 'AA' to 'CCC' categories may also include a plus (+) or minus (–) sign to show relative standing within the category.

A short-term rating is an assessment of the likelihood of timely repayment of obligations considered short term in relevant markets. Short-term ratings are graded into several categories, ranging from 'A-1' for the highest quality obligations to 'D' for the lowest. The 'A-1' rating may also be modified by a plus sign to distinguish the stronger credits in that category.

In addition to long-term and short-term ratings, Standard & Poor's has specific rating definitions for preferred stock, money market funds, mutual bond funds, financial strength and financial enhancement ratings of insurance companies, and programme ratings for derivative product companies.

Outlooks

An outlook notation indicates the possible direction in which a rating may move over the next six months to two years.

- 'Positive': may be raised.
- 'Negative': may be lowered.
- 'Stable': unlikely to change.
- 'Developing': may be raised or lowered.

CreditWatch

A CreditWatch listing highlights the potential for short-term change in a credit rating. It signals to investors that further analysis is being performed.

Exhibit 10.1 What the credit letter ratings mean

AAA: Extremely strong capacity to meet financial commitments. Highest rating.

AA: Very strong capacity to meet financial commitments.

A: Strong capacity to meet financial commitments, but somewhat susceptible to adverse economic conditions and changes in circumstances.

BBB: Adequate capacity to meet financial commitments, but more subject to adverse economic conditions.

BBB– (minus): This is the lowest rating before non-investment grade.

BB: Less vulnerable in the near-term but faces major ongoing uncertainties to adverse business, financial and economic conditions.

B: More vulnerable to adverse business, financial and economic conditions but currently has the capacity to meet financial commitments.

CCC: Currently vulnerable and dependent on favourable business, financial and economic conditions to meet financial commitments.

CC: Currently highly vulnerable.

C: A bankruptcy petition has been filed or similar action taken but payments or financial commitments are continued.

D: Payment default on financial commitments.

Ratings in the 'AAA', 'AA', 'A' and 'BBB' categories are regarded by the market as investment grade. Ratings in the 'BB', 'B', 'CCC', 'CC' and 'C' categories are regarded as having significant speculative characteristics. Ratings from 'AA' to 'CCC' may be modified by the addition of a plus (+) or minus (−) sign to show relative standing within the major rating categories.

The rating process in brief

A Standard & Poor's rating is assigned only when adequate information is available. The process includes quantitative, qualitative and legal analysis. S&P examines key business fundamentals, such as an issuer's industry, prospects for growth and its vulnerability to technological change or regulatory action. For sovereign (country) ratings, important factors include not only the basic underlying economic strength of the country, but also the political system and the social environment.

Price fluctuations in traded gilts and bonds

Gilts and bonds can be traded during the loan period and prices tend to reflect the market's view on future interest rates. Once the gilt or bond is traded the value of the coupon will no longer be guaranteed. This is because, when the price changes, so too does the value of the yield. In general, gilts and bonds are considered less volatile than shares, but there have been many exceptions that disprove this rule. Over an unusual period in 1994, for example, gilts fell by as much as 15%–20%.

Gilt interest is paid in arrears (see below) so the price will also take into account whether a recent interest payment has been made to the holder – in which case the price is ex-dividend. If the interest is still to be paid, the price is cum-dividend (the recent interest payment is still attached and therefore is purchased along with the gilt).

Gilts

Gilt-edged stocks are bonds issued by the UK government via the UK Debt Management Office (DMO), an executive agency of the Treasury. Investors can buy and sell gilts throughout the lifetime of the issue. The DMO website (see further information below) is an excellent source of information for students and maintains an up-to-date list of the gilts in issue. The most common category is the conventional gilt, which behaves like a conventional bond and pays interest twice a year.

Of increasing interest, however, are index linked gilts, where the capital and coupon both rise each year in line with retail prices. The advantage of this instrument is that, whatever happens to inflation, investors overcome the uncertainty of whether an asset will provide real growth after allowing for inflation. In other words, index linked gilts provide a guaranteed real return, if held to maturity, removing both the inflation risk of conventional fixed rate bonds and the growth uncertainty of equities. An example of how the return on this type of gilt is calculated is on page 133.

Rump gilts refers to issues where there are very few gilts in circulation.

DMO convention is to divide gilts into the following maturity categories although market convention is: shorts 0–5 years; medium 5–15 years.

- Shorts – gilts with 0–7 years to run to maturity.
- Mediums – 7–15 years.
- Longs – over 15 years.
- Undated – no fixed repayment date.

Certain gilts have two repayment dates – for example '2012–2015'. This means that the government can choose to repay the gilt at any time from 2012 onwards with three months' notice, but it must repay by 2015 at the latest. It is important to note that it is the government's choice, not the investor's.

Private investors can buy gilts in several ways. They can purchase through a bank or stockbroker that is a Gilt Edged Market Maker (GEMM). The intermediary will charge a commission for the transaction. It is also possible to buy through the Bank of England brokerage service direct (see Further information below) or via the Post Office. Information on gilt prices and yields is published in the *Companies and Markets* section of the *Financial Times* on weekdays and in *FT Money and Business* at the weekend.

How to assess gilt and bond income

The title of a gilt tells us most of the information we need to know before purchase. So, for example, a £1,000 investment in 6.5% Treasury Stock 2006 will provide an income of £65 per annum until 2006, when the government repays the original £1,000. However, the income only remains stable where the gilt is bought at launch and is held to maturity. To assess the income from traded gilts and bonds we need to look at three figures:

- The *nominal* value represents the original purchase price (which is not necessarily the price at which we buy). This is the amount we receive at redemption.
- The *coupon* tells us the interest rate that applies to the nominal value throughout the loan period.
- The *market price* is the present value if we buy or sell.

The coupon and nominal figures determine the level of interest but the actual return or yield will depend on the buying price. If the buying or 'market price' of a gilt or bond goes up, the yield goes down because we have paid more than the nominal value and therefore the interest rate will be smaller in comparison. So, if the nominal price is £100 and the interest rate is 10% but you buy at £120, then the interest is still only

10% of £100 – that is, £10, so the yield is 8.33% (£10 as a percentage of £120). If the situation is reversed, so the nominal is £120, the interest rate 10% and you buy at £100, you will still get 10% of £120, which is £12 – a yield of 12%.

Exhibit 10.2 How gilt prices are shown in the *FT*

UK GILTS - cash market

Apr 2	Notes	Price £	Chng	Wk % Chng	Yld Red	... 52 week ... High	Low
Shorts" (Lives up to Five Years)							
Tr 10pc '04	✤	100.66	–.04	–.1	4.26	107.02	100.66
Tr 5pc '04		100.15	–.02	.....	4.08	101.86	100.15
Cn 9½pc '04	✤	102.81	–.08	–.2	4.31	109.02	102.81
Tr 6¾pc '04		101.53	–.07	–.1	4.29	105.18	101.53
Cn 9½pc '05		105.05	–.15	–.3	4.45	111.44	105.05
Ex 10½pc '05	✤	108.31xd	–.21	–.3	4.54	115.78	108.31
Tr 8½pc '05		106.29	–.23	–.4	4.54	112.37	106.29
Tr 7¾pc '06		107.07xd	–.29	–.5	4.63	113.28	107.07
Cn 9¾pc '06	✤	112.32	–.34	–.6	4.68	120.24	112.32
Tr 7½pc '06		107.05	–.32	–.5	4.66	113.37	107.05
Tr 4½pc '07		99.51	–.32	–.6	4.68	100.13	99.51
Tr 8½pc '07		111.43	–.39	–.7	4.70	119.01	111.43
Tr 7¼pc '07		108.42	–.42	–.7	4.72	115.43	108.28
Tr 5pc '08		100.94xd	–.41	–.7	4.73	106.38	99.99
Tr 5½pc '08–12		102.44xd	–.58	–1.0	4.88	109.02	101.71
Tr 9pc '08	✤	116.79xd	–.53	–.8	4.82	125.75	116.79
Tr 4pc '09		96.65xd	–.49	–.9	4.08	101.96	95.12
Five to Ten Years							
Tr 8pc '09	✤	115.25xd	–.62	–1.0	4.80	124.08	114.75
Tr 5¾pc '09		104.73	–.59	–1.0	4.79	111.94	103.57
Tr 6¼pc '10		108.02	–.71	–1.2	4.82	116.12	106.79
Cn 9pc Ln '11		125.21	–.85	–1.3	4.84	135.92	124.45
Tr 7¾pc '12–15		117.19	–.86	–1.4	5.06	126.67	116.04
Tr 5pc '12		100.93xd	–.79	–1.5	4.86	108.42	99.18
Tr 9pc '12	✤	127.67	–.99	–1.4	4.91	138.62	126.66
Tr 8pc '13		123.59xd	–1.06	–1.6	4.86	134.66	122.28
Ten to Fifteen Years							
Tr 5pc '14		100.97xd	–.96	–1.7	4.88	109.00	98.97
Tr 8pc '15		127.59	–1.22	–1.7	4.87	138.76	125.75
Tr 8¾pc '17		137.65xd	–1.36	–1.8	4.89	149.74	135.54
Ex 12pc '13–17	✤	154.39	–1.27	–1.5	4.88	169.09	153.60
Over Fifteen Years							
Tr 8pc '21		136.65	–1.35	–1.7	4.83	147.98	133.89
Tr 5pc '25		102.78xd	–1.18	–2.0	4.79	110.90	99.89
Tr 6pc '28		118.13	–1.34	–1.9	4.75	127.33	114.68
Tr 4¼pc '32		92.83	–1.12	–2.1	4.71	100.09	89.68
Tr 4¼pc '36		92.78xd	–1.14	–2.1	4.69	100.19	89.69
Undated							
Cons 4pc	✤	78.47	–1.30	–2.7	–	88.54	74.61
War Ln 3½pc		73.72	–1.32	–2.9	–	82.74	70.08
Cn 3½pc '61 Aft.	✤	74.99xd	–1.36	–3.0	–	85.80	70.93
Tr 3pc '66 Aft.	✤	60.63xd	–1.07	–2.6	–	63.85	54.15
Cons 2½pc	✤	51.88xd	–.96	–2.7	–	56.08	47.18
Tr 2½pc		51.88xd	–.76	–2.5	–	57.58	49.21

	Notes	Price £	Chng	Wk % Chng	... Yield ... (1)	(2)	... 52 week ... High	Low
Index–Linked	(b)							
4⅜pc '04	(135.6)	135.75	–.04	–.1	–	–	138.53	135.75
2pc '06	(69.5)	264.54	–.47	–.4	0.73	1.20	268.20	259.19
2½pc '09	(78.8)	237.93	–.77	–.7	1.47	1.69	244.75	232.50
2½pc '11	(74.6)	253.55xd	–1.03	–.8	1.62	1.78	260.98	245.76
2½pc '13	(89.2)	214.06	–.86	–.9	1.68	1.80	220.17	205.75
2½pc '16	(81.6)	237.07	–.97	–.9	1.71	1.81	241.51	224.59
2½pc '20	(83.0)	238.09	–1.06	–1.0	1.72	1.80	240.55	222.98
2½pc '24	(97.7)	207.10	–1.09	–1.2	1.70	1.77	209.62	191.06
4⅛pc '30	(135.1)	200.69	–1.34	–1.3	1.65	1.71	203.43	183.73
2pc '35	(173.6)	111.25	–.84	–1.6	1.63	1.68	113.14	98.33

Prospective real redemption rate on projected inflation of (1) 5% and (2) 3%. (b) Figures in parentheses show RPI base for indexing (ie 8 months prior to issue) and have been adjusted to reflect rebasing of RPI to 100 in January 1987. Conversion factor 3.945. RPI for Jul 2003: 181.3 and for Feb 2004: 183.8.

● Source: Debt Management Office (DMO). All UK Gilts are tax-free to non-residents on application. xd Ex dividend. Closing mid-prices are shown in pounds per £100 nominal of stock.
Int yield: Interest yield. Red yield: Gross redemption yield. Prospective real Index-Linked redemption yields are calculated by HSBC Bank plc from Gemma closing prices. ✤ Indicative price. Gilts benchmarks and most liquid stocks, are shown in bold type. The full list of Gilts can be found daily on ft.com/bonds&rates.

Figure 10.1

Source: *Financial Times*, 3rd/4th April 2004.

Gilt prices shown in newspapers usually show the middle-market prices; that is, prices halfway between the buying and selling price. Like shares, gilt prices are changing constantly and we would need to go to a broker to get an up-to-date buying and selling price.

Index linked gilts

Index linked gilts guarantee to increase both the six-monthly interest payments and the 'nominal' or original capital investment due at redemption in line with increases in the Retail prices index (RPI). Since the starting RPI used is eight months before the date of issue, the final value of the investment can be calculated precisely seven months before redemption (RPI figures are published one month in arrears).

Like conventional gilts, the index linked variety is traded actively so the price and real value of the yield can fluctuate significantly between the issue and redemption dates. However, there is no inflation (RPI) risk for the investor in index linked gilts other than the eight-month period without indexation at the end of each stock's life.

Index linked arithmetic

The following calculation is drawn from the DMO.

$4\frac{1}{8}$% Index-Linked Treasury Stock 2030 was issued on 12 June 1992. Interest is paid on 22 January and 22 July each year. The gilt will be redeemed on 22 July 2030, at which time the final interest payment will also be made.

The base month for the Retail prices index for the gilt was October 1991, ie eight months before June 1992. The RPI in October 1991 was 135.1. Each interest payment (except the first, which related to a period of more than seven months) comprises £2.0625 (half the $4\frac{1}{8}$% annual coupon) adjusted for the movement in the RPI, as per the following formula:

Amount of dividend per £100 nominal of stock = Half the annual coupon × RPI eight months before the dividend is due/Base month RPI.

Therefore for the interest payment made on 22 January 2001 for $4\frac{1}{8}$% Index-Linked Treasury Stock 2030, the amount paid was:

£2.0625 × 170.7/135.1 = £2.6059 per £100 nominal of stock
(170.7 was the level of the RPI in May 2000).

Subsequent interest payments will vary according to the level of the RPI eight months before the payment is due.

The principal repayment depends on the level of the RPI eight months before the repayment date of the gilt and is calculated in the following way:

Repayment per £100 nominal of stock = 100 × RPI eight months before the repayment date/Base month RPI.

We do not, of course, know as yet what the RPI will be in November 2029 (eight months before the repayment date of $4\frac{1}{8}$% Index-Linked Treasury Stock 2030). Suppose that the latest RPI figure available is that for December 2000 (172.2). In order to produce an estimate for the value of the November 2029 RPI it is necessary to make an assumption about inflation over the period from December 2000 to November 2029. If we suppose that inflation over this period averages 3% per annum, this would give a published RPI for November 2029 of:

$$172.2 \times \left(1 + \frac{3}{100}\right)^{28\frac{11}{12}} = 404.8$$

The sum repaid to investors in $4\frac{1}{8}$% Index-Linked Treasury Stock 2030 in July 2030 would then be:

£100 × 404.8/135.1 = £299.6299 per £100 nominal of the gilt.

Source: Debt Management Office.

Comparing gilt yields with other investments

So, how does the gilt yield compare with the yields on equities? The income on index linked gilts is guaranteed to grow in line with inflation over the years but cannot grow more quickly. Equities offer no guarantees but historically have grown more quickly than the rate of inflation. However, under unfavourable economic conditions, such as those experienced over the past few years, equities can lag behind inflation by a significant margin. In today's volatile climate it is important to remember that index linked gilts have provided their return for a much lower level of risk than equities. For more detail on the relationship between equities and gilts, see Chapter 4.

Corporate bonds

Issuers and advisers may refer to the fact that in the event of a company becoming insolvent, bonds rank before shares in the creditors' pecking order. Frankly, it is unlikely that a company in these circumstances could afford to repay bondholders but not shareholders. In most cases, therefore, it is wise to view this apparent additional security with a degree of scepticism. In 2004, for example, Parmalat, the Italian dairy food company, collapsed with $7.2bn of investment rated debt. At the time of writing bondholders were expecting a paltry 10 cents in the Euro. One of the major concerns that remains, post-Parmalat, is that the company's debt had a BBB– rating from S&P, based on allegedly misleading information provided by Parmalat management.

Whether an individual is considering buying directly or via a collective fund, there are various risks to consider with corporate bonds – in particular credit risk and interest rate risk. A third risk is capital erosion. This can occur in funds that deduct the annual management charge from capital instead of income – a procedure that may be used to inflate the potential yield artificially.

In response to growing demand the corporate bond market is growing in range and complexity. This has brought with it concern over the risks to capital where, for example, a fund is able to offer a comparatively high yield by holding sub-investment grade bonds and debt from developing countries where the economies are unstable.

Until comparatively recently, retail bond funds would have been dominated by AAA-rated debt, but this is no longer the case and many funds focus on BBB–, which is the lowest level in investment grade debt, while yet others are buying into sub-investment grade debt. While the returns on sub-investment grade debt have been very attractive relative to AAA debt, these instruments are as risky as equities and should be treated as such. For these reasons, we should regard the corporate bond market as far from homogenous.

A change in interest rates will have an immediate impact on the price of individual bonds and corporate bond funds. This is because gilts and bonds have to compete with other interest-paying instruments. If banks and building societies raise the interest rates on deposits, bonds and gilts will look less attractive and therefore prices will fall to the point where the yield relative to the price is attractive once again. Rather like index tracking funds, charges are a more significant factor in the corporate bond fund selection process than is the case with equity funds. With a bond fund the gap in performance between the best and the worst is small, so differences in charges are highly significant.

Those with a substantial amount to invest can take advantage of index tracking bond funds, although these are rare. In due course it may be possible to find exchange traded funds (ETFs) that cover bond markets. These have some of the characteristics of unit trusts and may offer a cheap way to track bond markets.

Bond charges and yields

The Investment Management Association (IMA) has coordinated the way corporate bond fund yields are calculated by its members so that managers show yields on a consistent basis. The yield figures should not be examined without reference to the way the annual management charge is deducted. As mentioned, if this is taken out of capital, as opposed to the usual practice of deducting it from income, then the yields will look artificially high.

When it comes to the yield, there are two figures to consider: the **gross redemption yield** and the **running yield**.

- The gross redemption yield or 'projected total yield' takes into account both the income received and changes in the capital value of the bonds if they are held to maturity.
- The running yield or 'projected income yield' only takes into account the current rate of income received from the bonds. No allowance is made for any changes in the capital value so this could mask capital erosion, for example, if the annual charge is deducted from capital.

As a general rule the gross redemption yield is the better measure of the total expected investment return. A high gross redemption yield might be accompanied by a higher credit risk and often greater volatility in the capital value of the fund. The running yield is important for investors concerned about the income they will receive. A high running yield is often associated with capital erosion.

Activity 10.1

In a group or individually, examine two recent gilts tables from the *Financial Times*, with a week or so between publication dates. Explain what each heading means. Consider how the price change for specific issues has affected the yield both in terms of the weekly fluctuation and the price change since issue (the issue price shown is £100).

Comment: The Debt Management Office's *Private Investor's Guide* contains most of the information you need to answer these questions. You can download this from the DMO website. There is also a more detailed version on the website, *UK Government Securities: A Guide to Gilts*, which you may find useful.

Summary

This chapter took a closer look at how gilts and bonds work. It examined how the yield is calculated and why this will change where a bond or gilt is traded at a different price from that at launch. It also considered potential problems in the corporate bond market and discovered the potential pitfalls associated with capital erosion and with sub-investment grade debt.

Key terms

- Coupon p. 128
- Gross redemption yield p. 135
- High yield/junk bond p. 128
- Investment and sub-investment grade debt p. 128
- Junk bond p. 128
- Maturity or redemption date p. 128
- Nominal p. 128
- Running yield p. 135

Review questions

1 Explain why you would recommend funds rather than individual gilts and bonds to a private investor.

2 How is the yield calculated on a traded bond or gilt? Why does a rise in the gilt price reduce the yield?

3 What factors might affect the security of a bond fund?

4 What is the difference between the gross redemption and running yield?

Go to the Companion Website at **www.booksites.net/harrison_pfp** for a multiple-choice quiz to test your understanding of this chapter.

Further information

The Bank of England brokerage service: **www.bankofengland.co.uk**. A link appears on the DMO website.

The Debt Management Office (DMO): **www.dmo.gov.uk** (includes an online version of the informative *Private Investor's Guide*).

The Investment Management Association: **www.investmentuk.org**

Standard & Poor's: **www.standardandpoors.com**

Chapter 11 ● ● ● ●

Equities

Introduction

This chapter considers direct equity investment, while Chapters 12 and 13 examine ways of gaining an exposure to equities via collective funds. To understand the opportunities and risks associated with equity investment, we need to assimilate a large amount of information.

Objectives

After reading this chapter you will be able to:

● Understand the different ways in which shares are grouped – for example by size and by market.
● Explain how to value a share.
● Understand the dividend yield.
● Describe how we can use economic indicators to help assess a company's potential.
● Describe briefly high risk strategies such as contracts for difference and spread betting.

How shares are grouped

Shares are grouped in different ways to help potential investors assess their characteristics and investment prospects. Size and type of business are the two most obvious differentiators. In theory, large companies that are broadly diversified should be more stable than smaller companies and those focused on a very specific product or service. This is partly because of their sheer size and (apparently) deep pockets but also because, through diversification in the UK and overseas, they should be less vulnerable to market cycles and economic factors such as a rise or fall in interest rates or a recession. If one part of the company is affected by a fall in retail sales, for example, other parts of the group might still be thriving through diversification into financial services.

In this way an investment in a blue chip company carries an inherent spread of risk, whereas a small, specialist company is much more vulnerable to economic conditions and market sentiment. But students should note that this argument is a generalisation. If you believe that the US and main European markets behave in a similar way to the UK, then any Anglo-American or Anglo-Dutch company listed on The London Stock Exchange may react in a very similar way to a UK, US or Dutch-only company.

Smaller companies – typically those below the FTSE 350 – can double turnover in under a year but when they get into trouble the end can be swift and savage. Larger companies are less likely to experience such rapid growth – or to crash in such a spectacular manner, although there are always exceptions to this rule. In practice, of course, a large company can get into serious trouble or even crash unexpectedly. It is always a nasty shock to discover in retrospect just how well the directors can hide what should have been clear signs of impending doom. Enron, Worldcom and Parmalat have shaken investors' faith in the regulation of major quoted companies.

The FTSE UK Index Series

The quickest way to assess the size of a company is by looking at the FTSE UK indices, published each day in the *Financial Times*. This section considers the chief characteristics of the main equity indices that are likely to contain a private investor's most popular shares. Students should always bear in mind that these are *theoretical* characteristics. In practice, markets may move in a totally unpredictable fashion, so it is important to look at *actual* trends, not just the theory. Reading the *Financial Times* and following the fortunes of a selection of companies from different indices and sectors will teach you more about economic cycles and investment theory and practice than any individual book. The FTSE website is also of considerable interest to students.

The FTSE International indices are arithmetically weighted by **market capitalisation**, so that the larger the company the greater the effect its share price movement will have on the index. 'Market capitalisation' is the stock market valuation of the company, which is calculated by multiplying the number of shares in issue by their market price.

The FTSE UK Index Series includes FTSE 100, FTSE 250, FTSE SmallCap, FTSE All-Share and FTSE techMARK (technology stocks). Most of these are described, starting on page 52. Apart from the UK series there is a global equity series (which includes FTSE4Good, for socially responsible investors – see page 190), 'domestic, x-border & partner indices' (which covers a range of joint ventures between FTSE International and other index providers), bond indices and hedge fund indices, among others. For information on these series and individual indices go to **www.ftse.com/ indices_marketdata/Family_tree.jsp**.

All-Share companies that fall outside the FTSE 350 (the FTSE 100 and Mid-250 combined) are potentially more risky and volatile than the larger companies. However, this is an area in which private investors traditionally have done well. These companies are less sought-after by the professionals because very large funds cannot trade in these shares easily since the size of the deal might in itself push up or depress the share price. As a result, these companies usually are less well researched than the FTSE 350. Beginners and the risk averse should not commit too much money to any one company outside the 350 because this would concentrate the risk in the portfolio.

Once we get down to the Fledgling index we have to be extremely cautious. A small company that specialises in one or two products is very vulnerable to price competition and a sudden reduction in demand. Moreover, a signal from a tip sheet (a publication that gives buy and sell recommendations – often used as a derogatory term) to buy a small company's shares could be enough to send the price through the roof, while a panic to sell on the part of very few investors can be enough to force the share price down into the doldrums.

In conclusion, as planners we would suggest that intensive research and a strict ceiling on the amount an individual invests in any one company are essential. Also, these shares may not be very liquid, so buying and, in particular, selling can be a problem.

Classification by sector

The sectors used by the FTSE International categorise the All-Share group companies according to what they do. This is because the companies in a sector are likely to be affected by a similar range of economic factors. For example if we are in a dire recession people still need to eat, so companies in the 'Retailers, food' sector might be a good place to find some 'defensive' stocks, while 'Breweries, pubs and restaurants' and 'Leisure and hotels' might feel the pinch as consumers cut back on non-essential items. However, stock picking purely by sector is not necessarily a good technique. Some sectors represent a very concentrated market, whereas others – transport for example – represent a diversified range of companies. The point to remember here is that we must consider the profile of the sector and the company itself. Just because one company is experiencing good growth does not mean that we can pick any company in the sector and be guaranteed similar performance.

Sector classifications can help in determining an individual's investment position relative to the market. If the objective is to beat the All-Share index, for example, we need to have a clear idea of how the index is constructed and perhaps deviate where we feel a sector is likely to perform well under the current market conditions.

Shareholder perks

Some shares offer certain perks – for example a discount at the company's stores or free tickets to certain events. In most cases these are no more than the free gift in the cereal box but for some sport, entertainment or other enthusiasts the perks may well swing the decision to invest. If the perks are of interest we should check that private investors would qualify, particularly where they use a nominee account, which means that although they are the beneficial owners, the shares are held in the nominee company's name.

New issues

New issues include privatisations of public sector companies and the **demutualisation** of building societies and life assurance institutions. Demutualisation is where an institution converts from **mutual status,** where it is owned by its members, to public limited companies (plcs) owned by shareholders. Most demutualisations have been characterised by the large windfall share payments, where free shares in the new company were given to existing savers and borrowers.

What information will a company provide?

By law a company listed on The London Stock Exchange must produce a considerable amount of documentation for its existing and prospective shareholders (and, of course, the regulators, accountants and auditors, among others). Typically, this will include two sets of profit figures at six-monthly intervals. The first set in the company's financial year is known as the **interim results** while the second set, the **final results,** is produced at the company's financial year-end. These figures provide a detailed analysis of the company's trading year and its profits or losses. Students will learn a great deal from reading a range of annual reports and accounts, many of which are available free via the *FT* London Share Service (**http://ft.ar.wilink.com**).

How to value shares

A simple share valuation involves two basic exercises. First, we need to make a general assessment of how well or otherwise the company is doing compared with the market as a whole, and then compare its performance with its peers in the relevant sector. If you have access to **www.ft.com** or a similar newspaper archive it is relatively easy to check the company's recent history. This information can be used in conjunction with the annual report and accounts but bear in mind that this document will already be out of date by the time it is published.

The second exercise is to consider how the market views the share price. This is a more precise activity and requires an understanding of how professionals make their calculations. For some companies it is necessary to look at the **net asset value** (**NAV**) (investment trusts and property companies, for example). **Gearing** – or the amount the company has borrowed compared with what it actually owns – is also an indicator of the company's security and an investor's sensitivity to company performance. ('Gearing' is known as leverage in the US.)

The dividend yield

The dividend yield represents the income from an investment based on historic information. It is the annual gross dividend as a percentage of the market price. The figure shows the rate of gross income a shareholder would receive on an investment at that particular share price – rather like the way you might describe the before-tax interest paid on a deposit account. As with an ordinary deposit account, there is no guarantee that the dividend yield will be maintained.

The Barclays Capital Equity Gilt Study (see page 161) explains that a low dividend yield is associated with a high valuation for the stock market because it tends to be followed by low returns, whereas high dividend yields tend to be followed by high real returns, especially over the following 12 months.

We must never assume the past is a guide to the future. Much will depend on the economic environment. The Study explains that investment is more about gauging the direction of markets and appreciating the new valuation norms than about relying on past guidelines. Changes in the economic environment are the main determinant of changes in valuation standards. In particular, changes in the inflation rate are a major influence on the markets.

● ● ● ● Key indicators in practice

Dividends form an important element in the 'total return' – that is, 'dividends reinvested plus capital growth'. Clearly, there are no hard and fast rules with dividends because they reflect the current state of the business. If the company is prone to follow the dips and peaks of market cycles (see Chapter 13), this will be reflected in the dividend payments. Even some of the larger companies – including those on the FTSE 100 – cut dividends when times are tough.

As mentioned above, analysts tend to assume that a higher dividend indicates the shares are likely to produce above average total returns over the long term, while some very successful investors only invest in high yielding shares. However, a comparatively high dividend is always worth investigating to make sure there is nothing untoward going on behind the scenes. Look at the company's gearing (debt) to see if it is borrowing to shore up its dividend commitment. Very high dividends can be a sign that the company is in trouble.

Dividend cover

Remember what we learned about the term 'dividend cover' in Chapter 3 in relation to investment trusts. This is a stock market ratio that quantifies the amount of cash in a company's coffers. If the dividend cover is high this means the company could afford to pay out the dividend several times over from earnings per share. This indicates that profits are being retained for the business. When the cover is low it means the company had to struggle to scrape together the dividend announced and that it may even have subsidised it from reserves.

The price/earnings (P/E) ratio

This is the market price of a share divided by the company's earnings (profits) per share in its latest 12-month trading period. As a very rough guide, a high ratio means the market considers a company is likely to produce above average growth, while a low P/E ratio means the opposite.

P/E ratios are a handy benchmark to use when comparing shares of similar companies within a sector – two supermarket chains, for example. We also need to check the ratio against the average for other sectors, because it could be that at a particular point in the market cycle all shares in the sector in which we are interested might be marked down if they move in line with economic trends.

Both the dividend yield and the P/E ratio are shown in the *Financial Times* share prices pages (see page 82).

Net asset value

This is an important feature for certain types of company, particularly property companies and investment companies. Take investment trusts, for example. These are UK companies that invest in the shares of other companies. Investment trusts have a fixed number of shares that are subject to the usual market forces, so the share price does not necessarily reflect the total value of the shares the trust owns.

If the share price is lower than the value per share of the underlying assets the difference is known as the **discount**. If the share price is higher the difference is known as the **premium**. As a general rule, an investment trust share trading at a discount may represent good value.

Financial gearing

This is the ratio between the company's borrowings and its capitalisation – in other words, a ratio between what it owes and what it owns. Private investors should find out why a company is highly geared before they invest, particularly if interest rates are high. This is because servicing the debts could cause a considerable strain on the company's business and profits. However, we should also consider gearing in the context of the company's business plans. If interest rates are low, a highly geared company which is well run can make good use of its debts – for example to expand into a new and profitable market.

Another way of looking at gearing is to consider how the profits compare with the interest payments made to service the company's debt. The number of times profits can cover the interest payments is known as **interest cover**. Company analysts suggest that in very broad terms, a ratio of four times profits to interest owed is healthy. A ratio of 1 : 1 is definitely not.

The acid test

The acid test is the ratio of the company's current assets (excluding stock) to its current liabilities. The reason stock is excluded is that if a company is in serious trouble its stock may not be worth the full market value. Sales and auctions following liquidation usually sell at knockdown prices. Analysts suggest that the ratio ought to be about 1 : 1, so that if the company did get into trouble it could meet all its liabilities – including payments to bondholders and shareholders – without having to rely on whatever the liquidator could raise by selling off its stock cheaply.

Asset backing

This is another way of looking at what the company would be worth if all else failed and it became insolvent. This test is a common exercise in the analysis of a takeover bid because the acquiring company and the shareholders need to know the real value of assets per share in the target company in order to calculate an attractive price for the bidding process.

The pre-tax profit margin

This is the trading profit – before the deduction of depreciation, interest payments and tax – expressed as a percentage of turnover. The pre-tax profit margin is considered a useful guide to the company's general performance and the management team's competence because it reveals the profits earned per pound of sales.

The return on capital

This is the profits before tax, divided by the shareholders' funds, and indicates the return the company is making on all the capital tied up in the business.

Making comparisons

All of these ratios and measures must be considered in the context of a full financial picture of the company. Obviously if we focus on just one or two, we may miss something very important or get an unbalanced view of the company.

We should bear in mind that one of the main uses of ratios is to spot where the market ratings are inappropriate to the company's actual prospects. Clearly, to identify this situation we would require a great deal of knowledge about the company itself and to understand why the market has miss-priced it. For this we would need to refer to as many sources as possible for information about markets, inflation, the economy and individual companies.

Buying and selling

How we buy and sell shares (this includes investment trust shares) will depend on the nature of the agreement we have with a stockbroker or investment manager. In the case of a discretionary or advisory stockbroker, the firm will act on the individual's behalf once they have completed a terms of business agreement and paid a cash and/or stock deposit. The firm will automatically provide a tariff of charges. A **discretionary manager** makes the investment decisions, whereas with an **advisory manager** the decision-making is shared. An execution-only stockbroker simply buys or sells without comment. Online **execution-only** stockbrokers tend to offer the cheapest dealing rates.

It is possible to hold individual equities within a 'self select' Individual savings account (ISA), which offers certain tax breaks. Individuals can invest up to £7,000 each year in an ISA but this reduces to £5,000 from April 2005. The taxation and contribution rules are explained on page 178.

Higher risk investor strategies

Derivatives

As explained on page 56, derivatives literally derive their value from an underlying security. Broadly, these instruments allow investors to gain exposure to a share or index, for example, without actually making any purchases. For much less than the share price, the cost of the derivative provides that market position. One of the main attractions for the private investor is the fact that with derivatives it is possible to make money out of a market whether it is rising or falling – or even static. Contracts for difference are a type of derivative contract that allow the investor to bet on market movements (see below).

The best resource on derivatives for students is at the London International Financial Futures Exchange (**www.liffe.com**). You can register for free and then use the Learning Centre via the private investor link.

Day trading

Day trading is only for the very knowledgeable investor who can afford to take major risks. The process involves buying and selling shares on the same day with the aim of making a profit. Day traders rarely hold overnight positions – hence the name. Such investors require access to **real-time market information**, quoting and dealing services, and these services are expensive. They are up against professional dealers who will have access to the very best information sources.

Contracts for difference (CFD)

It is possible to borrow to invest with **contracts for difference (CFD)** – an agreement to trade the price movement of a share. Here the individual does not actually buy the share but wins or loses based on changes in the share price. This service is offered by certain stockbrokers to their wealthy clients who are prepared to take a significant punt on market movements.

Spread betting

Spread betting is a particularly dangerous activity – although the rewards can be spectacular. A spread is the difference between the buying and selling prices quoted by a stock exchange dealer. The dealer buys at the lower price and sells at the higher. The *Financial Times* described CFDs for private investors as a 'dangerous game even for those with nerves of steel' (7 June, 2003) and provided the following example:

> A dealer who quoted a price of 863.5p–868 for Company B would buy shares from you at 863.5p and sell them to you at 868p. [...] Spread betting firms will quote a slightly wider spread – for example 862–869 for Company B.
>
> If your bet was that Company B's price would fall below 862p, you would 'sell' or open a 'down bet' at 862p. If Company B's price fell and the spread moved down to, say, 830–837p, you could close out or 'buy back your down bet' at 837p making a profit.
>
> Conversely, you would lose money for every point the price rose above 862p. If you decided to close the bet when the spread had moved to, say, 888–894p then you would have to do so at 894p. [...] If the down or 'sell' bet was £20 per point, the profit would be £500 when the price moved to 837p. But the losses would be £640 if the price rose to 894p.

Exchange traded funds (ETFs)

Exchange traded funds (ETFs) are an alternative to index trackers and offer greater flexibility in achieving a particular exposure to an index or sector, and are about half the cost of trackers. The **total expense ratio (TER)** of a typical retail tracker is about 1% (although the cost comes down for larger investments), whereas for ETFs the TER is about 0.5%.

ETFs are hybrid products. Like collective funds they hold a basket of stocks, but they are traded on an exchange as though they were themselves a stock. This means that they can be traded all day, whereas a mutual fund is only priced once a day at the end of the exchange's trading session. This ease of trading and pricing means that there can be a much closer match between an ETF's market value and net asset value than might be the case with a mutual fund. However, this point is only of relevance to institutional managers and very sophisticated day traders.

The ETF market in the US is huge, closely followed by Japan. However in the UK and Europe it is only in its infancy. Nevertheless we should follow this development with interest as it can provide the private investor with a very flexible tool for changing asset allocation and market position.

Company share schemes

Shares purchased through an employee share ownership scheme can be very attractive price-wise but, like any equities, if an employee buys shares in an employer they are taking a risk. This is particularly true for directors and senior executives where the share options form a significant element of the total remuneration. Complications can arise if the executive leaves a company earlier than expected and in these cases planners would need to consider very carefully the timing of the share purchases and/or sales, plus any tax implications.

In falling markets there is a genuine concern that the value of shares purchased may plummet and be worth less than when an employee took out the option ('underwater' shares). As a general rule, therefore, individuals are wise to consider how well the company's shares fit in their overall portfolio before they take a major stake. We should always remember that a high concentration of an individual's capital in just one company is very risky.

Non-executive schemes

Share option schemes allow employees to buy shares in their employer's company at less than market value. It is also possible to avoid income tax on what is effectively a benefit in kind – that is, the difference between your buying price and the market price.

The important point to remember about these schemes is that the 'option' is a right to buy, not an obligation. If direct investment is not appropriate, but the share price is attractive, employees can exercise their option and sell immediately afterwards, pocketing any profits, in most cases with no tax to pay. Between one-third and one-half of employees do just that. In some cases the company even provides subsidised dealing facilities.

Under the save as you earn (SAYE) contract, for example, the employee agrees to save between £5 and £250 each month for either three or five years, after which they receive a tax-free bonus. With the five-year contract, if you leave your money in the account for a further two years you qualify for an extra bonus. The option to buy is valid for a maximum of six months after the contract matures.

The most attractive feature of the SAYE scheme is that the option price of the shares can be fixed as low as 80% of the market value at the date the option is granted – that is, when the employee starts the contract.

There is no annual interest as such but the scheme details should set out the equivalent rate by calculating what the value of the bonuses received at the end of the contract are worth when spread over the entire savings period. It is important to assess this rate carefully because if the individual decides not to buy the shares, this will be the rate their savings will have earned over the period.

There are over 5,000 companies in the UK with Approved Employee Share Schemes with about 3.5 million participating employees. These schemes offer tax benefits for employees who participate. The best source of information on the range of company share schemes is ProShare.

Activity 11.1

Accurate and professional reporting of a company's trading position, its profits and losses, and its gearing position, among other facts, are key to the institutional and private investor's research. Yet despite the apparently rigorous regulation of Western stock markets, major scandals occur. Three recent examples are Enron, Worldcom and Parmalat. Find out what went wrong in one of these cases, determine whether a financial planner could have spotted the irregularities, and debate whether the steps taken to prevent a repeat of the scandal will be effective.

Activity 11.2

Using the LIFFE private investor learning centre, provide one example of how an investor might use a futures contract in a portfolio and one example for an options contract. Explain why you think that such strategies are suitable or otherwise for the private investor.

Summary

This chapter examined the factors an investor should consider before buying shares in an individual company. It considered size, sector, the information provided by the company itself, and what economic indicators can add to this perspective.

Key terms

- Acid test p. 143
- Advisory management p. 144
- Asset backing p. 143
- Contracts for difference (CFD) p. 145
- Day trader p. 145
- Demutualisation p. 140
- Derivatives p. 144
- Discount p. 142
- Discretionary management p. 142
- Dividend cover p. 142
- Dividend yield p. 141
- Exchange-traded funds (ETFs) p. 146
- Execution-only p. 144

- Gearing (leverage) p. 141
- Interest cover p. 143
- Interim and final results p. 140
- Market capitalisation p. 138
- Mutual status p. 140
- Net asset value p. 141
- Price earnings (P/E) ratio p. 142
- Premium p. 142
- Pre-tax profit margin p. 143
- Real-time market information p. 145
- Return on capital p. 144
- Spread betting p. 145
- Total expense ratio (TER) p. 146

Review questions

1 Explain why companies are categorised by size and sector.

2 What can we learn about a company from the Annual Report? Why is this information limited?

3 Name four indicators and measures that would help you form a view about a company's share price.

4 Describe two of the high-risk investment strategies and comment on whether you think they are appropriate for private investors.

Go to the Companion Website at www.booksites.net/harrison_pfp for a multiple-choice quiz to test your understanding of this chapter.

Further information

The *Financial Times*: **www.ft.com**

FT free annual reports service: **http://ft.ar.wilink.com**

Investors' Chronicle: **www.investorschronicle.ft.com**

ProShare: **www.proshare.org**

Two books on interpreting financial pages in the *Financial Times* are *How to Read the Financial Pages*, M. Brett, Random House, and *The Financial Times Guide to Using the Financial Pages*, R. Vaitilingam, Financial Times Prentice Hall.

The Stock Exchange publishes useful leaflets on buying and selling shares: **www.londonstock-exchange.com**

Chapter 12 ●●●●

Collective funds 1

Introduction

It would be very difficult to cover such a huge subject as collective funds (known as mutual funds in the US) in one chapter and so this important aspect of personal financial planning is divided into three sections. This chapter looks at the basic structures for investment vehicles. These funds do not offer smoothing of returns (as is offered by profits funds), protection from the downside (as is offered by protected funds), or guaranteed income or growth (as is offered by structured products). Nor do the managers of these funds go short – that is, sell shares they do not own – a strategy used by hedge funds. All of these more complex structures and strategies are considered in the next chapter, while Chapter 14 explains how we can place funds inside different wrappers to improve tax and/or administration efficiency.

Objectives

After reading this chapter you will be able to:

- Understand the main features of unit trusts, open-ended investment companies, life office unit-linked funds and investment trusts.
- Explain the important tax differences that distinguish unit trusts from unit-linked funds.
- Understand why investment trusts are extremely flexible but incorporate more layers of risk than are present in unit trusts, for example.

The four basic structures

The four most popular types of collective funds in the UK are:

- Unit trusts.
- Open-ended investment companies (OEICs).
- Investment trusts.
- Life assurance funds.

Most of these funds can be held in tax-efficient wrappers, such as an Individual savings account (ISA) and Defined contribution (DC) pension schemes and plans (see chapter 14 and 23).

Although these funds share many features in common and offer a similar broad investment scope, there are differences in structure and taxation. The individual's choice will depend on the finer details.

The costs

The cost of a fund is important, although as a rule the aim is to ensure competitive pricing rather than the cheapest. There are three figures we might use to assess the cost and for comparison purposes:

- **Annual management charge (AMC).** This is the most frequently quoted cost and covers the fund management charge.
- **Total expense ratio (TER).** This shows the annual management charge plus any other costs that might be revealed in the annual report, such as audit fees, custody (safekeeping of assets by a third party (the custodian) – usually a bank) and administration.
- **Reduction in yield (RIY).** This is probably the most complete measure in that it shows the percentage reduction in the return or yield taking account of all costs over a known investment period. This is the figure the provider must show on the key features document for certain products.

Unit trusts and open-ended investment companies (OEICs)

Although there are technical differences between the unit trust and OEIC structure, as far as the private investor is concerned these two types of fund can be treated as being identical. For the sake of simplicity where we refer to a unit trust, this covers both products.

A unit trust is a collective fund with a specific investment aim. Unit trusts are 'open ended', which means the trust managers may create or cancel units on a daily basis depending on demand. Investors purchase units in the fund, the value of which fluctuate directly in line with the value of the underlying assets. These underlying assets might be equities, corporate bonds, preference shares and convertibles, among others.

The trade organisation for these funds is the Investment Management Association (IMA), which, among other functions, provides classification for the categories to which funds belong – for example Equity United Kingdom, Equity United Kingdom Income, Smaller Companies, Fixed Income GBP – Corporate, Equity Global and so on. Students should visit the IMA website to get a better idea of how funds are categorised. Some of the specifications for a category are surprisingly broad – for example the Equity United Kingdom category funds must have a minimum of 80% in the UK but can be actively and passively managed and the managers can gear by up to 100%.

The most obvious strategy for risk management over the medium to long term is diversification. A cautious **managed fund** offers modest growth potential through exposure to different asset classes but is predominantly invested in equities and bonds, typically with a ratio of 60 : 40. Within this category you can also find **distribution funds**, which tend to have a ratio of 40 : 60 in equities and bonds and are designed more for the income seeker. The aim of both types of fund is to exploit the inverse (or negative) correlation between these two asset classes to provide reasonable returns during most market conditions. The point with this type of fund is that it is completely transparent. There are no smoothing mechanisms, caps and floors to limit how high your investment will soar and how far it will plummet. Here you are paying for the skill of the investment manager rather than a questionable insurance policy.

Funds of funds

In recent years there has been a massive increase in the number of 'funds of funds' (FoFs). The managers of unit trusts invest in other unit trusts with the objective of selecting a winning team of managers that can achieve an aggregate return that more than compensates for the additional layer of charges. It is also possible for fund managers to act as 'managers of managers', where they appoint individual sub-managers to run separate mandates within a fund. Although they sound very similar, in theory at least the manager of managers should have more control over the underlying managers.

Investment trusts

An investment trust is a British company, usually listed on the London stock market. These companies invest in the shares of other quoted and unquoted companies in the UK and overseas. This means they can also invest in other investment trusts to create the equivalent of a fund of funds model.

As public companies, investment trusts are subject to company law and Stock Exchange regulation. The prices of most quoted investment trusts are published daily in the *Financial Times*, while monthly data is provided by the Association of Investment Trust Companies (AITC), which categorises the trusts in a similar way to the IMA classification of unit trusts.

Investment trusts are different from unit trusts in several important ways and offer the active investor additional opportunities. However, these opportunities also make investment trusts potentially more volatile than unit trusts. For example investment trust companies have a fixed number of shares, so unlike unit trusts, 'units' cannot be created and cancelled to meet increased and reduced demand. As with any quoted company, the shares are only available when other investors are trying to sell. This means there are two factors that affect investment trust share prices. The first is the performance of the underlying assets in which the company invests. This factor also affects the price of units in a unit trust.

Where unit trust prices directly reflect the net asset value (NAV) of the fund, however, investment trust share prices may not. (The NAV is simply the value of all company assets less all liabilities.) This leads to the second factor, which is that the market forces (supply and demand) to which investment trust shares are subject may make the shares worth more or less than the underlying value of the NAV. If the share price is lower than the NAV it is described as trading at a discount. If it is higher it is trading at a premium. Clearly it is more attractive to buy an investment trust that is trading at a discount, although in practice there may be reasons for the discount that would put off potential investors.

Investment trusts can borrow money to invest, a process known as gearing. This adds extra investment flexibility and if the assets purchased with the borrowed money do well, the company and its shareholders will benefit. A poor return on the shares will reduce the profitability of the company.

Split capital investment trusts

Investment trusts can have different types of shares. The main types are:

- Zero dividend preference shares (**zeros**). These have a target redemption value that will be paid to investors on a set date in the future. This is not guaranteed. This type of share does not attract dividends.
- **Income shares**. As the name suggests, these shares receive the dividends after any interest or borrowing costs. There is no target level of return at redemption, as the rate will depend on investment performance.
- **Capital shares**. Here the value depends on how much money is left after the zeros and income shares have been redeemed and any borrowings repaid.

'Splits' were the subject of a major mis-selling scandal at the turn of the century. In April 2004 the management groups concerned were still under investigation and investors' losses were put at £620m by the AITC. Some companies had high levels of investment in other similar trusts (a strategy known as cross holdings); others had high levels of borrowings. Where the two features occurred companies were in a very weak position during the bear market (see page 30).

There are several other types of share, each offering different features; for example stepped preference shares, which offer dividends that rise at a predetermined rate and a fixed redemption value which is paid when the trust is wound up.

Taxation of unit and investment trusts

In terms of taxation, the unit and investment trust route is very similar. Where these investments are held outside a tax-favoured wrapper the capital gains tax liability falls on the investor, who can offset any tax liability against the annual CGT exemption (£8,200 in 2004–2005). Investment trusts are generally lower cost than unit trusts, with the exception of index trackers. To summarise, unit trusts, with the exception of the index trackers, are generally considered slightly more expensive than investment trusts but less sensitive to market movements.

Life insurance investment bonds

Insurance funds are similar in scope of asset allocation to investment trusts but they are often sold for a specified term, in which case they are known as insurance 'bonds', which should not be confused with the asset class of that name. The trade body for these funds is the Association of British Insurers (ABI), which provides the categorisations in the same way as the IMA and AITC.

Like unit trusts, a lump sum premium in an insurance company 'bond' buys units, which directly reflect the net asset value of the fund's underlying investments. The charges for the two types of collective funds are broadly similar. However, the tax treatment is different (see below). Despite the confusing array of investments offered by insurance companies to the public, most fall into one of three main categories:

- **Maximum investment plans (MIPs)** are regular monthly or annual premium investments and usually run for 10 years. Once this term is complete the investor can either take the proceeds or leave the fund to continue to benefit from investment growth. It is also possible at this stage to make tax efficient annual withdrawals.
- **Insurance company investment bonds** are similar to MIPs but this is a single premium or lump sum investment.
- **Endowments** combine investment with a substantial element of life assurance and have been widely sold in the mortgage market.

With maximum investment plans and insurance company investment bonds, premiums are invested in a choice of funds, most of which are unit linked, similar in concept to unit trusts in that your premiums buy units in a collective fund and the value of those units rises and falls in line with the value of the underlying assets.

Although sold by life assurance companies, most of these regular and single premium plans offer minimal life cover, as their main purpose is investment. If the investor dies the company might pay out 101% of the original investment or the value of the fund, whichever is the greater.

Unit linked life assurance funds offer a similar range of investment opportunities as unit trusts.

As mentioned, the traditional endowment is most commonly used as a repayment vehicle for a mortgage, although sales have slowed considerably following the recent mis-selling scandal (see page 29). The distinguishing feature of an endowment is that it combines a significant element of life assurance with a savings plan so that if the policyholder dies during the term of the policy the combination of the value of the fund plus the life assurance is sufficient to repay the debt. It is possible to buy second-hand endowments where people have sold a policy to a market maker in order to get a higher price than would be available from the insurance company. Traded endowment policies (TEPs) are examined on page 166.

Early surrenders of life policies

Traditionally, long-term life assurance investments deducted the commission costs for the entire investment period during the first year or two. This is why so many people got back so little from their policies if they pulled out during this 'initial' period.

An endowment – or indeed any investment – is portable when it comes to mortgage repayment. If the policyholder buys another house and needs a larger mortgage, it may be best to keep the original policy and top up with a repayment or interest only mortgage backed by a new savings plan where necessary. If the policyholder is unable to continue premiums for some reason, there are various options that can give a better return than cancellation. It is possible to make the policy 'paid up' which means it is not necessary to pay any further premiums but the money is still tied up until the maturity date. The policyholder will still benefit from investment growth but it is important to check the ongoing charges and what penalties apply before taking this step.

Those who need access to their capital might be able to take a loan from the insurance company, based on the surrender value of the policy. Alternatively, it may be possible to get up to 30% more than the surrender value if it is sold in the second-hand endowments market. In this case buyers take over the commitment to continue the premiums in the hope that the final payout will be well in excess of the purchase price plus the cost of the outstanding premiums. The two main options are to auction the policy or to sell it to a market maker who, naturally, will charge a fee or take a percentage of the profit. (The profit is the difference between what you would have received as a surrender value from your insurance company and the actual price achieved.)

Taxation of life assurance policies

Life assurance taxation is notoriously complicated. Insurance company bonds pay tax broadly equivalent to the basic rate on income and capital gains. However, in the 2003 Budget the government reduced the top rate of tax paid by life insurers on onshore funds from 22% to 20%, but from April 2004 the tax credit for any gains made on these investments reduced from 22% to 20%. For basic rate taxpayers the position does not change but for higher rate taxpayers the effective rate of tax rises from 18% to 20% (that is, 40% minus the 20% paid by insurers – previously 22%).

Income tax paid within a life fund cannot be reclaimed by the investor, so generally, these bonds are not considered suitable for non-taxpayers. Moreover, the capital gains tax paid by the fund cannot be offset against an individual's exemption.

At the end of the investment period, the proceeds of a life assurance policy will be treated as though the fund had already paid the equivalent of basic-rate tax. For lower- and basic-rate payers that is the end of the story. But what happens next for higher-rate payers depends on whether the policy is classed by the Inland Revenue as **qualifying** or **non-qualifying**.

With a qualifying policy there is no further tax liability for higher-rate payers. However, to attract this special tax status the policy must abide by various conditions. First, it must be a regular premium plan where you pay a predetermined amount each month or each year. Second, it has to be a long-term plan – usually a minimum of 10 years. Third, it has to provide a substantial amount of life cover. This means that single premium investment policies are non-qualifying, but the regular premium MIPs may be classed as qualifying depending on the term and level of life cover provided. Mortgage endowments, which tend to be long-term regular premium plans, usually are qualifying due to the substantial element of life cover.

Unique tax feature of bonds

There are circumstances in which the unique features of investment bonds can be attractive to certain investors. With bonds there is no annual yield as such since income and growth are rolled up within the fund, but up to 5% of the original capital can be withdrawn each year for up to 20 years. The Inland Revenue treats these withdrawals as a return of capital and therefore at the time of payment they are free of tax so the higher rate tax liability is deferred until you cash in your policy. (Withdrawals above 5% are treated by the Inland Revenue as though they are net of basic rate tax, so the higher rate liability must be paid, and cannot be deferred.)

Top-slicing relief

Even with a non-qualifying life policy it may be possible to reduce or avoid the deferred higher rate tax bill due to the effect of 'top slicing relief'. Top slicing relief averages the profit over the number of years the bond has been held and adds this profit slice to an investor's income in the year the bond matures. If part or all of this falls into the higher rate bracket, it would be taxed. However, with careful tax planning investors can avoid this liability by encashing the bond when they become lower rate taxpayers – in retirement for example.

Higher rate taxpayers who have used their full CGT allowance may also find bonds and MIPs attractive because the 5% withdrawals do not have to be declared for income tax purposes in the year of withdrawal.

● ● ● ● Friendly society policies

Societies registered under the Friendly Societies Acts of 1896 and 1955 are set up for the provision of benefits for members. Many small societies exist to provide benefits to very specific groups; for example of a religious or ethical persuasion. Friendly societies are often snubbed as the small fry of the investment industry. However, in contrast to life assurance funds, which have to pay both income and capital gains tax, friendly society funds are tax free. Unfortunately, the amount that can be invested is small – £270 as an annual lump sum (£300 if premiums are paid on a more regular basis) and most plans run for 10 years. There are societies that accept a lump sum investment to cover payments for the full 10 years. We should always look carefully at past performance and charges for friendly societies and compare these with what is on offer from ISA managers and unit and investment trusts which offer low contribution regular savings plans.

● ● ● ● Offshore funds

In certain cases for more wealthy, risk-tolerant investors it may be appropriate to consider offshore funds. Whether this type of fund would be suitable will depend on the tax jurisdiction of the fund, the way the fund itself is taxed, and the individual's tax position.

Points to consider with offshore funds include the charges, which can be significantly higher than the equivalent onshore fund, and the regulation. We must always consider what protection is offered if the company collapses or the fund manager runs off with the investors' money. As a general rule for a UK investor investing in UK securities, unit and investment trusts are likely to prove more cost effective and simpler than offshore funds.

There are two main types of offshore insurance bond:

● Distribution bonds, which pay a regular 'income'.
● Non-distribution bonds, which roll up gross (interest is reinvested without deduction of tax).

Investors who may gain by going offshore include UK and foreign expatriates who are non-resident for UK tax purposes and who can benefit from gross roll up non-distribution bonds if they do not pay tax in the country where they live. Higher rate taxpayers may also benefit from the gross roll up but you do have to pay tax when you bring the money back into the UK, although of course you may have switched to the basic rate tax bracket if you have retired by the time the non-distribution bond matures.

Selecting collective funds

The financial plan will determine how much an individual can invest and whether this should be as an occasional lump sum (typically towards the end of the tax year) or as regular monthly premiums. One advantage of monthly premiums is **pound-cost averaging**. This term is used to describe the way that capital invested in small amounts on a regular basis can even out the impact of market fluctuations and saves the worry about when to make an annual investment.

Open architecture

The substantial investment in technology and in developing Internet capability has made it much easier for providers of investment products to offer what is known as an 'open architecture' approach to investment fund choice. This is a platform that accommodates the provider's own range of funds and the funds of a selection of external managers.

When it comes to selecting a good fund, there is plenty of advice on what not to do and very little on positive selection criteria, so what follows is to some extent subjective. The financial press and several firms of advisers produce surveys that highlight the best and worst performers in the various categories of funds. We must take great care when we examine past performance statistics because these can be very misleading. What the surveys do offer is some ideas on how to screen funds, so it is worth checking out the methodology used in the most authoritative publications – *Money Management*, for example.

We should also consider how funds are categorised by ratings agencies – Standard & Poor's Fund Research, for example, or Moody's. Top funds in terms of research capability and the investment management team, among other features, get an A, AA or AAA (the highest award). Fund objectives should be clearly defined and these objectives should be measurable, so that there are clear benchmarks against which performance can be judged. The asset allocation, stock selection, investment style and investment philosophy should also be set out clearly.

Although it is difficult to police the use of statistics, to ignore past performance altogether is unwise. In many cases past performance statistics can be a useful aid to gauge the future potential of a manager or fund, *provided* the performance is clearly attributable. To have any meaning such statistics:

- Must be coupled with a clear understanding of how past performance was achieved.
- Must be combined with an assessment of the current investment style of the management team.
- Must relate to the individuals currently responsible.
- Must relate to the current structure of the management company, which must continue to provide the same level of technical research and other support functions.

Activity 12.1

Using a recent copy of *Money Management*, examine the pages that set out Standard & Poor's rated funds. Select three funds and consider how S&P applied its screening criteria. Visit the S&P website at **www.standardandpoors.com** and the individual fund managers' sites. Compare S&P's methodology with Citywire, which tracks the individual manager rather than the fund. Visit the Citywire website at **www.citywire.co.uk**. Now compare these two approaches and explain the pros and cons of each method. Is there a clear relationship between the results for top funds and the results for top managers?

Summary

This chapter examined the main structures for collective funds. It explained how the structure affects the risk profile of the fund and how the taxation varies and may determine an investor's final choice. It also considered what factors might inform the choice of manager and how to use past performance in an appropriate way.

Key terms

- Annual management charge (AMC) p. 150
- Capital shares p. 152
- Distribution fund p. 151
- Endowments p. 153
- Funds of funds (FoFs) p. 151
- Income shares p. 152
- Investment bonds p. 153
- Managed fund p. 151
- Maximum investment plans (MIPs) p. 153
- Net asset value (NAV) p. 152
- Non-qualifying p. 155
- Pound-cost averaging p. 157
- Qualifying p. 155
- Reduction in yield (RIY) p. 150
- Total expense ratio p. 150
- Zeros p. 152

Review questions

1 Describe the four main categories of collective fund outlined in this chapter and point out any important differences.

2 What are the main types of fund sold by insurance companies?

3 Would you recommend an offshore fund and if so, in which circumstances?

4 What factors might we consider in selecting a fund?

Go to the Companion Website at **www.booksites.net/harrison_pfp** for a multiple-choice quiz to test your understanding of this chapter.

Further information

The Association of British Insurers: **www.abi.org.uk**

The Association of Investment Trust Companies: **www.aitc.org.uk**. (For an interactive version of the Monthly Information Service, which lists all of the member companies, go to **www.aitc.org.uk/misonline**.)

For details of fund supermarkets, see page 183.

The FSA publishes comparative tables of certain investments at **www.fsa.gov.uk/tables**.

The Investment Management Association: **www.investmentuk.org**

Standard & Poor's: **www.standardandpoors.com**. (For access to the fund information S&P provides for *Money Management* and its sister publications, go to: **www.ftadviser.com/fund research**.)

Useful websites for fund information include **www.moneyfacts.co.uk**; **www.trustnet.com**; **www.hemscott.net**.

The trade and technical press

It is impossible for the student to read every magazine and paper. Moreover some publications lack editorial integrity and are influenced too much by pressure from advertisers. A purely subjective selection of publications that provides good quality analysis and news coverage of the collective fund market would put *Money Management* (monthly) at the top of the list. For weekly coverage try *Investment Week* and *Financial Adviser*.

Chapter 13 ●●●●

Collective funds 2

Introduction

This chapter covers the growing range of collective fund structures that offer a mechanism to protect returns from stockmarket volatility and/or use sophisticated strategies to provide 'absolute' returns. Absolute returns are positive throughout the market cycles. This is the objective of 'alternative' strategies that do not adhere to any traditional benchmarks.

Objectives

After reading this chapter you will be able to:

● Understand the mechanisms and strategies that underpin with profits and traded endowments, protected and structured funds, and hedge funds.
● Debate the merits and drawbacks of each structure or strategy.
● Argue whether you do or do not believe that the additional potential for outperformance or the level of risk management offered is worth the additional cost.
● Discuss the potential for mis-selling complex products in the retail market.

● ● ● ● With profits funds

With profits funds have been with us for several decades and until comparatively recently formed the backbone of the long-term savings market, particularly for pensions and mortgages. These funds, which invest in equities, bonds and property, pay an annual bonus or return and in addition pay a final or terminal bonus. Originally the annual bonus was completely protected once allocated, but the more modern version of this product, the unitised with profits policy, offers a lower level of guarantee.

The aim of with profits is to enable the risk-averse investor to benefit from a significant exposure to equities without direct exposure to the corresponding short-term volatility. Put simply, to achieve this smoothing of returns the actuary reserves some of the profits in years of plenty to boost returns in years when investment markets are falling. However, 'with profits' refers to far more than this smoothing mechanism, as we shall see.

These funds have been the subject of harsh criticism in recent years and have lost their place as the nation's favourite long-term investment in the retail market. In particular the crisis at Equitable Life has revealed just how badly with profits can be managed (see page 166) and the scope of life offices to conceal problems. While much of the criticism about the opacity of the product and poor financial reserving is justified, students should not take the press coverage on board without questioning whether all journalists fully understand how these complex products work. As in any press campaign, bad news sells more copies of newspapers than good news.

The meaning of 'with profits'

Most investors (and journalists) assume 'with profits' refers to the smoothing mechanism that allows the appointed actuary at the life office to hold back profit in the good years in order to maintain a reasonable return when market conditions are poor. Certainly this mechanism is an important feature of with profits funds but the concept implies a great deal more. In most cases with profits policyholders also share in the profits and losses of the company's other lines of business – term assurance and annuities, for example. When a proprietary company suffers a loss this is borne by the shareholders as well as the with profits policyholders. For a mutual, which is owned by its policyholders, the 'with profits' policyholders are the owners of the business and ultimately benefit from the profits – but also suffer the brunt of the losses. In other words, 'with profits' also implies its corollary, 'with losses'.

This means that when we invest in a traditional with profits policy we are investing in the skill of the investment manager *and* buying into the company's fortunes – for good or for bad. Until recently being a member of a mutual was seen as a win-win situation and many have benefited from the windfalls that have followed demutualisation. After the Equitable Life scandal, policyholders will appreciate what should always have been made clear to them, namely that there can be a significant downside to mutual membership.

The market value adjuster (MVA)

Investors have also misunderstood the market value adjuster (MVA), which is a penalty applied on early termination of a policy and which represents an important feature of unitised with profits policies. With profits guarantees only apply where investors stay for the full term of the policy, and even then the smoothing mechanism will not fully insulate them from movements in the markets.

Companies justify the MVA by pointing out that when policyholders start leaving in droves the company is forced to sell investments for less than they are worth, often at a time of falling markets. The fund suffers as a result, and the MVA aims to share this suffering between those who leave and those who stay put. What is happening here is that the stated value of an individual's holding is actually higher than the true value, shown in the **asset share**, which we consider below. The three-year bear market that started in 2000 meant that the asset share dropped significantly. As policyholders pulled out, the run on funds forced companies to apply high MVAs (over 20% in several cases). Naturally this caused considerable anger among policyholders and highlighted the inflexibility of these investments.

The with profits market is far from homogenous; the operation of the smoothing process, the provider's financial strength, investment philosophy and process are all relevant in determining the outcome.

Future trends in maturity values will depend on the actuary's analysis of the relationship between the benchmark asset share over the next few years and the current payout. The asset share represents the policyholder's 'fair share' of the fund, and takes account of premiums paid, actual returns over the specific policy term to date, deductions for expenses, plus any relevant experience built into the formula – for example mortality within the with profits policyholders' pool, and profits and losses from other lines of business.

Where the theoretical payout (the apparent fund value of an individual's holdings) is higher than the asset share and the asset share is projected to keep falling – as is prevalent at present – the actuary will need to reduce payouts further in order to bring the position back into balance. Of course, if the company has over-declared annual bonuses in the past – as was very common in the late 1980s and 1990s – the actuary may not be able to recreate a healthy balance.

The misunderstanding of the role of the smoothing mechanism led investors in 2003 and 2004, for example, to expect to benefit immediately from the temporary upturn in the stock market and to see an increase in the annual bonus. Instead they got a reduction. This is a good example of investor expectations being out of line with reality. Even before the onset of the bear market in 2001, life offices were bracing themselves for a period of bonus cuts. This was partly because providers had competed for market share by paying out unrealistically high annual bonuses and did not hold back sufficient reserves during the good years. But it was also because it was necessary to adjust payouts to reflect the anticipated lower rates of inflation and the associated lower returns. The massive fall in the markets simply made matters worse. With or without the bear market, bonuses would have fallen.

Looking forward, the continuation of the low inflation environment dictates that asset shares on long-term policies will continue to fall over the next few years. However, not all companies are affected in the same way.

Exhibit 13.1 Key points on with profits

● With profits funds must never be confused with pure equity funds. The level of equities now held in these funds varies considerably and will provide a very different range of returns compared with pure equity funds. By 2004 the average equity component had fallen from a high of 60%–80% to about 25%, although there were exceptions where the equity allocation was 70%–80%, where the provider had a strong balance sheet to support the risk.

● Smoothing takes place over a period of many years. It is inappropriate to expect a single year of fairly strong equity performance to compensate fully for a three-year bear market and the impact will vary between companies.

● Those companies that strove to maintain maturity payouts beyond the high inflation/high return years may be forced to cut bonuses more significantly than more prudent providers.

● Other factors, such as profits and losses on other lines of business, are also taken into account.

Investment process

It is important to remember that good returns on with profits policies rely on successful investment management – not on the smoothing mechanism. Many of the life offices in the with profits market have a poor reputation for asset management and this factor should not be overlooked.

Evidence from the more successful providers indicates that investment strategies for with profits funds should be based on a robust financial strength that gives the fund manager the flexibility to maintain an appropriate weighting in equities throughout all market conditions. Financially weak life offices have been forced to reduce their equity weighting at the wrong time – selling equities at much lower prices than when they purchased. It is unlikely that some of these companies will be able to recover ground sufficiently to generate attractive returns over the longer term. At the time of writing about half of with profits funds were closed to new business. We can expect more funds to follow suit and possibly a spate of takeovers within the market. Some of the remaining mutuals may demutualise in a bid to shore up their falling financial strength.

Success in with profits also depends on a disciplined approach to long-term investment. The asset manager should be able to attribute returns to skill and not to market direction. A **contracyclical**, long-term approach to investment is ideally suited to the requirements of the risk-averse, long-term investor. This avoids market fads, such as the telecom, media and technology (TMT) boom–bust cycle, and directs new investment towards asset classes, sectors and stocks that are temporarily out of favour.

A diverse portfolio with a general tilt towards value investments ensures the with profits fund benefits from shares in companies that offer a track record of profitability, good cash flow, and asset backing.

Should with profits survive?

While we could argue that the concept of with profits has withstood the events of recent years and that a financially strong life office should continue to offer attractive returns, nevertheless we should also question whether it is appropriate for individuals to invest in the fortunes of a single company. This point is often overlooked. Arguably, an individual who allocates a high proportion of overall savings and investments to a with profits fund is placing a high concentration of assets in a single company. The combination of the opaque smoothing mechanism, the dominance of the appointed actuary, and the exposure to the profits and losses on other business lines makes the outcome of a with profits investment not so much unknown as unknowable.

The alternative to the traditional with profits structure is the smoothed managed fund, which operates like a unit-linked fund but with a separate mechanism for a limited degree of smoothing the annual returns. This type of fund attempts to emulate the attractions of traditional with profits but in a more transparent way and without the link to the company's overall fortunes.

Exhibit 13.2 The guaranteed annuity rate: an exercise in poor actuarial analysis

One of the controversial features at the heart of the Equitable Life crisis was the **guaranteed annuity rate (GAR)**, which applied to about 25% of individual pension policyholders at the time the problem became public. Policyholders swap their pension fund at retirement for an annuity, which provides the regular retirement income (see Chapter 24). The annuity rate – that is, the level of income an individual secures with their fund – depends largely on interest rates at the time of purchase.

The company started selling individual pension policies with a guaranteed annuity rate back in 1956 and stopped in 1988 when these policies were replaced by personal pensions. The GAR guaranteed pension investors that at retirement they would receive a minimum annuity 'rate' or income in return for their funds. In retrospect this was a very risky strategy on the part of Equitable Life because it relied on interest rates remaining high. Broadly speaking, interest rates reflect the yields on gilts – the instruments insurers buy to generate the income stream to annuitants – and can be very volatile over the long term.

Throughout the 1980s double digit inflation and interest rates continued to disguise the lurking liability in GAR policies. But by January 1994 interest rates had fallen far enough to make the guaranteed rates – typically between 9% and 12% depending on age and sex – look very attractive.

At this point Equitable effectively stopped honouring the guarantee but the way it did so was complicated. The value of a with profits policy builds up through the annual 'bonus' or return. At maturity (retirement in the case of pension plan holders) the company adds a final or 'terminal' bonus, which reflects more recent investment conditions. This can be worth over 50% of the total fund.

What Equitable did was to cut the final bonus on the GAR policies to bring down the total fund size. This meant it could pay the guaranteed annuity rate because it applied to a much smaller fund. In this way the company brought GAR policyholders' expectations in line with the non-GAR investors.

Initially very few people noticed this adroit move on Equitable's part because by the mid-1990s interest rates were up again. In 1997 the government gave the Bank of England independence over interest rates. Interest rates began to fall again and the GAR suddenly looked very attractive. It was then that policyholders and the press began to demand that Equitable pay the full terminal bonus and honour the GAR. The company could not afford to do so.

The Equitable policyholder pressure group was very articulate and influential and forced the company to agree to a court case to test its decision to cut final bonuses for GAR policies. In September 1999 the High Court upheld Equitable's bonus policy, but it also granted policyholders leave to appeal. Which they did. And they won. In a surprise reversal of the High Court's decision in January 2000, the Appeal court ruled against Equitable Life on a majority judgment. This appeal was upheld by five law lords in July 2000, who ruled that it was 'inequitable' for the company to treat policyholders in different ways.

This was the beginning of a major crisis for Equitable, which was still unresolved at the time of writing and from which it is unlikely to emerge intact. The high exit penalty (MVA) it imposed on those who wanted to leave increased its unpopularity. The Penrose Report of the Equitable Life Inquiry into the mutual's problems, which reported in 2004, was very critical of the mutual's 'over-bonusing', which the report argued had left it financially weak.

●●●● Traded endowment policies (TEPs)

Despite the uncertainty that surrounds with profits endowments it may still be possible to find good quality secondhand policies – **traded endowment policies (TEPs)**. Sellers argue that these can offer a high degree of security but students should be aware that TEPs are very complex products and must be selected with great care.

As discussed in the previous chapter, the mortgage endowment aims to build up a lump sum to repay the mortgage at the end of a fixed term. It also pays a death benefit, which together with the value of the fund will repay the mortgage if the investor dies before the policy matures. The value of the life assurance will vary depending on the size of the fund in relation to the mortgage.

The life assurance element of the endowment is not transferable so the TEP purchase relates solely to the investment policy. If the original policyholder dies before the maturity date then the TEP owner would receive the proceeds of the policy early.

The role of the secondhand market

A secondary market in the financial world arises where there are sellers and buyers – both of whom seek to benefit from the exchange. Between half and two-thirds of investors fail to maintain their with profits policies to maturity (a damning indictment of the market in itself). The 'surrender value' – that is, the amount the insurance company will pay if an individual stops a policy part way through the term – rarely reflects the actual value of the contract at that point in time, so the policyholder loses heavily. Early leavers with a unitised with profits policy could also be penalised through the application of the market value adjuster (MVA).

The discrepancy between the intrinsic value of a policy and its much lower surrender value led to the establishment of a secondhand market in the early 1990s where intermediaries match potential buyers with sellers.

The TEP market is big and was still growing rapidly at the time of writing, although it will not escape unscathed from the problems facing the with profits market as a whole. The number of policies coming up for sale continues to grow, however, due to the massive sales of endowment mortgages in the 1980s and 1990s. Sellers can usually get 15%–30% above the surrender value they would otherwise receive from the provider, if they sell privately. This leaves enough profit to pay for the intermediary's costs and provide an attractive deal to the purchaser.

The attraction of TEPs

Investors who buy TEPs are usually looking to achieve a reasonable rate of growth over the remaining investment period without taking on significant risk. When you purchase a policy you pay a lump sum and agree to maintain the monthly premiums until the policy matures. Each TEP will have a certain number of years left to run and so, as a buyer, your aim would be to get back more than your outlay – that is, the purchase price plus the cost of the monthly premiums. (It is possible to buy TEP funds, although with a few notable exceptions, these have not performed well.)

Buying individual policies with different maturity dates allows investors to use TEPs for specific financial goals – for example to pay for a child's university fees. The cost of a typical 3-year university course could be as high as £23,000 in London and £19,000 elsewhere. A series of TEPs with a potential value of £3,000–£5,000 each that matured at regular intervals might be a good way to meet the fees and accommodation costs. Another use for TEPs might be to supplement retirement income.

TEPs are most commonly sold by **market makers**. These companies will buy a policy outright and maintain the monthly premiums until they find a purchaser. It is also possible to buy policies at auction, although this is not a good idea unless the investor is very experienced in this market. A third way to buy is through agents who match buyers and sellers directly, in a similar way to an estate agent.

How to assess the TEP maturity value

The company selling the TEP should indicate the potential value of the policy but this **formula maturity value** is only an estimate based on investment assumptions. Clearly, as with any investment, there is a degree of risk. However, a policy that has been running for several years will already have an intrinsic value. Traditional with profits policies include a **basic sum assured**, which is the absolute minimum amount they will pay out at maturity. On top of this there is an annual return – known as a 'bonus'. With conventional policies, once a bonus has been allocated it is guaranteed, provided the policy is held to maturity. Over the rest of the term the policy should benefit from further **annual bonuses** and at maturity there should be a final or **terminal bonus**. The formula used to estimate the value of the policy at maturity takes all of these elements into account, assuming bonus (growth) rates stay at their current level, to provide a value. This value is discounted back to the present and also takes account of the premiums that must still be paid.

The calculation is complicated, as there are up to four elements that make up the final value of a TEP at maturity. On purchase the buyer will know the value of the 'sum assured' and the bonuses that have been paid to date (the 'accrued' bonuses). However, the buyer will not know the actual rate of bonus the insurance company will pay in the remaining years of the policy. Bonus rates are falling at present and may do so for some years, although in some cases they may remain attractive in comparison with other investments. The fourth element – the final or 'terminal' bonus allocated at maturity – is purely discretionary, although it can account for over 50% of the total payout. Recently some companies have decided not to pay this bonus.

To sum up, the TEP future returns will depend largely on the ability of the insurance company to maintain attractive annual and final bonuses. This in turn will depend on the asset mix of the fund, the skills of the investment managers and – most importantly – on the company's financial strength. The **realistic balance sheet** is one indicator of the level of reserves the insurer holds that are not related to liabilities. Comparative tables in specialist publications for intermediaries, such as *Money Management*, are useful. The higher the percentage, the better the free asset ratio. Students might also look at the credit rating awarded by Standard & Poor's or Moody's. The top S&P rating is AAA but an AA or A is perfectly satisfactory. Other analysts provide their own rating of life office financial strength. Details of realistic balance sheets and credit ratings should be available from the market makers that sell TEPs.

Protected and 'guaranteed' funds

Protected and guaranteed products offer a link to the return on an index or a basket of indices. The growth potential is limited but in return these products offer some downside protection. The provider might buy an option contract (see page 56) to protect itself from a severe fall in the relevant index or indices and can exercise this contract if the market falls beyond a certain point.

These products have always been controversial and serve to demonstrate that in most cases where a product is mis-sold or widely discredited, either the risks were not explained, or they were impossible for the layperson to understand.

For the record, students should appreciate that there is nothing intrinsically wrong with most high-risk investments, provided the investor understands the risks and can accommodate them. For this, investors require a clear appreciation of the risk to the **total return** – capital and income combined. This is important in relation to the **structured capital-at-risk products** (**Scarps** – the Financial Services Authority's description) that rely on the movements of different stock market indices. Such investments generally fulfil their stated obligations but there is often a huge gap between the product description, which may well provide a robust if highly technical analysis of the risks and probabilities of returns, and the consumer's perception. For example, individuals used to deposit accounts assume 'income' is separate from and additional to their capital deposit. However, where a Scarp advertises a high rate of 'income' this is not derived from interest income from cash or fixed interest investments, or dividends from shares. In many cases the original capital is at risk as this provides the income stream when markets fall below a certain point.

The Financial Services Authority (FSA) provides some useful examples of Scarps on its website and students will find these and the associated FSA Factsheet helpful in understanding the risks (**www.fsa.gov.uk/consumer**). The FSA's example assumes you have £5,000 to invest in a 'growth' Scarp. The product might offer growth of 30% over five years, but it may also state that if the FTSE 100 index falls by more than 20% at the end of the term, your capital is reduced by 1% for each 1% fall in the index. (This applies to the full amount of the fall, not just the excess over 20%.) If, after five years, the index fell by 50%, your £5,000 would indeed receive a 30% return in the form of growth (£1,500) but your original capital would be reduced to £2,500 (ie a 50% fall in the index = a 50% fall in the original capital). In total you would get back £4,000.

An 'income' Scarp might offer 6% pa for five years but it may also state that if the FTSE 100 falls at the end of the term your capital is reduced by 2% for each 1% fall in the index. If, after five years, the index fell by 25%, on your initial investment of £5,000 you would have received the 6% annual income (£1,500) but the capital would have reduced to £2,500, so again you would get only £4,000 back in total.

Most of the income Scarps (previously known as 'precipice bonds') have disappeared following a mis-selling scandal, where risk-averse investors bought the bonds as very low-risk investments, assuming that they offered something better than a deposit account. There were only three new versions of the income Scarp on the market at the time of writing. Dozens of growth Scarps were still active, however, and these are designed to appeal to the risk-averse investor who wants exposure to real assets but without the full downside potential.

Individuals keen to limit their downside should ask for clear information that helps them judge the probability of total loss. Financial planners should devise their own method of assessing these structured products or take advantage of an existing mathematical formula to determine this probability for structured products (for an example, see the adviser Bestinvest's website at **www.bestinvest.com**). For products available at the time of writing the probability of total loss according to Bestinvest ranged from 0% to 32%, so you can see how broad the risk-rating is in this market and why certain products, like those that link to the Nasdaq 100 or, even riskier, the FTSE/Xinhua China 25 index, are certainly not suitable for the risk-averse.

Students should keep track of new structured products that come onto the market. For example in 2003–2004 we witnessed the launch of the **constant protection portfolio insurance (CPPI)** products. These products link to an index or fund and the investor's money is split between the underlying fund and cash. The protection is provided by a switching mechanism that sells units in the fund and moves into cash when markets are falling and the reverse when markets are rising. Some products also buy additional insurance but the key difference between a Scarp and a CPPI product is that with the latter the capital is actually invested, whereas with a Scarp the money is usually held in cash with a derivative providing the exposure to the relevant indices.

Diversification and funds of funds

Finance theory suggests that while there are many strategies that may reduce investment volatility, in the retail market those with modest amounts to save have access to a limited number of options. The choice will depend on the period for which the individual is prepared to tie up capital, the level of downside protection required, the individual's tax position and the price they are prepared to pay.

The most obvious and reliable strategy for risk management over the medium to long term is diversification (see Chapter 5). A 'cautious managed' unit trust or OEIC, for example, offers modest growth potential through investment in equities and bonds, typically with a ratio of 60 : 40. Within this Investment Management Association (IMA) category you will also come across 'distribution' funds, which tend to have a ratio of 40 : 60 in equities and bonds and are designed more for the income seeker.

The ultimate diversification model blends asset classes, managers and investment styles and is the structure employed by **funds of funds** and **multi-manager funds**, which aim to reduce risk at the total portfolio level, although individual sub-funds might demonstrate quite volatile behaviour. Funds of funds have access to an extremely wide range of sub-funds, including manager of managers mandates, derivatives, cash, investment trusts, and direct equities and bonds.

The problem with diversification, however, is knowing when to stop. Over-diversification can lead to unnecessary costs and to style neutrality, at which point it would be simpler and cheaper to use a managed fund or an index tracker. Drawing the line where efficient diversification ends and counter-productivity begins is a task that continues to engage the best minds in the multi-manager business. These products are transparent but require careful analysis to ensure there is genuine value provided by the selector of funds or managers – otherwise this product will morph into what was commonly called a broker bond back in the 1980s, where the middleman merely served to add an extra layer of charges.

Alternative investments

Investments are described as 'alternative' where the risk profile and the return of the fund or asset do not correlate with conventional equity and bond markets. We could use the term 'alternative' to refer to commercial property but in the retail market generally the term is used to describe hedge funds and private equity.

Hedge funds

There is no statutory definition of a hedge fund. The term relates to the original funds that used specific strategies to 'hedge' risk – usually some form of derivative, such as an option (see page 56). The reputation of hedge funds as an extremely high-risk strategy in part derives from the spectacular collapse of the Long Term Capital Management (LTCM) hedge fund, which revealed in September 1998 that it had lost a cool $2.3bn.

Today the term covers a very wide spectrum, ranging from the comparatively low-risk strategies that actually hedge risk, to very high-risk strategies that rely on the expertise of individual managers.

Broadly speaking we can identify certain characteristics that apply to hedge funds:

- Aggressive leverage – that is, heavy borrowing to invest.
- The use of 'short' selling – that is, selling assets the fund has 'borrowed' but does not own (see below).
- Performance-related fees – typically an annual fee of 1%–2% of the assets plus anything from 5% to 25% of the profits.
- Opaque financial information – in other words, you never really know how much you are paying.

Following an investigation in the US, **market timing** has been discredited. Market timers typically bet on the value of international securities in mutual funds. Mutual funds are only priced once per day so the market timers can end up holding securities that have not traded for many hours. Large and rapid sales and purchases can exploit this anomaly.

The classic hedge fund holds undervalued stocks for the medium to long term in the same way as any active manager might. This is the 'long' element in a long/short fund. For a small premium hedge fund managers also 'borrow' stocks, which they believe are becoming overpriced, from the major institutional pension and insurance funds, many of which indulge in stock lending to boost their own returns. The hedge manager sells high and repurchases the stocks when the price drops so they can return them to the stock lender on the due date. This technique is known as **short selling** and allows managers to pocket the profit if the price of the stock drops. In this way these funds can sustain the annual return in falling markets – but only where the manager has out-standing skills. In theory it exposes the investor to an unlimited liability if the price of the stocks that are sold short shoots through the ceiling.

There are as many different styles as there are hedge fund managers. Some are comparatively low risk but others are very risky indeed, particularly where the fund is highly geared – that is, it has borrowed heavily to invest. Charges can be much higher than for conventional funds and more complex – for example there is usually a performance-related element for the fund manager. It is also important to appreciate that investing in a hedge fund involves placing money with a specific manager and that these managers tend to change jobs quite frequently.

Funds of hedge funds

The fund of hedge funds approach has proved most popular to date among institutional and private investors. This is where the fund invests in a range of hedge funds with different styles and strategies, reducing the exposure to any single hedge fund or manager. In theory a well-constructed fund of hedge funds should produce consistent absolute returns with a very low correlation to traditional equity and bond funds and so provide good diversification from traditional markets and investment styles. When included in a private investor's portfolio this should reduce risk at the overall level.

The manager selecting and monitoring the underlying hedge funds needs to be tough on performance attribution. A disciplined fund of hedge funds manager will hire sub-managers who can generate alpha – that is, returns based on skill rather than market movement. They should keep a close eye on the size of a hedge fund manager's assets under management. Smaller funds can move quickly and buy and sell comparatively large holdings with ease. Very large funds cannot always do this and where they do buy an exceptional stock, its impact on the overall fund performance may be modest compared with the impact on a much smaller fund. Part of the fund of hedge funds manager's skill, therefore, is in identifying why an operation is successful and in replacing the manager if the investment philosophy and processes fail to work as assets under management grow.

Authorisation

At the time of writing, hedge funds were not authorised investments, although the Financial Services Authority was in the process of allowing certain types of hedge funds onshore for institutional investors and very sophisticated private investors. It also planned to allow more flexible investment rules for authorised retail funds, so that they can invest in illiquid assets such as private equity and property.

The authorisation of the funds in which an individual invests is important. Individuals who have problems with any unauthorised investment cannot complain to the Financial Ombudsman Service (FOS) nor can they seek compensation from the Financial Services Authority (FSA).

Private equity

By its very nature an unquoted company is not an authorised investment under the Financial Services and Markets Act 2000. The British Venture Capital Association (BVCA) defines this asset class as the equity financing of unquoted companies at many stages in their life from start-up to the expansion of companies of substantial size, for example through management buy-outs and buy-ins. Private equity represents medium- to long-term investments in companies with growth potential. The investment capital is eventually released through trade sales or flotation on the public markets.

Private equity is a huge market. The BVCA says that private equity investors have holdings in some 11,000 UK companies that employ almost 3m people. This represents about 18% of the private sector workforce. By comparison, there are only about

2,200 quoted companies on The London Stock Exchange. Private equity funds returned 11.4% per annum over the five years to 31 December 2002, according to the BVCA. This is better than most other asset classes.

Needless to say there is a downside to private equity. Investing directly in an unquoted company is a very high-risk strategy, and the same is true of the specialist **venture capital trusts** (**VCTs**, see below), which are only suitable for the very wealthy investor who can commit for the long term. Venture capital is classed as a subset of private equity, covering the early stages of funding from seed to expansion capital.

Venture capital trusts

Venture capital trusts (VCTs) are quoted investment companies that invest in unquoted companies or companies listed on the Alternative Investments Market (AIM, see page 53.) The government recently changed the rules for investing in VCTs following the collapse of this sector, which at its peak represented £450m a year but had fallen to about £45m by 2003.

In 2004 the government doubled the annual allowance for individual investment in VCTs from £100,000 to £200,000. The purchase of shares qualifies for income tax relief at 20% and, from April 2004, provided the investment is held for a minimum of three years, there is an additional 20% relief for two years. However, this is paid directly to the VCT provider for additional investment on the individual's behalf. For each £1 invested, investors get 20p in tax relief and a further 20p invested in the fund: so for a net investment of 80p the investor buys assets of £1.20. At the same time as increasing the income tax relief the government removed the ability to defer capital gains arising on other assets up to the amount of the VCT investment.

The reason behind the change is that the CGT deferral feature led to the immense popularity of the scheme in the early years but also caused its collapse. During the long bear market of 1999–2002 wealthy investors did not have the gains to defer and so saw little reason to invest, particularly in companies that represented such a high risk during this period.

The additional income tax advantages are certainly attractive but investors should not base their decisions on tax breaks alone. Any investment in very small companies is going to be a very high-risk strategy. Planners should look at the track record of the management company and also consider the types of company in which they invest. Some VCTs avoid start-ups and focus instead on well-established companies with a good cash flow. A VCT that invests a significant proportion of its capital in start-ups and 'early stage' enterprises clearly represents a higher risk profile.

An **Enterprise Investments Scheme** (**EIS**) is a vehicle that provides private equity financing to smaller companies and offers long tax deferral opportunities. Unlike the VCT, this scheme retains its capital gains deferral feature.

The annual allowance for EISs from 2006 rises from £150,000 to £200,000 and there is 20% income tax relief. It is possible to invest in EIS portfolios, which invest in a range of schemes, making it less risky than investing in just one EIS, but also increasing the costs.

Students who want to find out more about private equity should start with the websites below. The success of the VCT, as with a hedge fund, will depend heavily on the skills of the management company.

An alternative route to hedge funds and private equity

One way to build an exposure to funds of hedge funds and private equity is to invest in an investment trust that either invests solely in one of these asset classes – for example a venture and development capital investment trust or a fund of hedge funds – or one that includes a substantial exposure to these classes but otherwise has a broad spread of assets.

Activity 13.1

'There is nothing intrinsically wrong with most high-risk investments, provided the investor understands the risks and can accommodate them. For this, investors require a clear appreciation of the risk to the *total return* – capital and income combined.'

In a group discuss this comment in relation to the design and marketing of the following products: with profits policies, endowment mortgages and structured capital-at-risk products. How can the regulators improve the marketing and sales of complex products in the mass market?

Summary

This chapter critically examined the structures of collective investments designed to manage volatility. As explained, the product designs generally are very complicated and the risks often are not understood by investors. We may question, therefore, whether such products are suitable for the mass retail market, yet this is often the primary target.

Key terms

- Annual and terminal bonuses p. 162
- Asset share p. 163
- Basic sum assured p. 167
- Constant protection portfolio insurance (CPPI) p. 169
- Contracyclical p. 164
- Enterprise Investments Scheme (EIS) p. 173
- Formula maturity value p. 167
- Funds of funds p. 170

- Guaranteed annuity rate (GAR) p. 165
- Hedge funds p. 171
- Market makers p. 167
- Market timing p. 171
- Market value adjuster (MVA) p. 163
- Multi-manager funds p. 170
- Realistic balance sheet p. 168
- Short selling p. 171
- Structured capital-at-risk products (Scarps) p. 168
- Total return p. 168
- Traded endowment policies (TEPs) p. 166
- Venture capital trusts (VCTs) p. 173

Review questions

1 Which aspects of with profits policies were not well understood by investors?

2 Why did guaranteed annuity rates (GARs) prove to be a poor actuarial decision?

3 Explain how we can assess the value of a traded endowment policy (TEP). Which aspects are known and which rely on investment assumptions?

4 Explain why structured capital at risk products are confusing for the unsophisticated investor?

5 Which are the two main types of alternative investment for private investors? What are the key risks?

Go to the Companion Website at **www.booksites.net/harrison_pfp** for a multiple-choice quiz to test your understanding of this chapter.

Further information

Association of Investment Trust Companies **www.aitc.co.uk**

British Venture Capital Association **www.bvca.co.uk**

FTSE Hedge index **www.ftse.com/hedge**

For more details about traded endowment policies (TEPs) go to the Association of Policy Market Makers (**www.apmm.org**).

Specialist advisers on private equity include **www.allenbridge.co.uk** and **www.taxefficient review.com**.

Chapter 14 ●●●○

Tax-efficient wrappers and administration platforms

Introduction

This short chapter looks at the different ways individuals can hold investments in order to enhance tax efficiency and/or administration and monitoring flexibility. Strictly speaking, personal pension plans, among other pension arrangements, should also be in this chapter. However, given that the subject of pensions and retirement planning covers such a huge area, this subject is dealt with separately in Chapters 21–24.

Objectives

After reading this chapter you will be able to:

● Describe **Personal equity plans (PEPs)** and **Individual savings accounts (ISAs)**.
● Explain how the tax features of ISAs have become less attractive in recent years.
● Discuss the objectives of fund supermarkets and wrap accounts.

Tax-efficient wrappers

Tax-efficient wrappers, like Individual savings accounts (ISAs) and personal pension plans (see Chapter 23), do not in themselves provide good investment performance. What they can offer is a tax-favoured environment in which individual equities and collective funds can be placed and where some or all income tax and/or capital gains tax is avoided legally.

The important point we must always remember is that we must set investment goals first and only then decide which types of assets are best held in the different tax efficient plans. This point is often misunderstood by investors towards the end of each tax year when the 'ISA season' gets under way and providers and advisers promote ISAs as though they were an investment in their own right.

Personal equity plans (PEPs)

Personal equity plans are to some extent investment history, but there are still many sizeable PEP funds in existence that require monitoring, even though it is no longer possible to make additional investments. Over the 12 tax years from January 1987 to April 1999 when PEPs were available, an individual could have invested a maximum of £85,000. After April 1999 it was no longer possible to contribute to a PEP but any existing funds built up could remain in the tax-efficient wrapper. Returns could either be reinvested or withdrawn.

Originally there were different categories of PEP and certain geographical restrictions but these rules no longer apply, so it is possible to change the asset allocation to create a more international spread of investments. In practice many investors who took advantage of the PEP rules from the beginning are now coming up to retirement. In this case they may prefer to change the asset allocation to reflect an increased income requirement and a lower risk tolerance. PEP investors also have access to a wide range of corporate bonds and to gilts and other fixed interest securities issued by European governments.

Individual savings accounts (ISAs)

ISAs were introduced in April 1999 and replaced PEPs and Tax-efficient special savings accounts (TESSAs) as the mainstream tax-efficient investment apart from pension plans. ISAs allow individuals to save up to £7,000 each tax year without paying tax on capital gains. Originally the equity income was tax-free as well but this perk disappeared on 6 April 2004. From this date ISA managers could no longer claim back the 10% tax credit on dividends paid into an ISA. For basic rate taxpayers who do not have capital gains, this removes much of the benefit of using ISAs to buy shares or equity funds. Higher rate taxpayers can still benefit from holding income-paying equities in an ISA as they avoid the additional 22.5% on gross dividends when these are paid outside an ISA.

Investors with bonds in ISAs will still be able to reclaim the tax paid on interest income from April 2004. This is because the income from bonds is defined as interest and is taxed in a different way from equity income. Investors in bonds are treated as though they have paid a 20% savings tax withheld at source. For bonds the tax credit remains at 20%.

ISA investment choice

The range of investments that can be held within an ISA is very broad and includes a wide selection of collective funds. It is also possible to use a **self-select ISA** to hold a portfolio of funds and individual shares and bonds (see below).

Clearly, if an individual has a comparatively small amount to invest it does not make sense to run a self-select portfolio because trading in small volumes is disproportionately expensive. For many investors, therefore, buying into collective funds through packaged ISAs is the best route. Moreover, if they are happy to stick within a range of unit trusts and open-ended investment companies (OEICs) it is possible to split the annual allowance between several managers where the investments are made through a fund supermarket.

The ISA contribution rules

At the time of writing it was possible to invest £7,000 a year in an ISA provided the investor was aged 18 or over and a UK resident. There are three types of ISAs: cash ISAs, stocks and shares ISAs and life assurance ISAs. Cash ISAs are similar to deposit accounts with additional tax advantages (see page 121).

There are two formats for ISAs, known as the mini-ISA and maxi-ISA. It is not possible to take out both types in the same tax year. This means an individual could invest in three separate mini-ISAs run by different managers: cash up to £3,000 and stocks and shares up to £4,000 (split £3,000 stocks and shares/£1,000 life assurance in 2004–2005).

Alternatively the investor could buy a single maxi-ISA with one manager and still invest in shares, cash and life funds. It is also possible to invest the entire allowance in individual shares. Fund supermarkets allow you to invest across a range of managers within the single maxi plan.

CAT-marked ISAs

'CAT' stands for charges, access and terms, and products that bear this label must agree to abide by certain rules, set out as follows:

CAT-marked equity ISAs

- Annual management maximum charge of 1%.
- Minimum regular saving from £50 per month or a minimum lump sum of £500.

CAT-marked cash ISAs

- Must not have charges except for additional services – for example extra statements.
- Must allow payments and withdrawals from as little as £10, with a maximum notice period of seven days.
- Must not impose other conditions – on the frequency of withdrawals, for example.
- If interest rates go up the ISA rate must follow within a month.

CAT-marked insurance funds

- Maximum annual management charge of 3%.
- Minimum premiums from £25 per month or £250 per year.
- Must not apply a penalty if account is closed and must provide at least the value of premiums paid three years or more before the date of encashment.

From April 2005 a new range of low-cost, medium-term savings products will be launched and it will be possible to hold these within an ISA as well. This will include a new stakeholder plan and Child Trust Fund and will replicate CAT standards – that is, incorporate such features as comparatively low charges (a maximum of 1.5% AMC), easy access and exit, and fair terms.

Self-select ISAs

Self-select ISAs offer maximum flexibility when it comes to direct investment and investing in funds. These plans are sold by stockbrokers and large firms of independent financial advisers. Some are available as low-cost Internet plans.

Apart from the wider investment choice, one of the immediate benefits of the self-select structure is that this enables the investor to make changes to the portfolio on the same day. With packaged ISAs it can take several weeks to switch between managers. This can be frustrating and costly in a rising market. It is also possible to hold cash within the self-select plan and earn interest on this while waiting to reinvest the money.

The cost will depend on the adviser's charges. This might be a flat annual administration charge, which could suit the larger portfolios, or the fee might be linked to the value of the fund (for example 0.5% per annum plus VAT). Some will have no annual fees, but will charge for dividend collection, which, on a large portfolio, could add up quickly. One thing to look out for is high dealing charges, especially on shares. What can appear cheap because of a low or zero annual management charge can prove costly if there is little or no discount on unit trust purchases and if share-dealing charges for buying and selling are in excess of 1%.

Finally, the self-select route can provide an individual with as much or as little advice as is required. With a discretionary service the stockbroker makes all the investment decisions; with an advisory service the investor and stockbroker discuss investments before buying; with an execution-only service the investor makes all the decisions and the stockbroker simply carries out these instructions.

Wrap accounts

Money Management publishes regular surveys on wraps, among many other topics, and students should refer to these if they wish to follow market developments. At the time of writing, wrap accounts did not represent a big market in the UK (it is huge in the US and Australia), although providers and advisers suggest they have tremendous potential and that we will see a major growth in this product.

A wrap account is an online platform that allows the investor to see in one place and to aggregate the value of their total range of savings and investments. For the planner these would bring considerable benefits as it would be possible to consider assets and liabilities in one place and to monitor asset allocation and the underlying investments more easily than if these are held as discrete products with separate online or paper-based access to information.

One of the biggest problems for the development of wraps is that providers will need to find a way of bringing on board an individual's existing products as well as any new investments. This will require a substantial investment in technology and cooperation between all providers. In particular, wrap providers will need to find a way to provide automatic valuations of life and pension investments.

Fund supermarkets

In many ways fund supermarkets already represent a wrap account for collective funds, whether these are purchased and held within or outside of an ISA and/or pension plan. Certain supermarkets offer asset allocation modellers and fund selection tools. It comes as no surprise, therefore, that some of the providers of wraps are the existing fund supermarkets, which have already developed the basic technology.

Activity 14.1

Visit the fund supermarket and wrap websites and compare and contrast the services and features offered. Which do you think would be most appropriate for a financial planner to use in conjunction with a client? Do you think that wraps will appeal to the average investor? Justify your argument.

Summary

This chapter considered how tax-efficient wrappers and administration platforms can be used to enhance the financial planner's and individual's efficiency and control over savings and investments. The fund supermarket and wrap account market in particular are experiencing tremendous growth and we can expect to see new generations of these services become available to the average investor in due course. However, at present they tend to be the province of the wealthier, sophisticated investor.

Key terms

- CAT-marked products p. 180
- Fund supermarket p. 181
- Individual savings accounts (ISAs) p. 178
- Personal equity plans (PEPs) p. 178
- Self-select ISA p. 179
- Wrap account p. 181

Review questions

1   Explain how the tax features of ISAs have become less attractive in recent years, particularly for basic rate taxpayers.

2   Which investments benefit most from the ISA tax wrapper?

3   What is a fund supermarket? Visit some of the websites below to help answer this question.

4   What is the longer-term objective of a wrap account? Why will providers find it difficult to accommodate an individual's existing products?

Go to the Companion Website at **www.booksites.net/harrison_pfp** for a multiple-choice quiz to test your understanding of this chapter.

Further information

The following is a selection of providers that offer a fund supermarket and/or wrap account. The source for this information was the *Money Management* March 2004 survey on wrap accounts. Only the sites that are accessible to students are mentioned here. Several – Cofunds and Transact, for example – are only available to advisers.

Fundsnetwork: **www.fundsnetwork.co.uk**

HL Vantage: **www.hargreaveslansdown.co.uk**

Selestia: **www.selestia.co.uk**

Seven IM: **www.7im.co.uk**

Skandia: **www.skandia.co.uk**

The following two companies are expected to launch wrap accounts:

FundsDirect: **www.fundsdirect.co.uk**

Lifetime Group: **www.lifetimegroup.co.uk**

Chapter 15 ●●●●

Ethical investments, pensions and banking

Introduction

This chapter considers ethical investment in terms of direct equity investment, collective funds, pension schemes, banks and services aimed at religious groups.

Taken together, ethics and finance do not represent a comfortable mix. If you ask 10 people what they think is ethical you will get 10 different answers. Ethical views, by their very nature, are subjective. Nevertheless, ethical or **socially responsible investment (SRI)** is an increasingly important subject within financial planning and this chapter considers how a planner might help an individual accommodate ethical, environmental and religious views within the overall plan. It also considers the growing availability of investments in the UK that are designed for different religions.

Objectives

After reading this chapter you will be able to:

● Explain what is meant by ethical and socially responsible investment.
● Describe how an ethical portfolio can be constructed through active selection or a passive screening process.
● Discuss the potential impact on a portfolio of shares or funds with relation to asset allocation and performance.
● Debate where to draw the line in terms of exclusions.
● Explain how the Ethical Investment Research Service (EIRIS) and the FTSE4Good index series can help the private investor.

What does ethical investment involve?

Ethical investment refers to the pursuit of an investment policy that takes account of personal opinions and beliefs to help select the companies in which to invest and to determine which to shun. From the planning perspective the objective is to help the individual articulate their views in the context of investment and to ensure they fully understand any implications of this approach.

In particular it is important to be able to explain the impact any ethical screening process will have on a portfolio or a fund's annual returns. An ethical fund will not have broad exposure to the FTSE All-Share, for example, which is the benchmark used to judge the performance of most general equity funds. An ethical fund, therefore, needs to have an appropriate performance benchmark and should not be expected to reflect market movements as a whole.

Fortunately, the launch in 2001 of the ethical stockmarket indices – the FTSE4Good series – makes it much easier to assess a company's approach to the environment, or to social issues such as exploitative wages, for example, and to see the impact of ethical screening in the performance.

Ethical Investment Research Service (EIRIS)

Ethical investment is a complicated subject and is not helped by the difficulty and cost of obtaining sufficient data upon which to form a view about the ethics or otherwise of a company. An excellent source of information for those interested in this subject is the Ethical Investment Research Service (EIRIS), which maintains a database of ethical funds and individual companies.

EIRIS was set up in 1983 by a number of organisations including Quakers, Methodists, Oxfam and the Rowntree Trust. It monitors the screening and performance of the ethical and environmental collective funds. It also offers a screening process for direct equity investors. The simplest way to use EIRIS research is to request an 'acceptable list' – a list of companies which meet the individual's ethical or environmental criteria. A 'portfolio screen' enables you to find out more about the shares in an existing portfolio, while, for the real enthusiast, EIRIS fact sheets provide all the information on the database on the companies in question.

EIRIS researches over 1,000 companies. The list of screening options (below) indicates how complex the screening process can be:

- alcohol
- animals (meat production and sale, leather/fur manufacture and sale)
- arms and sales to military purchasers
- community involvement
- corporate governance
- directors' pay
- environmental issues

- equal opportunities
- gambling
- greenhouse gasses
- health and safety convictions
- human rights
- intensive farming
- military contracts
- newspaper production and television
- nuclear power (fuel, components and construction of plants)
- overseas interests (wages exploitation in emerging economies, deriving profits from countries with poor human rights records)
- ozone-depleting chemicals
- pesticides
- political contributions
- pornography
- Third World involvement
- tropical hardwood
- tobacco
- waste disposal
- water pollution

Exhibit 15.1 Defining an ethical policy

The major exclusions in ethical funds tend to be arms, alcohol, tobacco, gambling, animal testing, environmental damage, pornography, and the payment of exploitative wages in developing countries. But the list could extend almost indefinitely.

Some funds adopt a **positive ethical screening** approach and aim to invest in companies that are working towards a desirable goal – 'green' companies involved in recycling or environmentally-friendly waste disposal, for example. Environmental funds can also be regarded as ethical. Here the choice of shares will depend on a company's environmental policy in terms of controlling pollution, ozone depletion, deforestation and waste management, among other criteria.

Where an individual has strong ethical views and adopts a **negative ethical screening** approach – that is, the elimination of unethical companies – they need to consider carefully where to draw the line. It is one thing to exclude tobacco and/or alcohol companies, but what about the supermarkets that sell their products? Gambling is also a typical exclusion but does this mean all the outlets that sell tickets for the National Lottery should be avoided? Some ethical investors might favour pharmaceutical companies because of their groundbreaking research in the war against cancer and AIDS, for example. Others might exclude the same companies on the grounds that they carry out experiments on animals.

In an extreme case, even apparently innocuous products like National Savings & Investments and gilts can cause problems because they are effectively 'sold' by the UK government. The same government that provides welfare for the poor is responsible for the massive expenditure on arms and animal experiments, via public and private sector agencies and universities.

In practice, many investors settle for a broad-brush approach that eliminates the obvious villains but does not go into the small print. Using the analogy above, this would exclude the tobacco companies but not the supermarkets that sell cigarettes. This approach would also screen out the companies whose primary business is armaments but could leave in companies with a minority interest in arms.

Some element of compromise is called for in most cases and the point where this is reached will vary from individual to individual. Ultimately investors must decide how far they are prepared to go to identify the ethical stars and whether they are prepared to accept the resulting restriction in investment choice. A cynic might argue that if we take ethical investment to its natural conclusion we will end up investing purely in property. This is not a good idea, nor is it a sound argument. As an investor in commercial property funds we have no control over the tenants appointed by the property managers.

Pension schemes

Ethical investors should consider whether to limit their views to their private portfolio of shares and funds or to take it further. For example members of company pension schemes may have limited influence over the investment objectives of the pension fund, although fortunately socially responsible investment is becoming a much more prominent issue for institutional pension funds. Those in Defined contribution (DC) schemes are usually offered a choice of funds from which to select. In some cases there may be an ethical option.

In 2002–2003 EIRIS undertook a study of the 250 largest occupational pension funds by capital value. This was the first study of its kind undertaken to ascertain whether and how members' pension funds were responding to ethical/socially responsible investment. The guide is available on the EIRIS website and allows members to find out more about their own scheme and to learn how they can play an active role in its evolution towards SRI.

By law, trustees of occupational schemes must state the extent to which SRI is taken into account, if at all. They must also set out their policy that directs the exercise of voting rights in the companies in which they invest.

Banks

Banks are very influential in the application or otherwise of SRI. They lend money to the local community, to large businesses and to governments. Some banks take a very positive SRI approach and also use their influence to reduce financial exclusion in the UK and to ease Third World debt. Others may lend to organisations and regimes that are guilty of unethical policies, environmental damage or human rights abuses. The EIRIS website provides a very detailed guide to these issues and highlights which banks are taking a positive approach, and it is also worth visiting Ethical Consumer at **www.ethicalconsumer.org**.

Islamic finance

Islamic finance is based on the principles of Shariah (Islamic) law. This attempts to maximise social welfare (Maslahah) by protecting the five pillars of Islamic society: faith, life, wealth, intellect and posterity. As a result Islamic investment excludes companies where the primary business does not conform to these objectives. In particular the screening process will exclude companies involved in tobacco, gambling, armaments, pork, financial institutions and pornography. Shariah law forbids paying or receiving interest, but dividends paid on shares are acceptable.

According to EIRIS there are about 150 Islamic institutions that manage US$100bn for customers worldwide. Western banks like Citibank, ANZ, Barclays and HSBC also have Islamic banking arms; and FTSE International has created a Global Islamic Index Series to measure the performance of companies that comply with Shariah law.

The impact of ethical screening on performance

Critics of ethical investment argue that performance suffers due to the exclusion of many major FTSE 100 companies, most of which have something distinctly unethical somewhere among their diverse operations. If a fund excludes the very obvious unethical villains it would lose access to about 8% of the stock market by value. This figure grows if you add animal testing, nuclear power and environmental damage, for example. The full EIRIS screening, as listed above, disqualifies up to 60% of the FTSE 100 companies.

This disqualification means that an ethical fund by its very definition will have a disproportionate weighting towards smaller and medium-sized companies, which tend to be more focused and where it is easier to examine the business range and environmental issues in order to take a confident view. As far as performance goes, smaller companies have the ability to outperform their larger counterparts. They are also inclined to be more volatile and must be selected with great care, as the performance of the FTSE 250 and SmallCap (the smallest 420 or so in the FTSE All-Share index) demonstrate. It is important in this respect to remember that when the SmallCap does well it is often due to the outperformance of a handful of companies rather than a consistently good performance across the board.

In addition, there is a danger that the ethical policy leaves a fund over-exposed to certain sectors that may only be classed as ethical by default – the hotel and leisure industry, for example. Moreover, the fund would be unable to reap the rewards of a boom in other sectors such as chemicals, engineering or pharmaceuticals.

A good year to illustrate this point is 1997, when most general ethical funds underperformed the market as a whole because they had limited exposure to the sectors that outperformed. Typical exclusions that proved regrettable from the performance perspective included banks (most lend money indiscriminately to non-ethical companies and countries with poor human rights records), integrated oils (environmental damage) and pharmaceuticals (animal testing and, occasionally, exploitation in tests on humans in emerging countries).

Alternative investments

EIRIS provides details of investments that it believes offer a distinct social value but which are not listed on The Stock Exchange. Examples include investment in a company that imports tropical hardwood from sustainable sources, or one involved in fair trade with developing economies.

The attraction of such companies is that as an investor you can help them to grow. However, the downside is that these shares may not pay dividends and can be difficult to sell. Moreover, once you look outside the All-Share the usual warnings about small companies apply with a vengeance.

FTSE4Good

FTSE4Good is a series of socially responsible indices launched by the FTSE Group in 2001 and forms part of the global series. There are eight indices covering the UK, Europe, the US and global equities, four of which are **benchmark** and four tradable. For example the benchmark FTSE4Good benchmark UK index has a tradable index, the FTSE4Good UK 50 (see Table 15.1). The excluded industries are:

- Tobacco producers.
- Companies providing strategic parts or services for, or manufacturing, whole nuclear weapons systems.
- Companies manufacturing whole weapons systems.
- Owners or operators of nuclear power stations and those mining or processing uranium.

All companies operating outside these industries are eligible for the socially responsible screening, which covers three areas:

- Environmental sustainability.
- Social issues and stakeholder relations.
- Human rights.

Information on the companies is based on EIRIS research and analysis under the direction of the FTSE4Good advisory committee.

This is a very proactive index series that continues to reflect changes in the consensus on what constitutes good corporate responsibility practice globally. In May 2002 the environmental criteria were raised and in March 2003 the human rights criteria were raised. In 2004 FTSE planned to raise the criteria relating to labour standards in the supply chain. For a more detailed explanation of the inclusion criteria go to the FTSE4Good section of the FTSE website.

Table 15.1 FTSE4Good UK 50 index

Last Updated: 26/04/2004 FTSE4Good UK 50 Index Constituents

Constituent	Inv mkt cap	Percentage wgt	Classification
Abbey National	6,223.677443	0.756954%	810
Alliance & Leicester	3,940.151673	0.479221%	810
Allied Domecq	5,092.989870	0.619434%	416
AstraZeneca	32,163.743958	3.911912%	486
Aviva	12,718.095000	1.546837%	840
BAA	5,649.390618	0.687107%	591
BG Group	11,855.662500	1.441944%	078
BHP Billiton	11,846.352139	1.440811%	048
BOC Group	4,600.294085	0.559510%	113
BP	85,533.409765	10.402992%	078
BT Group	15,649.411291	1.903358%	673
Barclays	33,392.711308	4.061385%	810
Boots Group	4,806.837746	0.584631%	527
British Sky Broadcasting Group	10,109.476021	1.229564%	543
Cadbury Schweppes	9,515.205223	1.157286%	435
Carnival	5,436.100758	0.661165%	538
Centrica	9,820.921531	1.194469%	773
Compass Group	7,840.890723	0.953648%	581
Diageo	23,724.552490	2.885496%	416
GUS	7,967.520000	0.969049%	527
GlaxoSmithKline	59,549.865467	7.242746%	486
HBOS	28,677.147984	3.487855%	810
HSBC Hldgs	72,382.981001	8.803573%	810
ITV	5,279.559900	0.642126%	542
InterContinental Hotels Group	3,939.101693	0.479093%	536
Kingfisher	6,706.903306	0.815726%	527
Land Securities Group	5,106.211042	0.621042%	862
Legal & General Group	6,321.861000	0.768896%	840
Lloyds TSB Group	23,814.924910	2.896488%	810
Marks & Spencer Group	6,371.866556	0.774978%	527
National Grid Transco	13,339.283125	1.622389%	775
Pearson	5,412.800000	0.658331%	547
Prudential	9,337.754853	1.135703%	840
Reckitt Benckiser	10,257.250824	1.247537%	475
Reed Elsevier	6,815.378776	0.828920%	547
Reuters Group	5,679.870000	0.690814%	547
Royal Bank Of Scotland Group	49,149.271959	5.977775%	810
SABMiller	6,396.787105	0.778009%	415
Sainsbury (J)	4,062.656250	0.494120%	630
Scottish & Newcastle	3,643.069000	0.443088%	415
Scottish & Southern Energy	5,910.680000	0.718886%	720
Scottish Power	7,170.240000	0.872080%	720
Shell Transport & Trading Co	33,938.837583	4.127808%	078
Smith & Nephew	5,457.957238	0.663823%	446
Standard Chartered	10,398.637104	1.264733%	810
Tesco	19,577.616149	2.381126%	630
Unilever	16,345.265000	1.987991%	435
Vodafone Group	67,467.804119	8.205765%	678
WPP Group	6,935.979698	0.843588%	545
mmO2	8,865.109679	1.078218%	678

Source: FTSE4Good.

Activity 15.1

Examine the London Share Services pages in the *Financial Times* and suggest which sectors might be eliminated automatically from an ethical portfolio in a negative screening approach to ethical investment. Now use the FTSE4Good and EIRIS websites to identify individual companies within these sectors that are positively selected for the indices and/or collectives funds because they are making a contribution to ethical concerns. Comment on the results. After this exercise have your views changed on negative and positive screening?

Summary

This chapter examined the increasingly important issue of ethical investment and considered how ethical views or beliefs can be accommodated within a sensible financial plan. In this area it is essential that the individual fully understands the potential impact of this approach.

Key terms

● Positive and negative screening p. 187
● Benchmark and tradable indices p. 190
● Socially responsible investment (SRI) p. 185

Review questions

1 Explain why it is difficult to define an ethical policy. Give two examples of companies that might be selected or rejected for different but equally strong ethical reasons.

2 What is the impact of ethical screening on asset allocation? Your answer should consider both company size and sector.

3 Explain the key criteria for Islamic banking and investment.

Go to the Companion Website at **www.booksites.net/harrison_pfp** for a multiple-choice quiz to test your understanding of this chapter.

Further information

Ethical Investment Research Service (EIRIS): **www.eiris.org**

FTSE4Good: **www.ftse4good.com**

For more information on Islamic finance go to the EIRIS site and also to **www.islamic-banking.com**.

The Investment Management Association (IMA) also provides information on ethical funds: **www.investmentuk.org**.

Life and Pensions Moneyfacts lists ethical and environmental life assurance fund, pension funds and unit trusts: **www.moneyfacts.co.uk**.

Chapter 16 ●●●●

Tangible (alternative) assets

Introduction

Low interest rates and the volatility of stock markets have led to an increased interest in tangible unregulated assets. While in Chapter 4 we used the term 'alternative' to refer to absolute return funds and private equity, for example, rather confusingly the term is also used to refer to tangible assets such as forestry and fine wine. In other words, these are assets that have physical form, as opposed to a solely monetary value, as is the case with an equity and units in a collective fund.

This chapter does not attempt to cover the entire range of tangible assets – which might include classic cars, antiques, fine art and virtually any 'collectible' item – but aims merely to give the student a flavour of the attractions and potential dangers.

Objectives

After reading this chapter you will be able to:

- Understand the difference between regulated and non-regulated assets.
- Comment on whether individuals should regard **tangible assets** outside property as investments.
- Explain why woodlands and forestry might appeal to ethical investors.
- Discuss how to avoid the **scams** (frauds) associated with investments in wine, precious metals and gemstones.

The regulation of tangible assets

Unless assets like forestry and wine are part of a collective scheme, they are not regulated by the Financial Services Authority. This means that there is no statutory system of regulatory protection and few, if any, controls over the information provided by the less scrupulous firms and individuals that rub shoulders with the experts in these markets. What these very disparate assets have in common – aside from their high-risk investment profile – is that they can combine a strong element of personal enjoyment with the possibility of profits.

Forestry

Woodland represents a long-term ethical investment that makes a positive contribution to the global climate. Growing trees emit oxygen and absorb carbon dioxide – one of the major greenhouse gasses. Woodlands also offer an environment in which flora and fauna flourish.

Britain is one of the least afforested countries in Europe. Only about 12% of the land is planted with trees. Yet soil and climatic conditions enable Britain to grow a wide variety of hardwoods, including beech, oak and ash, and softwoods such as Sitka, Norway Spruce, Douglas Fir, Larch and Scots Pine. Timber is one of the few major natural resources that is renewable. Currently new plantings are running at approximately 5,000 hectares pa. Britain imports 90% of its timber needs. There is no sign of a slowdown in demand and timber is again starting to compete with materials such as plastics, steel and concrete.

There are four main uses for timber:

- Timber products – including hardwood veneers, laminated products, furniture, and electricity and telephone transmission poles.
- Sawn wood – converted into boards and planks, building timbers, timber frames, flooring, fencing posts, rails and so on.
- Wood-based panels; for example chipboard.
- Paper and pulp production.

In addition, there are useful tax breaks to be earned by growing timber:

- The increase in value of a crop of growing timber is completely free from capital gains tax.
- The sale of felled timber or a crop of growing trees is free from income tax and capital gains tax.
- Forestry grants are not taxed (except annual payments under the Farm Woodland Premium Scheme).
- The whole forest may be exempt from inheritance tax (IHT) after two years of ownership.

On the downside:

- None of the expenses of preparing, planting and then maintaining the forest is tax deductible (although the investor may be eligible for a grant to help with costs).
- Any increase in the value of the actual land on which the forest is situated is liable to capital gains tax on disposal but indexation and taper relief can reduce this liability.

The Woodland Grant Scheme may help with the cost of planting, although to what extent depends on the type of tree planted, the size of woodland planted and the range of Woodland Grant Scheme grants available to the site. The scheme covers 50%–100% of planting costs and grants are mostly paid as soon as planting is complete. A retainer – 20% of the basic grant – is paid after five years if the trees are well maintained. A further retainer of 10% is paid after ten years. If the investor is a farmer they may be entitled to additional incentives from the Farm Woodland Premium Scheme. This provides subsidies – taxable as farm income – to encourage the planting of trees on farm land and to compensate for loss of agricultural income.

The market for timber is very long term. The ages at which commercially grown trees are felled vary among 20 years for poplars, 45–60 years for most conifers and 120 years for oaks. During the growing period thinning will be carried out to improve the quality of the remaining trees. By the time a conifer forest is about 25 years old it will become attractive to paper manufacturers and timber processors who want to protect their future supplies of raw materials. From 25 years to maturity, the forest will become increasingly attractive to individual investors perhaps because of the inheritance tax relief available to owners of forests or the fact that proceeds from felling the trees will be completely free from income tax.

The level of return quoted by industry experts is around 4%–6% per annum in excess of inflation and this is tax free. So it may be compared with yields of say 12%–15% from other taxed investments, assuming an inflation rate of 3% and tax rate of 40%. However, it is important to remember that trees are living things and may be attacked by various diseases. What's more, they may be damaged by fire or destroyed by high winds. Careful management may reduce the risk to an acceptable level, while insurance will also limit your potential losses through natural causes.

Given the long-term nature of this investment it is essential to consider its implications for inheritance tax planning.

●●●● Wine

The fine wine market grew strongly in the mid-1990s but it has been damaged by a series of frauds where people were persuaded to invest in wines and spirits that failed to yield a profit and in some cases could have been purchased more cheaply elsewhere. According to one of the leading experts in this field (**www.investdrinks.org**) an analysis of recent price movements of six leading Bordeaux properties between

September 1999 and April 2002 shows that gains are often modest. Based on price lists from Farr Vintners, a fine wine broker, few wines from the best vintages over the past 40 years showed an annual percentage increase of more than single figures during this period.

While the financial press tends to cover authorised investments competently, its analysis of wine as an investment cannot be relied upon and quotations of prospective annual returns of 20% should be viewed with caution. Of late this market has proved to be a rocky ride, with some huge losses on the way for those who got their timing – or their vintages – wrong.

Claret, the red wine from Bordeaux, is the most important investment market. Stocks of the great wines of Bordeaux are at their lowest levels for 30 years. The proprietors of the Bordeaux châteaux invested heavily in the late 1980s in new cellars and equipment. They believed they would continue to produce great wines as regularly as they did in the 1980s and that demand for their wines would continue to increase. Demand has continued to rise but there was no great vintage in the first half of the 1990s. That meant the châteaux had to sell off their stocks of older vintages to finance their investments.

Provided the investor buys the right wines at the right price and the right time, this may be a financially rewarding asset. For the individual investor, however, there are some sensible guidelines and points worth considering:

- Wine should only be a small part of the total investment portfolio – for example, 2%–3%.
- It is never wise to borrow in order to invest in wine.
- Like regulated investments the price of wine can fall as well as rise.
- There are no dividends from investing in wine so straightforward comparisons with a share index can be very misleading.
- It is wise to seek expert advice from a reputable merchant, wine broker or auction house before buying. These companies advertise in magazines like *Decanter*, *Wine* and the *Wine Spectator*.

Wine does have advantages as an investment. It is an internationally accepted commodity and there is a finite amount of investment quality wine. The average annual production of the top quality châteaux in Bordeaux is around 520,000 cases. But the amount available for investment decreases as it is drunk.

London is a major centre of the trade in wine for investment purposes and much of the wine remains there in bonded warehouses, notably Trapp's Cellars under London Bridge railway station. Traditionally, investors laid down their wine in cellars to appreciate in value but increasingly, new investors from the Far East are buying such wines to drink as well as for investment purposes.

Wine must be properly stored in carefully regulated conditions to maintain its quality and value. For most investors, this will mean in bonded warehouse cellars. Investors storing wine with a merchant or in bond must stamp each case with their name. This is to protect them in the event of bankruptcy of the supplier or the cellarers. Many investors were caught out in the early 1970s with the bankruptcy of the London Wine Company. They learned the hard way that if there is no way of identifying your wine, there is no way the receiver is going to let you have it. If a case does not have your name on it, you cannot prove it is actually yours.

Selling and taxation

The sale of wine is not normally subject to capital gains tax, because the Inland Revenue believes it is a diminishing or wasting asset. But some fortified wines may be subject to CGT if they have a lifespan of more than 50 years. CGT on wine may be applied if the Inland Revenue thinks an individual has gone into the wine trade, in which case it may tax the gain as business profits. Provided individuals purchase wine under bond from a reputable merchant wholesaler, they will be able to avoid paying both duty and VAT, which are only levied when the wine is released from bond.

Theatre

The entertainment industry provides opportunities for investments that are highly speculative. But it also offers perks that may sway an investor with a passion for the theatre or films, for example, who may be attracted by the prospect of attending a first night and going to the party afterwards, possibly alongside megastars and royalty.

Lucky theatre investors may find themselves in on the ground floor of another *Cats*, which has returned over £28,000 plus the original stake for every £1,000 invested back in 1981. The international award-winning production cost around £445,000. Distributed profits total over £20 million. Unfortunately, spectacular misses are more frequent in this business and in recent years London theatres have been badly hit by the drop in tourism that followed 11 September, 2001.

Investors interested in a London theatre might look for productions that offer a promotion that will bring the audience in from the provinces, perhaps providing coaches and hotel accommodation as part of the theatre ticket package. Foreign tourists are also a major part of most West End audiences, but we should remember that a production that does well in the UK provinces may not necessarily appeal to an international audience.

The most obvious way to invest is via a theatre production company. Such companies organise and administer the staging of a production, starting with finding a suitable script or idea and continuing right up to the end of the final performance. Once an idea has been conceived and a script has been written, the producer must find appropriate performers to take the leading roles. He must also prepare the budget for the production and locate a suitable theatre. Budgeting includes a contingency fund to sustain the show until it is on its feet. The production manager also has to work out the weekly running costs, the cost of hiring the theatre and equipment, paying the cast, orchestra and crew wages, the creative team royalties and the marketing. Based on this information the production manager will produce a **recoupment schedule** that shows how many weeks the show must run to cover costs. The aim is to put together a package that can recover 75% of costs within 39 weeks.

With these steps in place the manager will start to seek funding. The production company may put up some capital but it is more common for funding to be provided by outside backers, known as **angels**. Assuming the show is a success, the angels' investment is paid back first and profits are then split between the producers and the angels. The producers will generally take 40% of the profits and the angels, 60%.

It is important for investors to understand what is being sold – for example does the investment include the role of the author, the play and/or its stars – as well as the role of those behind the proposal? Celebrity authors are attractive but do not guarantee success. Stars sell tickets, especially if they are TV names, but will be expensive and dislike long runs. Established directors/producers usually do better than newcomers, seeing the best scripts first and getting the best terms from theatre owners.

To apply for producers' prospectuses, visit the Theatrenet website, which explains how being an angel works (go to the bottom right hand side of the home page at **www.theatrenet.co.uk**) and provides links to current projects. Alternatively, contact the Society of London Theatre (SOLT) and ask to be put on its mailing list. The Society maintains a list of potential angels under a scheme where producers may approach confirmed potential investors with independently approved prospectuses. The producers are not given your details. The Society operates its list as a confidential mailing service to give members of the public access to information (**www.officiallondon theatre.co.uk**). Another good source of information on theatre angels can be found on The Stage website (go to 'how to' guides on the home page of **www.thestage.co.uk** and look for 'how to invest in theatre shows').

Film financing

In the 2004 Budget the chancellor announced a major change to film financing that takes effect in 2005. The reform introduces a tax credit of 20% against profits that is paid directly to producers. It is designed to stamp out investment partnerships that took advantage of the previous tax relief provisions that allowed the production costs of a film with a budget of less than £15m to be written off over a year. Such partnerships tried to turn what was intended as a tax deferral mechanism into permanent tax avoidance. Tax practitioners suggest that the move will eliminate film partnerships and encourage financing from specialist banks and lenders, but film directors are now looking for different ways to allow private investment to continue.

At the time of writing it was too early to tell what investment routes would remain or be developed for the private investor. Whatever emerges, interested investors should take care to ensure that they understand the downside and their position on recoupment (division of assets in the event of closure), which should be first or possibly second after a bank.

Gemstones

This section is not so much a lesson in investing as a wealth warning. While certain gemstones may gain in value, the market has been undermined by a series of frauds. Professional dealers can make a handsome profit on the mark-up on stones and jewellery shown in shop windows. This can be between 50%–100% of the intrinsic value. With this level of mark-up, there is little chance of buying new jewellery and selling it on for a profit. Antique jewellery is potentially far more profitable, provided you choose wisely. In the early 1990s a 60-year-old Cartier platinum and diamond watch might have gone for £10,000 but would have been worth £14,000 at the end of the decade. Fabergé Eggs have also done remarkably well.

Unfortunately, gemstones have attracted the serial fraudsters. Some investors have been persuaded to buy stones that they are told will sell for a profit of several hundred percent at a later date at an auction. All too often the auction never takes place and the company is wound up. To add insult to injury, the original scam company sells its list of gullible investors to a second company. This company then approaches the investors and explains that for a further investment the company can find a buyer for the gemstones. Interested investors should watch out for glossy brochures offering gemstones at apparently cheap prices that can be sold in due course for a remarkable profit.

Antiques and fine art

Much of the advice above applies to antiques and fine art. Most auction houses warn against buying collectables as investments and suggest you should only buy what you like. The cost of keeping larger items coupled with the insurance can rapidly reduce your 'investment'. Selling via a major auction house is expensive and between the auctioneer's commission and the 'buyer's premium' you can lose about half of the actual hammer price. Sotheby's maximum commission in the UK is 15% plus insurance of 1.5%. It also charges commission to sellers at 20% on the first £70,000 and 12% thereafter. If you prefer to go to a dealer do shop around, as they will take a big slice of the selling price.

Summary

This chapter looked briefly at a range of investments that fall outside the regulatory environment and which tend to attract enthusiasts. While such investments can provide an attractive return it is important to look very carefully at the credentials of the company making the sale, as certain investments such as fine wine and gemstones have been the subject of serial frauds.

Key terms

- Angel p. 200
- Recoupment schedule p. 200
- Scams p. 195
- Tangible assets p. 195

Review questions

1 Explain the difference between regulated and non-regulated investments.

2 Explain the difference between tangible and non-tangible assets.

3 As a planner would you advise an investor to consider any of the assets covered in this chapter and if so, why?

4 Which 'investments' in particular would you recommend an individual should avoid?

Go to the Companion Website at **www.booksites.net/harrison_pfp** for a multiple-choice quiz to test your understanding of this chapter.

Further information

Part of the information in this chapter was drawn from the Independent Research Services' 'lesson' on alternative investments (**www.irs-spi.co.uk**).

The Association of Art and Antique Dealers: **www.lapada.co.uk**

The Forestry Commission: **www.forestry.gov.uk**

For information about wine investment and fraud go to **www.investdrinks.org**.

The Society of London Theatre: **www.officiallondontheatre.co.uk**

The Stage: **www.thestage.co.uk**

Theatrenet: **www.theatrenet.co.uk**

Chapter 17 ●●●○

Property

Introduction

This important chapter considers the various ways the private investor can buy property as a home and as an investment. The investment category is divided into residential 'buy-to-let' and commercial property, which is accessed via collective funds. The chapter concludes with equity release, where older homeowners need to reverse the investment process and either borrow against their home or sell a proportion of its value in order to free up some of their capital.

Objectives

After reading this chapter you will be able to:

- Describe the main types of residential mortgage.
- Explain which types of insurance are suitable for borrowers and which are less effective.
- Discuss the opportunities and pitfalls of buy-to-let.
- Explain how individuals can invest in commercial property funds.
- Debate the risks of equity release for the elderly.

● ● ● ● Buying the main family residence

The process of buying a house or flat can be very fraught, not least because of the sharp practice that prevails in certain sectors of the market. Fortunately from 31 October 2004 the sale of most residential mortgages fell under the remit of the Financial Services Authority (FSA), which should ensure more consistent regulation. Until this point the FSA only regulated the sale of investments sold to repay a mortgage – for example Individual savings accounts (ISAs).

There are plenty of sources of information on mortgages and home ownership but probably the best guides to the basics are published by the Council of Mortgage Lenders (CML), 'How to buy a home', and the FSA's 'Guide to mortgages' (see p. 219). The CML is the central body for the various types of mortgage lender including the banks, building societies, finance houses, insurance companies and specialist mortgage companies.

This chapter looks at specific mortgage protection insurance but for the bigger picture on protection insurance, see Chapter 7. The Association of British Insurers (ABI) publishes free fact sheets on mortgage protection insurance and building and contents insurance.

Leasehold versus freehold

To buy a property **freehold** involves the purchase of the land, as well as the bricks and mortar. For most people this is the most satisfactory arrangement. However, many properties – particularly flats – are sold on a **leasehold** basis. In this case the buyer has the right to live in the property for 99 years, or whatever term is left on the lease. Once the lease expires the property reverts to the owner.

Leaseholders are required to maintain the property and pay towards these costs. If the owner (the freeholder) allows the property to become run down, they can demand a considerable sum for renovation. These problems can usually be avoided if there is a clear agreement that explains where the various responsibilities lie. A solicitor should always check the terms very carefully indeed.

The mortgage

A mortgage is a **secured loan** and represents the legal charge on the property, which the borrower gives to the lender as security. Together with any special terms and conditions, the **mortgage deed** is the legal contract between you and the lender. The most important features of the mortgage deed are:

- The names of the parties to the contract – that is, the borrower and the lender.
- The amount of the loan and the borrower's acknowledgement of receipt of the loan.
- A promise by the borrower to repay the loan, with interest, on the stipulated terms. These include the amount of the initial repayments and any special terms; for example a fixed rate or a discount on the lender's variable rate for the first two years.

- The granting of the legal charge of the property to the mortgage lender until the loan is repaid.
- The borrower's commitment, if applicable, to any insurance policies and to carry out any repairs and alterations – for example the lender may insist the house is reroofed within the first three months of ownership to maintain the property's value.

As this is a secured loan, if the borrower breaches the terms of the mortgage contract by failing to keep up the monthly payments, the lender has the power to take possession of the property and to sell it in order to recoup the loss. Repossessions are a last resort but unfortunately they were an all too familiar feature of the late 1980s and early 1990s when many borrowers had over-stretched themselves and could not keep pace with the sharp rise in interest rates.

Provided the individual has a reasonably stable income, there will be a huge range of mortgage facilities available and a good mortgage broker will have access to the latest offers. The planner's role is to ensure the individual takes out the best mortgage for their circumstances, selects an appropriate term and, where possible, avoids any mortgage packages that could present difficulties at a later date; for example early repayment penalties. The term should reflect the period during which the individual can afford repayments and so in most cases should not extend beyond retirement. Shorter-term repayment mortgages result in higher monthly repayments but reduce the overall amount paid in interest.

As with the mortgage itself, the range of repayment options has developed considerably in recent years and some lenders require little more than a verbal assurance that the borrower *will* save one way or another in order to repay the debt. Once it is clear how much the buyer can afford to raise – and this will depend largely on the lender's criteria, the individual's income and the condition of the property – the buyer makes a formal offer and applies for the loan. The lender will insist on a valuation to check that the property is priced correctly. This is not the same as a structural survey, which is strongly recommended.

The mortgage lender will offer an advance and if the conveyancer, who looks after the legal side of the process, is satisfied that all is in order the purchase will proceed to **exchange of contract**. This is when the buyer must make a formal commitment to buy, and the owner of the house makes a formal commitment to sell. At this stage the conveyancer may ask the buyer for a deposit of between 5% and 10% of the purchase price. A few weeks later, on **completion**, the buyer takes ownership of the house and must pay the balance.

Lending criteria

Lenders differ in the amount they will offer but in general this is likely to be up to three times annual earnings, less any existing commitments such as hire purchase agreements and other outstanding liabilities. For a joint mortgage the multiple is likely to be three times the higher income plus once the lower, or up to two and a half times the joint income. The lender will want to see confirmation of the income and this is likely to take the form of a letter from the employer or, for the self-employed, copies of audited accounts for several previous years.

Clearly the amount of debt an individual can comfortably manage will depend on their circumstances. Couples should be careful not to over-commit themselves if they plan to start a family in the near future and expect one of the incomes to substantially reduce or disappear altogether for several years. It is also important to be aware of the potential for negative equity where there is a very high **loan-to-value ratio**. Should house prices fall, the loan could outstrip the market value of the property. This was very common in the early 1990s.

The mortgage and any capital available from savings need to cover several items other than the price of the house itself. Surveys, conveyancing fees, stamp duty, land registry fees and the removal costs can all mount up and it is important to get an estimate of these costs before making a formal offer.

Stamp duty is a government tax on the purchase of properties and must be paid where the purchase price exceeds £60,000. The current rate is 1% and this is paid on the full price, not just the tranche that exceeds £60,000. This rises to 1.5% for purchases between £250,000 and £500,000 and 2% for houses above this level. Land registry fees must also be paid for either registering the title to the property or the transfer, where the title has already been registered. The fee for a £100,000–£150,000 house was about £350 at the time of writing. The individual will also need to consider buildings and contents insurance, life assurance and, depending on existing cover, a payment protection policy.

Self-certification

An increasing number of lenders offer self-certification mortgages, which are appropriate in cases where earnings may be reliable but erratic, where the standard lending formula is not appropriate. This type of mortgage used to be offered to the self-employed but it is increasing in popularity as more people work on short-term contracts, or rely on bonuses and dividends for the bulk of their earnings. A steady income stream from investments is also acceptable to certain lenders.

In theory self-certification should require no proof of earnings but in practice lenders vary considerably in their requirements. Some require a minimum period of continuous employment or ask to see at least two years' accounts. Some will accept irregular income but not investment income. Proof of residency and a previous lender's reference may also be required.

Which type of mortgage?

There are two basic types of mortgage: the repayment and the interest only. The latter may or may not be backed by an investment plan.

● Repayment

With a repayment mortgage the monthly payments cover interest and capital so that at the end of the mortgage term the borrower has paid off the entire debt. Where the mortgage is arranged on a **standard variable rate,** or a discount of this, the repayments will rise and fall in line with the corresponding fluctuations in the lender's variable rate, which in turn is affected by interest rates set by the Bank of England. There may be a penalty for early repayment of the mortgage.

To simplify administration, lenders often calculate the interest payments at the start of their financial year for the whole of that year, so this will not take account of any extra capital repayments you make during the year that reduce your debt.

● *Interest only*

The alternative to a repayment mortgage is an interest-only loan where the borrower makes interest payments each month but the capital debt remains static. Most people who borrow on this basis are either required or encouraged to save through an investment vehicle so that by the end of the mortgage term there is sufficient capital to repay the debt. Unless buyers opt for an endowment mortgage (almost certainly not a good idea – see page 29) they will also need to take out sufficient life assurance to repay the loan if they (or their partner in the case of a joint mortgage) die before the fund has grown to the required level. This can be simple term assurance or decreasing insurance that reflects the amount of capital paid off through the repayment mortgage or the amount saved through the investment scheme.

These days it is very rare for a new borrower not to be able to find some sort of special deal on the interest rate but this is usually offset by a degree of inflexibility. A typical example is where the lender insists that the borrower stick with the loan for a minimum number of years. If the borrower repays early then there could be a penalty.

The annual percentage rate (APR)

Before looking at the various options it is helpful to understand how the interest rate is calculated and applied. There are many variations on this theme – for example a lender might calculate and charge the interest on a daily, monthly, quarterly or even annual basis, all of which will affect the annual rate charged.

The APR was introduced to help borrowers make meaningful comparisons between lenders' offers (see p. 110) and represents the total charge for credit, taking into account:

● The amount of interest charged.
● The frequency of payments.
● Certain other costs, such as the valuation fees and lender's conveyancing charges, which are not included in the nominal rate.

The APR must be quoted in a standard way but it does not take into account any other costs – for example if the lender insists the borrower buy its buildings insurance in order to qualify for a lower rate of interest. Moreover, the APR quoted for fixed rate or discount schemes only applies to the offer period; it does not take into account the full variable rate, which will take effect after the reduced rate has finished. Nor does it reflect the additional cost if there are early repayment penalties.

Standard variable rate

Lenders usually adjust their interest rates in line with fluctuations in base rates. Where the institution has both borrowers and savers – the building societies and banks for example – the margin between the two interests rates represents their profit. If they have to pay more to savers to keep rates competitive they will have to pass on this increase to mortgage customers.

Fixed rate

This type of mortgage is particularly attractive to borrowers who want the security of knowing what their liabilities will be for several years ahead in order to budget accurately. Typically lenders are prepared to fix for one or two years, sometimes up to five. When the fixed rate period ends the borrower would switch to the lender's variable rate or might be offered the chance to fix again.

The factors that influence a decision to go for a fixed rate as a borrower are similar to the considerations facing a saver, albeit in reverse. If general interest rates rise the borrower will be protected from an increase in mortgage repayments for the period of the fixed rate. However, if interest rates fall the borrower is locked into an uncompetitively high rate.

As with savers who go for a fixed rate bond, for example, fixed rate borrowers must watch out for early redemption (repayment) penalties. Quite often these are so high that borrowers are forced to stay put because it is too expensive to get out, even when they take into account much better rates elsewhere.

Discounted rates and cashback

Most lenders offer a discount of 1%–2% on their variable rate, usually for a period of one or two years. On top of this a lender may provide a 'cashback' payment where a lump sum is paid to the borrower once the mortgage has been settled – typically 3%–5% of the amount borrowed. Alternatively the lender pays the cost of legal fees and/or buildings insurance for the first few months. This type of package can be very attractive for buyers who need to keep payments down during the first few years but again it is important to understand the penalties for early redemption. Where a mortgage is repaid within a specified term it is usually necessary to repay any offers, including the difference between the discount and standard variable rate paid so far.

Base rate tracker

This is similar to a standard variable mortgage but the interest rate is guaranteed to be a specified amount above the Bank of England or another base rate.

Cap and collar mortgages

Under a cap and collar mortgage the lender sets an upper and lower limit on fluctuations in the interest rate. This means the borrower knows that the rate cannot exceed the upper limit, but if interest rates fall below the collar, the borrower would be saddled with an uncompetitive package, in the same way as applies with a fixed rate. Penalties are likely to apply if the borrower wants to remortgage to take advantage of better rates elsewhere.

Shared appreciation mortgages

These are particularly attractive to young people making their first purchase and also to elderly people who want to release some of the capital in their homes (see p. 214). As the name suggests a third party takes a share in the property and in this way secures the relevant proportion of any gains or losses in the value of the home when it is resold. Typically the third party might be a housing scheme. (A housing scheme is an organi-sation – usually with charitable status – that is dedicated to the provision of affordable housing, often for specific categories of people or in target areas.) With this arrange-ment it is important to document the allocation carefully and to be clear at the outset which party is responsible for buying costs such as stamp duty and legal fees.

Flexible and current account mortgages

Lenders are becoming more willing to cater for those whose lifestyle and job circumstances change. For example, it might be possible to fluctuate the payments where income also fluctuates and it may be possible to negotiate an increase in the loan. A more structured approach to the flexible mortgage is offered by the current account mortgage (CAM) and the 'offset' mortgage. The concept is attractive. If you have a mortgage with an interest rate of 5% and a savings account that pays 3%, then it makes sense to transfer any money in the savings account to repay the mortgage.

In the current account mortgage there is just one account with an overall lending limit. Interest is charged on the actual amount borrowed. The offset mortgage is more complex in that there are separate accounts for the mortgage and savings. The savings account earns no interest but its credit value is offset against the outstanding mortgage capital and so the interest payable is reduced accordingly. In most cases individuals will benefit from this type of arrangement, as the mortgage interest saved will be greater than the savings interest given up. However, it is important to make sure that the mortgage rate is competitive. Some providers charge a higher rate than average and so the benefit is lost.

Remortgaging

According to the independent market analyst Datamonitor, remortgaging accounts for over 45% of total gross advances in the mortgage market and is expected to rise to 48% by 2008. This is somewhat surprising given that in all but the most straight-forward of mortgages there tend to be penalties on early repayment. These penalties, in theory, should make it difficult for borrowers to take advantage of new offers and clearly they should make careful calculations before proceeding, to ensure that the new deal plus penalties is not more expensive than the old deal. The FSA provides comparative tables for those looking for a first mortgage or to remortgage.

CAT standards

As with Individual savings accounts (ISAs – see page 178), CAT stands for certain standards in the charges, access and terms of the mortgage. Full details of these are set out in the FSA guide to mortgages. The important point to note about CAT-marked mortgages (or any other CAT-marked product) is that while they may represent reasonable value for money, they are in no way intended to be a recommendation by the government or the FSA.

Mortgage related insurance

Due to the substantial size of the loan and the value of the property, borrowers must make sure they have the right type of insurance. In some cases this will be a compulsory requirement by the lender although usually the borrower has the right to choose the insurer.

Buildings and contents insurance are essential and both the CML and FSA guides offer some good advice for buyers. This chapter, however, is limited to the examination of the mortgage related insurance that protects the lender if you default, and the personal insurances which either pay off the debt in the event of your death or help you maintain repayments in the event of long-term illness.

Mortgage indemnity

Financial institutions like to protect themselves if they lend more than 75% of the value of the property. The risk they face is that if the borrower defaults they would need to repossess the house and sell it, possibly for less than the purchase price. To protect against such losses on a high loan to value advance, lenders require borrowers to take out mortgage indemnity insurance, which would reimburse them for some or all of the difference between the outstanding mortgage and the actual selling price. The important point to remember about the mortgage indemnity fee (it might also be called an additional security fee or high percentage loan fee) is that it protects the lender, not the borrower.

Life assurance

Life assurance is examined in Chapter 7, but briefly this should pay off all the individual's outstanding liabilities where they would otherwise fall on to a connected person (typically, the immediate family). The mortgage is likely to be a family's main debt in the early years but it is important to factor in any other liabilities, whether they are debts or regular commitments.

Payment protection

This is a variation on critical illness and/or permanent health insurance (see page 95). If the borrower suffered a chronic illness or became disabled, this type of policy would cover the cost of the mortgage and any related costs – insurances for example. The critical illness element would provide a lump sum if the individual suffered a major illness.

Borrowers might also be offered an accident, sickness and unemployment (ASU) insurance. This covers the monthly mortgage payments if the individual becomes too ill to work or is unemployed. The accident and sickness element is like a short-term income protection policy. Unemployment insurance is available through a few specialist insurers but generally is very expensive, so ASU may be the only way to get it. However, individuals should treat this type of insurance as a way of buying some breathing space if they need to reassess their finances in the light of illness or unemployment. It does not provide a long-term replacement income.

The same caveat applies to the limited versions of income protection offered through a mortgage protection scheme. The main point to note here is that, while the lender is concerned to ensure the borrower maintains monthly repayments, in practice they would need a great deal more than this to cover all the monthly outgoings and liabilities. Full income protection is particularly important for the self-employed who do not have access to a group scheme at work.

Mortgage related savings

For a discussion on medium- to long-term collective investments, see Chapters 12 and 13. Where a borrower wants to set up an investment earmarked to repay the mortgage, it makes sense to follow a 'lifestyle' asset allocation strategy; that is, to switch gradually from equities into bonds and cash in the five years before the mortgage term ends. In this way it is possible to avoid the problems that would otherwise occur where equity markets tumbled shortly before the individual needed to repay the debt. (For more on lifestyle, see page 293.)

Second homes

An increasing number of couples buy a second home for personal use at weekends and holidays, possibly with the intention of turning it into a retirement home. Where a property is bought for personal use, owners may be reluctant to rent it out during periods when it would otherwise be unoccupied. This means that there will be no income to offset costs and that security may be a problem.

The tax position for those with more than one home is as follows. Within two years of the second purchase you need to inform the Inland Revenue which home is your principal residence. You can change this election at a later date. Any gain on the home that is not the principal residence will be subject to capital gains tax. For this reason it makes sense to choose the home most likely to increase in value as the principal residence, as this does not have to be the place where you spend most of your time. For the same reason, if it is likely that you will make a loss on a property then this should not be the principal residence as this would not be an allowable loss to offset against gains.

Residential homes overseas

A second home overseas manifests all of the potential problems of a second home in the UK, although in addition there will be local laws, taxation and, where applicable, currency fluctuations to consider. UK residents and UK domiciled individuals who rent property overseas will be liable to tax on this income, less any expenses and mortgage interest. Capital gains tax (CGT) will also be payable on any gain when the property is sold. Foreign taxes can usually be offset against tax paid in the UK. Expert local advice is essential and it will be necessary to make a foreign will to cover any assets overseas. Planners must bear in mind that in some countries, for example Spain, the property is divided according to the law on the death of a parent.

Buy-to-let

About 2m households rent through the private sector in the UK and according to the letting agents there is a national shortage of rental property in every area, from the executive home to the studio flat. Yet according to the financial press the buy-to-let market is saturated and newcomers are finding it difficult to find suitable tenants. Clearly any purchase for this purpose must be considered very carefully.

The objective of buy-to-let is for the investor to cover the mortgage repayments and all other costs, *and* make a profit. The average gross return on rental income in Britain today is about 8%–10%. The gross return is the amount the landlord receives before deducting the costs of letting (including the mortgage where applicable) and the management fees, where the property is let via an agency. Where capital appreciation exceeds retail prices inflation the owner will also achieve capital growth. However, this outlook is over-optimistic. Such figures assume the property is let continuously. If the individual does not choose the property with care it may stand empty for several months at a time, which will put a serious dent in the return.

Regulation

Where an individual buys residential property directly, rather than through a pooled fund such as an authorised unit trust, they are not covered by the Financial Services and Markets Act, even if the purchase was made through an adviser who is FSA authorised. This means that there is no protection in the case of bad advice or if the property turns out to be poor quality.

Taxation

Taxation is discussed in Chapter 19. As far as investment property is concerned, **net rental income** (income after expenses) is subject to income tax at the individual's marginal rate (22% or 40% in 2004–2005). Expenses include the loan interest, but it is possible to claim for a 'wear and tear' allowance of 10% of the rent, less water rates, where the property is furnished.

Any growth in the value of the property between purchase and sale is subject to capital gains tax (CGT) although the actual amount will depend on the length of time the individual has held the property as an investment. In due course it appears that it will be possible to hold residential property in a personal pension, which may prove very tax-efficient for the right investor, as the sale would be free of CGT.

Letting agents

About 50% of rentals are arranged through letting and managing agents, most – but not all – of which are members of recognised professional organisations. Buy-to-let is the initiative launched by the Association of Residential Letting Agents (ARLA) and is supported by several major mortgage lenders. Its aim is to stimulate the rented property market by encouraging private investors to take advantage of low interest rates and the medium- to long-term potential for capital growth in property.

The loan

Historically investors in property who wanted to raise a loan for a buy-to-let property found that lenders imposed a hefty surcharge on retail mortgage rates and would not take the rental income into consideration when calculating the maximum loan. Now many lenders offer rates comparable to those extended to owner-occupiers, and they take the rental income into account when assessing the maximum loan that the borrower can service.

Loans can be arranged for a single property or a mini property investment portfolio of up to five houses and flats. Loans of between £15,000 and £1m per investor are available for periods of between five and 45 years. Typically the loan will cover up to 80% of the valuation. Methods of servicing the loan are flexible in most cases and mirror terms available to owner-occupiers. There are even loans which allow for over-payment and use the surplus to provide a repayment holiday or to cover future periods when you may be short of cash if the property is temporarily empty.

Which type of property?

ARLA's advice is to keep the choice of buy-to-let property simple. 'The common denominators sought by potential tenants are location, amenities and facilities,' it says. Investors should not make the mistake of buying somewhere quaint because they could see themselves being very happy there. 'Ignore personal tastes and avoid property with potential maintenance problems such as a lot of woodwork or a large garden. These features will add nothing to the rental value but cost a lot to keep up,' ARLA warns. In addition, mortgage lenders may have their own stipulations. For example, they may not like properties with more than one kitchen and four or five bedrooms in case they are converted to bedsits.

Rentals tend to be short term – typically six months to three years. A good letting agent will vet tenants carefully and make sure there is the minimum amount of time between lets. Typically you could expect an ARLA agent to charge 10% of the rent for finding the tenant and to cover the inventory and paperwork. For a full management agreement, where the agent will assume full responsibility for the property, this will cost an additional 5%–7%. These fees are tax deductible.

Most lets, unless for very high rentals, are arranged under an assured shorthold tenancy. This covers tenancies from six months upwards but usually there would be a cap at 12 months with an option to renew. This will list all the dos and don'ts and set out any rules; for example on children and pets.

Commercial property

Commercial property as an asset class behaves in a very different way from equities and bonds and therefore represents a good diversifier (see page 59). It can generate a useful income and can also benefit from capital growth. The simplest and, for most investors, the only way to invest in this type of property is via collective funds.

The Investment Management Association (IMA) lists the unit trusts that invest in commercial property, while the Association of British Insurers (ABI) lists the relevant life and pension funds. The rules for investment vary. For example authorised property unit trusts can invest up to 80% of assets in direct property or property company shares. Bear in mind that where funds invest in the shares of commercial property companies, this is quite different from investing in property directly, as you would be exposed to the profits and losses of the business. These unit trusts also tend to hold a higher level of cash than other unit trusts in order to maintain sufficient liquidity for unit cancellation.

Pension funds and unit linked life funds invest in property and both types tend to have less in cash as they are used for longer-term investment. Investment trusts can also invest in property, as can offshore funds and limited partnerships. Partnerships invest in a single or multiple buildings let to tenants. This usually requires a minimum of £25,000 and is a very long-term investment.

For the taxation of different types of collective fund see Chapter 12. For personal pensions, which are likely to be allowed to hold direct residential property from April 2006, see Chapter 23.

Equity release

There are several ways elderly home occupiers who are 'house rich, cash poor' can tap into the equity in their homes and use this to generate an extra income or capital sum. For older people who do not need residential care this might be attractive, as they don't have to sell up and move. It is possible to take the money as a regular income or as a lump sum, depending on the scheme rules.

These schemes are complex and the implications for an elderly homeowner can be very significant. This market is likely to increase rapidly as the government cuts the real value of state pensions, employers reduce their commitment to occupational schemes, and individual investors struggle to make a decent return with their Defined contribution (DC) pensions. For many people going into retirement or who have been retired some years, the family home is the most valuable asset by far.

The FSA has a good fact sheet on the subject, 'Raising money from your home', which provides sensible advice and cautionary warnings in equal measure. Other organisations also provide advice and these are listed at the end of the chapter.

The **home income plans** (**HIPs** – see below) sold in the late 1980s led many pensioners to make unwise investments and they were banned in 1990. But with increased longevity, cuts in state welfare and low interest rates, asset rich, cash poor pensioners are once again turning for financial assistance to a second generation of much more respectable equity release plans. Following the bad publicity of the earlier plans, several providers joined together in 1991 to form SHIP, the Safe Home Income Plans Company. The website, listed at the end of the chapter, provides contact details for the member companies. The code of practice offered by members of SHIP includes the following features:

- You have complete security of tenure and are guaranteed the right to live in the property for life, no matter what happens to interest rates and the stock market.
- You have freedom to move house without jeopardising your financial situation.
- You will be guaranteed a cash sum or fixed regular income; your money will not be sunk into uncertain investments.

There are two basic types of safe equity release scheme – those where the home-owner negotiates a fixed rate loan against the property, known as a **lifetime mortgage** and those which involve the sale of part or all of the property, known as **home reversion** where the buyer will take the proceeds of the sale or loan out of the estate when the individual dies and the house is sold.

Lifetime mortgage

Lifetime mortgages (also known as mortgage annuities) are still available but have been much less popular since the 1999 Budget, which abolished tax relief on this type of mortgage. Nevertheless, depending on the individual's age and circumstances, this might still be an option worth considering. A lifetime mortgage allows the homeowner to remortgage part of the value of the house – usually up to £40,000 to £50,000. The lump sum is repaid with the proceeds of the house sale when the individual dies. The mortgage may be in the form of:

- A home income plan.
- An interest-only mortgage.
- A roll-up mortgage, where the interest is added to the loan.

With a home income plan the lump sum secured by the mortgage is used to buy a **purchased life annuity** from the lender, which guarantees a regular income for life. This income pays the fixed rate of interest on the mortgage and what is left is for the individual to spend how as they wish. The annuity rate (the annual income per £1,000) is generally unattractive for the under-80s. Until the 1999 Budget the mortgage interest for home income plans was net of **mortgage interest relief at source (MIRAS)** at the concessionary rate of 23% but only loans taken out before April 1999 continue to qualify. This move has made the reversion plans (see below) more suitable in most cases.

An interest-only mortgage is no different in principle from the standard variety, except the loan will not be repaid until the borrower dies and the house is sold. The main issue here is to be sure the individual can afford the interest payments, which may be variable. The roll-up mortgage can look more attractive but the effect of the roll-up of interest means that the actual loan will increase rapidly, as is shown in Table 17.1.

There are more flexible arrangements coming onto the market – for example, the drawdown mortgage, which the individual can draw upon as and when necessary. Some lifetime mortgages include a 'shared appreciation' element (see page 209).

Table 17.1 A £45,000 roll-up mortgage: how the amount owed increases

Loan period	5% pa	7% pa	9% pa
5 yrs	57,433	63,115	69,293
10 yrs	73,301	88,522	106,532
15 yrs	93,552	124,157	163,912
20 yrs	119,399	174,136	252,100
25 yrs	152,387	244,235	388,039

Source: FSA.

Reversion plans

Under a reversion plan the homeowner sells, rather than mortgages, part of the house but continues to live there rent free. As a rough guide, they could expect to receive up to 50% of the value of the portion sold, as the price takes into account the fact that the company will not be able to take the proceeds of the sale until the individual's death. Interest rates on these mortgages tend to be 1%–2% higher than is available elsewhere in the market.

There are two types of reversion plan. With a **reversion annuity** the purchase price is used to buy an annuity, which provides an income for life in the same way as the home income plan described above. The income is higher because there is no mortgage interest to pay but because the individual has *sold* rather than mortgaged, they will not gain from any rise in house prices on that portion of the property. Under the cash option, again the homeowner sells part (or all) of the home in return for a lump sum, which is tax free, provided the house is the main residence. The individual continues to live there, rent free, until they die. The money could be used to buy an annuity but this is not obligatory.

The proportion of their house an individual or couple decides to sell will depend on how much income or capital is required. This in turn should be balanced with the desire to pass on the value of the house to children. Having said that, those who eventually move into a residential or nursing home would almost certainly be expected to use any remaining proceeds of the house to pay towards fees.

The minimum sale is usually between 40% and 50% of the value of the property and with some companies you can sell up to 100%.

Qualifying conditions

To qualify for a reversion plan homeowners must have full ownership. Also, the property must be in good condition, otherwise the company concerned may have trouble selling it in the future.

Age is an important consideration and in general only the over 70s will find equity release attractive, although some lenders consider younger applicants. Where a couple live in the home it is important to arrange the scheme in both names to ensure that after the first death the survivor can continue to live in the home until they die. The annuity income is based on the yields available on gilts and corporate bonds, which are comparatively low at present. It is also based on life expectancy, so the longer the insurance company expects the individual to live, the lower the income it will pay.

Tax and social security benefits

Equity release is a big step and can affect other aspects of the individual's financial position. For example, it is important to look at the impact of the additional income on the individual's tax position and the possible loss of means-tested social security benefits. In particular, care is needed if the individual is eligible for council tax benefit and pension credit as these are means tested and may be reduced or lost altogether. Clearly the home income plan benefits must more than compensate for any such loss. Moreover, before entering into an agreement, individuals should also check what would happen if they had to move into sheltered accommodation or a nursing home later in retirement.

Finally, it is essential to consider all the costs involved – for example the survey, legal fees and administrative charges. Some plan providers make a contribution but the amounts vary.

Activity 17.1

A civil servant, age 40, married with two children, would like to reduce his mortgage repayments now that the second baby has arrived and his wife has stopped work for a few years. Currently the couple has a joint repayment mortgage, variable rate, with 15 years to go. They have mortgage protection insurance and critical illness insurance, both of which policies were sold with the existing mortgage 10 years ago. What are the points to consider here?

Comment: Your answer should take into consideration the term of the mortgage and the different options. It should also consider what type of mortgage protection insurance, if any, this family requires.

Activity 17.2

An elderly couple, both in their late 70s, need to increase their income. Their main asset is the family home and so they are prepared to consider equity release. Their two main concerns are first, what impact the additional income might have on their social security benefits, and second, how equity release would affect their desire to pass on the value of the house to their two children. Advise the couple on their options.

Summary

This chapter covered a great deal of important ground. The family home should not be regarded primarily as an investment but increasingly couples are selling down at retirement to increase their scope for investing for income, and/or using equity release for similar reasons later in retirement. The chapter looked at various ways to invest in property and raised concerns over the growth of the buy-to-let market. It also considered the place of a collective commercial property fund in an individual's asset allocation.

Key terms

- Annual percentage rate (APR) p. 207
- Completion p. 205
- Exchange of contract p. 205
- Freehold p. 204
- Home income plans (HIPs) p. 215
- Home reversion p. 215
- Leasehold p. 204
- Lifetime mortgage p. 215
- Loan-to-value ratio p. 206
- Mortgage deed p. 204
- Mortgage interest relief at source (MIRAS) p. 216
- Net rental income p. 212
- Purchased life annuity p. 215
- Reversion annuity p. 216
- Secured loan p. 204
- Standard variable rate p. 207

Review questions

1 Explain the purpose of the annual percentage rate (APR) and which factors it must take into account. What are some of the potential problems inherent in this calculation?

2 Given the very high rate of remortgaging (45% of new advances), do you think that all cases are likely to benefit the borrower? What factors might make a remortgage difficult?

3 What are the attractions and dangers of buy-to-let?

4 Why is a collective commercial property fund a suitable diversifier in an individual's portfolio?

5 Explain the ways an elderly couple can gain access to the equity in their home. What are the key issues they should address?

Go to the Companion Website at **www.booksites.net/harrison_pfp** for a multiple-choice quiz to test your understanding of this chapter.

Further information

Association of Residential Letting Agencies: **www.arla.co.uk**

The Council of Mortgage Lenders (CML): **www.cml.org.uk**

FSA guide to mortgages is at **www.fsa.gov.uk**, while the comparative mortgage tables are at **www.fsa.gov.uk/tables**.

For advice on state benefits try the Citizens' Advice Bureau **www.nacab.org.uk** and **www.adviceguide.org.uk**; also Counsel and Care **www.counselandcare.org.uk**.

Home Improvement Agencies: England **www.foundations.uk.com**; Scotland **www.care-repair-scot.org.uk**; Wales **www.careandrepair.org.uk**; Northern Ireland **www.foldgroup.co.uk**.

The Home Improvement Trust is a not-for-profit organisation that arranges equity release schemes to fund repairs and home improvements/adaptations: **www.hitrust.org**.

The Investment Management Association lists the unit trusts that invest in commercial property: **www.investmentuk.org**. For life funds go to the Association of British Insurers site at **www.abi.org.uk**.

The Mortgage Code Compliance Board (MCCB): **www.mortgagecode.org.uk**

Safe Home Income Plans Company: **www.ship-ltd.org**

Useful fact sheets for older homeowners are available from the FSA (see above), Age Concern **www.ace.org.uk** and Help the Aged **www.helptheaged.org.uk**.

Case study 17.1

Background

Kate Benjamin, 35, and Phil Cane, 37, are both non-smokers and in good health. Phil is employed as an IT manager for a large firm of lawyers in Leeds. Kate is employed as a fulltime nursery nurse. Phil earns £40,000 and Kate earns £20,000 gross pa. The couple lives in a quiet leafy suburb of Leeds in a semi-detached house that they bought seven years ago.

They have a repayment mortgage with 13 years to run with an outstanding balance of £60,000. They have just finished their fixed rate period and the mortgage has reverted to the variable rate. The house is valued at £140,000.

Problem

Kate and Phil have big plans. They have obtained planning permission to build a single storey extension to the side of their house. Kate is a qualified piano teacher and wishes to go part time in her existing job, to three days a week, and teach the remainder of the time using the newly built room.

Case study 17.1 (*continued*)

They have given the builders the go ahead and expect the costs to amount to about £20,000. They have £25,000 cash reserved to pay for these works. Kate would also like to buy a grand piano, estimated cost £40,000, before she starts teaching. They have no cash reserves for this and do not wish to use capital invested elsewhere. They have sufficient disposable income to meet existing retirement and protection objectives, plus they have approximately £400 per month left over to pay for the piano.

Advice

They have seen an advert on the television telling them about an offset mortgage and although they don't really understand how it works, they are interested to find out more including if it is the answer to Kate's dreams, so she can buy a new piano sooner rather than later. The couple may get married in the next five to seven years but do not feel it is a priority. They may, however, need more capital at that time and wish to simplify their mortgage finances now so that they can have easy access to up to a further £5,000 if they do decide to get married. They seek your advice to help meet their objectives both now and in the future, with minimal fuss. They would like you to explain both the pros and cons of any available options that may meet these objectives.

Source: Money Management, Financial Planner of the Year Awards 2003, *FT Business*.

An additional case study relevant to this chapter is available from the Companion Website at **www.booksites.net/harrison_pfp**.

A full solution to this case study is available to lecturers via the password-protected area of the Companion Website at **www.booksites.net/harrison_pfp**.

Chapter 18 ●●●●

Lloyd's of London

Introduction

This chapter looks at the Lloyd's of London insurance market as an investment opportunity for very wealthy individuals who are prepared to take a significant degree of risk. Despite the return to profits for this market in recent years and the limitation on liability, heavy insurance losses could wipe out the individual's investment.

Objectives

After reading this chapter you will be able to:

- Understand why individual investors (Names) have suffered such great losses.
- Debate the merits of investment under the limited liability regime.

●●●● Developments in the market

Over the past three decades Lloyd's has provided wealthy individual investors with exciting returns and frightening losses in equal measure. The losses experienced by **unlimited liability** individual members or **Names** in the second half of the 1990s and the 2000–2002 period triggered a dramatic overhaul of the structure of Lloyd's and the role of these investors. Since then the Lloyd's insurance market has achieved strong profits on an annually accounted basis. In 2004 it was able to accept premiums of over £15bn.

It is still possible to invest in this historic insurance market but it is no longer possible to become a new Name with the associated unlimited liability. For wealthy investors this can be attractive but extreme caution is necessary. While the 2,000+ existing Names continue to operate on an unlimited liability basis, this chapter briefly considers how new investors can participate under the limited liability regime in place at the end of 2002. By 2004 private investors accounted for about 20% of the market share at Lloyd's.

Before examining participation options it is helpful to understand the attraction of Lloyd's, how it works and the background to the most recent overhaul of the system. The capital individuals 'deposit' with Lloyd's is usually in the form of a **letter of credit** or **bank guarantee** rather than cash. This means that in effect the investor's capital is working three times over, rather than just once:

- Investors continue to receive the income and capital gains arising from investing the capital elsewhere.
- Membership of Lloyd's syndicates entitles them to a share of the profits arising from the excess of premiums received over the costs of meeting claims, reinsurance and operating expenses.
- Premium income is invested by the syndicates, so providing income and capital gains, which are shared among the syndicate members.

It is possible, for example, for a wealthy investor to unlock the capital in a second or third home by using it as security. So becoming a Name need have no effect on the individuals' assets unless, of course, they are subsequently called in to pay for losses.

●●●● How Lloyd's works

Insurance risks at Lloyd's are taken up by its members, the individual Names and companies that provide the supporting capital on which the market is based. Members form groups known as **syndicates**, which are annual ventures that are owned by their investors. Each syndicate is a joint venture run by a managing agent, a professional underwriter and support staff. Members pay a management fee and commission on profits earned by the syndicate. These charges are deducted from the premium trust fund. Syndicates compete for business and may specialise in one of the main areas of business – marine, aviation, catastrophe, professional indemnity or motor – or may write risks across the whole spectrum of the market. Under the reforms introduced in September 2002 the Franchise Board imposes the best underwriting practices on all syndicates to create a uniformity of standards.

Historically, Lloyd's has demonstrated that it has some of the best underwriters in the world, but unfortunately some less competent underwriters have inflicted heavy losses. The reforms will give managing agents a franchise to operate within the Lloyd's market. Some managing agents are quoted companies listed on The London Stock Exchange; others are private companies. Occasionally managing agents act as capital providers to the syndicates they manage and so have a multiple role as corporate members of the market, agents and, from 2003, franchisees.

When profits are paid

Traditionally, Lloyd's syndicates did not close their accounts for a particular calendar year until two years after the end of that year. This was supposed to allow enough time for any outstanding claims to be settled. At the end of the two-year **running off period**, any claims that are still outstanding are reinsured with the next account and the books are closed. So the books for an Underwriting Account are closed on 31 December two years later. Any reinsurance premiums that must be paid into the next year's account are deducted from the profits, which are then distributed to the syndicate members in May or June after the Account has been closed.

If a syndicate's account is not closed because its managers are still uncertain about the extent of its liabilities for a particular year, the year is left 'open' and the syndicate members are left in doubt about their potential commitment. However, in a move designed to make Lloyd's activities more transparent and attractive to potential investors, it is proposing to move to an annual accounting basis by 2005.

Reform

In the late 1980s and early 1990s Lloyd's saw unprecedented losses, due to three main factors:

- Claims for asbestos, pollution and health hazards resulting from policies written many years previously, predominantly in the US.
- The spate of natural and man-made disasters between 1987 and 1992, including the Piper Alpha explosion and the Exxon Valdez oil spillage.
- A concentration of reinsurance liability. This meant that rather than spreading catastrophe losses around the market, they were focused on a small number of syndicates.

In the past Names would ride out the occasional bad year in the reasonable expectation that any losses would be more than made up in the future. Unfortunately, the losses of £7.9bn experienced between 1988 and 1992 wiped out all the profits Lloyd's had ever made in the whole of its previous 300-years history.

More recently, the terrorist bombing of the World Trade Centre on 11 September, 2001 had dramatic repercussions for many participants in the insurance and reinsurance markets and Lloyd's was no exception. At the time of writing Lloyd's had paid out about US$4.5bn and reserved a similar amount for further claims.

At that point it became clear that radical reform was required to keep the market viable. Individuals had learned to their cost that investing in Lloyd's as an unlimited liability Name really did mean accepting unlimited liability for losses. Some were forced to sell their homes to pay their liabilities. The scandals and bad years made many forget the corollary: profits are unlimited as well. The remaining unlimited liability members now believe that there are good years ahead for them at Lloyd's and hope to recoup their losses.

Changes to the market

In its response to the problems of the 1980s and early 1990s, the Lloyd's Council drew up plans for far-reaching reforms that allowed companies to invest with only limited liability, and for new investors to be protected against losses resulting from business written before 1992. But there were even more radical changes to come. These were not just a reaction to 11 September, 2001 but were also a response to the threat that rival emerging insurance markets – for example in Bermuda – would undermine Lloyd's pre-eminence in world insurance markets. In fact many of the corporate investors at Lloyd's are from Bermuda and the US and some threatened to return to their home markets if reform did not go ahead.

In September 2002 Lloyd's introduced a package of reforms:

- An end to new members joining the Society with unlimited liability.
- A plan to close run-off years, thus freeing members from the uncertainties of old, unquantifiable liabilities.
- The establishment of a Lloyd's Franchise.
- The formation of the Franchise Board, led by Lord Levene of Portsoken. This is a single unitary board with clear accountability to oversee the market's commercial and regulatory needs.
- A new Compliance Committee to provide reassurance to all members that they will continue to be treated fairly and to ensure regulatory compliance.
- The introduction of an internationally recognised standard of accounting.

New investors should benefit from these reforms. In particular they will make it easier to compare Lloyd's with other investment opportunities. In theory, existing Names with unlimited liability should also benefit from these reforms, whether their intention is to stay put until they have recouped their more recent losses or to make a longer-term commitment to Lloyd's. However, in the light of damaging tensions between corporate and individual members, Lloyd's has put pressure on Names to convert to limited liability. Names have resisted this move because they are concerned that they will not be able to 'roll-over' their huge losses from recent years and offset them against future profits. In the autumn of 2002 Lloyd's entered discussions with the Treasury and the Inland Revenue to consider the implications that arise when an unlimited liability Name converts to limited liability. Unlimited liability Names, for their part, remain determined to retain their existing rights. This battle between traditional Names and Lloyd's has not helped investor confidence nor does it aid potential investors in their search for information.

Investment opportunities

Now that limited liability companies are allowed to invest in Lloyd's it may seem that there is little to be gained as an outsider from investing in the market. It is in the nature of the business that some risks are more dangerous than others. Insiders who work in the insurance business day by day have a better chance of recognising a risk that may turn into a liability. Many individual members, however, feel very strongly that Lloyd's' success depends on their continued involvement and that individual members have generally been more successful than corporate members as they are more prudent, given they are investing their own money. Following the September 2002 reforms, the two options for new private investors are:

- To buy shares in a Lloyd's quoted company. At the end of November 2002 there were 13 Lloyd's managing agents listed on The Stock Exchange.
- To invest on a limited liability basis by setting up a limited company, known as a **Nameco** or a **Scottish Limited Partnership**.

Investing in a Lloyd's company

Originally, there were two main roles at Lloyd's, the provision of risk capital and decision-making. The Names did the former and managing agents the latter. When corporate capital arrived in 1994 it came in two main forms. **Spread trusts** were investment trusts that behaved just like Names. They raised money through share issues and joined syndicates, the aim being to boost returns by successful underwriting. Management of the capital played second fiddle to the underwriting and was doled out to a variety of managers and tracker funds. At the same time managing agents set up funds dedicated to underwriting on the syndicates they managed themselves.

The spread trusts were not terribly successful, rarely trading at a premium to their assets and often charged high fees because they hadn't raised as much money as they had planned. However, spread trusts are still in existence and have their own managed syndicates.

A **Lloyd's vehicle** or **ILV** ('I' is for 'integrated') that integrates the capital provider and managing agent offers an alternative structure. Here, the company owns the managing agent and the capital. All the managing agent's business is backed by its own capital – it takes a 100% share of the syndicates it manages. This is ideal when insurance is doing well – the ILV gets all the profit. The reverse is also true.

Once the managing agent that is to be responsible for the ILV's underwriting has been identified a reasonably confident valuation may be made by looking at the historical underwriting returns made by the syndicates the potential insurer is to manage and the amount of capital it has now. The next step is to work out how much it will cost to get it there. Adding that to the current valuation has often revealed cheap shares.

A good source of information on ILVs is the Association of Lloyd's Members' *Lloyd's Market Results and Prospects Yearbook*, published by Moody's, or Moody's own *Lloyd's Syndicates Ratings Guide*, which includes an overview of the managing agencies and listed Lloyd's vehicles. Moody's syndicate insurance Financial Strength Ratings allow investors to compare the prospects for Lloyd's syndicates with other insurance companies rated by the agency, as the same triple-A through to C ratings symbols are used throughout.

The main cost of making the transition is buying **capacity**. Capacity is the tool used to divide up the spoils of a syndicate, to limit the risks it takes and to determine the amount of capital the syndicate members must provide. In that sense it is rather like shares in a public company. It is measured in pounds and the total capacity is the maximum amount in premiums the syndicate can take in one year. It is owned by the members of a syndicate and is now traded through a series of auctions throughout the summer. The idea is to work out how much capacity the firm must get hold of, and how it will be funded by a mixture of investments, subordinated loans and re-insurance. Then, having guessed at a price, work out how many shares will have to be issued. Once that is done, valuation is a matter of calculating the value of the capital and the value to the firm of the capacity, capitalising the funding costs and dividing by the number of shares to see if the transformation will boost the share price. That may sound tough, but once you have got hold of information about the performance of the syndicate, your calculations – though lengthy – are comparatively straightforward. Of course, there are still some dangerous pitfalls:

- Illiquidity.
- Bad syndicates.
- Consolidation. The current trend of consolidation affects prospects for future profitability and the continuity of certain syndicates.
- Prices. Valuation depends on the insurance market and on the investment market – the latter is generally more predictable.
- Timing. As mentioned above, Lloyd's has made some spectacular losses over the past decade and further losses may occur. Investment companies try to balance their assets between insurance business and other investments, according to the relative prospects of each.
- Tax status. As they become ILVs, the investment trusts have to pay tax on their capital.

Investing through a Scottish Limited Partnership or Nameco

For investors who prefer a more hands-on approach there are two options, both of which limit the individual's liability: Scottish Limited Partnerships and Namecos. Of these two routes the Scottish Limited Partnership is generally considered to be the easier and there is substantial underwriting capacity available through these vehicles.

These partnerships must have a general partner, usually provided by a professional, and up to 19 limited partners. In practice, however, the investor may prefer to be the only limited partner – or perhaps to include members of their family in this category. Where limited partners do not know each other or do not share the same aims and objectives this can create problems.

To invest, the individual needs an absolute minimum spare capital of £0.5m. This must be available if the underwriters call on it, but in the meantime the individual can invest this elsewhere and enjoy the income/growth and retain the investment rights. As mentioned above it is necessary to provide a letter of credit or a bank guarantee to demonstrate to Lloyd's that the capital really is available.

The limited nature of this investment means that the maximum loss is the capital put forward – in this case £0.5m. Should the underwriting losses exceed the capital the individual would not be asked to provide any further money.

One of the most attractive taxation aspects of the limited partnership is that it is possible to offset losses made at Lloyd's against other sources of income. When the individual leaves the partnership they also leave behind any remaining liabilities.

The Nameco, although also a mechanism for limiting liability, is a very different legal entity. A Nameco is treated by the Financial Services Authority as a mini insurance company. As such the cost of administration and meeting the regulatory requirements is considered unattractive in many circumstances. Equally, if the individual wants to terminate the investment, the Nameco has to follow similar winding-up procedures to an insurance company and this can be time consuming. Moreover, as a company, any losses can only be offset against future gains within that company, so it is not possible to use an underwriting loss as part of the individual's general income and capital gains tax planning strategy.

Summary

This chapter took a brief look at the attractions and dangers of the Lloyd's of London insurance market for very wealthy investors. Even with limited liability the minimum investment is £0.5m and it is possible to lose the lot, so this is not a market for the faint-hearted.

Key terms

- Capacity p. 226
- Letter of credit/bank guarantee p. 222
- Lloyd's vehicle (ILV) p. 225
- Name p. 222
- Nameco p. 225

- Running off period p. 223
- Scottish Limited Partnership p. 225
- Spread trust p. 225
- Syndicate p. 222
- Unlimited liability p. 222

Review questions

1 Why do we say that capital invested at Lloyd's works three times over?

2 Why are the remaining unlimited liability Names so reluctant to change status to limited liability?

3 Do you think private investors should consider a limited liability role at Lloyd's and if so, to whom might this appeal?

Go to the Companion Website at **www.booksites.net/harrison_pfp** for a multiple-choice quiz to test your understanding of this chapter.

Further information

Lloyd's (**www.lloydsoflondon.com**) provides a lot of information about the recent changes to the market and includes a Managing Agents site. A good source of information for would-be as well as existing investors is the Association of Lloyd's Members, which represents the majority of Names, both limited and unlimited. The website is at **www.association-lloyds-members. co.uk**. Another lobby group is the High Premium Group at **www.hpg.demon.co.uk**. The global ratings agency Moody's publishes *Lloyd's Syndicates Ratings Guide*. For details telephone 020 7772 5420 or go to the website **www.moodys.com**. Certain stockbrokers specialise in Lloyd's. To find a firm go to the website for the Association of Private Client Investment Managers and Stockbrokers (APCIMS) at **www.apcims.co.uk**.

Chapter 19

Taxation

Introduction

Taxation comes into virtually every area of personal financial planning and while planners would not necessarily be expected to be taxation experts they must understand the rudiments of the subject and know when to delegate to a tax specialist. This is particularly important with trust arrangements and all arrangements for individuals who are non-resident or who are not domiciled in the UK. Pension planning forms an important aspect of this subject and its tax attractions are considered in Chapters 22 and 23.

Objectives

After reading this chapter you will be able to:

- Explain the difference between tax evasion, avoidance and mitigation.
- Debate the implications of the 2004 disclosure requirements for tax avoidance.
- Understand how the personal allowances and exemptions enable a family to redistribute income and assets to make best use of each member's annual personal allowances and exemptions.
- Understand how appropriate inheritance tax arrangements can help the family retain its wealth when the parents die.
- Explain the basic use of trusts, which allow the donor to specify who will receive the benefit of certain assets but which allows trustees to retain full or partial control of the distribution for a specified period.

Keep it legal

The hallmark of good tax planning is that it will pass the Inland Revenue's scrutiny with flying colours, even where complicated family trust arrangements and considerable wealth are involved. The Revenue distinguishes between different ways taxpayers try to minimise their tax liability. In particular we need to understand and carefully distinguish between the terms **evasion, avoidance** and **mitigation**. Although these tend to be used indiscriminately, their meanings are *very* different.

- **Evasion.** If you deliberately omit something from your tax return, or give a false description, that is evasion. You have not just been dishonest – you have acted criminally and could be fined or imprisoned.
- **Avoidance.** This is on the right side of the law but can include arrangements that use tax loopholes – that is, procedures the Revenue may frown upon but has not yet got around to closing. The Inland Revenue has cracked down on any schemes deliberately established to avoid tax (see below).
- **Mitigation.** If your tax saving has been encouraged by the government – for example you put your investments in an Individual savings account (ISA), or a pension scheme – that is mitigation and it is positively endorsed by the Revenue and the government.

Clearly financial planners should recommend mitigation wherever appropriate. Tax avoidance, however, has become a fraught area in recent years and so it is essential to keep up-to-date with the Inland Revenue's thinking on this important subject. 'Creative' tax planning should be avoided. From the mid-1990s the Revenue has waged an effective war against tax abuse, although until 2004 it had to close down avoidance schemes on a piecemeal basis. In the 2004 Budget the chancellor made it clear that while taxpayers are entitled to take advantage of the law to minimise their tax bill, the creation of devices designed deliberately to avoid tax would no longer be tolerated.

In the 2004 Budget the Revenue was given far-reaching new powers in the form of disclosure requirements that force accountants, lawyers and bankers to submit details of any tax avoidance schemes they sell. Each scheme is given a reference number by the Revenue and taxpayers must include these on the annual tax return. Moreover, tax advisers have to inform the Revenue about all existing schemes on which they advise that were sold after 18 March 2004. Failure to notify results in fines of £5,000, backed up by daily late payment penalties of £600.

Personal tax allowances and exemptions

Successful tax planning requires common sense and expert advice, in equal measures. This means that we should always be clear that the particular use of a tax-favoured arrangement has a genuine benefit. In some cases the cost of setting up and maintaining

Table 19.1 The main personal tax allowances and exemptions for 2005–2006

Income tax allowances	2005–2006 (£)
Personal allowance	4,895
Personal allowance for people aged 65–74	7,090
Personal allowance for people aged 75 and over	7,220
Income limit for age-related allowances	19,500
Married couple's allowance for people born before 6 April 1935	5,905
Married couple's allowance – aged 75 or over	5,975
Minimum amount of married couple's allowance	2,280
Blind person's allowance	1,610

The rate of relief for the continuing married couple's allowance and maintenance relief for people born before 6 April 1935, and for the children's tax credit, is 10%.

Taxable bands 2005–2006 (£)	
Starting rate 10%	0–2,090
Basic rate 22%	2,021–32,400
Higher rate 40%	Over 32,400

	2005–2006
Trusts	40%
Schedule F Trusts	32.5%

The 10% starting rate of Income Tax includes savings income. Where individuals have savings income in excess of the starting rate limit they will be taxed at the lower rate of 20% up to the basic rate limit and at the higher rate of 40% for income above the basic rate limit.

The rates of tax for dividends are 10% for income up to the basic rate limit and 32.5% for income above the basic rate limit.

Source: data from the Inland Revenue.

the arrangement can outweigh any tax savings. All transactions must comply with current tax law and be carefully documented. The taxation of trusts must be considered carefully. In 2003 the government undertook a major consultation on the taxation of family trusts and from April 2004 the special tax rate within a trust rose from 34% to 40%.

There are three main personal allowances and exemptions and these usually rise in line with retail prices inflation each year in the spring Budget. A full set of figures is provided in Table 19.1, but briefly, for the 2004–2005 tax year, each member of a family has:

● The income tax annual personal allowance of £4,895.
● The capital gains tax (CGT) annual exemption of £ 8,500.
● The inheritance tax annual exemption for gifts of £3,000.

Income tax personal allowance

The personal allowance is the amount of income an individual can receive before paying income tax. The source is irrelevant – it can be earned income, investment income and/or income from a pension scheme or plan.

Most families are not tax efficient because their combined wealth – both in terms of earned income and assets – tends to be concentrated in the hands of the main bread-winner. They, therefore, are also responsible for paying most of the tax, usually at the top rate.

One of the best ways to save on income tax is to share income between the spouses to make use of the non-working or lower-earning spouse's allowance. The most common redistribution techniques are to give income-generating assets to the lower-earning spouse and, where an individual runs a business, to pay the spouse a salary. This can lead to an overall annual saving of several thousand pounds. With regard to the salary it is important to be able to justify the payment to the Inland Revenue, and provide evidence that it is actually paid.

It is also possible to give income producing assets to children who can make use of their own allowances and, where necessary, their lower and basic rates of taxation. Here it may be necessary to set up a trust, so that the income is not classed as the parent's (see page 241). Finally on this point, gift of assets must be unconditional otherwise the Revenue will see through the arrangement and continue to tax the individual on the asset's value.

Capital gains tax

The annual exemption of £8,500 for the 2005–2006 tax year is the amount of capital gains an individual can make before paying CGT at the marginal rate of income tax (see Table 19.2). Marginal in this context simply refers to the individual's highest rate. We incur a CGT liability when we make a **chargeable gain** – that is, when we sell an asset and its value has increased since the time of purchase. Remember, CGT is not charged on the asset itself but on its gain in value. The gain is the difference

Table 19.2 Capital Gains Tax: Individuals and Trustees

Annual exempt amount	2005–2006 (£)
Individuals etc*	8,500
Other trustees	4,250

* Individuals, trustees of settlements for the disabled, and personal representatives of the estate of a deceased person.

The amount chargeable to CGT is added onto the top of income liable to income tax for individuals and is charged to CGT at these rates:

- below the starting rate limit at 10%,
- between the starting rate and basic rate limits at 20%,
- and above the basic rate limit at 40%.

CGT indexation allowance: Individuals and others within the charge to capital gains tax are not entitled to indexation allowance for any period after April 1998. To calculate indexation allowance up to April 1998 on disposals on or after 6 April 1998, use the table below. You work out the indexation allowance by multiplying the amount you spent by the indexation factor.

Source: data from the Inland Revenue.

Table 19.3 CGT Indexation allowance

Year	Month Jan	Feb	Mar	Apr	May	Jun	Jul	Aug	Sep	Oct	Nov	Dec
1982			1.047	1.006	0.992	0.987	0.986	0.985	0.987	0.977	0.967	0.971
1983	0.968	0.960	0.956	0.929	0.921	0.917	0.906	0.898	0.889	0.883	0.876	0.871
1984	0.872	0.865	0.859	0.834	0.828	0.823	0.825	0.808	0.804	0.793	0.788	0.789
1985	0.783	0.769	0.752	0.716	0.708	0.704	0.707	0.703	0.704	0.701	0.695	0.693
1986	0.689	0.683	0.681	0.665	0.662	0.663	0.667	0.662	0.654	0.652	0.638	0.632
1987	0.626	0.620	0.616	0.597	0.596	0.596	0.597	0.593	0.588	0.580	0.573	0.574
1988	0.574	0.568	0.562	0.537	0.531	0.525	0.524	0.507	0.500	0.485	0.478	0.474
1989	0.465	0.454	0.448	0.423	0.414	0.409	0.408	0.404	0.395	0.384	0.372	0.369
1990	0.361	0.353	0.339	0.300	0.288	0.283	0.282	0.269	0.258	0.248	0.251	0.252
1991	0.249	0.242	0.237	0.222	0.218	0.213	0.215	0.213	0.208	0.204	0.199	0.198
1992	0.199	0.193	0.189	0.171	0.167	0.167	0.171	0.171	0.166	0.162	0.164	0.168
1993	0.179	0.171	0.167	0.156	0.152	0.153	0.156	0.151	0.146	0.147	0.148	0.146
1994	0.151	0.144	0.141	0.128	0.124	0.124	0.129	0.124	0.121	0.120	0.119	0.114
1995	0.114	0.107	0.102	0.091	0.087	0.085	0.091	0.085	0.080	0.085	0.085	0.079
1996	0.083	0.078	0.073	0.066	0.063	0.063	0.067	0.062	0.057	0.057	0.057	0.053
1997	0.053	0.049	0.046	0.040	0.036	0.032	0.032	0.026	0.021	0.019	0.019	0.016
1998	0.019	0.014	0.011									

Source: data from the Inland Revenue.

between the original price and the selling price after making an adjustment for inflation, known as the **indexation allowance** (see Table 19.3). This allowance applies up to April 1998, after which **taper relief** applies. Taper relief reduces the rate of CGT according to how long the individual has held the asset.

It is also possible to crystallise a capital loss if an individual sells an asset that has lost value since purchase. Here the loss can be offset against gains in the current tax year or it can be rolled over for use in future tax years.

As gifts between spouses are exempt from CGT the tax-efficient couple should consider sharing assets to make use of both exemptions. Until the March 1998 Budget it was possible to **bed and breakfast** shares. This involved selling shares to realise the capital gain and to make use of the annual allowance. The following day the seller bought back the same number of shares. In the absence of B&B it might be worth considering a **bed and spouse** arrangement, where one spouse repurchases the shares the other sells. The shares must be sold and repurchased – they cannot be transferred directly.

Clearly there is a danger during volatile markets that the share price might rise in the interval between sale and repurchase. However, the overall objective for those with large shareholdings is to realise capital gains at regular intervals to keep the CGT bill within the annual exemption.

CGT and shares

In practice most investors manage to avoid capital gains tax without making any special arrangements, simply because their liability regularly falls within the annual

CGT exemption. Investors who receive 'windfall' shares when a life assurance society or building society converts from a mutual to plc status (demutualisation) should bear in mind that the proceeds of any sales will be classed as a pure capital gain unless they are held in a tax-exempt investment such as an Individual savings account (ISA).

●●●● Inheritance tax planning

When a person dies their estate is liable to inheritance tax (IHT) on anything over the nil-rate band (£275,000 for the 2005–2006 tax year). This is a tax on individual wealth at death and is deducted from the estate before it can be passed on to the heirs. There is no IHT liability on assets left to a spouse, but once they die, then the value of the estate in excess of the exemption is taxable. This means that leaving everything to a spouse loses the opportunity to use the nil-rate band, so tax practitioners often recommend that assets up to the level of the nil-rate band should be passed on to children on the first death, for example, or that a trust is set up to this effect (see below).

There are several ways to mitigate an inheritance tax bill but the allowances are not inflation linked, so their value today is very modest. Each year it is possible to give away up to £3,000, free of CGT. The allowance can be rolled over for one year, so if a couple did not use the allowance it can be added to the current year's figure, giving a total gift option of £12,000 per couple.

In practice there is nothing to stop individuals giving away any amount in excess of this exemption but if they die within seven years the tax assessment is based on when they made the gift and the date of death. A sliding scale of tax rates is used so the longer the period between the two dates the lower the liability. This arrangement, known as a **potentially exempt transfer** (**PET**), may be abolished in a future budget along with other IHT-avoidance measures.

Many parents consider giving their house to their children but in practice this can raise tax complications. If the donor continues to live in the home the Revenue treats it as their own property for IHT purposes. Even where the donor pays a commercial rent there are other problems. For example, the children would be liable to CGT on any gain in the house price between the date of the gift and the date of the eventual sale. Moreover, the donors could find themselves homeless if the children ran into financial difficulties and there was a forced sale of the house.

A simple option for those who anticipate a large IHT liability is to take out a life assurance policy, which will cover the IHT bill on death. Joint life, second death whole of life policies are often used for these purposes (see page 93). The policy should be written in trust for the successors (the children, for example) to make sure the policy itself does not form part of the individual's taxable estate on death.

There are several other useful IHT exemptions. For example, parents can give children £5,000 on marriage, free of any IHT liability, while grandparents can give up to £2,500. One underused exemption is modest gifts from income. These are gifts that are 'normal or habitual' and leave sufficient income for the donor to maintain their standard of living. A good example of this might be where a parent pays the premiums on a life policy for a son or daughter.

Enduring power of attorney

While most people recognise the need to establish a procedure for dealing with their finances when they become very elderly, it is prudent to put in place such arrangements to cover unforeseen events, where an individual might be unable to continue to act rationally. An enduring power of attorney authorises a person or persons of the individual's choice, who will act on their behalf.

Trusts in estate planning

A **trust** is a legal structure that recognises there can be two owners of assets – the **trustees,** of whom there must be at least two and who have legal control of the assets, and the **beneficiaries,** who are entitled to the income and/or capital but only under the terms of the trust. The person who transfers assets to the trust is called the **settlor.**

Trusts are useful in estate planning and it is important to select the most appropriate trust for the purpose, taking into account its tax treatment, the role of the trustees and the ability to dictate the terms under which the beneficiaries receive income and capital. **Interest in possession** or **life interest** trusts allow an individual to receive the income from an asset for life or a fixed period. On death or at the end of the fixed period other nominated individuals have the right to the capital.

Married couples can use **discretionary trusts** to transfer assets up to the value of the nil-rate band on death. The surviving spouse can be included as a beneficiary along with the children. The trustees can pay income and capital to the spouse but when they die the trust does not form part of the estate and instead the capital can go to the children free of IHT.

The important point to remember about trusts is that the trustees have the right to distribute the capital and income – not the beneficiaries. Having said that, trustees should follow the wishes of the settlor where possible. A settlor will often provide a letter of guidance to trustees. When an individual transfers assets into a trust this is treated as a disposal and so there may be a capital gains liability. This can be held over until the trustees sell the asset. The same is also true where assets are transferred from the trust to a beneficiary. (See page 241 for an explanation of **bare trusts** for children.)

Similar to a discretionary trust is an **accumulation and maintenance** trust, which gives parents or grandparents the flexibility to provide funds for the benefit of children. A transfer of assets into this type of trust is classed as a PET and so the donor is not restricted to the nil-rate band.

The taxation of trusts changed in the 2004 Budget when the rate rose from 34% to 40%.

● ● ● ● Domicile and residence

The rules on residence and domicile are complicated and only a snapshot is provided here. The Inland Revenue website is the best source of information for those who want a more detailed guide. The guide IR20 'Resident and non-resident liability to taxation in the United Kingdom' is available at **www.inlandrevenue.gov.uk/pdfs/IR20.pdf**. For chapter and verse you would need to consult the residency manual on the website or a tax reference book, such as the *Zurich Tax Handbook* (details at the end of the chapter).

At the time of writing the government was reviewing the whole area of domicile and residence with regards to taxation and it is important that the student keeps up to date with any developments.

Under our tax system an individual who is resident in the UK is usually taxed on their worldwide income. For tax purposes the UK is classed as England, Scotland, Wales and Northern Ireland, but does not include the Republic of Ireland. Non-residents are taxed on income that arises in the UK but not elsewhere. Residence is determined by the amount of time an individual spends in the UK and applies if the individual is here for six months (183 days) or more during the tax year, and also if they are present for an average of three months (91 days) or more per annum measured over a period of four tax years.

Slightly different tax treatment applies to those who are 'resident but not ordinarily resident'. An individual is ordinarily resident where they come to the UK with the intention of staying for at least three years.

Domicile is particularly complicated and this is the Revenue's key focus for reform as it is possible for individuals who live in the UK but who are not domiciled here to take advantage of very favourable tax concessions. Broadly speaking, domicile is the country that is the individual's permanent home. This has nothing to do with an individual's nationality, citizenship or residence, although these can influence the determination of domicile. All individuals have a domicile of origin. Usually this is the domicile of the father at birth. Until age 16 the individual's 'domicile of dependency' is that of the parent or guardian – that is, the person on whom they are legally dependant. After 16 an individual can change their domicile (domicile of choice) but this is only possible where they move permanently or indefinitely to a new county. This must involve dissolving financial ties with the former home.

To make matters more complicated the Revenue has a term for those who it believes are domiciled in the UK even if they declare otherwise. If individuals are 'deemed domiciled' in the UK this will affect their tax position, particularly with relation to inheritance tax. The idea is to prevent people moving assets out of the country shortly before they die in order to escape the tax net.

Charitable giving

If an individual wishes to give to charity they should ensure this is achieved in a tax-efficient manner. The Charities Aid Foundation (CAF) sets out the following four main options:

- **Gift Aid**: For every £1 given by taxpayers, charities can claim an extra 28p from the Inland Revenue. Donors need only confirm their tax status and address. Using their self-assessment forms, higher rate taxpayers can claim back the additional tax they have paid on a donation, or pass all or part of the tax rebate on to the charity of their choice.
- **Payroll giving**: Donors can give money out of their pre-tax earnings to a church or charity, if their employer or pension provider is registered with a payroll giving agency.
- **Gifts of quoted stocks and shares**: Gifts of shares in any listed companies or units in unit trusts and open ended investment companies (OEICs) are free of capital gains tax and can be offset against the donor's taxable income. For example an employee earning a taxable salary of £50,000 can donate £5,000 worth of shares to charity and pay income tax on £45,000.
- **Legacies**: Donors can pledge a specific sum or assets to charities in their wills, which can reduce the IHT bill on an estate.

Also, from April 2004 taxpayers will be able to donate all or part of a tax repayment from the Inland Revenue to charity via the self-assessment tax return. The list of charities participating in the scheme is available on the Inland Revenue website.

Making a will

For most people, making a will is a simple and cheap exercise, and represents a small price to pay for peace of mind and for the ease and comfort of our family. Yet only one in three adults bothers.

If an individual dies **intestate** – that is, without a valid will – then the laws of intestacy will decide which of their dependants receive the estate. In particular, where young children are involved, the individual would not have the chance to make careful arrangements for their inheritance of capital (this would happen automatically at age 18 under the intestacy rules), and will not have appointed the executors, the trustees and the children's guardians who will oversee their upbringing.

Planners should remember that there are certain events that render it essential to rewrite a will – marriage or remarriage, for example. As a general guide, even if there are no major changes relating to marriage or children, individuals should check their will is up to date every five years.

Making a will does not involve a huge amount of work, unless the individual's finances are very complicated. However, there are certain common mistakes that can be easily avoided. For example, an individual should ensure full disposal of all of their estate, otherwise the result could be partial intestacy. It is also important to make provision for the fact that one of the main beneficiaries may die before the donor. Above all, we must consider the legal rights of dependants. If individuals do not make suitable provision they may be unable to claim their right to a sensible provision under the law. In this context 'children' refers to those born inside and outside marriage, and adopted children, although it does not usually include stepchildren.

The will should also specify any gifts to charities or gifts of assets to particular beneficiaries (for example jewellery to a daughter/granddaughter). The powers of the trustees should also be set out here. There is also scope within the will to establish burial preferences.

It is important that individuals discuss any specific role with an appointed executor or trustee before putting it in writing. These responsibilities can be onerous or may conflict with some other role the individual already performs. Where there are young children, the appointment of willing and responsible guardians is essential.

Finally, if the individual owns any property overseas they should draw up a separate will under the terms of that country, with care to ensure consistency with the UK will.

Executors and trustees

The executor is responsible for collecting the individual's estate and distributing it in accordance with the law. This can include paying any outstanding taxes and dealing with other financial affairs. The executor takes over from the date of death but is not officially appointed until the will is 'proved' and the appointment is confirmed by a grant of probate.

Most people appoint as an executor a spouse or close relative together with a professional – for example a solicitor or accountant. Where the will includes a trust it is helpful if the executor and the trustees are the same people.

Intestacy

To summarise, the main disadvantages of dying intestate are as follows:

- Your estate may not be distributed in accordance with your wishes.
- The appointed administrators may not be people whom you personally would have chosen – or even liked.
- It may take longer for the estate to be distributed, whereas when a will has been made an executor can take up their duties immediately after death occurs.
- The costs may be greater, leaving less to pass on to your beneficiaries.
- Children will receive capital automatically at age 18, whereas you may have preferred this to take place later at a less 'giddy' age. What is more, the family home, where your widow or widower lives, may have to be sold in order to raise the capital.
- A testamentary guardian is not appointed for young children.

- Trusts may arise under intestacy that give rise to complications, including statutory restrictions on the trustees' power to invest and advance capital.

Distribution of an estate under the laws of intestacy

The following details refer to the law in England and Wales. The laws that apply in Northern Ireland and in Scotland differ. 'Issue' refers to children (including those born inside and outside marriage, and adopted), grandchildren and so on. It does not include stepchildren.

If the deceased dies leaving:

- *A spouse but no issue, parent, brother, sister, nephew or niece*: The spouse takes everything.
- *A spouse and issue*: The spouse takes £125,000, personal 'chattels' (car, furniture, pictures, clothing, jewellery etc) plus a life interest – that is, the income only – in half of the residue. The children take half the residue on reaching age 18 or marrying before that age. In addition, on the death of the deceased's spouse, the children take the half residue in which the spouse had a lifetime interest.
- *A spouse, no issue, but parent(s), brother(s), sister(s), nephew(s) or niece(s)*: The spouse takes £200,000, plus personal chattels, plus half the residue. The other half goes to whoever is living in order of preference: parents, but if none, brothers and sisters (nephews and nieces step into their parents' shoes if the parents are dead).
- *No spouse*: Everything goes to, in order (depending on who is still alive): issue, but if none, parents, but if none, brothers and sisters (nephews and nieces step into their parents' shoes). The pecking order then moves on to half brothers and sisters or failing them, their children, but if none, grandparents, but if none, uncles and aunts (cousins step into their parents' shoes), but if none, half uncles and aunts (failing that, their children). If all of these relatives have died then the estate goes to the Crown.

Where part of the residuary estate includes a dwelling house in which the surviving spouse lived at the date of death, the spouse has the right to have the house as part of the absolute interest or towards the capital value of the life interest, where relevant.

Under certain circumstances it is possible for a beneficiary to redirect certain property to another person within two years of the death of the donor.

●●●● Self-assessment

Each year in April the Revenue sends out about 8.8m self-assessment forms to tax-payers. The administration burden for both the Revenue and the individual will reduce if the scheme to allow about 1m people to complete a simplified tax return system takes off in April 2005. Apart from the self-employed, employees required to complete a return in the past will fall into the self-assessment category as will anyone whose tax affairs are even remotely complicated (see below).

Individuals who pay income tax through the pay as you earn (PAYE) deduction at source may not receive a return but should not assume they are automatically exempt. Under self-assessment, the onus is on each person to check and, if necessary, to ask for the right forms.

The basic return, which is now available online, has eight pages but many people need additional pages or 'schedules' for self-employment, employment and capital gains tax, among other aspects. Apart from the website the Inland Revenue has a helpline (0645 000 444) open weekday evenings from 5pm to 10pm, and at weekends from 8am to 10pm.

It is a legal requirement to maintain accurate records to support a tax return. The Revenue selects cases at random for an investigation but will automatically investigate if it suspects an individual has paid the wrong amount. Employed taxpayers should keep all documents for at least 22 months after the tax year to which they relate; for the self-employed this period is five years and 10 months.

Those in the following categories must complete a self-assessment return:

- Self-employed.
- Business partners.
- Company directors.
- Employees or pensioners with more complex affairs (see below).
- Trustee and personal representatives.

'More complex' tax affairs include individuals who:

- Have capital gains in excess of the annual exemption.
- Pay income tax at 40%.
- Received income from more than one source.
- Received a lump sum or compensation payment from their employer.
- Lived abroad for all or part of the tax year in question.
- Wish to claim complicated pension contribution reliefs or tax relief for the more sophisticated investments such as enterprise investment schemes or venture capital trusts.

January 31 is the deadline for filing the main tax return for the previous tax year. So, 31 January 2004 was the deadline for the 2002–2003 tax year. This is also the time when the first instalment is due on account for the 2003–2004 tax year. The Revenue tolerates no excuses; it imposes fines for late payment. In the light of this automatic fine schedule it is essential to get the payments in on time even if a taxpayer is in dispute with the Revenue about the amount.

The January tax bill covers two periods. First, there may be an amount outstanding for the previous tax year. The self-employed will already have paid two instalments for that year – in January and July – so the balance may be modest. There may even be a refund.

Second, it is necessary to pay the January instalment on account for the next tax year. This is calculated as half of the individual's total bill for the previous tax year.

> ## Exhibit 19.1 Key self-assessment dates for the calendar year

Students should remember that the whole system works in advance. This means that taxpayers often pay tax for a year before they have actually calculated the correct assessment – hence the balancing of the books in January.

January 31 2004

1 Last date for filing the 2002–2003 return. This must include the calculation of tax owed. Penalty for failure: £100 (£200 if it is still outstanding by 31 July 2006).

2 Payment of any outstanding tax for 2002–2003. Penalty for failure: interest is charged on a daily basis from 31 January (currently at 9.5% per annum) on any late payment. In addition: 5% surcharge on tax not paid within 28 days; 10% surcharge on tax not paid within 6 months.

3 First payment on account for tax year 2003–2004. Penalty for failure: interest due from 31 January.

April 2004

Self-assessment tax returns for the 2003–2004 tax year issued.

July 31 2004

Second payment on account for 2003–2004. Penalty: interest due from 31 July.

September 30 2004

Submission of tax return for 2003–2004 if the taxpayer would prefer the Inland Revenue to calculate the liability.

January 31 2005

Final deadline to file the 2003–2004 tax return with own computations. Final payment for 2003–2004. First payment on account for 2004–2005.

Taxation and investing for children

As was explained on page 232, children have personal allowances and exemptions in the same way as adults. This means that they can earn income and own assets, using the income tax allowance and CGT exemption in the usual way. However, most parents would baulk at the idea of their children owning valuable assets or capital directly. One of the most commonly used trusts in this area of personal financial planning is the **bare trust**. Where a parent or grandparent invests on behalf of a child a bare trust is created automatically. Under a bare trust the gift is outright and the child has an absolute interest in the income and capital. The trustees allow the investment to be transferred to the child's name when they reach age 18.

Income is classed as the child's as the beneficiary, but if it exceeds £100 a year it will be classed as the parents', if they were the settlors. In the case of grandparents, the income will be taxed as the child's even where it exceeds £100 pa.

IHT may be payable, as the gift is regarded as a potentially exempt transfer (PET) and so a sliding scale of tax will be charged if the settlor dies within seven years.

Child trust funds

The government introduced the Child Trust Fund in 2003 and proposed that it should be paid to every child born after 1 September 2002, although the scheme is unlikely to start before April 2005. At the time of writing this was expected to be a gift of £250 on birth (double this for children in very low-income families, defined in 2004–2005 as less than £13,230 pa and those who receive child tax credit). The government may make an additional payment at age seven. The money will accumulate until age 18, at which time the 'child' will gain access.

The government hopes that parents will invest more in the account to give the child a start in life – towards further education costs, for example. Clearly £350 is a drop in the ocean. Assuming annual growth at 5% this would be worth £770 by age 18. However, a further £1,200 pa can be added by parents, guardians and family friends. There will no tax relief on contributions but the fund will be tax exempt.

Other tax efficient investments for children worth considering and covered elsewhere in this book, include the following, which offer special deals for the under 18s:

- National Savings & Investments (page 119).
- Friendly societies (page 156).
- Personal pensions (page 289).

A planner should always consider the amounts available for investment and where appropriate should recommend a higher risk/reward, equity-based investment, given the long-term nature of many children's savings. A low-cost global investment trust might be a good option here.

Generally the accounts that offer promotional materials based on children's favourite cartoon and fictional characters have comparatively high expenses due to the cost of the promotion material.

Source: The information on making a will is based on Chapter 15 of *The Deloitte & Touche Financial Planning for the Individual*, S. Philips, Gee Publishing, 2002. Sections reproduced are by kind permission of the author.

Activity 19.1

Toby and Wendy are both approaching 65 and plan to retire next year. The family home is worth £400,000, they both have adequate pension provision, and in addition they have £250,000 in a portfolio of investments. They realise that it is timely to consider estate planning.

At present in their wills they leave everything to each other on first death, and on second death the estate is divided equally between their two children, John (44) and Caroline (37), who each have two children in turn. Unfortunately John's elder son Richard is physically disabled and although very bright, will need considerable help if he wishes to go to university when he finishes school. Toby and Wendy would like to help him.

Discuss in broad terms what steps Toby and Wendy might consider immediately and over the coming years to help achieve their objectives.

Summary

This chapter covered a great deal of ground, starting with the personal tax allowances and exemptions, and progressing through inheritance tax planning, domicile and residence, the use of trusts, and concluding with making a will and tax-efficient investing for children. Clearly there is considerable scope for research and learning for the student who wishes to take a closer interest in this subject. We strongly recommend in these cases that students consult the recommended reading below and make full use of the Inland Revenue website.

Key terms

- Accumulation and maintenance trust p. 235
- Avoidance p. 230
- Bare trust p. 235
- Bed and breakfast p. 233
- Bed and spouse p. 233
- Beneficiary p. 235
- Capital gains tax exemption p. 232
- Chargeable gain p. 232
- Child Trust Funds p. 242
- Discretionary trust p. 235
- Enduring power of attorney p. 235
- Evasion p. 230
- Gift aid p. 237
- Gifts of quoted stocks and shares p. 237
- Income tax allowance p. 231
- Indexation allowance p. 233
- Inheritance tax exemption p. 234
- Interest in possession/life interest trust p. 235
- Intestate p. 237
- Legacy p. 237
- Mitigation p. 230
- Payroll giving p. 237
- Potentially exempt transfer (PET) p. 234
- Settlor p. 235
- Taper relief p. 233
- Trust p. 235
- Trustee p. 235

Review questions

1 Explain the difference between tax mitigation, avoidance and evasion. What new powers did the Inland Revenue gain in 2004 to combat avoidance schemes?

2 Suggest two ways an individual might prevent an inheritance tax bill falling on the heirs.

3 What are the four main methods used in charitable giving?

4 Why is it so important that an individual makes a will? What are the consequences of failing to do this?

Go to the Companion Website at **www.booksites.net/harrison_pfp** for a multiple-choice quiz to test your understanding of this chapter.

Further information

A good reference text for personal taxation is *The Zurich Tax Handbook*, A. Foreman, Pearson, Harlow, 2003.

The Inland Revenue: **www.inlandrevenue.gov.uk**

For more information about the Child Trust Fund go to: **www.inlandrevenue.gov.uk/ctf/ index.htm**.

Case study 19.1

Background

Debbie and Peter Jones are both 68 years old, non-smokers and in fair health. They have planned well over the years and retired when they were 65 on a total pension annuity income of £20,000 gross pa and £5,000 net savings income. Their pension and savings income is split equally. Their pension incomes will reduce by half on the first death and increase in line with RPI.

Peter has just received several investments from the estate of his elder brother John, who died in September 2002. These consist of:

- Cash   £100,000
- UK smaller companies OEIC   £16,000
- European smaller companies unit trust   £18,000

The couple own their own bungalow worth £100,000 in Tenby, Wales, and have wills leaving all to each other and then to their only son George.

Problem

Both Debbie and Peter have utilised their 2003/4 capital gains tax exemptions. They wish to invest Peter's inheritance to achieve several objectives.

1 To pay for a lavish party for their ruby wedding anniversary in June 2007 at an estimated cost of £10,000 in today's terms.
2 To invest to increase their net income by £4,000 so they can go on an extra holiday each year in Europe.
3 To invest the remainder aggressively to accumulate the maximum capital lump sum to pass on to George and any future grandchildren.

The expenditure amounts to £16,000 pa. They are very happy with their other limited investments and have an emergency fund held on deposit of £50,000. Peter holds £15,000 nominal of Treasury 10% 2003 gilt.

Case study 19.1 *(continued)*

Advice

Debbie and Peter require help to meet their various objectives whilst keeping overall control of all their money in case they need it for any medical care or wish to change their minds about letting George inherit all if he marries an unsuitable girl. The couple were not expecting this inheritance and live comfortable, active and happy lives so they have a fairly aggressive attitude to risk regarding its investment.

Source: Money Management, Financial Planner of the Year Awards 2003, *FT Business*

An additional case study relevant to this chapter is available from the Companion Website at **www.booksites.net/harrison_pfp**.

A full solution to this case study is available to lecturers via the password-protection area of the Companion Website at **www.booksites.net/harrison_pfp**.

Chapter 20 ●●●●

Education fee planning

Introduction

This chapter considers the costs involved for parents who decide to send their children to private primary and secondary schools, and for all parents whose children go on to university. Education fee plans should not be considered in isolation but should be fully integrated with the main financial plan. What is required is a clear understanding of the costs, and a schedule for when the fees fall due. The objective is to achieve an appropriate cash flow schedule, backed by a range of suitable investments. Insurance is important but once again this should be seen in the context of the overall financial plan.

Objectives

After reading this chapter you will be able to:

- Research specific school fee and further education costs using the Internet.
- Suggest a series of short-, medium-, and long-term savings and investments that can be used to generate the fees when they fall due.
- Consider insurance in the context of the overall financial plan rather than as a separate item.

The importance of education fee planning

An increasing number of parents send their children to fee-charging independent schools. The reasons for doing so vary. In many cases the parents are seeking academic excellence and the benefits of smaller classes. Parents may have views on the 'traditional' or religious values upheld by certain schools, or a child may have special needs or a particular talent that would flourish under more focused guidance. Whatever the reasons, sending children to public school is a major financial commitment and should not be undertaken lightly. Education advisers stress that a child who begins their school career in private education may find it difficult to adapt to a move to a state school, although a move from state to private can be an easier transition.

State school admissions

If parents cannot afford to pay for private schooling out of income and capital, and yet are concerned about the standard of local state schools, one option is to move to an area with a better reputation. Living in a catchment area is no guarantee of a place, however, but it will certainly help unless the eligibility rules change significantly.

For parents considering this step it is sensible first to check the school's admissions policy before making a move. By law parents have the right to apply to any school, but where a school is very popular – and state schools with a good academic reputation are always oversubscribed – the school's admission priorities will place brothers and sisters of existing pupils, and the children of staff, above children of the local catchment area. Some state schools base admission on academic excellence, others on language abilities, and yet others on church attendance. The admission rules are set out clearly in a prospectus, which each school must provide free on request.

What does private education cost?

The best centralised source of information on independent schools is the Independent Schools Council Information Service (ISCIS) website and handbook (details provided at the end of the chapter). However, while ISCIS is strong on school research, it is weak on financial advice. Its handbook lists a very small number of advisers who can offer school fees plans and a limited number of companies that offer dedicated insurance products. ISCIS, to its credit, states that inclusion of these details is not a recommendation, but parents should be aware that any experienced financial planner will take education fee planning into account within the main plan – not as a discrete feature. Insurance company school fee plans – especially those that involve with profits endowments – should be viewed with caution, as the structure can be unnecessarily complex and the asset management unsatisfactory. Having said that, for most parents who want private schooling for their children, planning ahead in a constructive way for fees is essential and that means starting well ahead of the date the child is expected to start. School fees vary considerably but at the time of writing, secondary schools charged between £2,500 and £4,000 per term, and for full boarding parents should expect to pay anything from £3,500 to £6,000.

Fees are usually payable in advance, although some schools operate a monthly payment system. Typically fees increase at about 5% per annum, which is greater than retail prices. Parents should find out about the cost of the uniform (this can be substantial), extra-curricula activities, and any other payments – for example, for examinations, meals and school trips. ISCIS suggests all of this could add up to 10% to your bill.

In practice most parents aim to pay the fees from a mixture of earned income and savings. Grandparents often contribute and an injection of capital can be a very welcome boost. Many senior schools, and a few junior schools, offer scholarships to particularly bright children, although these rarely cover the full costs. Further financial help may be offered through a bursary, which is a grant from the school to help with the fees. These details are provided in the ISCIS handbook.

How to meet the costs

As stated at the beginning of this chapter, successful planning for school fees requires good cash flow management backed by a range of suitable investments. To construct the right portfolio of investments for the parents' circumstances the planner needs a clear idea of what the fees will be and how many years there are between the initial investment and the date the payments start. This will establish the length of the accrual and drawdown periods.

On top of this we need to factor in school fees inflation, salary inflation (if the individual intends to fund partly from income) and a sensible annual investment return. If the parents have some capital to invest at the outset and/or are prepared to pay part of the fees from income, this will reduce the level of savings required. As mentioned, we should avoid or at least be wary of ready-made packages that invest mainly or wholly in insurance company products. Like endowment mortgages, these cannot offer guarantees but can only target the capital sums required. Parents should also avoid plans and trusts that are linked to particular schools, as these may prove inflexible if the child does not pass the relevant entry examinations or prefers to go elsewhere.

Which investments?

The parents' attitude to risk and tax status will help define the asset allocation and the choice of particular funds, as will the timeframe. The last point is important because whichever investments are selected, the planner must cater for phased encashment to pay the fees when they fall due.

Where there is a family trust this might also be an appropriate source of income. Here the trustees may be able to release capital or income to help cover the costs.

If grandparents are keen to help they might set up an accumulation and maintenance trust for their grandchildren's education fees, or alternatively transfer assets to a bare trust, which could be administered by the parents, for example. Trusts are examined in chapter 19.

Parents should also consider additional insurance, where necessary, to cover the cost of education fees if one or both die or become disabled and can no longer save. However, this is better dealt with in the overall context of the family's assets and liabilities, rather than as a separate 'school fees protection' policy, which is likely to be a packaged combination of life assurance and critical illness insurance, for example. See Chapter 7 for protection insurance.

Entry requirements

For secondary schools, money alone will not buy a place. Most independent schools require prospective pupils to pass the Common Entrance Examination, which is usually taken at age 11, 12 or 13. Although the exam is set centrally, the papers are marked by the school to which you apply, and each school has its own pass mark to ensure applicants will be able to cope with its specific academic standard.

The scope of the Common Entrance Exam is broadly in line with the national curriculum. However, independent preparatory schools spend the last two years preparing pupils for the exam, so clearly this gives children from independent schools a head start. If a child attends a state junior school, parents should find out if there are specific subjects covered, where private coaching would help their child to pass.

Before parents begin their search they should consider the following points to narrow down the choice:

- Day or boarding.
- Senior, junior or both.
- Single sex or co-educational.
- Academic or special requirements.
- Religious requirements.

Tertiary education

Even where parents are able to find good state schools for their children's primary and secondary education, the costs of tertiary or further education have risen dramatically in recent years. At the time of writing a year at university would cost about £7,000, including the student's contribution towards fees.

Students can borrow most of this through the Student Loan Company. The interest rates on the loan are preferential and repayments are not required until the April after the student has finished college, provided they earn at least £15,000 a year.

University fees are a political hot potato and very much on the front line of any election campaign. It is important to keep up to date with any changes the government plans to introduce. For the 2004–2005 academic year the government introduced a range of changes to the financial support for students. Details are available at the Department for Education and Skills website at **www.dfes.gov.uk/studentsupport**. There is also a new interactive online service, including an application form and entitlement calculator, at **www.studentfinancedirect.co.uk**. The Local Education Authority (LEA) provides details of financial support on its website.

The costs in detail

At the time of writing, the government paid for about three-quarters of the bill for fees. Typically, a full-time course would cost about £4,000 a year and the government puts about £3,000 towards it. That leaves two aspects to fund:

- The student's contribution to tuition fees; and
- Living costs.

The local education authority (LEA) handles the applications for tuition fee support, student loans and supplementary grants. The relevant LEA telephone number can be found in the phone book under the local council. The LEA booklet 'Financial support for students' is a useful guide.

As soon as the student has an offer of a place at college or university – even if this is only conditional – it is important that they apply to the local education authority for help with fees and for a living cost loan. Even where parents do not expect to qualify for a loan they should still make their application, otherwise the student may lose the right to any help with tuition fees.

Tuition fees have to be paid for each year or term up front. Most colleges accept the fees in instalments. Scottish students do not have to pay for their fees in their fourth year at university if the degree course is the equivalent of a three-year course in other parts of the UK.

Living costs loans

Depending on the individual's circumstances it is possible to apply for three types of financial support to cover living costs:

- Loans.
- Supplementary grants for students in particular circumstances.
- Access to Learning Fund.

These loans are offered on an annual basis so it is necessary to reapply each year. Again, the first port of call is the LEA. Student loans are available to help meet living costs while studying. Interest is pegged to the rate of inflation, so this is a cheaper source of borrowing than the commercial banks or other lenders. The LEA will explain the maximum loan to which the student is entitled and ask how much of this maximum is required. Students should inform the Student Loans Company (SLC) on what has been agreed. The SLC is responsible for actually transferring the money into the student's account at the beginning of each term.

Most students will automatically qualify for about three quarters of the maximum loan. The remaining quarter is means tested.

The size of the loan depends on several factors, including where the student lives and where they intend to go to college, the type and length of course, and the family's contribution. Table 20.1 shows the maximum basic loans for 2004–2005. The loan is lower in the final year of study because it does not cover the summer holiday.

Table 20.1 Summary of loans

The maximum amount of loan available in 2004–2005 is:

£4,095 for students living away from home.
£5,050 for students in London and living away from home.
£3,240 for students living at home.

Notes: 'London' refers to the area covered by the City of London and the Metropolitan Police District. Outside this area, students qualify for the standard rate. If the student studies abroad for eight or more weeks in a row during any academic year as a compulsory part of the course, they may be eligible for a higher loan. If the course lasts longer than the standard 38 weeks the student may be able to get an additional means tested loan to cover each additional academic week. Seventy-five per cent of the maximum loan is available to all eligible students regardless of any other income they have. The remaining 25% depends on the student's income and that of their family. This will be assessed by the LEA. The loan is repayable once the student leaves and starts earning in excess of £15,000.
Source: DfES.

Additional grants and loans

There are additional sources of means tested support for those in particularly difficult circumstances or who are disabled. Information about these is supplied by the LEA.

● ● ● ● Changes for university students from 2004 to 2005

In 2004–2005 the maximum amount that any student will be asked to contribute towards his or her fees is £1,150. Most students will be asked to contribute less than this depending on their household income.

New students from September 2004 may be eligible for the Higher Education Grant. This annual grant is to help with the costs of living and studying. The amount of help a student receives will depend on the individual's or the household income. This grant does not have to be repaid.

The Higher Education grant will be worth up to £1,000 a year but is means tested. If the family income is £15,200 or less, the student will be entitled to the full amount of grant. If the income is between £15,201 and £21,185, the student will receive part of the grant. If the income is over £21,185, the student will not be eligible.

Table 20.2 shows the level of Higher Education (HE) Grant you could receive. If your household income is in between the amounts shown, you will receive a different amount of grant.

Table 20.2 Eligibility for the Higher Education Grant

Household income	Amount of HE Grant
£0–£15,200	£1,000
£16,000	£873
£17,000	£715
£18,000	£556
£19,000	£397
£20,000	£238
£21,185	£50

Source: DfES.

Exhibit 20.1 Department for Education and Skills timetable for university fees application

1 Get an application form from the LEA. For new students this is called a PN1. For continuing students it is called a PR1. If they have not sent your child a form you should contact them to get one. A list of LEA contact details is on Student Finance Direct website at **www.student financedirect.co.uk**. This form will also ask your child to say whether he or she wishes to take out a student loan.

2 The LEA will inform the student whether they are eligible to receive help and if so, how much. It will also inform parents if they are expected to contribute towards fees and living costs. Payments are normally made at the start of the term.

3 The DfES strongly recommends that if the student needs the first instalment of financial support to be available at the start of term, they should return the application form as soon as possible. They can apply from the March before the start of the academic year and no later than the beginning of July (new students) or the end of May (current students). Late applications may result in late payments. Remember to read 'Financial Support for Higher Education Students' available from the LEA or from Student Finance Direct online.

Activity 20.1

Assume that parents want to save in order to send their five-year-old son to an independent secondary school at age 11, and to university at age 18. They do not want him to build up any student debt.

Comment: Use the figures provided in this chapter and on the websites above to estimate the total cost to the parents. Explain which figures you are using for secondary and university education and what factors you have assumed for inflation and investment returns, among others. With reference to earlier chapters in this book, suggest the types of savings and investment vehicles that might be appropriate

Summary

This chapter quantified the costs involved in sending a child to an independent school and to university. It examined how best to structure the investments that might fund part or all of the fees, taking into account the length of the potential investment period and the drawdown period, during which fees fall due.

Review questions

1 What are the key factors to consider in order to ensure fees can be paid?

2 Would you advise a parent to take out a dedicated school fees plan?

3 What changes are taking place in further education funding in the 2004–2005 academic year?

Go to the Companion Website at **www.booksites.net/harrison_pfp** for a multiple-choice quiz to test your understanding of this chapter.

Further information

Department for Education and Skills (DfES): **www.dfes.gov.uk/studentsupport**

The DfES online service, including an application form and entitlement calculator: **www.studentfinancedirect.co.uk**

Independent Schools Council Information Service (ISCIS): **www.iscis.uk.net**

National Union of Students: **www.nus.org.uk**

Case study 20.1

Background

Debbie and Martin Arthur, aged 50 and 53 respectively, are both non-smokers and in good health. Debbie works part time as a legal secretary and earns £14,000 pa. Martin works full time as a civil engineer and earns £31,200 pa. They have the following assets and liabilities.

Their repayment mortgage should finish in 12 years' time. Their current total annual expenditure is approximately £40,500 pa, which includes the additional costs of books, outward bound courses and hobbies for their two children, who attend the local state school. Their eldest child, Steven, has just applied for a job as an insurance clerk and does not wish to enter further education. Eric, however, has just started his A levels and wishes to continue to university to study history. The family takes annual holidays costing in the region of £2,800 pa. The cost of these holidays is taken from capital saved in their bank account. They were advised to make wills by a previous financial adviser in January 2000 but have not done so.

Case study 20.1 (*continued*)

Problem

The couple have an annual income deficit and are worried about paying off their credit card bills. At the moment they pay the minimum monthly amount of 5% of the balance. The couple would like to review their mix of assets to ensure that their income deficit is covered. They would like to give a lump sum of £25,000 in today's terms to each child when they reach age 25. Steven has just reached his 18th birthday and Eric is 16. The couple would also like to ensure that they have sufficient funds to help Eric with his further education. They anticipate he would need approximately £3,000 pa (for a three-year course). They wish to pass the remainder of their estate on to their children when the last partner dies but nothing in the meantime other than that already detailed. The couple pay 10% of their salaries towards their retirement provision and are happy that when they retire, the accumulated capital will be sufficient to meet their income requirements. They intend to retire when Martin reaches 60. No details of their retirement provision have been provided and they do not wish to be advised on this area. The couple describe themselves as having a realistic attitude to investment risk, realising that they may have to take limited equity risk in order to achieve their desired objectives. Debbie has indicated that she is more cautious than Martin.

Advice

You are asked to advise Debbie and Martin about their various objectives. They would like you to explain all the options available clearly and give clear reasons for any recommendations made. They are happy to utilise all their assets to ensure their various objectives are met, particularly the lump sum gifts.

Source: *Money Management*, Financial Planner of the Year Awards 2003, *FT Business*

A full solution to this case study is available to lecturers via the password-protected area of the Companion Website at **www.booksites.net/harrison_pfp**.

Chapter 21 ●●●●

State pensions

Introduction

Investing for retirement through pension schemes and plans is one of the most important areas of financial planning. There are three main sources of pensions: the state, occupational schemes and individual plans. In addition many people build up separate savings for retirement through Individual savings accounts (ISAs), for example, which are not bound by the pension rules and are therefore more flexible if slightly less tax efficient.

This chapter examines the state schemes and in the two following chapters we look at occupational schemes and individual plans. Chapter 24 explores how these investments can be used at retirement to generate the required income and, where appropriate, to plan for inheritance.

Objectives

After reading this chapter you will be able to:

- Explain how the basic state pension works and where to find further information.
- Understand how the second tier of the state pension operates and the eligibility rules.
- Discuss why state pensions for women in particular are so complicated.
- Debate the problems associated with a means-tested top-up to the basic pension.
- Find your way around the Department for Work and Pensions website sections.

The framework for state pensions

Despite the comparatively low level of the state pension when compared with social security pensions in other European countries, for many people this still forms an important element of their overall retirement income. It is helpful, therefore, to understand how the state pension is earned and how it relates to private schemes and plans. The system is extremely complicated partly because of the sheer scale of the benefits system and partly because successive governments have changed benefit levels and in some cases the entire structure, particularly with relation to the second tier pension.

The state pension has two elements – a flat rate pension, known as the **Basic state pension (BSP)**, and the **Additional pension** – a pension that is currently linked to earnings and is also known as the **State second pension** or **S2P**. The State second pension was introduced in April 2002 and replaced SERPS (State earnings related pension scheme), which began in 1978. Members of SERPS retain their rights built up to that date.

Eligibility to both state pensions is built up through the compulsory payment of **National insurance contributions (NICs)**, which are levied on employee and employer earnings. Purists might argue the point but in practice NICs can be regarded as another form of direct taxation on earnings from employment and self-employment.

The DWP website lists all of the current rates for NICs and pension benefits. The maximum single person's basic state pension for the 2005–2006 tax year is £82.05 per week, while the maximum additional or SERPS pension is about £143 per week. It is too early to quote relevant figures for S2P. State pensions rise each year in line with retail prices, are taxed as earned income and should be included in the end of year tax return.

Equal pension ages

The official pension age – currently 65 for men and 60 for women – is the minimum age at which men and women can claim a state pension in the UK. By the year 2020 the UK will have a common pension age of 65 for both men and women. This move to equal pension ages will result in a rather complex phasing period. Women born after 6 April 1950 will retire at a later age than 60, while women born after April 1955 will have to wait until age 65 to claim. There is a ready-reckoner for precise details provided with The Pension Service guide 'Pensions for Women'. The phasing period will last 10 years, between 2010 and 2020.

National insurance contribution record

Many people assume, mistakenly, that they will qualify automatically for the full BSP if they have worked for about 40 years before retiring. This is not the case.

The pension is based on the entire working life, which starts at 16. The career pattern of the vast majority of people is interrupted by further education, periods of unemployment, periods spent not working in order to raise a family, and a whole host of other variables, so they may have to be in work for longer than 40 years from the starting date.

State pensions come under the general heading of 'social security benefits', which also include benefits paid to people who are sick, disabled, out of work or on a very low income. Eligibility to benefits relates to the individual's NIC record, and in some cases will be means tested. National insurance for employees is levied at 11% on what are known as **band earnings**; that is earnings between the **primary threshold** and the **upper earnings limit**. These are £94 and £630 per week for the 2004–2005 tax year. (There is also a **lower earnings limit** of £82, which used to be the starting threshold for payment.) Employees also pay 1% on earnings above the upper threshold. The contributions are deducted automatically from an employee's pay packet while the self-employed pay a flat rate contribution each month to the Department for Work and Pensions, and an earnings-related supplement, which is assessed annually through the tax return. Employers pay a slightly higher rate at 12.8% on all earnings above the lower threshold.

The 'married woman's stamp'

State pensions for older women are particularly complicated due to a two-tier National insurance contribution system which still allows those who were married or widowed before 5 April 1977 to pay a reduced rate, known as the 'married woman's stamp'. This is 4.85% of earnings between the primary threshold and upper earnings limit, plus 1% for earnings above the latter. The married woman's stamp originally was popular because it meant a much lower deduction from the weekly or monthly pay cheque. However, women who pay this rate do not build up a right to a basic state pension in their own name. Instead they can claim through their husband's NIC record for a 'Category B' state pension, which is worth about 60% of the full rate.

Eligibility for the basic state pension

To get the full weekly rate of the BSP, worth £82.05 in 2005–2006, an individual must have 'qualifying years' for about 90% of their working life – broadly speaking that is tax years in which they paid the full rate of NIC for the complete period. Part years do not count but it is possible to pay voluntary contributions to make them complete. To get the minimum basic pension payable (25% of the full rate) normally an individual needs a minimum of 10 or 11 qualifying years.

Those in receipt of certain benefits are treated as though they had paid NICs. This applies to those who receive sickness benefit or who cannot work because they care for a disabled relative, for example.

Deferment of claim

It is not possible to claim the state pension before the official pension age but it is possible to defer claiming for up to five years and earn increments of about 7.5% for each year of delay. From 2005 at the earliest it will be possible to defer the BSP indefinitely and the annual rate of increase for deferment will be 10.4%.

Married couple's pension

The combination of the single person's BSP (£82.05) and the spouse's pension (Category B £49.15) together represent what is known as the married couple's state pension, which is worth about £131.20 for the 2005–2006 tax year.

The pension credit

The government offers a range of benefits to provide extra support to very low-income pensioners. Until October 2003 it provided the **minimum income guarantee (MIG)**, paid through Income Support, which topped up the basic pension to £102.10 in that year for those who qualified. Any private pension income would reduce the amount of the top-up pound for pound, leaving those with private pensions of between £10 and £20 per week in the same position as if they had no private pension income. Clearly this gave low-income groups very little incentive to save modest amounts in pension arrangements.

The **pension credit** replaced the MIG in October 2003 and is means tested, although over 70% of pensioners are eligible. For 2005–2006 the DWP said that a single person with a weekly income less than £109.45 would be eligible for an element of the credit, as would a married couple with a weekly income under £167.05.

The offset for those who have private pensions is 40p in the pound rather than pound for pound. The credit aims to reward pensioners who have small private pension plans and/or occupational pensions by allowing them to claim means-tested help higher up the income scale.

There is still a great deal of confusion about the impact of the pension credit. Organisations as diverse as the Association of British Insurers (ABI) and the Institute of Fiscal Studies have argued that the credit still acts as a disincentive for low-income families to save and that it is still an unfair penalty on those with very modest private pensions.

BSP and occupational pension schemes

Integrated company schemes are very common. Under this system, the level of pension promised by the company scheme makes an allowance for the basic state pension. Effectively this means that the employer does not provide any pension for earnings up to the lower earnings limit or a multiple of this. Low earners and those who do not qualify for a state pension in their own right are the groups most affected by this practice. In these cases, the spouse might consider paying a contribution to a Stakeholder scheme for the lower earning partner (see page 289).

Additional pension (SERPS)

Those who retired before April 2002 will not be affected by the replacement of SERPS with the State second pension. Those who retire after this date may build up benefits under both schemes, which will make the calculation of expected income almost impossible for the layperson, and indeed for the financial planner. SERPS is worth a maximum of about £143 and is paid at the same time as the Basic pension, that is, at age 65 for men, and between age 60 and 65 for women depending on their official state pension age.

Employees who were not contracted out of SERPS, either through a company pension scheme or an 'appropriate' personal pension plan, would automatically have been a member and earned a right to the pension through their NICs.

The value of the pension depends on the level of the individual's earnings and the contribution period. It will also depend on when the individual reaches pension age because the government reduced SERPS for those who retired after 5 April 1999. This, combined with the planned phased increase in women's pension age from 60 to 65, which commences in 2010, makes the calculation of the additional pension an extremely complicated exercise.

How SERPS is calculated

Broadly, the SERPS pension will be worth 25% of an individual's National insurance band earnings averaged over the period 6 April 1978 to 6 April 1999. For benefits built up after this date but before April 2002, the formula is reduced over a 10-year period from 25% to 20% of band earnings averaged over the individual's entire working life. Note that the SERPS calculation refers to band earnings – that is earnings between the lower and upper earnings limit rather than commencing with the primary threshold.

Where individuals are members of a company pension scheme that was contracted out of SERPS or had an 'appropriate' personal pension used for contracting out on an individual basis, their additional pension would be replaced by the private scheme or plan.

'Inherited' SERPS

In October 2002 a new rule came into force that reduced the maximum amount of SERPS pension from 100% to 50% a widow or widower could inherit on the death of the spouse. This reduction does not affect anyone who was widowed before this date or whose husband/wife reached retirement age before this date.

The State second pension (S2P)

The State second pension or S2P is intended to offer a more generous benefit for low earners, certain carers of invalids and the elderly, and people with a long-term disability. At the time of writing S2P was an earnings-related benefit but it is expected to convert to a flat rate benefit in due course.

Although it is not yet compulsory, all earners who do not fall into the above categories will be encouraged to opt out of the S2P and use the rebate of NICs to start a private pension scheme or plan.

Pension forecasts

The calculation of the pension is undoubtedly complicated. The first step for individuals who want to find out what they can expect from the state scheme is to ask the Department for Work and Pensions for a pension forecast (form BR19 – also available online). This should provide a fairly intelligible explanation of the entitlement. It is possible to get a pension forecast provided the individual has more than four months to go to pensionable age. Each forecast takes between three and six weeks to process, longer if you are widowed or divorced, where the assessment will be more complicated.

Appeals

Given the complexity of the state pension system it is not surprising that from time to time the DWP makes a mistake in the calculation of benefits. Those who suspect an error in their social security benefit and are unsatisfied with the decision that was made by the adjudication officer or adjudicating medical authority, can request a review or make an appeal. The DWP leaflet 'If you think a decision is wrong' sets out the process.

Summary

This chapter looked at how the state pensions work and the eligibility rules. While planners would not be expected to be able to make complex calculations based on opaque DWP formulae, it is important to keep up to date with the main benefits rates and know how to request more detailed information.

Key terms

- Additional pension p. 258
- Band earnings p. 259
- Basic state pension (BSP) p. 258
- Integration p. 260
- Lower earnings limit p. 259
- Married woman's stamp p. 259
- Minimum income guarantee (MIG) p. 260
- National insurance contributions (NICs) p. 258
- Pension credit p. 260
- Primary threshold p. 259
- State earnings related pension scheme (SERPS) p. 258
- State second pension (S2P) p. 258
- Upper earnings limit p. 259

Review questions

1 Explain how eligibility to the basic pension and to SERPS and S2P is built up.

2 What is a qualifying year and how many do you need for the BSP?

3 What are the deferment rules for those who wish to delay drawing their state pension?

4 Give three examples of why state pensions are so complex for women.

Go to the Companion Website at www.booksites.net/harrison_pfp for a multiple-choice quiz to test your understanding of this chapter.

Further information

Citizens' Advice Bureaux: www.nacab.org.uk

The Pension Service (part of the Department for Work and Pensions): www.thepensionservice. gov.uk; the DWP's 'Pensionguide' website provides information to help individuals plan for retirement: www.pensionguide.gov.uk. Students who wish to specialise in social security benefits and welfare should also consult the section of the main site dedicated to advisers at www.dwp.gov.uk.

Chapter 22

Defined benefit occupational pension schemes

Introduction

The entire tax regime for occupational and private pensions changes on 6 April 2006 (A-Day). The new tax rules are not retrospective and so for the period leading up to A-Day and for a good while afterwards planners will need to understand both regimes (well, the new regime and the previous eight in fact). This chapter and the next examines the pre-A-Day regime and looks at planning exercises necessary to avoid losing important tax benefits over the next few years.

Before looking at the structure of occupational schemes it is important that we understand the context in which employers are attempting to deliver these valuable employee benefits today; why these multi-million pound funds ran intro trouble; and the events that led up to the government's decision to introduce the Pension Protection Fund (PPF) in April 2005.

Objectives

After reading this chapter you will be able to:

- Explain why so many pension funds were in crisis in the early years of the 21st century.
- Describe the role of the Pension Protection Fund.
- Debate the significance of the move away from Defined benefit (DB) to Defined contribution (DC) schemes.
- Explain how different types of DB schemes work, including a 'sixtieths' scheme and a 'career average revalued earnings' scheme.
- Explain how DC schemes work and how to achieve optimal results.

The occupational pension scheme 'crisis'

Under **Financial Reporting Standard 17 (FRS17)**, which came into effect between 2001 and 2003, UK companies were required to show changes in the market values of their pension funds as they happened, rather than smoothed over many years, as had been the case previously. The rule hit companies during the worst bear market for decades and the result was sudden shock headlines showing a severe drop in asset value of most of the UK's occupational pension funds. The seriousness of the situation emerged during 2002, when the FTSE 100 companies went from a collective position of virtually no FRS17 deficit at the end of May, to a £60 bn deficit by the end of the year.

This development placed members of Defined benefit (DB) schemes in a very vulnerable position as many employers, hoping to cut benefit costs and keep shareholders happy, started to close their schemes, replacing them with Defined contribution (DC) schemes, which would enable them to contain, and in most cases cut, future costs (see Figures 22.1 and 22.2).

By law the pensions of DB scheme members are guaranteed by the sponsoring employer. Employers have the right to close (**wind up**) a scheme provided they follow the rules laid down by the trust deed. Generally when a scheme is wound up, the assets are sold and the proceeds are used to buy **annuities** from insurance companies to secure members' guaranteed salary-linked retirement income. These annuities pay an immediate income to retired members and provide a future income to those who have not yet reached the retirement age for the scheme.

Until recently an employer could wind up a scheme that was underfunded and therefore unable to pay the promised benefits. This led to a scandal that raged from 2002 to 2004, when thousands of employees lost a substantial chunk of what they thought were guaranteed pensions after working for companies for 30 years and more. In the

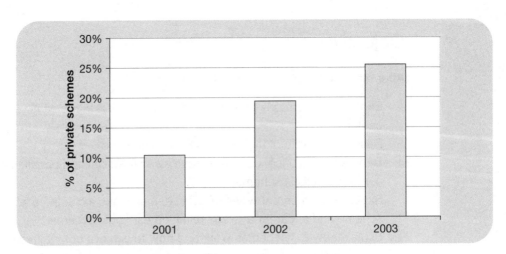

Figure 22.1 Final salary schemes closed to new entrants during the year
Source: National Association of Pension Funds.

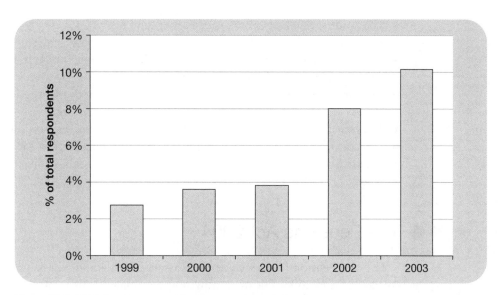

Figure 22.2 DC schemes opened for new members during the year
Source: National Association of Pension Funds.

worst cases the employer became insolvent and the employees also lost their jobs. Understandably they were shocked to discover there was no safety net to protect them.

Employers keen to maintain the solvency of their DB schemes are taking various steps to underpin them. Some have issued bonds as a provision on which they can draw if necessary; almost all doubled contributions in 2004, according to the consultant Watson Wyatt.

The reasons for the serious underfunding position of most DB schemes are legion and in certain cases go back many years. FRS17 quantified the position at a very vulnerable time for pension fund investment. The following factors are particularly relevant:

● The decision of the Conservative government during the 1980s to tax pension fund surpluses. These surpluses are needed for times when stock markets fall, as they did in the late 1990s, and as schemes mature the balance between 'active' members paying contributions shifts in favour of retired members drawing pensions.
● The 1995 Pensions Act forced schemes to provide index-linked pensions (capped at 5% pa). While this was a valuable benefit, by making it compulsory schemes were put under financial pressure. The Act also introduced the now discredited **Minimum Funding Requirement (MFR)**, as a measure of scheme solvency. The MFR was far from adequate, to the extent that a fund that met the requirement on winding up would only be able to pay at most 40%–60% of active members' accrued benefits, and often a lot less. This is partly because the Act insisted that those in retirement should have all of their benefits paid in full, which could wipe out most of the fund, leaving little for those still working.

- The gradual removal of advanced corporation tax (ACT) relief over successive governments significantly reduced the return funds could achieve.
- The use of pension funds by employers in the 1980s and 1990s to fund early retirement as part of mass redundancy programmes.
- **Contribution holidays** on the part of employers, again during the 1980s and 1990s.
- The bear market from 1999 to 2002, and continued low interest rates.
- The cost of annuities, which has gone up due to falling interest rates.
- We are living longer and therefore drawing a greater total income from pension schemes.

The Pensions Act 2004

The new Pensions Act received royal assent in 2004 and will be phased in between April 2005 and 2006. The main provisions, examined below, are:

- The Pension Protection Fund.
- A new Pensions Regulator.
- A new solvency requirement for schemes.
- A change in the priority order for payment of pensions and deferred pensions for schemes in wind up.
- A reduction in the maximum statutory indexation of pensions from the current rate of 5% to 2.5% (or inflation, if lower).

The Pension Protection Fund

From the date of implementation, the Pension Protection Fund (PPF) will pay pensions up to a maximum of £25,000 pa, where an employer becomes insolvent and the scheme cannot afford to pay the promised benefits. This is in addition to the Pension Compensation Scheme, established by the 1995 Act, which steps in where the employer deliberately stole or 'misappropriated' assets from the scheme. The PPF is expected to be funded by a levy on occupational schemes based on the number of members and solvency position.

The background to the PPF is that, briefly, until June 2003 it was perfectly legal for an employer to wind up a scheme provided it met the very inadequate Minimum Funding Requirement (MFR). Several high-profile cases hit the national press and television headlines, highlighting a major flaw in occupational pension scheme law. Maersk, the Danish shipping giant, closed its UK Sea Land pension fund and wound it up in 2002, leaving members with about half of the value of their benefits. Yet Maersk is a profitable company. In June 2003 the government introduced emergency measures that prevent a solvent employer from walking away from its pension promises. Since then employers can only wind up a scheme where it pays for the full **buy-out cost** – that is the full cost of the immediate and deferred annuities.

Similar problems for members arose with companies that went into liquidation with underfunded schemes, like Allied Steel and Wire (ASW), which did just that in July 2002. Shortly afterwards the trustees announced that the two pension schemes that covered the Sheerness and Cardiff plants were being wound up and that the benefits of hundreds of members would be reduced by about 55%.

New solvency measure and regulator

The government and actuarial bodies have argued for a long time over what is an appropriate measure of solvency for company schemes but there was universal condemnation of the MFR, which assumed funds could rely on high equity returns. Under the Pensions Act 2004, MFR is replaced with a **scheme-specific funding requirement,** supported by annual actuarial reports. Another measure of the Act is to replace the current pensions regulator, the Occupational Pensions Regulatory Authority (OPRA) with a more proactive Pensions Regulator.

The priority order on wind up

One of the problems with the 1995 Act was that it insisted that a fund in wind up should be used to secure the full cost of pensions in payment – that is pensions to those who have already retired. Anything left would be divided between those still working. In practice this meant that an individual who had just retired would have the whole of their benefits secured, whereas an employee with 30–40 years' service who is just about to retire might get only 40% of their benefits. This is being changed so that a fairer division of the fund is achieved across all member categories.

Pension tax 'simplification' in April 2006

On 6 April 2006 (**A-Day**) the government will introduce a new 'simplified' tax regime for all private occupational and personal plans. When considering the importance of this radical overhaul to the pensions tax regime, we must remember that it is not retrospective. This means that DB pension rights and DC funds built up before A-Day will remain.

The new regime includes the following features:

- A single tax regime; the eight existing tax regimes for occupational and individual pension arrangements are reduced to one.
- Simpler guidelines for maximum contributions: there will be an annual ceiling on tax-favoured contributions of 100% of earnings up to a ceiling, initially set at £215,000.
- The **lifetime allowance**. Maximum benefits will be calculated over the entire career and tax-favoured treatment will only apply to those that do not to exceed the lifetime allowance, which is set at £1.5m for the 2006–2007 tax-year.

Any pension funds in excess of this limit will suffer a tax charge of 55% (known as the **lifetime allowance charge**), although it is possible to protect larger funds built up before A-Day. To assess the impact, members of DB schemes, where the pension is expressed as a proportion of the salary at or near retirement, should multiply their accrued pension by 20, to convert it to a monetary fund. A final salary pension worth £75,000 pa, therefore, is equal to the £1.5m cap.

For the vast majority of people, pension tax simplification will do as the name suggests. However, for about 5% of the working population at the top end of the earnings scale, adapting to the new regime will require detailed planning. In the following sections we examine the rules in force until April 2006, and we then look at planning issues for those with substantial accrued benefits and/or high earnings.

Introduction to company pension schemes

For many employees membership of the company pension scheme represents the most important benefit after the salary itself.

Company schemes are tax efficient in the following ways:

- The employer's contributions are tax deductible.
- The employee's contributions are paid free of basic and higher rate tax.
- The pension fund builds up virtually free of tax; and
- A significant chunk of the final benefits – typically 25% – can be taken as tax-free cash at retirement.
- However, the pension, whether drawn from a company scheme or from a life office in the form of an annuity, is subject to the individual's top rate of income tax.

There are two main types of occupational schemes: **Defined benefit (DB)**, also known as 'final salary' (although this is only one type of DB scheme); and **Defined contribution (DC)**, also known as 'money purchase'. For simplicity we refer to these as DB and DC. With a DB scheme the employer bears the investment risk and backs the pension guarantees. With a DC scheme the investment risk falls on the member and there are no guarantees. There are also hybrids between the two. The general trend is away from DB and towards DC.

Stakeholder schemes

These new DC schemes, introduced in April 2001, represent a comparatively low-cost private pension scheme for employees who do not have access to a more traditional company scheme. Those who earn less than £30,000 can pay into both a company scheme and stakeholder scheme. As stakeholder schemes are essentially a group of personal pension plans, we examine them in the next chapter on page 287.

Defined benefit (DB) explained

Defined benefit schemes are still the most prevalent among larger employers in the UK, although in the majority of cases these schemes are now closed to new members. Under a typical DB scheme the member's pension is based on the number of years of membership ('service') and their salary at or near retirement. Again a typical scheme might guarantee to provide a pension that builds up ('accrues') at the rate of one-sixtieth of the member's final salary for each year of service up to an Inland Revenue maximum of forty-sixtieths – that is, two-thirds of final salary at retirement (restricted for some higher earners – see page 277).

While **sixtieths** schemes are still the most common type of DB arrangement, some employers are looking to reduce the cost of DB schemes and yet still retain the salary link, which is highly valued by members. One option is to reduce the rate at which the benefit builds up, so instead of earning one-sixtieth of salary for each year, the member might earn one-eightieth. This would give a maximum pension of half of the member's salary after 40 years rather than the two-thirds achievable with a sixtieths scheme.

Career average revalued earnings (CARE) schemes

Another option that is gaining in popularity is to change the structure of the salary link – for example from final salary to an employee's average salary over their career. DB schemes that link the pension to average salary (career average revalued earnings or 'CARE' schemes) are complicated but have certain attractive features. With this type of scheme each year's benefit is linked to the salary in that year, so that instead of a pension worth, say, 50% of *final* salary, the member might end up with 50% of each year's salary, averaged over their career. To calculate the total pension, each year's salary is increased (revalued) to the date when the member retires. This might be in line with retail prices inflation (RPI) or a lower figure. The overall effect is that the pension will be based on the member's average earnings – revalued in line with inflation – over the period they were in the scheme. Another variation is **cash balance** where the scheme provides a cash amount based on final or average salary and this is used to buy an annuity.

As with most pension arrangements there are winners and losers. Clearly those whose earnings rise rapidly through seniority and promotion will do less well under a CARE scheme than they would under a final salary arrangement. However, some employees will be better off. For example, manual workers who include a lot of overtime in their early career can benefit from a career average earnings formula, as it is easier to take account of a variable earnings pattern. So too can those whose earnings peak mid-career or who actively seek a lower paid and less stressful position in the years preceding retirement.

Multi-employer (industry-wide) schemes

Multi-employer pension schemes are considered a sensible solution to providing good quality pensions via smaller employers, who can benefit from the economies of scale that this arrangement confers. Britain's leading pensions organisation, the National Association of Pension Funds (NAPF), whose members are responsible for running about £600bn in pension scheme assets, is promoting multi-employer occupational schemes in a bid to ensure all employees have access to good quality retirement provision.

The chief target is smaller companies, which often find it difficult to provide adequate pensions, particularly in industries where earnings patterns are fragmented. According to the independent research organisation the Pensions Policy Institute, in 2003 only one in seven companies with less than 50 employees offered a scheme. This is in spite of legislation that requires all companies with five or more staff that do not already provide a scheme to offer access to a stakeholder pension and deduct contributions via the payroll. (A rather controversial aspect of stakeholder legislation is that employers only need to provide a scheme if employees make a request.)

Multi-employer (industry-wide) schemes are not a new concept. One of the biggest schemes in the private sector is the multi-employer Universities Superannuation Scheme and there are also several large multi-employer arrangements that formed after the privatisation of the railways, electricity and water industries, for example. Two particularly innovative schemes operate in the voluntary sector and the building and construction industry. The Pensions Trust, which runs pension schemes for 3,500 charities and voluntary organisations, has a membership of about 105,000. The Building and Civil Engineers' Benefits Scheme (B&CE) is a not for profit organisation that provides pensions and other financial services to about 7,000 employers, through which it has over 220,000 individual policyholders.

Multi-employer schemes have the potential to provide much more than retirement pensions. An efficient contribution collection facility allows providers to distribute other important benefits at attractive prices.

●●●● Contributions to company schemes pre-April 2006

Under the rules that apply until April 2006, employees can contribute up to 15% of gross pay to an occupational scheme. The most common rate is about 5%–6%, but this is rising in many schemes as both employers and members accept the need to pay higher contributions in order to maintain the stability of the scheme and to prevent closure – see Figure 22.3. 'Pay' in this context is defined as basic salary plus, in some cases, benefits such as overtime, bonuses and the taxable value of fringe benefits. The employer does not pay a fixed contribution but is advised by the scheme actuary to pay whatever is necessary to maintain the scheme's solvency.

Salary exchange or 'sacrifice'

Salary exchange is a way for the employee to improve their pension position without having to increase contributions. Under salary exchange the employee agrees to forego

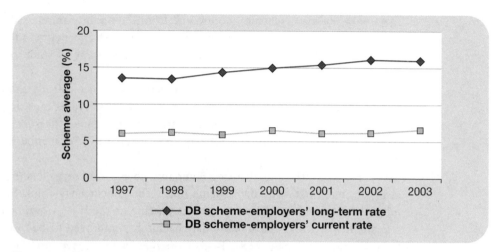

Figure 22.3 Employers' contribution in the private sector

Note: The graph excludes schemes with zero member contributions.

Source: National Association of Pension Funds.

a slice of salary and the employer instead directs this into the pension scheme to improve the level of pension. The employee does not have to pay any tax or NICs on this slice of salary and the employer is able to reduce its NIC bill, or redirect the savings into the scheme as a further boost to the member's benefits. This is a complicated strategy and must be carefully documented. In particular it is important that the employee does not lose out on benefits linked to the level of salary, otherwise the value of important protection insurances, for example death-in-service lump sums and disability pensions, would fall.

Topping up a company pension

By law every scheme, with a few minor exceptions, must provide an **additional voluntary contribution (AVC)** scheme, which allows members to top up their company scheme benefits within the 15% maximum contribution per annum. In most private sector schemes the AVC arrangement would be set up on a DC basis and run by a third party – usually a life office. This means that although the main scheme may provide a pension linked to salary, the AVC scheme would invest the contributions to build up a fund, which, at retirement, is used to buy an annuity from a life office.

The tax attractions are as follows:

● Full tax relief on contributions.
● The fund grows virtually tax free.
● A tax-free cash lump sum may be taken at retirement where the member joined before April 1988. All schemes may pay a cash element from A-Day.
● Where tax-free cash is not available the value of the AVC fund can be used in the tax-free cash calculation for the main pension.

As with the main scheme, the income from the annuity purchased with the AVC fund is taxable. Generally the member would take AVC benefits at the same time as retiring from the company main scheme, although there is some flexibility in the timing.

An important aspect of AVCs is the investment choice. Ideally the AVC provider would offer access to other companies' funds in addition to its own. It is important to check the flexibility of the contribution structure. Some life offices lock members in to regular monthly contributions and may apply a penalty if the member stops or reduces payments.

From April 2001 a member of a company scheme who earns less than £30,000 can also pay in to a stakeholder scheme under the **concurrency** rules. Some employees might be better off using a stakeholder scheme as the top up rather than the AVC scheme. In particular the stakeholder scheme is guaranteed to be low cost and have flexible terms (see page 289). It also provides a tax-free lump sum. Many of the discrepancies between different arrangements will disappear after April 2006.

The rules for taking the proceeds of AVCs are complex and it will depend on when contributions started. After A-Day the rules wll be simplified.

- Where AVC contributions began before 8 April 1987, the whole fund can be taken in cash provided the total cash taken from AVC and main scheme combined are within Revenue limits.
- From 17 March 1987 the Revenue restricted the level of salary on which the tax-free cash calculation was based. The ceiling was £100,000 so that the maximum cash taken from AVC and main scheme pension combined was £150,000 (one and a half times the £100,000 salary limit).
- Where contributions to the AVC scheme started on or after 8 April 1987, the whole of the fund must be taken in the form of pension although its value is taken into consideration when the tax-free cash from the main scheme is calculated.

AVC schemes are provided by the employer. It is also possible for employees to buy an individual top up plan known as a free-standing AVCs (FSAVCs). However, unless the individual is looking for a much wider investment choice, AVCs are likely to be more cost effective as the employer bears some of the running costs, whereas with a FSAVC the individual has to bear the full burden.

In conclusion, AVCs can be attractive in certain circumstances but individuals should bear in mind that the proceeds must be used to buy an annuity. To improve flexibility it makes sense to use a range of investments to supplement the main pension; for example Individual savings accounts (ISAs).

Pension transfers

This is one of the most complex pension issues. Employees who change job after two years' membership in a scheme cannot claim a refund of contributions but instead have three main options:

- Leave the pension where it is. This is known as a preserved or 'deferred' pension since the individual's right to draw the pension from that company scheme is deferred until they reach pension age. By law the value of a deferred pension must increase by retail prices (RPI) up to a cap of 5%. This is known as limited price indexation (LPI). However, LPI is being reduced to 2.5% from April 2005.
- Transfer the benefits to the new company scheme. This has the advantage of keeping all the benefits under one roof, but the individual may not receive the same number of 'years' in the new scheme as they had built up in the old scheme. This is due to the **transfer value (TV)** calculation, which does not have to reflect the full value of the member's benefits. The number of years bought in the new scheme will also be reduced where the individual is gaining a significant salary increase.
- Take a transfer to a personal pension or similar arrangement. In this case the individual would lose valuable salary-linked guarantees but would have more flexibility over the investment of the fund, the level of income drawn, and over inheritance tax planning (see Chapter 23).

The decision will be based on whether the individual is more concerned to preserve the salary-linked benefit or to take control of the investment management. For those with substantial transfer values (TVs), a transfer to a Self-invested personal pension (SIPP) and, at retirement, into **income drawdown** can offer considerable flexibility in the investment of the fund, in the level of pension drawn and in estate planning (see page 310).

Pension 'unlocking'

In recent years the Inland Revenue and FSA have cracked down on the unscrupulous practice of **pension unlocking,** where the individual is persuaded to transfer from a DB scheme into a personal pension in order to receive the tax-free cash early. Usually this would not involve a change of jobs. The advisers who promote this type of scheme take substantial commissions from the proceeds – as they did with the personal pension mis-selling scandal of the late 1980s and early 1990s.

An individual who converts a pension fund into cash and an annuity in their early 50s would receive a very small annuity. The FSA has warned against such schemes, which are only likely to be of benefit where the individual has a serious health condition. In this case an 'impaired life' annuity might offer better value than the company pension scheme. (See Chapter 24 on annuities).

Integration

About 50% of company schemes reduce the pension by 'integrating' with the basic state pension. Where a scheme is integrated, no pension is paid for the first slice of salary up to the NI lower earnings limit (see page 260). No employee or employer pension contributions are levied on this amount either.

Contracting out of S2P

Most DB schemes are contracted out of the State second pension (and, previously, SERPS). As a result the employer and employees pay a reduced rate of NIC with the balance invested in the company pension fund. Where the scheme is not contracted out the employee would receive the SERPS and/or S2P pension and the company pension on top of this.

The decision to contract out should not just be based on the mathematical calculations of the benefits each route might provide. It is also necessary to take account of the individual's desire to make their investment decisions. We might also take into consideration the habit of consecutive governments to reduce state pensions. Having said that, no government has succeeded in making retrospective cuts ... so far.

Tax-free cash

The maximum tax-free cash available from a company pension scheme typically is one and a half times final salary after 40 years' service. This is limited in the case of some higher earners and will depend on when the member joined the scheme.

- Pre-17 March 1987 there are no restrictions.
- From 17 March 1987 the Revenue restricted the level of salary on which the tax-free cash (but not the pension) calculation was based. The ceiling was £100,000 so that the maximum cash was £150,000 (one and a half times the £100,000 salary limit).
- In April 1989 the government introduced the 'earnings cap' (see below), which restricts the salary on which both the pension and the tax-free cash is based to £105,600 in 2005–2006. The maximum tax-free cash, therefore, would be £158,400.

Taking tax-free cash involves giving up part of the pension – a process known as **commutation**. In the public sector schemes the process is different, as the lower pension accrual (eightieths) allows automatically for the member to take full tax-free cash.

Pension increases

Company schemes typically increase pensions by 3%–5% each year. The minimum requirement to increase by LPI will change in April 2005 from a maximum of 5% to 2.5%. Most public sector pensions automatically increase in line with the full retail prices index.

Family protection benefits

DB schemes provide other important family protection benefits in addition to the pension itself; for example death-in-service benefits worth up to four times annual salary, widow's and dependent children's pensions and similar death-in-retirement benefits. Disability pensions and private medical insurance are also common features of the overall benefits package. However, if a member is not married it is important to check whether their partner is still entitled to the benefits. An increasing number of private sector schemes permit the trustees to award a discretionary pension to unmarried partners, including same-sex partners, although few make this a guaranteed benefit. Most public sector schemes will only pay a pension to the lawful spouse, as is the case with the state scheme.

The position of higher earners pre- and post-April 2006

Since 1989 the government has restricted the pensions of certain high earners. By now most executives and directors are subject to the **earnings cap** (£105,600 in 2005–2006), which is the maximum amount of salary on which contributions and the final pension can be based. The cap applies to members of final salary schemes set up after the 1989 Budget and members who joined any final salary scheme after 1 June 1989. For these employees the maximum contribution for the 2005–2006 tax year is £15,840 (15% of £105,600), while the maximum pension will be £68,000 and the maximum tax-free cash £158,400. The earnings cap is not retrospective and so only applies after the individual changed scheme and triggered the restriction. After April 2006 the cap will no longer apply for future accrual.

'Unapproved' company schemes

There are two main types of pension to cater for earnings above the cap. **Funded unapproved retirement benefit schemes (FURBS)** are company schemes that are recognised by the Revenue but are 'unapproved' for tax purposes. Under a FURBS, the employer sets aside contributions to build up a pension fund for the employee's earnings in excess of the cap. FURBS usually operate on a DC basis. The FURBS member will still remain in the main company scheme and receive benefits in the usual way up to the level of the cap.

Under a FURBS the member is taxed on the employer's contributions, which are classed as a benefit in kind, rather like membership of the company's private medical scheme. The employer can treat these contributions as a trading expense for corporation tax purposes, although it is necessary to pay employer NICs on the amount. The FURBS fund is subject to income and capital gains tax.

Where the fund is used to buy an annuity the income is subject to tax. However, the entire benefit can be taken as a tax-free lump sum on retirement – a far more attractive option and the most common choice. The death-in-service lump sum benefits can be paid under a discretionary trust and therefore should be free of inheritance tax.

An alternative option under Inland Revenue rules is the **unfunded unapproved retirement benefit scheme (UURBS)**. In these arrangements the employer does not pay any contributions and there is no fund earmarked for the employee. Instead, the pension benefits are paid out of company funds when the employee retires. At this point the employer receives an allowance to offset corporation tax.

There is no tax liability until the member receives the benefits but at that point all lump sums and pensions are taxed as earned income. Death benefits, as with the FURBS, should be free of inheritance tax if paid under a discretionary trust.

The impact on FURBS of the Pensions Act 2004 and simplification 2006

Two rafts of legislation affect FURBS. First, they became less attractive after 5 April 2004 due to tax changes within the fund, which increase the level of taxation on trusts from 34% to 40%. Second, any fund built up from contributions paid *after* 5 April 2006 will be taken into account for the lifetime allowance.

Primary and enhanced protection

All higher earners, whether or not they are capped, need to analyse the two ways to register funds before A-Day (**primary and enhanced protection**) to avoid the recovery charge tax of 55% that will apply to funds in excess of £1.5m taken as cash. Where the excess is taken as taxable income the charge is 25%. While those with very substantial funds should automatically register for protection, those with smaller funds that are expected to grow rapidly should also consider taking this step.

Under primary protection the individual's fund would be crystallised on A-day as their personal lifetime allowance and this will be expressed as a percentage of the statutory lifetime allowance of £1.5m. So, for example, a fund worth £3m on A-day would give the individual a personal lifetime allowance of 200%. Once established, the personal lifetime allowance will increase broadly in line with prices. If the fund grows faster than this the excess will be subject to the recovery charge.

Enhanced protection is designed to protect any *growth* in the fund value provided there is no further accrual. This means that post A-Day it will not be possible to make further contributions to a money purchase or Defined contribution (DC) scheme but it will be possible to enjoy the full investment growth of the existing fund within the tax-favoured environment. For DB schemes, the individual will not be allowed to accrue any further 'years' in the scheme but the pension will continue to reflect any salary increases in full.

Those who opt for enhanced protection should discuss with their employer ways to maximise accrual before A-Day, as this will increase the size of their personal lifetime allowance. There are three possibilities here. Under the current rules employees can make a maximum pension contribution of 15% of salary. Since most schemes only require an employee contribution of about 5%, this leaves plenty of scope for AVCs if the individual is not capped but very limited scope if they are.

A second method is salary exchange, whereby the individual gives up some of their annual salary and the employer redirects this into the scheme. As mentioned above, the problem with salary exchange is that a reduction in basic earnings will have an impact on other salary-linked benefits, such as death-in-service lump sums and disability benefits.

The third method is for the employee to redirect annual bonuses into their pension scheme. Bonuses are not usually taken into account for the pension itself or for death benefits, so the impact is minimal. Whether employees use AVCs, salary sacrifice or bonuses to boost their pension this will almost certainly go into a DC scheme. Ideally this should be set up under the main scheme trust, as this may provide greater flexibility when it comes to taking tax-free cash on retirement.

It is important to bear in mind the value of simplicity and flexibility when planning for the lifetime allowance. For those with over 10 years to go to retirement it might be simplest and most efficient to fund beyond the lifetime allowance and pay the recovery charge. Once this is paid the individual can take the excess fund as cash.

Separate occupational schemes for executives

Senior executives often belong to a fast stream version of the main company pension scheme that builds up the pension more quickly and provides better benefits all round. But executives and directors can also be provided for through an entirely separate insurance arrangement known as an **Executive pension plan** or **EPP**. EPPs, although providing a pension linked to final salary, are occupational money purchase schemes. In the past EPPs have been popular but today a self-invested personal pension (see page 295) is likely to offer better value and be simpler.

Special schemes for small family companies

Owner-directors of small family businesses and high earning executives can benefit from what is widely regarded as the one of the most tax efficient and flexible occupational pension arrangements in Britain, known as a **Small self-administered scheme** or **SSAS**. However, while the new tax regime for pensions that comes into force in April 2006 will simplify the SSAS rules it will also raise important issues for those who have built up substantial funds.

SSASs are designed primarily for family businesses and enable members to build up a fund at retirement that can pay a tax-free cash lump sum and a taxable pension of up to two-thirds of salary. The maximum number of members is 12 and typically all of these would be trustees and actively involved in the investment decisions.

Many of the 35,000–40,000 SSASs in Britain have used the fund to purchase the company's business premises. The fund can then lease the property back to the principal employer, provided a commercial rent is agreed. This frees the company from paying for property directly, while the fund benefits from the appreciation in the value of the property.

The pre-2006 contribution rules for SSASs are more flexible than for personal pensions because they are based on the projected salary at retirement rather than an annual percentage of earnings. Employers can often pay a large percentage of the member's salary for older members with long service in good years and less in years when profits are poor. The employer's contributions are tax deductible and are not subject to employer or employee national insurance. Where the employee pays contributions, these are limited to a maximum of 15% of salary.

SSASs currently permit a high degree of **self-investment**, which means members can use up to 50% of the SSAS fund to invest in their own company. It is also possible to take a loan from the scheme (a 'loan-back') provided the company pays a commercial rate of interest. This feature is useful for smaller companies, which can find it difficult to get good quality loans.

The rules will change after April 2006. In particular:

- All pension schemes will have the same investment choice, including residential property.
- Self-investment, where the scheme buys shares in the employer's company, will be limited to 5% of the fund value.
- Loans from the scheme to employers will be limited to 50% of the fund value.
- Scheme borrowing, for property purchase, for example, will be limited to 50% of the scheme assets.
- Where a scheme asset is used by members of individuals connected to them, this will trigger a benefit-in-kind tax charge on the member.
- SSASs will no longer have to appoint a pensioneer trustee to ensure the scheme follows the trust deed and rules on winding up.

Pensions and divorce

For most married couples the chief breadwinner's company pension is the most valuable asset after the family home. Over one-third of marriages in the UK end in divorce but until recently there was no legal obligation to split the main breadwinner's (usually the husband's) pension fairly. Today, however, the court will be able to demand an immediate split of the funds, so the lower earnings spouse can invest their share of the pension in a personal pension fund. This whole area is very complex and it would be necessary to request an actuarial assessment of the calculation of each partner's pension rights where one or both has built up a substantial pension, particularly where this is in a DB scheme.

Activity 22.1

Assume you earn £60,000 pa and have been in a DB pension scheme for 20 years. Your employer is a small IT specialist and there are rumours that the company may be in financial difficulties. You are planning to change jobs and you are concerned about what to do with your pension benefits. Outline your main options and consider what factors might lead you to a conclusion. What problems does this exercise raise for those who advise on occupational pensions, pension transfers and the security of benefits?

Summary

This chapter covered occupational pension schemes and examined the major changes that are coming into effect between April 2004 under the Pensions Act 2004 and April 2006 under the Pension Tax Simplification. The years preceding and following simplification will be extremely busy ones for planners and occupational pensions consultants as they assess the best way to implement the changes.

Key terms

- Accrual p. 271
- A-Day p. 269
- Additional voluntary contributions (AVCs) p. 273
- Annuity p. 266
- Buy-out cost p. 268
- Career averaged revalued earnings scheme (CARE) p. 271
- Cash balance p. 271
- Commutation p. 276
- Concurrency p. 274
- Contribution holiday p. 268
- Defined benefit p. 270
- Defined contribution p. 270
- Earnings cap p. 277
- Executive pension plan (EPP) p. 279
- Financial Reporting Standard 17 (FRS17) p. 266
- Funded unapproved retirement benefit scheme (FURBS) p. 277
- Income drawdown p. 275
- Lifetime allowance p. 269

- Minimum funding requirement (MFR) p. 267
- Multi-employer/industry-wide scheme p. 271
- Pension tax simplification (A-Day) p. 269
- Pension unlocking p. 275
- Primary and enhanced protection p. 278
- Recovery charge p. 270
- Salary exchange or sacrifice p. 272
- Scheme-specific funding requirement p. 269
- Self investment p. 280
- Sixtieth scheme p. 271
- Small self-administered scheme (SSAS) p. 279
- Transfer value (TV) p. 275
- Unfunded unapproved retirement benefit scheme (UURBS) p. 277
- Wind up p. 266

Review questions

1 Give a brief overview of the events that led to the severely underfunded position of occupational pension schemes by the end of 2002.

2 Explain what steps the Pensions Act 2004 takes to re-establish the stability of occupational schemes.

3 Describe the key features of Pension Tax Simplification. Why will this prove so complicated for those with substantial pension funds?

4 What are the most important differences between a Defined benefit (DB) and Defined contribution (DC) scheme?

Go to the Companion Website at **www.booksites.net/harrison_pfp** for a multiple-choice quiz to test your understanding of this chapter.

Further information

Details about pension tax simplification can be found at the Department for Work and Pensions website: **www.dwp.gov.uk.**

Further information on multi-employer schemes: The Pensions Trust is at **www.thepensions trust.org.uk**; B&CE is at **www.bandce.co.uk.**

The National Association of Pension Funds **www.napf.co.uk**

Case study 22.1

Background

Hazel Holmes and Neil Robinson have been living together for 24 years. They are not married. They have two children: Jason, aged 19, and John, aged 21. Hazel is 42 and Neil is 44. They are both in good health and are non-smokers.

Neil owns a 55% share in a cardboard packaging company based in Birmingham that makes various types of packaging for numerous fast food outlets. He started the company with two friends in 1983. He draws a salary of £80,000 pa and, in addition, receives dividends of £50,000 pa. Hazel has been employed by an advertising agency since 1 March 1990 and earns £60,000 pa.

The couple's assets are currently valued as follows:

House (unencumbered and owned as tenants in common with ownership being split 50 : 50)	£1.8m
Neil's self-invested personal pension (SIPP)	£1m
Hazel's contracted out money purchase scheme (joined 1 June 1990)	£300,000
Various OEICs, owned jointly and investing in International Equity funds all excluding the UK	£1m
Joint bank account paying 2% gross interest	£200,000

Case study 22.1 (*continued*)

On 1 February 2000 Neil bought 1,200 Pearson Group and 3,000 British Airways shares. The couple's joint annual expenditure is £120,000. Neil's company pays a pension contribution of 10% of his basic salary; he does not contribute personally. Hazel pays 6% of her salary annually into her pension scheme. Her employer matches this amount. The couple have a fairly speculative attitude to investment risk.

Problem

Three months ago the company was valued at £3m (excluding the premises). John has shown an interest in entering the business and Neil believes he has the skills eventually to take over the business when he retires at age 60. Jason, however, shows no interest in the business. Neil is particularly concerned about passing on his shareholding to John and any impact that might have on Jason's future inheritance. Neil wondered whether he should give a small number, say 10%, of his shares to Jason. The company has outgrown its current rented premises, and is considering purchasing an old factory unit on an industrial estate in the West Midlands valued at £2m. The remainder of the SIPP is made up of 50% UK Equity unit trusts and 50% in an International Equity insured fund.

Advice

The couple would like to retire when Neil reaches 60 and they anticipate their annual expenditure to be approximately £100,000 pa in today's terms. Neil is concerned about how his SIPP will be affected when the new pension rules come into force and wondered if he should do anything now to ensure that his various objectives can still be met. Neil would like to consider whether the company's new premises could be held more effectively in a SIPP.

You are asked to set out the options and make recommendations for the couple to consider when trying to meet their objectives. In all cases you are asked to explain how each recommendation meets their objectives.

Source: *Money Management*, Financial Planner of the Year Awards 2003, *FT Business*.

A full solution to this case study is available to lecturers via the password-protected area of the Companion Website at **www.booksites.net/harrison_pfp**.

Chapter 23 ●●●○

Defined contribution (DC) schemes and plans

Introduction

Historically Defined contribution (DC) schemes were associated almost entirely with the retail pensions market but this is no longer the case, with DC schemes now the most common type of new employer-sponsored arrangement. This chapter looks at the company and individual plans that rely on the DC structure to deliver retirement incomes.

Objectives

After reading this chapter you will be able to:

- Explain how Defined contribution schemes and plans work.
- Understand what determines the retirement income that can be bought with a DC fund.
- Explain the differences between a personal pension and its predecessor, the retirement annuity plan.
- Describe the additional investment opportunities offered by a Self-invested personal pension (SIPP).

● ● ● ● DC explained

With a DC pension arrangement the individual member bears the investment risk and there is no guaranteed pension linked to salary. Students will find that when it comes to the investment of contributions to a DC scheme or plan it will be helpful to refer to earlier chapters that explain the important asset classes and how to build an appropriate portfolio of shares and collective funds. The investment strategy should take into consideration the individual's objectives at retirement, whether this is to draw an income directly from their funds, or to convert the fund to an annuity to provide a guaranteed income.

Personal pension plans, Group personal pensions (GPPs), Stakeholder schemes and Contracted in money purchase schemes (CIMPS) are all DC arrangements. The contribution and benefit rules vary, however, depending on whether the individual belongs to a scheme based on personal pension legislation – for example a Group personal pension or Stakeholder scheme – or on occupational scheme rules, such as a Contracted in money purchase scheme. These particular rules will merge after April 2006 under Pension Tax Simplification (see page 269).

Under most DC schemes contributions are invested to build up a fund that is used at retirement to provide a tax-free lump sum and to buy an **annuity**, which pays an income for life. Annuity 'rates' – that is, the level of income each £1,000 of the fund will buy – depend largely on long dated gilt yields. It is possible to defer the annuity purchase and to draw an income directly from the fund, keeping the rest fully invested. **Income drawdown** and a similar arrangement known as **phased retirement** are complicated, and require in equal measure a substantial fund size and expert advice. (Annuities and drawdown are covered in the following chapter.)

To summarise, the level of income generated by a DC arrangement is not guaranteed but will depend on several factors, including:

- The level of the total employee and employer contribution.
- The investment performance of the fund.
- The level of charges deducted by the provider.
- Annuity 'rates' – that is, the level of income the fund will secure at retirement (or later in retirement in the case of drawdown).

Clearly it is important to ensure the individual's contribution is adequate. This is likely to be 10%–20% of earnings, depending on age and existing provision. Employers may contribute but at the time of writing this was not obligatory. The annual **statutory money purchase illustration (SMPI)** statement will show in real terms an estimate of what income the individual's fund should secure at retirement (see page 295). If this is less than the individual requires then some adjustments to the financial plan will be necessary, for example an increase in the contribution, an increase in savings outside the pension plan, and/or a later retirement date.

As mentioned, certain occupational DC schemes – particularly those operated by larger employers – follow the same maximum contribution and benefit rules as final salary schemes (see CIMPS below). However, most employers are choosing the Group personal pension or Stakeholder scheme route, as these are simpler in structure and easier to run. Under a GPP – which is effectively a group of individual plans – the individual can use their plan to contract out of the State second pension and to invest additional regular or single premiums to boost the pension provided by the National insurance contribution (NIC) rebate (see page 290).

All DC schemes will comply with Pension Tax Simplification in April 2006 but until then personal pension contribution limits start at 17.5% pa of **net relevant earnings** (equivalent in this context to **pensionable pay**) for employees up to age 35, and rising in stages to 40% for employees aged 61 and over. Employer contributions, where applicable, must be included in these limits. There is no limit on the benefits that the fund can secure at retirement.

Contracted in money purchase schemes (CIMPS)

Contracted in money purchase schemes (CIMPS) are Inland Revenue approved occupational pensions and as such may either follow the same contribution and benefit limits as defined benefit schemes or, in a minority of cases, will elect to follow the rules for Group personal pensions. Until April 2006 the maximum employee contribution is 15% of salary (restricted for higher earners – see page 277). However, although the member's maximum pension is calculated as a proportion of salary, the retirement income will actually depend on the size of the fund at retirement and annuity rates, provided benefits do not exceed the maxima for occupational schemes. This makes CIMPS one of the most idiosyncratic, not to say complex, of pension arrangements.

Stakeholder schemes

In April 2001 the government introduced stakeholder schemes to encourage those who do not have access to a more traditional company pension arrangement to save for their retirement. Its intention through these and other private arrangements is to increase the percentage of people with private pensions from 40% in 1998 to 60% by 2050. Stakeholders follow the same rules as personal pensions but to qualify for stakeholder status they must offer moderate costs, easy access and fair terms – for example penalty-free exit. This is similar to CAT-standard Individual savings accounts (see page 180).

One of the unusual features of the regime introduced in 2001 for all types of personal pension, including stakeholder, is that it is possible to contribute up to £3,600 a year (£2,808 after basic rate tax relief) even if an individual has no earned income. Previously all contributions had to relate to net relevant earnings. At retirement under a stakeholder, GPP or individual personal plan, it is possible to take up to

25% of the fund as tax-free cash while the remainder is used to buy a regular income in the form of an annuity. Other retirement investment options are available for those with a substantial fund who want to draw an income direct rather than convert to an annuity. Options at retirement for DC schemes are examined in the following chapter.

Stakeholder schemes are mainly available through employers that do not provide a more traditional occupational pension scheme, but they are also available directly from many financial institutions. Clearly if an individual does not have a pension then the stakeholder scheme provided by their company is likely to offer reasonable value for money, particularly where the employer is prepared to make a contribution.

In practice the difference in cost between stakeholder schemes and modern personal pension contracts is not significant, as the introduction of a 1% cap on the **annual management charge (AMC)** for stakeholder schemes is used for most GPPs. In 2005 the new stakeholder schemes can charge up to 1.5%.

For those who want a larger choice of funds it may be relevant to consider multi-manager personal pensions, although these tend to be more expensive than 1%. If cost is an issue, several investment trusts offer personal pensions and these may be cheaper than stakeholder schemes over the long term. Having said that, we must always be aware that the cheapest is not necessarily the best. What we should look for is charges that are competitive for the type of asset management provided.

● ● ● ● Contributions to stakeholders and personal pensions

Until April 2006, for personal pensions and stakeholders the maximum annual payment varies according to age. Table 23.1 shows the percentages of annual earnings an individual can pay into a personal pension/Stakeholder scheme. If an employer contributes, this must be included in the overall maximum. Personal pension contributions are restricted by the earnings cap, so the maximum salary on which contributions are based is £105,600 in 2005–2006. However, there is no cap on the maximum benefits, so the retirement income will depend to a large extent on the returns achieved.

Stakeholder and GPP contributions are deducted from the member's salary through the payroll system and forwarded to the provider. Members pay contributions net of

Table 23.1 Annual contribution limits for personal pensions pre-April 2006

Age	% Net relevant earnings*
Up to 35	17.5
36–45	20
46–50	25
51–55	30
56–60	35
61–74	40

* All personal pension contributions (but not the emerging pension itself) are subject to the earnings cap, which limits the amount of salary that can be used for pension purposes to £105,600 for the 2005–2006 tax year.

the basic rate of tax. The pension provider reclaims this tax from the Inland Revenue and credits it to the employee's fund. However, individuals are responsible for claiming any higher rate relief to which they are entitled through the annual tax return.

Retirement annuities

Many people still have **Retirement annuity plans (RAPs)** – the predecessor to the personal pension. After July 1988, sales of these contracts stopped but existing policyholders can continue to contribute to their plans.

The contribution and benefit rules for RAPs differ slightly from personal pensions, although again, these distinctions disappear in April 2006. Retirement annuity contribution limits are lower in terms of percentages than for personal pensions but the total earnings on which these contributions are based is not subject to the earnings cap. The limits are shown in Table 23.2.

Table 23.2 Annual contribution limits for retirement annuities pre-April 2006

Age	% Net relevant earnings
Up to age 50	17.5
51–55	20
56–60	22.5
61–74	27.5

Note: The earnings cap does not apply. It may be possible under these plans to pay a larger contribution by mopping up unused tax relief from 6 previous years.

It is possible to make use of unused tax relief from previous tax years with a RAP to boost the contribution in the current year. Under the **carry forward** rules, unused relief from the previous six tax years can be added to the current year, once the current year's limit is reached.

Under the pre-2006 rules, depending on the individual's age at retirement and the prevailing annuity rates, it may be possible to take more than 25% of the RAP fund as tax-free cash because the calculation is not a straight percentage of the fund but instead is based on the level of annuity the fund can purchase. The other main difference between the two arrangements is that it is not possible to contract out of the S2P with one of these older contracts – for this it is necessary to use an 'appropriate' personal pension.

Finally, it is possible to contribute to both a personal pension and retirement annuity, but where this is done within the same tax year the personal pension contribution rules apply.

Pensions for children and spouses

The new tax regime for personal pensions introduced in April 2001 offers attractive tax planning opportunities for the wealthier investor because it breaks the traditional link between earnings and pension contributions. For the first time it became possible for individuals to contribute to pension schemes and plans on behalf of others. There are three main tax-planning opportunities here. It is possible to pay up to £3,600 pa (£2,808 after tax relief) on behalf of:

- A child.
- A non-earnings spouse/partner.
- A spouse/partner who is in a company scheme but earns less than £30,000.

In each case it will be necessary to consider the long-term investment requirements of the individual for whom provision is being made to decide whether a stakeholder, a multi-manager personal pension or a self-invested personal pension is appropriate (see page 295). There are no exit charges on a stakeholder scheme so it might make sense to start with one of these and then transfer to a personal plan with wider investment scope once the fund has built up to an appropriate level.

There has been considerable interest in children's pensions, but we should bear in mind that pension tax breaks do not come unfettered. If a parent's or grandparent's chief concern is saving for school or college fees, for example, or providing a deposit on a house, then a stakeholder is inappropriate because the 'child' will not have access to the tax-free cash and income until at least age 55.

As far as spouse's/partner's pensions are concerned, it is not just the non-earner who can benefit from third party contributions. The **concurrency** rules allow an employee who earns less than £30,000 and who is a member of an occupational pension scheme to pay up to 15% of salary (that is, up to £4,500) into the main scheme and additional voluntary contribution scheme (AVC) combined and in addition to pay up to £3,600 into a personal pension or stakeholder scheme. This provides an excellent opportunity for the higher earner to fund the spouse's or partner's stakeholder pension.

●●●● Contracting out of the state scheme

Personal pensions and stakeholder schemes can be used to contract out of the State second pension (previously the State earnings related pension scheme) on an individual basis and in return receive a rebate of National insurance contributions to invest in an individual plan or stakeholder scheme. Employees who are not contracted out, will automatically belong to S2P. The self-employed do not pay into the S2P so this point is not applicable. (See Chapter 21 for details about the state pension schemes.)

●●●● How to choose a personal pension

It is essential to remember that a personal pension is no more than a tax-favoured wrapper in which to hold collective investments. The plan provides a legal and administrative framework; the success of the plan depends on the level of contribution, the asset allocation, and the quality of investment management. As with any long-term savings, asset allocation should be considered across all the individual's investments, not just within the pension plan.

The choice of pension providers should involve an examination of the following features:

- The financial strength of the provider. It is important to be confident that the company can survive in what is a very competitive market, which is in the throes of major consolidation. It is not sufficient to rely on household names.
- The performance track record of the provider and of the third-party managers available through the plan, with the emphasis on consistency over the long term and stability of the people responsible for the performance.
- The level of charges deducted throughout the investment period. Charges should be competitive and not necessarily the cheapest, although cost is a key factor with passive funds.
- The flexibility of the contract; for example there should be no penalties for reducing and stopping contributions, transferring the fund and early retirement. This feature is guaranteed with stakeholder schemes.

Options at retirement

This subject is covered in the next chapter but briefly, the fund built up from the NIC rebates in an appropriate personal pension is known as **protected rights** – a misleading term given that the plan itself provides no protection from stock market volatility, for example. There are certain restrictions on what you can do with this fund at retirement. Pre-April 2006, it cannot be used to provide tax-free cash and the pension must be taken at the same age as the state pension, currently 65 for men and 60 for women (rising to 65 between 2010 and 2020). The annuity purchased with the fund must provide for a spouse's pension worth 50% of the personal pension plan holder's own pension, and the annuity payments must increase, typically by 3% pa. We can expect many of these restrictions to disappear from April 2006. There are no restrictions on the annuity that can be purchased with the proceeds of the main plan.

It is possible to run more than one personal pension plan provided total contributions fall within the limits shown in Table 23.1, but here we must consider the impact of start up charges. It is only possible to take out one plan for the annual rebate of NICs where the individual contracts out of the S2P. This can be reviewed on an annual basis – the only requirement is not to split the rebate for any given tax year.

Charges and terms for DC arrangements

It is important to be aware that the quality of DC contracts varies considerably. Some of the earlier insurance company group and individual personal pensions sold in the late 1980s and early 1990s will look unattractive compared with the modern contract. In particular they may still incorporate high charges, very restrictive access to investment management, and impose penalties if the individual wants to reduce or stop contributions, or transfer the fund to another provider. Planners should automatically check any new contracts before purchase and where necessary change an existing contract, provided the penalties are not prohibitive.

Checklist for DC

A good DC scheme or plan should:

- Invest minimum employer and employee total contributions of between 10%–20% of annual salary, depending on age (the older the individual the higher the contribution).
- Delegate the investment management to an institutional fund manager that has a proven track record.
- Incur competitive administration and investment charges.
- Impose no financial penalties for those who leave the scheme, reduce contributions or retire early.

The DC 'default' option

DC schemes and plans usually offer a range of funds that cover the main asset classes. For details on the choice of unit linked and unit trust funds, see Chapter 12. However, between 80% and 90% of individuals take the 'default' option, according to actuarial consultants. While this may be suitable, it is important to examine the option carefully, otherwise the individual could end up in the wrong assets classes for their age and circumstances, and/or suffer poor investment management.

In older schemes the default might be a single fund run by a life office. According to the 2003 survey of pension schemes by the National Association of Pension Funds, where DC schemes offer life office managed units linked and with profits funds, 22% and 19% respectively of the entire scheme assets were invested in these options. For most members these may prove to be a poor compromise for such a long-term investment. Both types of fund rely on a 'balanced' approach to asset allocation, and following the bear market and falls in financial strength of life offices, this could mean anything from 30% to 80% in equities, depending on the provider's view of world markets. Some of the life offices that run unit linked funds have a poor reputation for asset management, while many of the with profits providers are unable to invest with confidence for the long term because they are financially weak. This constrains their investment philosophy and forces them into a very low-risk/reward strategy, which would entail an allocation to equities that would be inappropriate for younger investors.

Lifestyle investment strategies

A more sophisticated default option is the lifestyle fund. This recognises that an individual's risk profile and asset allocation requirements will change according to the number of years to retirement. For this reason the strategy gradually switches the individual out of equities and into gilts and cash over the last few years before retirement. The general objective is that by retirement the investor is 75% in bonds and gilts to align the fund with the assets that back annuities, and 25% in cash to provide the tax-free lump sum. This way sudden movements in the markets will not significantly alter the individual's annuity income and tax-free cash expectations.

The biggest problem with the early lifestyle model is that this is a dynamic asset allocation model that links the phased switch from equities to gilts purely to the number of years to retirement, at which point it is assumed the investor will buy an annuity. This is not a flexible model, nor is it responsive to stockmarket conditions. In practice few employees can predict their actual retirement date with any certainty. An unexpected early retirement/late redundancy could pitch the investor into the annuity purchase market at precisely the wrong time if they are still heavily, predominantly, in equities and markets recently have fallen. Nor does lifestyle cater beneficially for those who go into drawdown, as the phased switch into bonds and cash will be premature.

More recently actuarial consultants and investment managers have come up with better alternatives, for example a simple choice of asset class funds, which can be used as the basic building blocks for the portfolio of funds. Behind the scenes the consultant or a separate manager of managers will ensure that each fund is run within strict risk/return parameters and will hire and monitor the underlying managers. From the investor's point of view, what you get is access to top managers within a range of asset classes, all via a single pension investment vehicle.

While multi-manager asset class funds are ideal for the more knowledgeable investor, many members would still prefer a dynamic and automated asset allocation strategy. A comparatively new model from the consultant Lane Clark & Peacock uses a mathematical formula that links the automated switch from equities into bonds primarily to actual performance rather than to the period to retirement. This locks in gains in favourable markets by switching a proportion of the member's fund to bonds when predetermined targets are met. Regular reviews and easy Internet access allow each member to keep abreast of progress and to take timely decisions to reduce or increase contributions where this is necessary to keep on target for the desired retirement income. The idea – and it is one many investors will appreciate – is to take the unwelcome surprise out of DC retirement arrangements.

Bear in mind, however, that even with a sophisticated lifestyle strategy, much will depend on the trustee or employer's choice of investment managers for the equity and bond funds. A well-monitored multi-manager structure is ideal, provided the costs do not undermine the return.

Exhibit 23.1 The automated asset allocation strategy for DC

The automated switching programme ('DCisive') developed by the actuarial consultant Lane Clark & Peacock is linked primarily to the returns achieved and not to the number of years to retirement. Broadly speaking it works as follows:

● The trustee or employer sets the return target or benchmark, typically at 2% above 'risk-free' assets such as investment grade bonds.

● The two main funds are 100% equities and 100% bonds. Member contributions are invested initially into the equity fund.

● A gradual switch to the bond fund takes place over the course of the member's years to retirement. This is based on a mathematical formula that takes account of performance achieved in relation to the benchmark. The aim is to ensure that the member's overall return for the entire period in the scheme stays on target.

● The better the performance the quicker the move from equities to bonds. Where performance has been good, by retirement the member can expect to be 75% in bonds and 25% in cash. As annuities are backed by bonds this aligns the main fund with annuity rates, while the 25% in cash can be taken as a tax-free lump sum.

● Two years before retirement, where the member is not on target for 75/25%, bonds/cash, an additional switching mechanism expedites the process.

● Members have regular access to their fund's progress. Where equity returns have been less favourable, the member can see the impact on the desired retirement income and can change the contribution rate or perhaps plan to work longer.

● Members who want to retire early can change their retirement date, thereby accelerating the switching process.

● Those who want to retain a high equity exposure – for drawdown purposes for example – can set a later planned retirement date to slow the phased switching, or simply exit the strategy at any stage, without penalty, and take control of their investment decisions.

Family protection benefits

Death benefits under DC schemes and plans can be minimal, particularly in the early days, as this is likely to be just a return of fund. Clearly it will be necessary for the individual to top up family protection insurance through additional life assurance. Individuals will also need income replacement insurance if this is not provided by the employer. Private medical cover could also be considered (see Chapter 7).

Pension statements

Between April 2003 and 2004 all investors with DC pensions gained the right to an annual statement that calculates the real value, in today's prices, of the income they can expect to buy with their pension fund at retirement. In the past many providers simply set out the current fund value. The new statutory money purchase illustration (SMPI) statements show a projection of what an individual's fund might be worth at retirement assuming certain growth rates. In addition it will show the level of guaranteed lifetime income the fund might secure when the individual buys an annuity. The SMPI assumes 2.5% inflation between the date of the statement and the individual's retirement, and a maximum real equity return of 4.5% (less for other asset classes). In addition it assumes that the annuity purchased rises in line with retail prices, although it is not a requirement to buy an inflation-linked annuity.

Which type of pensions must provide an SMPI?

- Money purchase occupational schemes.
- Stakeholder schemes.
- Personal pensions.
- Self-invested personal pensions (SIPPS).
- Executive pension schemes (EPPs).
- Small self-administered schemes (SSASs).*
- Additional voluntary contributions (AVCs).
- Free standing AVCs (FSAVCs).
- 'Buy-out bonds' (deferred company pensions) arranged by trustees.

Note: * Not compulsory if every member is a trustee.

Excluded:

- Final salary company schemes.*
- Retirement annuities (the precursor to personal pensions).**
- State pensions.***

Notes: * Employers should provide annual statements automatically.
          ** In this case it will be necessary to convert the statement to a pension in today's prices.
          *** The Department for Work and Pensions will provide a forecast on request: ask for form BR19.

Self-invested personal pensions (SIPPs)

Self-invested personal pensions (SIPPs) follow the same basic rules as standard personal pensions but in addition they allow the individual to exercise much greater control over their investments. The appeal of the SIPP lies in the product's ability to separate the two key features of modern pension plans; namely the administration and the investment management. This means policyholders can run their own funds or appoint an investment manager (the financial planner or possibly a stockbroker, for example) to construct and run the portfolio for them. If the investment manager is unsatisfactory it is possible to change the firm without having to change the underlying administration arrangements.

SIPPs can also be used by partnerships and professional practices, which cannot use company-sponsored Small self-administered schemes (SSASs – see page 279). Many firms have made use of the SIPP rules to buy new business premises for the practice in a tax-favoured environment (see below).

An increasing number of SIPP providers run a low-cost online version. Before selecting a SIPP it is important to consider how frequently the individual intends to trade and to check the annual charge (if applicable) in conjunction with dealing costs, as these vary considerably. Planners should also consider the set up costs and the range of services offered.

Investment choice for SIPPs

The choice of investments for SIPPs is very wide and includes the following:

- Stocks and shares quoted on The London Stock Exchange and including securities on the Alternative Investment Market.
- Stocks and shares traded on a recognised overseas exchange.
- Unit trusts and investment trusts.
- Insurance company managed funds and unit linked funds.
- Deposit accounts.
- Commercial property.

Buying property with a SIPP fund

A SIPP fund cannot purchase a firm's existing business premises from the partnership but it can buy new offices into which the partnership can move, provided the property is leased back on a commercial basis. It is possible to use the SIPP fund to borrow on the strength of its assets to help with property purchase. However, the SIPP cannot lend part of the pension fund back to the investor.

New investment opportunities for DC from April 2006

The new tax regime that comes into force on 6 April 2006 introduces a wider investment choice for all personal pensions. This is expected to include residential property. It will not make sense to hold the main home within the fund, as whatever property is bought by the fund must be used to generate a retirement income and in most cases it would be necessary to sell the property at or shortly into retirement to do this.

At the time of writing the full rules for residential property had yet to be published. However it is certain that any use of property or other assets held by the pension plan must be established on commercial terms. In other words, if an individual bought or transferred a second home into the pension plan they would have to pay the plan a commercial rent or face an offsetting personal tax charge. Property bought purely for investment purposes could be a very attractive prospect, as the pension fund would provide a shelter against tax on both rental income and capital gains and there would be no offsetting personal charge.

The borrowing rules under the new regime are less flexible as it will be possible to borrow 50% of the amount in the fund at the date the loan is taken out (pre-April 2006 this was 75% of the property value). This will apply to commercial and residential property.

Exhibit 23.2 Key features of tax simplification for DC

- A single set of investment standards.

- 'Self-investment', where the scheme buys shares in the employer's company, will be limited to 5% of the fund value.

- Loans from the scheme to employers will be limited to 50% of the fund value.

- Scheme borrowing, for property purchase, for example, will be limited to 50% of the scheme assets.

- Where a scheme asset is used by members or individuals connected to them, this will trigger a benefit-in-kind tax charge on the member unless a commercial rent is paid.

Activity 23.1

You have been asked to help Fred, who is 39 and earns £50,000 pa, to select a pension plan. His wife, Jane, earns £60,000 and is in the Civil Service pension scheme, which is a defined benefit arrangement. What factors would lead you to recommend to Fred, in turn, a stakeholder scheme, a multi-manager personal pension plan or a self-invested personal pension (SIPP)? What asset allocation would you recommend?

Activity 23.2

Fred's parents want to set up a pension for their two grandchildren, Amy and Ben, who are aged 2 and 4. What are the main considerations in this choice? What type of plan would you recommend? What about asset allocation?

Summary

This chapter examined the main group and individual defined contribution schemes and considered the factors that influence the retirement income that the DC fund will buy. While the cost of the DC arrangement is relevant, it is important to remember

that this type of pension scheme or plan is simply a tax-favoured wrapper in which the individual holds funds and, in the case of SIPPs, individual equities and property as well. The choice of asset allocation and the underlying funds is paramount.

Key terms

- Annual management charge (AMC) p. 288
- Annuity p. 286
- Carry forward p. 289
- Concurrency p. 290
- Contracted in money purchase schemes (CIMPS) p. 287
- Default/lifestyle DC investment p. 293
- Income drawdown p. 286

- Net relevant earnings p. 287
- Pensionable pay p. 287
- Phased retirement p. 286
- Protected rights p. 291
- Retirement annuity plans (RAPs) p. 289
- Statutory money purchase illustration (SMPI) p. 295

Review questions

1 Explain what a DC pension arrangement, such as a stakeholder scheme or individual personal pension, provides at retirement.

2 How does the earnings cap affect personal pensions and retirement annuity plans pre-April 2006?

3 List three factors that determine the outcome of a personal pension.

4 What are the potential flaws in a default option under a DC scheme or plan?

5 What additional investment choices does a SIPP offer compared with a standard personal pension?

Go to the Companion Website at **www.booksites.net/harrison_pfp** for a multiple-choice quiz to test your understanding of this chapter.

Further information

For a full list of stakeholder providers go to Occupational Pensions Regulatory Authority: **www.opra.gov.uk**.

The FSA publishes comparative tables of stakeholder schemes and personal pensions at **www.fsa.gov.uk/tables**.

The SIPP Providers Group: **www.sipp-provider-group.org.uk**.

Chapter 24 ●●●●

DC funds and the retirement income

Introduction

Until recently it was assumed that members of company pension schemes would draw their tax-free cash and guaranteed pension at the official company pension age, while those with private plans would take their tax-free cash and use the rest of the fund to buy an annuity, which provided the guaranteed income for life.

In this chapter we recognise that today there is a need for considerable flexibility when it comes to the timing of drawing retirement benefits, the level of the income, and estate planning. While flexibility and choice are both very important, it does mean that financial planning in the run up to retirement is extremely complicated, and for many individuals the complexity continues through a good part of the retirement.

Objectives

After reading this chapter you will be able to:

● Describe the range of retirement income choices for individuals with DC pensions.
● Discuss the advantages and potential problems associated with a move from a defined benefit scheme into a DC retirement option such as income drawdown.
● Explain how to secure a basic guaranteed income before considering other riskier options.

Market developments

It is an undeniable fact that at retirement every investor with a Defined contribution (DC) pension arrangement deserves access to the best products on the market to maximise income in the most appropriate manner. This is as important for the investor with a small fund, for whom access to the **open market option (OMO)** can be restricted or even impossible, as it is for the wealthier individual who might benefit from a well-structured combination of conventional annuities, investment linked annuities and drawdown arrangements. Moreover, it is vital for those with a health or lifestyle factor to secure a rate that takes this into consideration.

Financial planners are not expected to operate state-of-the-art annuity and drawdown interactive websites. The trend in the market is for planners who might hitherto have struggled to conduct their own annuity business to refer clients to a specialist. This is a pragmatic approach given that the annuity and drawdown market will become more rather than less complicated in future.

There are important regulatory issues here. The key to successful introducer business lies in the professionalism, expertise and resources of the specialist. It also lies in the use of a clearly worded introducer or referral agreement that satisfies the concerns of both parties. Such agreements are in force and have been proven to work. However, it is important for the introducing adviser to understand the nature of the service the specialist will provide and to be comfortable with the level of contact the specialist will have with the client. The specialist will almost certainly want to deal directly with the client, make a full fact find, and offer a full end-to-end service. This is an important point. If an adviser wants a specialist to take full responsibility for regulatory and compliance issues, then clearly it must carry out a full fact find to ensure the client gets the best results. The agreement therefore must be clear-cut and avoid any confusion over who is responsible for what.

Basic retirement income objectives

Given our increased longevity (see Table 24.1), individuals with DC funds and other investments, who are coming up to retirement, tend to focus on one or more of the

Table 24.1 Life expectancy

Current age	Life expectancy (yrs)	
	Male	Female
55	29	32
60	24	27
65	19	22
70	15	18
75	11	14

Source: Continuous Mortality Investigation Bureau.

following concerns:

● That they might outlive the resources set aside for retirement income and capital.
● That there will be nothing left to pass on to their children when they die.
● That an overly frugal approach to drawing income, combined with an unexpectedly early death, will leave an excessive amount to their heirs at the expense of their own lifestyle.

No investment strategy can entirely remove these threats but the risks can be managed – at a price.

Conventional annuities

Annuities represent one of the biggest markets for retired investors, who hand over about £6bn to annuity providers each year, most of which is used to secure an income stream that is guaranteed for life – irrespective of investment returns and longevity. This guarantee represents the insurance element of the annuity contract and is not available through any pure investment or savings product.

Conventional annuities are not pure investments. Rather, they are bond-based insurance contracts and it is important to understand that like any insurance product, risk is pooled and, therefore, there are 'winners' and 'losers' among the members in that pool. The risk we insure is the uncertainty over how long we will live. By **annuitising** the DC fund we establish a protection mechanism that will avoid the possibility that we might outlive our capital and income. Put simply, the pooling mechanism uses the funds of those who die early to subsidise the income of those who live longer than average. Those blessed with longevity are the 'winners' and benefit from what is known as the **mortality cross-subsidy**.

A strong insurance element is also present in the state schemes and in DB company pension schemes. The *primary* purpose of a salary linked company pension, for example, is to guarantee an income stream that is based on the member's length of membership and salary. It has no direct link with the contributions paid or the investment returns of the fund.

In recent years the income from annuities has fallen, which has led investors to believe that these products offer poor value for money. This is not necessarily the case. The fall in interest rates and the increase in longevity have had a major impact on annuity rates but they do not necessarily represent poor value for money. Double-digit yields on annuities are associated with the 1980s when there were double-digit returns on the stock market but also double-digit rates of inflation. The real returns and yields on investments and savings generally fell into single figures. The point is, we cannot look at annuity rates in isolation from economic and demographic patterns.

● ● ● ● Options for DC investors at retirement

As explained in the last chapter, DC arrangements fall into two categories. The first is based broadly on personal pension legislation and includes:

- Personal pensions.
- Retirement annuities.
- Stakeholder schemes.

The second includes certain occupational schemes:

- Occupational money purchase schemes.
- Executive pension plans (EPPs).
- Small self-administered schemes (SSASs).
- Additional voluntary contributions (AVCs) and 'free standing' AVCs (FSAVCs).

The distinction between personal pension and occupational rules is important because it affects the timing as well as the way the individual can take benefits. For example, it is possible to take the benefits from a personal pension any time from age 50 onwards (rising to 55 by 2010) – although annuity rates tend to be very low indeed for younger investors because the insurance company has to pay the regular income over a longer retirement period. Investors with occupational pension schemes usually have to wait until the scheme's normal retirement age (NRA) before taking benefits. If they want to take benefits earlier then almost certainly there would be an actuarial reduction for each year between actual retirement and normal retirement age.

Under personal pension rules there is no limit on the income an individual can secure with their fund, whereas occupational scheme rules limit the maximum benefits and these will be based on the member's length of service and salary at or near retirement. These rules are changing in April 2006 (see page 269).

With a personal pension or similar arrangement it is possible to take up to 25% of the fund as tax-free cash. (The major exception here is AVCs started after April 1987 and all FSAVCs – see page 274.)

For the risk-averse who will rely solely on their pension fund for a retirement income, the most prudent option is to use as much of the fund as is necessary to buy an annuity to cover the basic income requirement. In terms of a guaranteed income for life, an annuity is a hard act to beat. This is because the mortality cross-subsidy, mentioned above, increases the annual income you might otherwise achieve if you invested your fund in gilts and bonds and lived off the yield and withdrew a proportion of the capital each year. The growth you would have to receive from an investment just to match that cross-subsidy might be worth an additional 7.5% at age 80 and almost 15% at age 85.

The cross-subsidy is an important feature of all annuities irrespective of the underlying investments. For this reason it is very difficult to compare an annuity, with its combination of insurance and investment features, with the returns from a pure investment – for example a bond or equity fund – or even with income drawdown, which allows you to defer the annuity purchase (until April 2006 this is limited up to age 75) and instead draw an income direct from your fund.

Of course, for those with large funds or with other sources of income in retirement, it is worth considering a more flexible arrangement. However, an individual who opts for anything other than a conventional annuity runs the risk of capital loss, which in turn could reduce future income expectations. It also increases costs.

It is important to remember that provided an individual's fund is large enough, they can divide it between different arrangements. As mentioned above, in this way an individual could, for example, secure a basic income that is guaranteed for life through a conventional annuity, while at the same time keep part of the fund in an arrangement that invests in the stock markets, in the hope of increasing the income during retirement and/or passing on capital to heirs.

Summary of DC choices at retirement

To summarise, at retirement a DC investor's options fall into five broad categories, considered in more detail below.

- If there are other sources of income it is possible to defer the annuity purchase and leave the fund in the pension plan or scheme until age 75 at the latest. Hopefully it would continue to benefit from investment growth in this tax-favoured environment, although there are no guarantees.
- The traditional choice at retirement is to buy a conventional annuity from an insurance company. Unless investors pay for a guarantee, once they hand over their money it is gone for good. Those in poor health may be able to secure a much higher than average income from an impaired life annuity (see page 306).
- A few insurance companies offer investment-linked annuities where the income is determined partly by the mortality cross-subsidy (as with the conventional annuity) and partly by the performance of the underlying investments.
- Flexible annuities provide a link to a range of stock market funds and allow the individual to vary their income and the amount that can be passed on to heirs on death. This comparatively new generation of annuity offers many advantages to the more sophisticated investor with a substantial fund.
- Income drawdown and similar arrangements allow the individual to keep the fund fully invested and to draw an income directly from the fund. This is not an annuity, so there is no mortality cross-subsidy to enhance the income.

Leaving the fund in the personal pension

Individuals who plan to phase in retirement by switching to part-time work can expect to draw a reduced salary for several years. Some will have private sources of income – for example from a business. In these cases it may make sense to leave the pension fund where it is. This has three distinct advantages:

- It is simple.
- There are no annuity purchase costs at this stage.

- If the individual dies, the entire fund passes on to his or her dependants free of inheritance tax. (Death benefits under DC occupational schemes rules vary.)

It is not necessary to remain with the same pension provider and a transfer might be worthwhile if charges and/or performance are unsatisfactory. Those in DC occupational pension schemes may be required to transfer to a personal pension if the scheme rules do not allow members to defer taking benefits. Those with a large fund and who would like a more flexible investment choice might consider transferring to a Self-invested personal pension (SIPP), which allows the policyholder to invest directly in equities and bonds as well as in a wide range of collective funds. A SIPP is an ideal vehicle from which to move into income drawdown.

As soon as the individual wants to draw an income or take the tax-free cash it is necessary to vest part or the whole of the fund. **Vesting** means taking the money out of the personal pension and moving it into one of the other options outlined above. Among other things, this releases the tax-free cash.

How conventional annuities work

What makes annuities so complicated is the fact that they combine investment with insurance. This means we cannot compare the 'return' from an annuity with the return from, say, an equity or gilt fund because the pure investment route offers no lifetime guarantee. When we look at annuities it is helpful to keep in mind these two elements and examine how they interact.

To calculate the **annuity rate** the insurance company, after deductions for expenses, assumes it will return the individual's capital over the number of years it expects them to live. On top of this it adds a rate of interest. This is broadly equal to half the yield on bonds at the time of purchase. The reason it is only half is that the capital runs down over the payment period. On top of this there is a cross-subsidy from the pool of lives within the annuity fund.

To summarise, the annuity income guaranteed by the insurance company in return for a lump sum investment is based on:

- A return of capital spread over the individual's expected lifetime (based on mortality tables).
- The yield on long-dated gilts and bonds (and occasionally, property) – the assets insurance companies buy to generate the guaranteed income.
- A mortality cross-subsidy between the annuitants who die early and those who live longer than expected.

Women live about five years longer than men on average and so the income they secure will generally be lower than that for a man of the same age. Those in poor health may be able to secure a higher than average income if their condition is expected to reduce their life expectancy.

The open market option

There is no obligation to buy an annuity from the existing pension provider. The 'open market option' allows policyholders to take the proceeds of their pension fund away from the plan provider and to buy an annuity from a more competitive company. This is important. The top names in personal pensions are quite different from the top names in annuities, and rates change frequently in what is a very competitive market. The difference between the best and worst annuity rates at any given time can be as much as 25% and even among the top 10 companies there could be as much as a 10% difference. Financial planners must weigh up any penalties or loyalty bonuses that affect an individual's fund if he or she moves it away from the original company. These may negate the better terms available elsewhere. Also, for small funds of less than £20,000, the cost of using the open market option can outweigh the slightly higher rate of income available. Many firms of advisers will not handle pension funds less than £50,000. Fortunately the advent of online annuity websites is helping to reduce the administration costs, so making it easier for those with small funds to get a competitive rate.

The situation is different for members of occupational money purchase schemes. Here the trustees usually buy the annuity, although it is important to check that, using an annuity specialist, they are shopping around for the best rates.

Those who use their pension scheme or plan to opt out of SERPS or S2P must use the fund built up from the rebates of national insurance contributions in a specific way. The rules vary depending on when the individual was contracted out, but generally these funds must buy a spouse's pension and must increase by a set amount each year (typically 3%), although these restrictions are likely to be relaxed under the new tax regime in April 2006.

Annuity features

When we look at annuity rates we must remember that the benchmark figures, often quoted in tables, relate to the level of annuity for a single male – that is, to an income that remains static throughout the payment period. There are several useful features sold as optional extras in addition to the basic annuity. Some may be essential, depending on the individual's circumstances and preferences, but they come at a cost in the form of a reduction in the income. Once the annuity is purchased it is not possible to change providers or the options.

Those who are concerned about passing on their wealth cannot leave a lump sum for a dependent but can secure a lifetime income. An alternative for those who purchase their annuity later in retirement is to buy a 10-year guarantee so that the income continues for up to a decade if they die soon after buying the annuity.

The impact of annuity options as a reduction in the initial income

- **Guarantee period**. Most annuities are guaranteed for five years, which means that if you die after two years the remaining payments over the following three years are paid to your estate. The maximum guarantee is for 10 years. The reduction in initial income for a five-year guarantee: 1% at age 60; 5% at age 75.

- **Joint life annuity.** This pays the individual's spouse, partner or other dependant person a pension if he or she dies. The individual's health and life expectancy will affect the price. Reduction in initial income for a 50% dependent's pension: 12% (assuming a male annuitant aged 60 with a spouse aged 57).
- **Escalating annuities.** Here the income rises in line with full retail prices inflation or at a fixed rate each year – for example 3%. Reduction in initial income for a 3% annual increase or link to retail prices: 30% at age 60.

A higher income for those with shorter life expectancy

Annuity rates are based on average life expectancy, so those in poor health are at a disadvantage. Fortunately several companies offer annuities that pay a higher than average income – in some cases double or treble the standard rate – because they assume the individual will have a lower than average life expectancy. These annuities are divided into 'enhanced', for minor conditions and lifestyle features, and 'impaired life'.

Enhanced rate annuities

According to research from Britannic Assurance, an estimated 40% of the population may qualify for an enhancement. At a time when annuity rates are perceived as comparatively low, the additional 10%–20% available to smokers, for example, represents a significant uplift. Enhanced rates for smokers assume that the annuitants on average will die five years earlier than non-smokers – hence the 20% uplift on the rate for a male smoker aged 65, compared with the rate for a non-smoker. It may come as a surprise to discover that smokers qualify for a higher rate than those who have had a triple heart bypass in the last 12 months. Medical advances have now enabled insurance companies to relegate the triple bypass to the 'slightly impaired' annuity category.

Apart from smoking, clients may qualify for an enhanced rate if they are significantly overweight, have diabetes, have had a career in manual employment, and even if they live in certain parts of the country. It is not a daunting process for clients or their advisers to find out if an enhanced rate is available since this type of underwriting only requires the completion of a questionnaire – not a full medical.

Impaired life annuities

This is a particularly valuable option for those with a very serious condition who need the maximum income possible to allow them to enjoy a better quality of life for their remaining years (see Table 24.2). But even those with a less serious condition might be able to increase their income by a significant amount if the policy is

Table 24.2 The value of the impaired or enhanced rate

Medical condition	Male 60 (£)	Female 60 (£)
Secondary/inoperable cancer	21,421	21,353
Advanced Parkinson's disease	11,060	8,932
Liver cirrhosis	9,017	7,429
Stroke (severe)	6,119	5,305
Heart failure	5,427	4,560
Benchmark rate	4,000	3,725

Note: Rates are intended as a guideline only to the different levels of enhancement. They are based on a single life annuity, purchase price £50,000, no guarantee, paid monthly in arrears.

Source: Pension Annuity Friendly Society/William Burrows Annuities.

individually underwritten. Typical conditions which qualify for an 'impaired life' and an enhanced rate annuity are shown in Table 24.3.

Table 24.3 Typical conditions that qualify for higher annuity rates

Impaired health:

- Heart attack, heart surgery, angina
- Life threatening cancers
- Major organ diseases – for example liver or kidney
- Other life threatening illnesses – for example Parkinson's
- Strokes

Enhanced rate:

- Smoking
- Overweight
- Manual occupation and living in the north of England among other areas

Table 24.4 Questionnaire details

The standardised forms for enhanced and impaired life annuities would cover the following factors:

- Age, sex, height, weight
- Occupation prior to retirement
- Alcohol consumption
- Tobacco consumption
- Blood press
- Cholesterol
- Mobility
- Physical conditions: heart attack, angina, bypass or angioplasty, diabetes, asthma, cancer, stroke, impaired kidney, bladder/liver complaint, digestive or bowel complaint, MS, Alzheimer's or Parkinson's disease.

The form would seek specific information on date of onset of condition, treatment and medication.

To underwrite an impaired life annuity insurance companies require the completion of a detailed questionnaire and may request a medical report from your doctor (see Table 24.4).

With both enhanced and impaired life annuities the options available under a standard annuity are also available, but where the spouse is in good health this will reduce the rate available to the main annuitant. Where an individual wants to provide a pension for their spouse, for example, it may be better to use another source of capital for this purpose.

Investment-linked annuities

Increased longevity goes hand in hand with increased financial commitments in retirement, particularly in later years when some form of residential care may be required. With returns on traditional annuities at an historically low level, investors who can tolerate stock market risk may be willing to consider annuities that offer the potential to boost their future income. Having said that, any investor with a substantial fund should also consider drawdown. For the wealthy investor the investment-linked and flexible annuity is often an appropriate choice at age 75, rather than at retirement (see below).

Currently the market for investment-linked annuities is very small and there is no consensus among specialist annuity advisers over which type of product is the more attractive. Several providers withdrew their with profits annuities following the difficulties facing with profits policies in the late 1990s and early years of the new century.

One of the problems planners face with investment-linked annuities is the difficulty in explaining the structure to the layperson. Even a conventional annuity, which is associated with the dull but predictable, is complex. Impose a stock market overlay and the product morphs into something that is incomprehensible to the average investor. Nevertheless, those with a substantial DC fund might consider a more flexible alternative to a bond-based conventional annuity, which provides a guaranteed income for life but offers limited scope for inheritance planning and no potential for investment growth.

One way to reduce the impact of charges and investment risk is to divide the fund between different arrangements. For example, we could consider allocating half of an individual's fund to buy a conventional annuity to secure a basic guaranteed income, and with the other half invest in the stock markets in the hope of increasing the individual's income during retirement, or enabling them to leave a large portion of the fund to the heirs on death.

Clearly individual circumstances vary but as a general guideline 'substantial' funds means a minimum of £100,000, where there are other secure sources of income, and at least £250,000 if this is the individual's main source. Some advisers put the figure as high as £500,000. Given the uncertainty over these figures, a more appropriate exercise is to consider how much guaranteed income is actually required to support the individual's basic expenditure. This can be secured with the conventional annuity, leaving the individual free to take more of a risk with the remainder.

A conventional annuity is more accurately described as a non-profit policy because policyholders get a guaranteed level of income irrespective of whether the insurance company makes a profit or loss on the funds invested. Investment-linked annuities enable the individual to benefit from investment profits – but equally, to share in the downside risks. As with any approved pension arrangement the fund continues to grow in a tax-favoured environment. This type of product is still an annuity, so the fund reverts to the insurance company when the annuitant dies, unless they buy a pension for their partner or a guarantee to ensure that the income would be paid for at least 5 or possibly 10 years from the date of purchase.

The big advantage of annuitising the fund, however, is that the annuitant will benefit from the mortality cross-subsidy.

Some investment-linked annuities allow you to convert to a conventional annuity at any age up to 85, although you cannot move to a different provider at this point.

Choice of fund links

The main structure used for investment-linked annuities is the with profits fund. It is possible to buy a unit-linked annuity but there are very few on the market. (See page 162 for an explanation of how with profits funds work.) With profits funds have been the subject of criticism in recent years due to their lack of transparency and the problems that policyholders with Equitable Life have experienced. However, some advisers believe that their use as a retirement investment vehicle is appropriate because of the smoothing of investment volatility, which avoids significant stockmarket volatility being passed on as fluctuations in the annual income.

How the with profits annuity income is calculated

The income for the first year is broadly based on what could be expected from a standard annuity but can be varied between a minimum, which assumes there will be no investment growth and an upper limit, which assumes the maximum investment growth permitted by the provider.

The individual can vary this level of income by assuming a certain rate of return over the course of the year the **anticipated bonus rate (ABR)** – typically between 0% and 4%. Providers may use a single reversionary (regular) bonus or two-tier bonus structure, which combines regular and discretionary (top up) bonuses. The way these different bonuses operate is complicated and therefore it is important to consider this feature of the contract before selection.

If the overall investment return is greater than expected the individual can increase the income for the following year – or leave it in the fund so that a potentially higher income is available later. If the return is lower than predicted then the income will fall.

Who might benefit from a with profits annuity?

- Those with substantial pension funds and/or other assets. However, they must be able to cope with the possibility that the annuity income might fall in future.
- Those who want to diversify their annuity portfolio – for example by buying a mix of non-profit (conventional) and with profit.
- Those who want an alternative to income drawdown.
- Those with very small supplementary funds – for example from an additional voluntary contribution (AVC) scheme.

Flexible annuities

The standard investment-linked annuity usually offers a choice of funds run by the provider. However, the latest products also offer access to a range of external managers and clearly this is an important feature, particularly given the length of modern retirements.

Investment choice is not the only important new feature. The new generation of annuities (only available from Prudential, Canada Life and London & Colonial at the time of writing) gives the individual much more control over the level of income and the death benefits. The upper limit for the income is about the same as an individual would get from a conventional annuity, but if they want to conserve the fund it is possible to take as little as 50% of this figure. (After April 2006, the minimum annual income will be a token £1, allowing annuitants complete flexibility.)

The death benefits issue is important. Under a conventional annuity it is possible to buy a guarantee to ensure the income is paid for a minimum number of years even if the annuitant dies. This is possible because the income is based on gilts and so the yield is known and the cost of the guarantee can be assessed.

With an investment linked annuity the income cannot be assessed accurately because the returns will vary. However, a flexible annuity allows the annuitant to ring-fence a proportion of the fund that the individual wants to pass on, in the form of income, to dependants. Under the current rules after 10 years any ring-fenced fund is automatically converted to the main annuitised fund.

Drawdown and phased retirement

For those who want maximum flexibility over income and death benefits it is worth considering **phased retirement, income drawdown,** or a combination of the two, known as **phased drawdown.** These are high-risk strategies for those in retirement, however, as any capital losses cannot be recouped through future earned income. Investors who went into drawdown in the late 1990s saw their funds decimated by the long bear market and in many cases thoroughly regretted their choice in retrospect.

Under phased retirement the individual builds up the required annual income by withdrawing only part of the pension fund, leaving the remaining fund invested in the original plan. Most personal pensions are segmented, so it is possible to vest several segments without disturbing the rest of the fund, which continues to grow (hopefully) in the tax-favoured environment. For each segment withdrawn, 25% can be taken as tax-free cash and 75% used to buy an annuity. This pattern is repeated each year.

Phased retirement is not suitable for investors who want to use their tax-free lump sum for a capital project because the cash forms an important part of the annual income. However, for those who don't need the tax-free cash, phased retirement is particularly attractive as a means of passing on capital to their heirs, as the fund that remains in the original personal pension unvested can go as a lump sum to the nominated beneficiaries on death and is not subject to inheritance tax.

Under income drawdown plans the individual takes the full amount of tax-free cash and then draws a taxable income direct from the remaining fund. The income level is flexible although it must fall between a minimum and maximum set by the Inland Revenue, based broadly on the annuity rate that would otherwise have been payable at retirement. If the individual dies the fund goes to their dependants, but where it is taken as cash there is a tax liability.

The main risk with phased retirement and drawdown – as with investment-linked annuities – is the lack of any guarantee that the individual's income will remain steady. There is little point in investing the bulk of the capital in cash and gilt funds, as these are very unlikely to generate sufficient capital growth to cover the cost of the arrangement and to outstrip what would have been payable under an annuity. The most flexible investment vehicle for drawdown is the Self-invested personal pension (SIPP).

Phased drawdown combines the two arrangements. Here the individual draws their income from the fund directly but makes use of the tax-free cash in the same way as for phased retirement. It is not necessary to purchase annuities and so this increases the death benefits but at the expense of the guaranteed income the annuities would provide.

Abolition of the compulsory annuity purchase at age 75

Until 5 April 2006, when the individual in drawdown or phased retirement reaches age 75 it is necessary to convert any remaining fund to an annuity, although this can be an investment-linked version if the individual is keen to maintain a stock-market-based investment.

After this date it will still be possible to buy an annuity or an investment-linked version but in addition the government intends to introduce the **alternatively secured pension (ASP)**. This allows a restricted form of income withdrawal beyond age 75 and any funds remaining in the plan on death must be used to provide an income for dependants. If there are no dependants the individual can pay the money to a charity tax free or, in the case of group DC schemes (including GPPs and group SIPPs), it can be allocated to other members. Where the scheme is sponsored by an employer – for example a SSAS – it can be paid back to the employer less a tax of 35%.

For many people, however, it will make sense to purchase an annuity to consolidate the income for later retirement and in this case the individual should plan ahead. Where they plan to buy a conventional annuity it would be sensible to phase the switch from equities and into safer asset classes well before the planned date of conversion. An alternative would be to transfer the fund into an investment-linked or flexible annuity or, if the fund is still sufficiently large, to divide it between different arrangements according to the individual's basic income requirements and risk profile.

Summary of income drawdown plan rules

If you have a personal pension or similar plan, at retirement you can take part of the fund (typically one-quarter) as tax-free cash and use the rest to buy an annuity. If you choose to defer the annuity purchase using an income drawdown plan, the following rules apply:

- You can buy the plan from age 50 but must convert the fund to an annuity by age 75.
- You cannot make further pension contributions to the plan once it is in operation.
- During the deferment period investment income and capital gains continue to roll up virtually tax-free.
- The income you draw must fall between a minimum and maximum set by the Inland Revenue and be based on the annuity rate you could have purchased at retirement.
- Your plan must be reviewed every three years to ensure the income level you are drawing is still appropriate. If the fund has fallen too much you must convert to an annuity immediately.
- If you die before age 75 there are three options:
  - Your spouse can use the fund to buy an annuity.
  - Your spouse can continue to draw an income but must convert the fund to an annuity by the time you would have reached 75.
  - The fund can be taken as cash (less a 35% tax charge).

Summary of phased retirement rules

- The pension fund is divided into segments. Each year you withdraw however many you need to provide tax-free cash (usually 25% of each segment) and to buy a conventional or invested annuity to provide a lifetime income.
- If you die before age 75 the death benefits will be in two parts:
  - The full fund in the pension plan will go tax-free to your beneficiaries (different rules apply if you transferred from an occupational scheme)
  - The balance of any guaranteed or spouse's pension on the annuities you have arranged each year.

Summary of phased drawdown rules

- The pension fund is divided into segments.
- No tax-free cash is taken, so the fund remains unvested.

● Income is drawn from the fund.
● On death the remaining fund can be paid tax-free to beneficiaries.

Activity 24.1

Mary has a DC fund worth £600,000 and this is her only source of retirement income, apart from £40,000 held in cash and an ISA worth £50,000. She wants to keep control of her fund and is therefore considering income drawdown. However, she needs a guaranteed minimum income of £20,000 pa. What are Mary's options and what would you recommend? Give reasons for your answer and explain how the websites mentioned below helped.

Summary

This chapter considered an individual's options at retirement if they have a DC pension fund. Clearly it is important to weigh up the need for a secure lifetime income with the desire to maintain a stock market link over what could be a long retirement. Although the range of annuity and drawdown-style products is considerable; in certain areas, such as investment-linked and flexible annuities, there is very little competition. Now that the framework for pensions tax simplification is known we can expect more products to come onto the market to increase choice and competition.

Key terms

● Alternatively secured pension (ASP) p. 311
● Annuitisation p. 301
● Annuity rate p. 304
● Anticipated bonus rate (ABR) p. 309
● Conventional annuity p. 301
● Enhanced rate annuity p. 306
● Flexible annuity p. 310
● Impaired life annuity p. 306

● Income drawdown p. 310
● Investment-linked annuity p. 308
● Mortality cross-subsidy p. 301
● Open market option (OMO) p. 300
● Phased drawdown p. 310
● Phased retirement p. 310
● Vesting p. 304

Review questions

1 What is the unique feature of the conventional annuity?

2 Explain why the open market option is so important.

3 How can those in poor health or who smoke, for example, get a higher annuity rate?

4 Explain how investment-linked and flexible annuities work.

5 Describe income drawdown, phased retirement and phased drawdown.

6 What new type of annuity will be available from April 2006?

Go to the Companion Website at **www.booksites.net/harrison_pfp** for a multiple-choice quiz to test your understanding of this chapter.

Further information

The FSA publishes comparative tables of annuities at **www.fsa.gov.uk/tables**.

The following websites all offer a good guide to annuities:

The Annuity Bureau – **www.annuity-bureau.co.uk**

Annuity Direct – **www.annuitydirect.co.uk**

Hargreaves Lansdown – **www.hargreaveslansdown.co.uk**

Wentworth Rose – **www.wentworthrose.co.uk**

William Burrows Annuities – **www.williamburrows.com**

Chapter 25 ●●●●

Working and retiring abroad

Introduction

Financial planning for those who plan to work or retire overseas is complex, as it must take account of both the UK and the local tax environment. Unless financial planners choose to specialise in this field they would not be expected to be experts but should be aware of the circumstances that require specialist expatriate taxation and legal advice.

Objectives

After reading this chapter you should be able to:

- Discuss circumstances where specialist taxation and/or legal advice are necessary.
- Consider what features should be provided in an expatriate's employee benefits package.
- Explain how to ensure that individuals retiring abroad are taxed only once on worldwide income in their country of residence.
- Describe how pension payments are paid to those living overseas.

● ● ● ● Overseas assignments

A two-year posting to Brussels for an employee of a major multinational should run smoothly, as the company will have a formal benefits package for all standard overseas placements. More difficult locations are another matter. Employees posted to the Middle East, for example, should look to their employer to cover the cost of a speedy evacuation to get the family home safe and sound in the event of any social or political unrest. A hardship allowance is also required for employees assigned to a country that has an uncongenial climate, has tough rules on alcohol and entertainment, or is unstable politically, where the individual's freedom of movement may be restricted.

The contract should set out clearly how the employee will be paid for tough assignments. An excellent guide to all these personal safety issues is the international consultant Mercer's *Quality of Living Report 2003*, which assesses the political, social, economic and medical conditions of 215 cities worldwide. The degree of hardship is generally measured through a quality of life index that would compare conditions in the home city with those of the assignment location. Allowances are not the only focus, however. The amount of special leave is also important, especially in remote locations, when regular visits to the family back home are vital for the individual's or family's well-being.

Pension arrangements

When it comes to the standard benefits in the package we should pay particular attention to the individual's pension arrangements, as the number of multinationals offering a Defined benefit (DB) pension scheme for expatriates has almost halved over the last 10 years. If the company offers a Defined contribution (DC) arrangement, where contributions build up a fund that is used at retirement to buy an annuity, it may be wise to seek actuarial advice to make sure that what is on offer is broadly equivalent in value to the home package.

In some cases the employer may set up an offshore trust to fund the pension. But even this can cause problems; for example if the country of assignment taxes employer contributions as income. Until recently it was quite common to have an unfunded pension promise, but, post-Enron, employees are understandably anxious to have a funded arrangement rather than a promise that a benefit will be paid out of company funds when they retire. With an unfunded promise, if the company becomes insolvent the employee could be left empty-handed.

Apart from the main benefits and security considerations it is vital to consider the cultural impact of working abroad. Employers report it is often the 'soft' issues that make or break an overseas assignment. Extra cash will not help the family adapt to a very different local culture and language, so it is wise to insist on a pre-departure intensive language course and cultural briefing for both the employee and their partner. Where business practices differ widely it can be very limiting and potentially damaging to go into your first meeting without an appropriate understanding of the business culture and practices of the host country as well as some basic language skills. Many executives who function really well in London and New York find they cannot function in the new environment, which may require a much more conciliatory approach and a lot of patience.

We must also consider the return after the assignment has finished. Ideally the individual's employment contract will guarantee that their current position is held open, but only 50% of international companies give this assurance. Where the assignment was long it will help to attend a repatriation briefing programme. This is particularly helpful if the assignment was cut short by unforeseen and possibly very upsetting circumstances.

Exhibit 25.1 Checklist for a successful overseas assignment

The big multinationals tend to have formal benefits and pay structures for expatriates, but if the company is venturing overseas for the first time the value of the employee's package will be directly linked to his or her bargaining skills. The following checklist applies to individuals going on a two to three year assignment accompanied by the family. The total cost to the employer is typically up to four times base salary but can be much higher in difficult locations.

Cash compensation and benefits
- Base salary.
- Bonus.
- Cost of living allowance.
- Hardship allowance for uncongenial locations.
- Foreign service premium (an extra perk linked to the assignment).
- Company cars (if this is the usual practice in country of assignment).
- Children's education.
- Compensation for loss of spouse/partner earnings (for example assistance with cost of job search or retraining).

Employee benefits
- Retirement pension.
- Medical insurance.
- Long-term disability insurance.
- Accidental death and injury insurance.
- Travel insurance.
- Club memberships (golf, for example, if this is an important cultural feature).

Holidays and home leave
- Home leave: usually one return trip (economy) per annum.
- Holidays/leave/vacation.
- Hardship leave (extra time out if you are working in a tough location).
- Compassionate leave.

Pre-assignment
- Trip to host country.
- Physical examinations.

- Cross-cultural training.
- Language lessons.
- Tax briefing.

Taxation and social security
- **Tax equalisation** – additional payments to ensure the individual is not disadvantaged by a more punitive regime while overseas.
- Assistance with local social security arrangements.
- Tax return.
- Exit and re-entry tax briefings.

Relocation assistance
- Travel to the new location.
- Shipment of goods and personal effects; air freight.
- Insurance.
- Storage of goods/personal effects in home country, if applicable.
- Time off for moving.
- Relocation allowance (may be in lieu of or in addition to actual relocation costs).

Housing
- Sale of home or lease breaking, if there is a penalty for breaking the tenant's agreement.
- Temporary living expenses.
- Housing and utilities allowance.

Source: Adapted from Mercer Human Resource Consulting.

Retiring abroad

The prospect of retiring in the sun is very appealing, but if an individual or couple want a financially healthy retirement the most important task is to arrange for all pensions and other sources of income to be paid abroad without double tax penalties. Expert advice on pension and inheritance tax planning is essential for would-be expatriates but here provide a brief overview of the steps to take before leaving the UK.

Today's flexible career patterns tend to result in a variety of retirement benefits, but essentially there are three main sources of pension:

- State schemes.
- Company schemes.
- Private individual plans.

State pensions

Chapter 21 deals with the UK state pensions in detail. Briefly, the pension, which builds up through payment of National insurance contributions, is made up of two elements – a basic flat rate benefit and an additional pension, which from April 2002 was known as the State second pension. The S2P replaced SERPS (State earnings related pension scheme) but any SERPS benefits built up to that date remain intact.

The pension is paid at age 65 for men and between age 60 and 65 for women, depending on the date of retirement. (The female state pension age is due to be raised in line with the male pension age and there is a transition period between 2010 and 2020 to achieve this.)

Cost of living increases

The state retirement pensions and widows' benefits can be claimed from anywhere in the world. However, annual cost of living increases are only paid if the individual lives in a European Union country or a country with which Britain has a social security agreement that provides for uprating (the list is available on the DWP website: see the end of this chapter). This means that those who retire to Australia, Canada and New Zealand, for example, will find that their state pension is frozen either at the date of departure from the UK or, for those already abroad when they reach state retirement age, at the time of the first payment.

Clearly, the loss of the annual cost of living increases will rapidly erode the value of the pension over a 15 to 20 year retirement and extra income from other sources will be required to compensate. As a rough guide to the impact of inflation, £100 today would be worth £64 after 15 years, assuming 3% annual inflation, and just £48, assuming an annual inflation rate of 5%.

If an individual later returns to the UK, their state pension will be paid at the full current rate. UK expatriates on a temporary visit home can also claim the full rate but only for the period spent in this country.

Payment abroad

For those who go abroad for short periods, the Benefits Agency has special arrangements that cover the payment of the pension. No action is necessary where the period is less than three months and in this case the pension payments can be collected on return. For periods between three and six months it is possible to arrange for the individual's UK bank to transfer payments to a bank overseas. For periods over six months the Benefits Agency, on request, will pay a sterling cheque to an overseas bank. Alternatively you can collect the lump sum on your return.

For periods abroad of over 12 months, a more permanent arrangement is made to pay the pension by automated credit transfer to the individual's overseas bank. However, it is possible to leave the pension for up to a maximum of two years and to collect the lump sum on return to the UK.

Company and private pensions

Company and private individual pensions can also be paid abroad. When calculating the individual's income from pension we should bear in mind that most statements from employers and pension providers assume retirement is within the UK, so it is essential to check how retiring abroad will affect the individual's tax position. For example the tax-free cash lump sum that is an important feature of UK private pensions is not recognised in certain countries and if an individual receives the benefit while overseas it may be taxed along with the pension.

We must also remember that in most cases the income will be subject to currency fluctuations. If the local currency in the retirement country rises against the pound, then the value of the individual's UK pension will reduce in real terms.

Pensions from previous employment

Most people change jobs several times before reaching retirement so it will be necessary to contact previous employers to check the value of any benefits left in the former employers' schemes. These benefits are known as **deferred pensions**. Where a company has been taken over or become insolvent and it is difficult to track down the trustees, the Pensions Register will trace benefits free of charge.

Pensions from work overseas

If the individual's career included overseas employment with foreign state and company pension entitlements, the tracing problems could become more complicated. Moreover, foreign pensions may fall due at a different retirement age from the rest of the individual's UK pensions.

As a general rule, whether it is a state or company pension, outside the UK it is up to the individual to keep track of their benefit rights and to make the claims. There is no central source of information about foreign state pensions, so it will be necessary to contact each authority, although where there is a social security agreement with the UK, the Department for Work and Pensions will help.

Taxation of pensions

Most of the tax details need to be sorted out at the time of retirement but it is useful to know in advance how the system works and where the pitfalls lie. Expert advice is essential here as it is essential to be conversant with the tax and pensions rules in the country of retirement. The object of the exercise is to pay tax on pensions and invest-ment income just once – usually in the retirement location.

Where the country has a double taxation agreement with the UK (there are over 80 of these agreements in operation), the Inland Revenue will allow pensions to be paid gross provided the individual has a declaration from the foreign tax authorities stating that he or she is being taxed on worldwide income.

This declaration should be sent to the individual's UK tax office. If there is a delay, pensions will be taxed twice – once in the UK, at the basic rate of income tax, and once again in the country of retirement. However, in these cases the Inland Revenue will repay the tax withheld when it receives the declaration from the foreign tax authority.

Individuals should not fall into the trap of thinking that if they move to a no-tax environment they would escape with their pensions tax free. In these cases there will be no double tax treaty with the UK in operation and if there is no local equivalent of the Inland Revenue, it will not be possible to get the declaration mentioned above. As a result the Revenue will impose the withholding tax on all pensions paid from the UK.

Other issues

The planner should review all of the individual's investments and decide whether some of these need to be moved to a different location – either offshore or to the retirement country. The UK wills should be rewritten to take account of the overseas property, and it will also be necessary to make a will in the new location.

In many cases when the couple edge towards late retirement, with its associated frailty, or when one of the partners dies, a return to the UK may be necessary. Ideally, therefore, those retiring overseas will take this possibility into account and make provision for a return to smooth the passage, particularly as this is likely to be at an emotionally difficult time of life.

Summary

This chapter considered some of the important taxation and personal issues that must be addressed where an individual plans to work or retire overseas. In the case of working overseas, while the benefits package is important it may also be necessary for the individual and their family to receive pre-departure cultural briefings, depending on the country of assignment. Those retiring abroad need expert tax advice that takes account of tax practice in the UK and the country of retirement.

Key terms

- Deferred pension p. 320
- Tax equalisation p. 318

Review questions

1 List six important features of the expatriate employee's benefits package.

2 Why might a cultural pre-departure briefing be so important?

3 What step should an individual take to avoid double taxation when retiring abroad?

Go to the Companion Website at **www.booksites.net/harrison_pfp** for a multiple-choice quiz to test your understanding of this chapter.

Further information

The Department for Work and Pensions provides leaflets and advice on retirement overseas and lists the countries with which the UK has a social security agreement that includes payment of the annual uprating for the state pension: **www.dwp.gov.uk**.

Mercer Human Resources: **www.mercerHR.co.uk**

Appendices

Appendix 1 ●●●●

Glossary of terms

This section provides a brief description of the terms used in this book. For full details refer to the index and find the relevant page where the term is used. A term in italics used in the description will have its own entry. For broader definitions and a more comprehensive dictionary of financial terms I recommend *Lamont's Glossary* (**www.lamonts-glossary.co.uk**).

A-Day See *Pension Tax Simplification*.

Absolute return fund A fund that aims to achieve a positive return throughout the market cycles and irrespective of movements in the equity and bond markets. See *correlation*.

Absolute performance A return above the rate of inflation.

Account aggregation The provision of information across a range of online accounts on one website.

Accrual In *defined benefit* pension schemes this the rate at which a member's benefits build up each year – for example one-sixtieth of final salary.

Accumulation and maintenance trust A *trust* that gives parents or grandparents, for example, the flexibility to provide funds for the benefit of children.

Acid test A ratio of the company's current assets (excluding stock) to its current liabilities.

Active investment management An investment style that aims to increase a fund's value by deviating from a specific benchmark – for example a stock market index. See *bottom up* and *top down*.

Additional pension The generic term used to describe the *State second pension*, introduced in 2002, and its predecessor the *State earnings related pension scheme*.

Additional voluntary contribution (AVC) An investment used to top up benefits from a company pension scheme.

Advisory manager A service from an investment manager, for example, where the manager discusses opportunities with the individual and offers advice, but no action is taken without the individual's approval.

Alpha Outperformance of a fund generated by the manager's skill rather than market direction. See *beta*.

Alternative investment An asset that is not correlated to the two major classes, equities and bonds. See *correlation*.

Alternative Investment Market (AIM) The market for companies that are too small to join the Official List – the main London Stock Exchange market.

Alternatively secured income (ASI) A very restricted form of *income drawdown* for pensioners over age 75. On death any funds remaining in the plan must be used to provide an income for dependants or, where it is a company-sponsored plan, the fund can revert to the scheme for the benefit of other members.

Angel An external backer of a (usually unregulated) venture.

Annual bonus On a with profits policy this is the annual 'return' calculated by the life office actuary and allocated to the policy.

Annual management charge (AMC) The fund management charge.

Annual percentage rate (APR) A standard way of assimilating the different methods credit card issuers and other lenders use to calculate the interest charged on a loan. It should express the *total credit charge* as a standard measure to take into account the size, number and frequency of the payments and any other built-in charges.

Annuitisation The process of converting a lump sum into an *annuity*.

Annuity Sold by insurance companies, these guarantee to pay a regular income for life in return for a lump sum investment.

Annuity rate The annual rate of income provided by an *annuity* in return for the investment of a lump sum.

Anticipated bonus rate The expected annual return on a with profits annuity. This is used to determine the annual income.

Asset backing What a company would be worth if it became insolvent.

Asset share In a *with profits* fund this is the policyholder's 'fair share' of the fund, and takes account of premiums paid, actual returns over the specific policy term to date, deductions for expenses, plus any relevant experience built into the formula – for example mortality within the with profits policyholders' pool, and profits and losses from other lines of business.

Band earnings An individual's earnings on which *National insurance* is paid.

Bare trust Where a parent or grandparent invests on behalf of a child a bare trust is created automatically. The gift is outright and the child has an absolute interest in the income and capital. The trustees transfer the investment to the child's name when they reach age 18.

Basic state pension (BSP) A flat rate benefit paid in retirement and based on an individual's national insurance contribution record.

Basic sum assured On a conventional *with profits policy* this is the minimum value at maturity irrespective of investment returns.

Bear market Where share prices are falling.

Bed and breakfast Banned from April 1998, B&B involved selling shares to realise the capital gain and to make use of the CGT annual exemption. The following day the seller bought back the same number of shares to retain the portfolio position.

Bed and spouse A replacement for *bed and breakfast* where one spouse repurchases the shares the other sells.

Benchmark index A benchmark index is constructed for the purposes of performance measurement by selecting a representative range of assets from the main (tradable) index.

Beneficiary One of two types of legal owners of the assets of a *trust* – the other being the *trustees*.

Beta A statistical measure of volatility that indicates the sensitivity of a security or portfolio to movements in the market index.

Bid price The price at which institutions buy and at which investors sell securities and funds.

Blue chip Refers to major companies, in particular to those in the FTSE 100. Blue is the highest value chip in poker.

Boiler room A high-pressure call centre from which fraudsters target their victims to sell unattractive, often non-existent, shares.

Bond A contract issued by borrowers that in return for the loan of your money, agrees to pay a fixed rate of interest (the *coupon*) for the loan period and to repay the original capital sum on a specified (maturity or redemption) date. Also referred to as 'fixed interest' assets because the coupon is fixed. However, the actual yield will depend on the price of the bond if it is traded.

Bottom up An investment style that considers individual companies before looking at the performance and prospects for the relevant sector, the local market, and national and international economic factors.

Bubble An over-priced range of stocks or stock market as a whole, driven by panic buying. When prices collapse the bubble is said to have burst.

Bull market Where shares are rising.

Buy-out cost The full cost of purchasing immediate and deferred *annuities* to meet a pension scheme's liabilities to its active and retired members.

Call option A type of derivative contract that confers the right but not the obligation to buy a fixed number of shares at a predetermined price on a fixed date or within a predetermined period of time.

Capital asset pricing model (CAPM) An economic model for valuing assets that assumes that the expected excess return of a security over a risk-free asset will be in proportion to its *beta*.

Capital gains tax (CGT) A tax on chargeable gains above the annual exemption. The gain is the difference between the purchasing and selling price of an asset. There is an adjustment for inflation, known as the indexation allowance, which applies up to April 1998, after which *taper relief* applies. Taper relief reduces the rate of CGT according to how long the individual has held the asset.

Capital gains tax allowance The amount of capital gains an individual can make in a given tax year before becoming liable for *capital gains tax* (CGT).

Capital shares See *split capital investment trust*.

Career averaged revalued earnings scheme (CARE) A type of *defined benefit* scheme that links the *accrual* to average earnings rather than final salary.

Carry forward The facility to mop up unused tax relief from up to six previous tax years to boost contributions to a *retirement annuity plan*.

Cash balance A hybrid between a *defined benefit* and *defined contribution* shceme.

Cash flow planning A strategy that ensures sufficient liquidity for known cash requirements, to avoid forced selling of medium- to long-term assets such as equities.

CAT-marked product A regulated product that must offer fair Charges, flexible Access, and reasonable Terms – hence 'CAT'.

Chargeable gain See *capital gains tax*.

Civil offence A crime under civil law, which relates to private and civilian affairs. Civil law aims to compensate the victim. See *criminal offence*.

Commission-free A financial product that does not incorporate an allowance for sales commission in the pricing.

Commutation Swapping pension for tax-free cash in a company scheme.

Completion When a buyer takes ownership of a property and must pay the balance.

Concurrency Dual membership of a company scheme and a stakeholder or personal pension plan.

Constant protection portfolio insurance products (CPPI) Investment products that link to an index or fund, where the investor's money is split between the underlying fund and cash. The protection is provided by a switching mechanism that sells units in the fund and moves into cash when markets are falling, and the reverse when markets are rising.

Consumer Prices Index (CPI) The Harmonised Index of Consumer Prices (HICP), better known as the CPI, was introduced in December 2003 as the main UK domestic measure of inflation for *econometrics* purposes.

Contracted in money purchase scheme (CIMPS) An occupational *defined contribution* pension scheme that does not contract members out of the State second pension.

Contract for difference (CFD) An agreement that allows an individual to borrow to invest, in order to trade the price movement of a share. Here the individual does not actually buy the share but wins or loses based on changes in the share price.

Contracyclical An investment strategy that avoids stock market fashions.

Contribution holiday A period when an employer does not contribute to the company pension scheme.

Conventional annuity See *annuity*.

Convertible A type of *equity* that is more akin to a *bond*. It pays a regular income, has a fixed *redemption date* and confers the right to convert to an ordinary share or *preference share* at a future date.

Corporate bond A bond issued by a company, which pays interest (the yield) and returns the original capital on a predetermined redemption or maturity date.

Corporate bond funds Collective funds that hold a range of individual corporate bonds of *investment grade* and, in some cases, *sub-investment grade*.

Correlation The relationship between two variables – typically indices or asset classes.

Correlation coefficient A statistical measure of the extent to which two or more variables – asset class price indices, for example – follow the same path or direction.

Coupon The income payable on a *bond* or *gilt*. This remains static irrespective of any price fluctuations of the bond itself.

Covered warrant A listed *derivative* launched by The London Stock Exchange in 2002. See *warrant*.

Credit card Allows holders to pay for goods immediately but defer payment until later.

Criminal offence Broadly, a crime against society. Criminal law aims to punish the offender. See *civil offence*.

Critical illness insurance An insurance policy that pays a lump sum on the diagnosis of a range of serious medical conditions.

Cumulative performance Results measured and aggregated over a period of time, which can even out a very volatile return pattern. See *discrete performance*.

Current account mortgage A combined account that covers both saving and borrowing, with an overall lending limit. Interest is charged on the actual amount borrowed.

Day trading Buying and selling shares on the same day with the aim of making a profit.

Debit card An 'electronic cheque'. The amount of the purchase is debited to (deducted from) the individual's account, usually two or three days later.

Debt consolidation Where an individual takes out a loan or other credit agreement in order to pay off two or more existing debts.

Debt management A strategy that ensures debt is repaid over a sensible period and that the terms of any loans are the most competitive.

Default 1. Not able to meet interest payments on a loan. 2. Not able to pay compensation claims, usually because the company has stopped trading or is insolvent.

Default/lifestyle DC investment A predetermined investment option for *defined contribution* pension schemes and plans that makes the asset allocation and fund management choices. See *lifestyle*.

Deferred pension A pension benefit – usually in a former employer's scheme – that will be paid when the individual reaches the scheme's official pension age.

Defined benefit (DB) A type of occupational pension scheme that links the benefit to earnings.

Defined contribution (DC) A type of company and individual pension arrangement that invests contributions to build up a fund, which generally is used to buy an *annuity* at retirement.

Definition of disability The definition used to assess whether an individual qualifies for disability income from a private insurance policy or the state.

Deflation A measure of the increase in prices in an economy over a period of time, typically based on a basket of household goods and expenditure.

Demutualisation The process by which a mutual life company, which is owned by its policyholders, becomes a proprietary company, which is owned by its shareholders.

Depolarisation Under depolarisation advisers are allowed to call themselves 'independent' only if they make advice available (but not compulsory) on a fee basis to clients. Other advisers can have ties with a range of product providers (multi-tied).

Derivatives Financial instruments that derive their value from the price of an underlying security. The generic term given to *futures* contracts and *options*.

Designated professional body Professional institutes may regulate members that do not provide specific investment advice and so do not need FSA authorisation – for example the Law Society for solicitors and the Institute of Actuaries for actuarial consultants.

Discount broker An adviser that offers access online to a wide range of products (collective funds, for example) at a competitive price and with a high-speed service.

Discount (trading at) An equity with a net asset value higher than the share price.

Discrete performance Results measured year on year rather than on a *cumulative* basis.

Discretionary management A form of advice where the investment manager makes all the decisions on behalf of the client.

Discretionary trust A trust where the trustees have absolute discretion over the payment of income and capital.

Distribution fund 1. A collective fund run by a life office that distributes income. 2. A comparatively cautious fund run by a life office or unit trust group for example; that typically has a 60 : 40 bond/equity weighting.

Dividend cover This shows the number of times the dividend could have been paid out of net profits and is a ratio of profits to dividends, calculated by dividing the earnings per share by the gross dividend per share.

Dividend yield For equities this is the dividend paid by a company divided by that company's share price.

Domicile A complex tax status but broadly this is the country that is the individual's permanent home.

Downside gearing Common in *precipice bonds*. When the index to which a product is linked falls below a certain level the provider reduces the investor's original capital by an equivalent or multiple percentage amount.

Earnings cap Introduced in the 1989 Budget, the cap restricts the level of earnings on which pension contributions and, for occupational schemes, benefits are based.

Econometrics The application of mathematical and statistical techniques to economic theories.

Economic indicators Statistical snapshots that show the state of the economy.

Efficient frontier A graphical representation of the relationship between risk and reward, which aims to show the greatest expected return for a given level of risk.

Efficient market A capital market for which there is a large amount of analysis available to potential investors and where new information is reflected quickly in the share prices.

Endowment A life policy that combines investment with a substantial element of life assurance.

Endowment mortgage A combined life assurance and investment product that aims to provide a capital sum to repay the loan by the end of the mortgage term or on the death of the borrower, whichever is first.

Enduring power of attorney A legal document that authorises a person or persons of the individual's choice to act on his or her behalf.

Enhanced rate annuity An *annuity* that pays an above-average income or rate because the individual has a lifestyle feature, such as smoking or obesity, that will lower life expectancy.

Enterprise Investments Scheme (EIS) A vehicle that provides private equity financing to smaller companies and offers long tax-deferral opportunities.

Equity Literally a 'share' in the ownership of a company. UK equities are the quoted shares of companies in the UK.

Equity release An arrangement that allows elderly homeowners to sell or *mortgage* a part share of their home in return for a regular income or lump sum.

Equity risk premium (ERP) The relative value of equities in comparison with lower risk assets.

Ethical investment Also known as *socially responsible investment (SRI)*, this is where an investor or fund manager applies ethical, environmental and/or religious screening in the selection of funds and securities.

Ethical Investment Research Service (EIRIS) An independent research service that maintains a database of ethical funds and individual companies, among other information.

Eurobonds *Bonds* denominated in sterling but issued on the Eurobond market – an international market where borrowers and lenders are matched.

Exchange of contract A formal commitment on the purchaser's part to buy, and on the owner's part to sell, a property.

Exchange traded fund (ETF) A basket of stocks that is used to track an index or a particular industry sector.

Execution-only The sale of an investment on the request of the investor and therefore without advice.

Executive pension plan (EPP) A supposedly 'fast-track' pension plan for executives that is used in certain cases instead of the main scheme.

Family income benefit (FIB) An insurance policy that provides a level or increasing income from the date of death until the end of the insurance period.

Final results Second set of annual results produced at the listed company's financial year-end.

Financial planning certificate (FPC) The regulatory examination requirement for those selling financial products. There are different levels, FPC1 being the most elementary. Much higher qualifications are required for complex sales, such as sophisticated investments and pension transfers.

Financial reporting standard 17 (FRS17) A snapshot accounting view of a pension scheme's funding level based on equity prices. In 2004 this was replaced by *scheme-specific funding requirements*.

Financial Services Authority (FSA) The chief financial regulator for financial services under the Financial Services and Markets Act 2000, which came into force in December 2001.

Financial Services Compensation Scheme (FSCS) The FSCS can investigate a claim of mis-selling where the alleged culprit is no longer trading. It can award compensation.

Flexible annuity Used to describe a small but varied range of *annuities* that offer flexibility over the death benefits.

Formula maturity value Indicates the potential value of a second-hand with profits *endowment* policy based on investment assumptions.

Fraud Financial fraud is regarded as theft by deception in the UK.

Free asset ratio An indicator of the level of reserves an insurance company holds that are not related to liabilities. See **realistic balance sheet**.

Freehold A freehold property purchase confers ownership of the land, as well as the bricks and mortar. See *leasehold*.

FTSE 100 This index consists of the 100 largest UK companies by market capitalisation.

FTSE 250 This index consists of the 250 companies below the *FTSE 100* and can include or exclude investment trusts.

FTSE4Good A series of *socially responsible investment* (*ethical*) indices launched by the FTSE Group in 2001 as part of its global series.

FTSE All-Small The *SmallCap* and *Fledgling* indices combined.

FTSE Fledgling This index covers all of the companies that are too small to be in the *All-Share* index but otherwise are eligible to join The London Stock Exchange. Together the *SmallCap* and *Fledgling* indices are known as the *All-Small index*.

FTSE SmallCap This index does not have a fixed number of constituent companies but instead it comprises all the remaining companies in the *All-Share*, which are too small to qualify for the top 350.

FTSE techMARK An index of technology stocks.

Funded unapproved retirement benefit scheme (FURBS) A funded 'unapproved' pension arrangement employers use for employees restricted by the *earnings cap*.

Fund of funds A *unit trust* or *OEIC* that invests in other funds with the objective of selecting a winning team of managers that can achieve an aggregate return, which more than compensates for the additional layer of charges.

Fund supermarket A facility offered by investment managers and large advisers, which provides access to a wide range of funds at low cost and with easy switching. These usually offer cheap or free *Individual savings accounts* and *personal pension* wrappers in which to hold funds from different managers.

Future A *derivatives* contract that represents an agreement to buy or sell a given quantity of a particular asset, at a specified future date, at a pre-agreed price.

Gearing (leverage) Financial gearing is the ratio between the company's borrowings and its capitalisation – in other words, a ratio between what it owes and what it owns.

Gift aid A scheme that enables employees to make regular tax-efficient deductions for earnings that are paid to a nominated charity.

Gilt-equity yield ratio This ratio tracks the yield on gilts divided by the yield on equities.

Gilts *Bonds* issued by the UK government.

Gross redemption yield On a bond fund the gross redemption yield or 'projected total yield' takes into account both the income received and changes in the capital value of the bonds if they are held to maturity. See *running yield*.

Growth investing An investment strategy where the objective is to find companies that will achieve above average earnings growth.

Guaranteed annuity rate (GAR) This guarantees *defined contribution* pension investors that at retirement they will receive a minimum *annuity rate* for their funds.

Guaranteed income bond (GIB) Provides a fixed rate of interest over a specific term.

Guaranteed/protected products Offer a link to the return on an index or a basket of indices. The growth potential is limited but in return these products offer some downside protection.

Headline inflation The full rate of *retail price inflation*, including mortgage interest costs.

Hedge fund There is no statutory definition but the term relates to the original funds that used specific strategies to 'hedge' risk – usually some form of *derivative*, such as an *option*. Today the term covers a very wide spectrum of strategies that are classed as *alternative investments*.

High yield/junk bond Usually refers to *sub-investment grade debt*.

Hire purchase A form of borrowing where the borrower does not become the legal owner of the goods until they have completed payments.

Home income plan (HIP) A type of *equity release* where the lump sum secured by the mortgage is used to buy an *annuity* from the lender, which guarantees a regular income for life.

Home reversion An *equity release* arrangement where the homeowner sells part of the house in return for a lump sum or an *annuity*, and continues to live there rent-free. On their death the buyer recoups the proportionate value of the property, including any capital growth.

Impaired life annuity An *annuity* that pays a higher than average rate because the provider assumes the individual has a lower than average life expectancy. See *enhanced annuity*.

Income drawdown This allows an individual with a personal pension fund to draw an income directly and keep the fund invested, rather than buy an *annuity*.

Income protection insurance This pays a replacement income if the policyholder is too ill to work.

Income shares See *split capital investment trust*.

Income tax allowance The amount of income an individual can earn in a given tax year before income tax is applied.

Independent financial adviser (IFA) Until the end of 2004 an IFA was an adviser who could select products from the entire range available on both a fee or commission basis. See *depolarisation, tied agent.*

Indexation allowance An adjustment for inflation on a *chargeable gain.* This allowance applies for assets held up to April 1998, after which *taper relief* provides the adjustment factor.

Index linked gilts *Bonds* issued by the UK government that guarantee to provide interest payments (the *coupon*) and a redemption value that increase in line with annual inflation.

Index tracking See *passive management.*

Individual savings account (ISA) Introduced in April 1999, this wrapper replaced *Personal equity plans* and *Tax-efficient special savings accounts* for new contributions as the mainstream tax-efficient investment apart from pension plans. Standard ISAs can hold collective funds, but see also *self-select ISAs.*

Inefficient market A capital market where there is a comparatively small amount of available research on companies and where the economic and political environment is less predictable.

Inflation A measure of the increase in the general price of goods and services.

Inflation shock A sudden and unexpected change in the inflation rate.

Inheritance tax (IHT) A death tax on the value of an individual's estate above the nil-rate band.

Inheritance tax allowance The amount an individual can pass on to his or her heirs before paying inheritance tax.

Initial commission The upfront sales commission paid by a provider to an adviser. Commission is calculated as a percentage of the investment or premium.

Insider dealing/trading This refers to an individual or company that trades in shares when it is in possession of price-sensitive information that is not known in the market at large.

Integration A company pension scheme can be integrated with the basic state pension so that it does not pay any pension for the first slice of salary up to the *National insurance lower earnings limit.* No employee or employer pension contributions are levied on this amount either.

Interest cover The number of times a company's profits can cover the interest payments.

Interest in possession/life interest trust A legal structure that allows an individual to receive the income from an asset for life or a fixed period.

Interest-only mortgage A mortgage where the borrower makes interest payments each month but the capital debt remains static and must be repaid in full at the end of the loan term.

Interest rate The amount charged for borrowing.

Interim results First set of (usually) twice-yearly profit figures in a company's financial year.

Intermediaries People and organisations that mediate between the providers of financial products and services, and the consumers who make the purchases.

Intestate Where an individual dies without making a valid will the laws of intestacy will determine the division of the estate between dependants.

Investment bond Run by insurance companies, this is similar to a *maximum investment plan* but is a single premium or lump sum investment. The bond usually runs for 10 years.

Investment grade debt Bonds that are rated BBB– and above by credit agencies.

Investment-linked annuity An *annuity* that invests the capital in order to provide an income with a stock market link.

Investment term The period to which an investment commits the individual. Early withdrawal may incur a penalty.

Investment trust A British company, usually listed on the London stock market, which invests in the shares of other quoted and unquoted companies in the UK and overseas.

Islamic (Shariah) finance Based on the principles of Shariah (Islamic law). This attempts to maximise social welfare (Maslahah) by protecting the five pillars of Islamic society: faith, life, wealth, intellect and posterity.

Joint life policy A joint life policy that covers more than one person – typically a husband and wife. It may be written to pay out if just one of the spouses dies ('joint life first death') or only when both have died ('joint life second death').

Junk bond Slang for sub-investment grade bonds.

Large cap Companies with a high *market capitalisation*; for example those in the *FTSE 100* index.

Leasehold Ownership of property on a leasehold basis confers the right to live there for the duration of the lease. Once the lease expires the property reverts to the *freehold* owner.

Legacy A gift by will.

Letter of credit/bank guarantee Used by Lloyd's investors, for example, as evidence of the availability of capital. However, the capital can remain invested elsewhere unless it is called upon to pay a claim.

Leveraged investors Those who borrow in order to invest in the stock market.

Lifetime allowance Under pension tax simplification, which comes into force in April 2006, this is the maximum total pension fund an individual can build up in a tax-favoured environment. It is possible to register in advance for protection for larger funds.

Lifetime mortgage/mortgage annuity An arrangement where an elderly homeowner remortgages part of the value of the house. The lump sum is repaid with the proceeds of the house sale when the individual dies.

Lloyd's vehicle (ILV) A way of raising money at Lloyd's where the company owns the managing agent and the capital.

Loan-to-value ratio The ratio between the value of a property and the amount of the loan secured against it.

Long-term care insurance An insurance policy that pays part or all of the fees for residential and nursing home case.

Lower earnings limit See *National insurance contributions*.

Managed fund A single fund that is split between different asset classes but is predominantly invested in equities and bonds.

Manager of managers An asset manager that appoints individual sub-managers to run separate mandates within its funds.

Market capitalisation The stock market valuation of the company, which is calculated by multiplying the number of shares in issue by their market price.

Market makers With reference to *traded endowment policies* these companies will buy a policy outright and maintain the monthly premiums until they find a purchaser.

Market timing By betting on the value of international securities in mutual funds, which are only priced once per day, market timers can gain access to securities that have not traded for many hours and where the price has since moved.

Market value adjuster (MVA) A penalty applied on early termination of a *with profits* policy.

Married woman's stamp A reduced rate of *national insurance contribution* that women can still pay provided they were married or widowed before April 1977. The rate does not build up an entitlement to the *basic state pension*, among other benefits.

Maturity/redemption date The date when a *bond* repays the nominal (original) capital.

Maximum investment plans (MIPs) A life office regular monthly or annual premium investment that usually runs for at least 10 years.

Mean expected outcome The mean is the average amount or value, so this is the expected outcome based on a range of potential outcomes divided by the number in the set.

Means-tested benefit A social security benefit that is only available where the individual can prove eligibility – usually by providing evidence that total earnings and capital fall below certain levels.

Mid-cap Companies with a mid-ranking *market capitalisation*. In the UK this usually refers to companies in the FTSE 250 index.

Minimum funding requirement (MFR) A now defunct method of assessing a pension scheme's ability to meet its liabilities. See *scheme-specific funding*.

Minimum income guarantee (MIG) A means tested benefit paid to raise a pensioner's income to a certain minimum level. Replaced in October 2003 by the *pensions tax credit*.

Mis-selling An advised sale that does not meet the FSA's standards. This is a regulatory offence and the FSA has statutory powers to investigate and impose fines.

Mitigation Arranging your affairs to reduce the impact of taxation in ways that are approved by the Inland Revenue.

Money laundering Where money from illegal sources is made to appear legal – for example by 'washing' it through legitimate bank accounts, or investing it and then withdrawing the capital.

Monte Carlo modelling See stochastic modelling.

Moratorium clause On a private medical insurance policy this method of underwriting would not require disclosure of a full medical history but all pre-existing conditions would be excluded for a period of time – typically two years – after which they would also be covered.

Morbidity A measure of state of health and the likelihood of illness.

Mortality A measure of life expectancy.

Mortality cross-subsidy The pooling mechanism for annuity policyholders by which the income of those who live longer is subsidised by the early deaths.

Mortgage The contract for a *secured loan* that represents the legal charge on the property. The borrower gives this to the lender as security.

Mortgage deed The legal contract between the borrower and the lender.

Mortgage indemnity insurance An insurance policy that is paid for by the borrower but will reimburse the lender if the property is repossessed and there is a difference between the outstanding mortgage and the actual selling price.

Mortgage interest relief at source (MIRAS) Tax relief on mortgage interest repayment that applied to *home income plan* mortgages taken out before April 2000.

Multi-employer/industry-wide scheme A single occupational pension scheme to which a range of employers have access.

Multi-manager funds Funds that invest in a range of sub-funds run by different specialist asset managers. See *fund of funds* and *manager of managers*.

Mutual A life office owned by its policyholders.

Mutual (collective) funds Funds that spread the individual's risk by pooling the investments of many to invest in a wide spread of a particular asset class – for example UK equities, commercial property.

Name A corporate or individual member of Lloyd's who puts up finance for the insurance business.

Nameco A vehicle for investing at Lloyd's that limits the individual's liability.

National insurance contributions (NICs) An additional tax on earnings between a lower and upper level. NICs help fund social services benefits and state pensions.

National Savings & Investments (NS&I) A savings and investment institution backed by the Treasury, which guarantees customers' deposits and allows the government to borrow public money for public spending.

Negative equity Where the value of an asset is exceeded by the loan(s) secured against it.

Negative ethical screening A method of screening that automatically eliminates companies that are involved in certain lines of business; for example alcohol and tobacco.

Negative (inverse) correlation As one variable increases linearly, the other decreases by the same or a similar amount. See *correlation coefficient*.

Net asset value (NAV) The approximate value of the underlying assets owned by the company.

Net relevant earnings The earnings that can be taken into account for the calculation of a *defined contribution* pension contribution an individual may make. Where applicable the employer contribution must be taken into account for maximum contribution purposes.

Net rental income The taxable income on an investment property after expenses.

Net worth statement A personal balance sheet.

Nominal The amount of capital that a bond will repay at maturity.

Non-correlation Indicates that there is no linear relationship and so the variables are not related. See *correlation coefficient*.

Non-systematic risk Factors that only affect that specific investment and not the market as a whole.

Non-tangible asset Most regulated investments under the Financial Services and Markets Act 2000 are non-tangible in that they have no intrinsic value but represent a financial asset; for example shares, gilts, bonds and collective funds.

Offer price The price at which institutions sell and investors buy securities and funds. See *bid price*.

Offset mortgage An arrangement where there are separate accounts for the mortgage and savings. The savings account earns no interest but its credit value is offset against the outstanding mortgage capital and so the interest payable is reduced accordingly.

Offshore Generally refers to tax havens or locations where the tax regime is more favourable than in the UK.

Offshore investment bond Run by offshore insurance companies. Two main types are distribution bonds, which pay a regular 'income', and non-distribution bonds, which roll up gross.

Open architecture This is a product/platform that includes the provider's own range of funds and the funds of a selection of external managers.

Open-ended investment company (OEIC) A collective fund similar to a *unit trust* but with a corporate structure.

Open market option (OMO) The facility to use the fund from a personal pension or similar defined contribution arrangement and to buy an *annuity* from a company other than the original provider.

Option A derivatives contract that gives the holder the right, but not the obligation, to buy or sell a specified underlying asset at a pre-agreed price on or before a given date.

Passive managers These aim to track or replicate an index performance (hence index tracking) by buying all or a wide sample of the constituent shares.

Pay-as-you-go (PAYG) A system of welfare where the *national insurance* contributions of those in work pay for the benefits of those who are unable to work or are retired.

Pensionable pay The amount of salary on which company pension scheme contributions and benefits are based.

Pensions tax credit A means-tested benefit, which replaced the minimum income guarantee in October 2003, aims to help pensioners who have small private or company pensions.

Pension tax simplification (A-Day) In April 2006 a new tax regime comes into force for all pension arrangements.

Pension unlocking Denounced by the FSA, here the adviser persuades a *defined benefit* pension scheme member to transfer to a personal pension in order to 'unlock' the tax-free cash early. Advisers who promote this type of scheme take substantial commissions from the proceeds.

Permanent income bearing shares (PIBS) These form part of the permanent capital of a building society but have no repayment date and are more like an irredeemable loan than ordinary equities.

Personal equity plan (PEP) The predecessor to the *Individual savings account*. A tax-efficient wrapper in which to hold funds and individual securities, available for new investment January 1987 to April 1999.

Personal pension A tax-approved investment where the proceeds are used to provide a retirement income.

Phased drawdown A variation on *income drawdown* that does not involve *annuitising* but makes use of tax-free cash to generate part of the income.

Phased retirement An alternative to *income drawdown*, here the individual vests a small number of personal pension plan segments each year to release the tax free cash element and to use the rest to buy an *annuity* to provide the required income.

Polarisation A regulatory system under which advisers were either tied to one provider for the distribution of one or more products or were independent financial advisers (IFAs), who could select products from the entire range available. *Depolarisation* replaced polarisation at the end of 2004.

Positive correlation Where one variable increases in line with another. See *correlation coefficient*.

Positive ethical screening An investment approach aim to identify companies that are working towards a desirable environmental or social goal.

Potentially exempt transfer (PET) Where an individual gives away an asset and dies within seven years, the tax assessment is based on the date of the gift and the date of death. A sliding scale of tax rates is used, so the longer the period between the two dates the lower the liability.

Pound-cost averaging An argument in favour of smaller regular contributions to an investment rather than an occasional lump sum is that capital invested in small amounts on a regular basis can even out the impact of market fluctuations. In theory the average unit or share purchase price over a given period is lower than the arithmetical average of the market prices.

Precipice bond A type of *structured product* that offers apparently high returns but in practice *downside gearing*, where the indices on which performance is based fell below a certain level, can result in overall loss of original capital.

Preference shares These carry no voting rights but have a fixed dividend payment.

Premium Bonds UK Government securities issued in units of £1 under the National Loans Act 1968.

Premium (trading at) Where the *net asset value* is lower than the share price.

Pre-tax profit margin The trading profit – before the deduction of depreciation, interest payments and tax – expressed as a percentage of turnover.

Price/earnings (P/E) ratio The market price of a share divided by the company's earnings/profits per share in its latest 12-month trading period.

Primary and enhanced protection A way of protecting pension funds from the *recovery charge* after *pension tax simplification* is introduced by securing in advance a personal *lifetime allowance*. This is expressed as a percentage of the statutory lifetime allowance of £1.5m.

Primary threshold The threshold at which an individual starts to pay *national insurance contributions*.

Private equity The equity financing of unquoted companies.

Private medical insurance (PMI) An insurance policy that pays for private treatment for acute curable conditions, not for emergency treatment or chronic illness.

Professional indemnity insurance (PII) A requirement for all authorised financial firms. PII covers compensation claims against the firm – for example for *mis-selling*.

Protected/guaranteed products Offer a link to the return on an index or a basket of indices. The growth potential is limited but in return these products offer some downside protection.

Protected rights The pension fund built up from rebates of *national insurance* contributions for those who are contracted out of the *additional pension*.

Public sector borrowing requirement (PSBR) The amount by which government spending (including local authorities and nationalised industries) exceeds the income from taxation, rates and other revenues.

Purchased life annuity (PLA) An annuity pays an income for life in return for a lump sum investment. A PLA is bought with spare capital, as opposed to a compulsory purchase annuity, which is bought with the proceeds of a pension arrangement.

Put option A type of *derivative* contract that confers the right but not the obligation to sell a fixed number of shares at a predetermined price on a fixed date or within a predetermined period of time.

Qualifying and non-qualifying Life assurance investment policies with different tax treatment depending on the level of life assurance.

Realistic balance sheet A new measure of an insurance company's free assets less liabilities. See **free asset ratio**.

Real return The investment return adjusted for *inflation*.

Real-time market information Asset prices at their current trading level.

Recoupment schedule A schedule for theatre investors, for example, that shows how many weeks the show must run to cover costs.

Recovery charge A new tax to be introduced in April 2006. This applies to pension funds that exceed the personal *lifetime allowance* and are not registered for *primary* or *enhanced protection*.

Redemption date/maturity The date when a *bond* repays the *nominal* (original capital).

Reduction in yield (RIY) The most complete measure of a collective fund's cost. It shows the percentage reduction in the return or yield, taking account of all costs. This is the figure the provider must show on the key features document that is provided to investors.

Regular premium The amount paid by the investor or policyholder to an investment or insurance policy. Usually monthly but can be annually.

Relative return/performance Performance relative to an index or a peer group.

Repayment mortgage A mortgage where the monthly payments cover interest and capital, so that at the end of the term the borrower has paid off the entire debt.

Resident For tax purposes a UK resident is taxed on their worldwide income. Non-residents are taxed on income that arises in the UK but not elsewhere. Broadly, residence is determined by the amount of time an individual spends in the UK.

Retail Prices Index/Inflation (RPI) Published by the Office for National Statistics every month, until 2003 this was the most common measure for inflation. The RPI is calculated by constructing a basket of goods and services used by the typical household. See *Consumer Prices Index*.

Retirement annuity plan (RAP) The predecessor to personal pensions. No new RAPs were sold after 1987 but it is still possible to contribute to existing plans.

Return on capital The profits before tax, divided by the shareholders' funds

Reversion annuity See *home reversion*.

Risk In financial terms this is the standard deviation of the (arithmetic) average return. For the private investor we usually think of risk in terms of loss of capital, and erosion due to inflation, but also in terms of the risk of not achieving a personal investment objective.

Risk management The control of risk in a manner that reflects the individual's circumstances, risk tolerance and investment horizon.

Running off period A two-year period after the end of an accounting year for a Lloyd's syndicate that provides time for outstanding claims to be settled.

Running yield For a *bond* fund, the running yield or 'projected income yield' only takes into account the current rate of income received from the bonds. No allowance is made for any changes in the capital value, so this could mask capital erosion, for example, if the annual charge is deducted from capital. See *gross redemption yield*.

Salary exchange/sacrifice Where a cut in an employee's salary is redirected into the pension scheme.

Scam See *fraud*.

Scheme-specific funding requirement The requirement that occupational pension schemes adopt a funding level that is appropriate to the scheme's liabilities.

Scottish Limited Partnership A vehicle for investing at Lloyd's that limits the individual's liability.

Sectors Used within indices to categorise companies according to the goods and services they produce.

Secured loan A loan that is secured against a property, for example, so that in the event of default, the property is taken in lieu of repayments.

Securities The general name for all *stocks* and *shares*.

Securities and Investments Board (SIB) The predecessor of the *Financial Services Authority*. See *self-regulatory organisation*.

Self-certification mortgage In theory, a mortgage where the lender does not require proof of earnings. In practice lenders vary considerably in their requirements.

Self-investment In pension scheme terms this is where the pension fund invests in the shares of the sponsoring employer.

Self-regulation A system established in 1986 where the financial services institutions were responsible for regulating their own kind. See *self-regulatory organisation*.

Self-regulatory organisation (SRO) The original Financial Services Act (1986) established a series of SROs to regulate different types of financial institutions and firms under the overall supervision of the *Securities and Investments Board (SIB)*.

Self-select ISA An *Individual savings account* that can be used to hold individual securities and cash, as well as collective funds, in a tax-favoured wrapper.

Settlor The person who transfers assets to a *trust*.

Shared appreciation mortgage A third party takes a share in a property and in this way secures the relevant proportion of any gains or losses in the value of the home when it is resold.

Shareholder activism Institutional investors use their voting power in sensitive areas such as executive pay and boardroom appointments.

Share option schemes These allow employees to buy shares in their employer at below market value. It is also possible to avoid income tax on what is effectively a benefit in kind – that is, the difference between the buying price and the market price.

Shares Broadly these are *securities* with no fixed *coupon* or *redemption date*.

Short selling Borrowing assets to sell them high, buy back at a lower price, and then return them to the lender.

Single life policy An insurance or annuity policy that runs only for the lifetime of the named individual, as opposed to a joint life policy, which terminates on the second death.

Single premium A one-off or lump sum payment to a pension or life assurance investment plan.

Sixtieth scheme A type of *defined benefit* pension scheme where the pension accrual is one-sixtieth of final salary for each year of service.

Small cap Companies with a comparatively small *market capitalisation*. Generally taken as those below the FTSE 350 (100 and 250 indices), which fall into the *FTSE Small Cap* index.

Small self-administered scheme (SSAS) A small company pension scheme designed primarily for family businesses.

Smoothed managed fund Operates like a unit-linked *managed fund* but with a separate mechanism for a limited degree of *smoothing* the annual returns.

Smoothing To reduce volatility the fund manager or, in the case of a *with profits* fund, the actuary, reserves some of the profits in years of good performance to boost returns in years when investment markets are falling.

Socially responsible investment (SRI) See *ethical investment*.

Split capital investment trust The 'split' refers to a special type of investment trust that has different types of shares – typically one providing income, and one providing a predetermined sum after a specific period.

Spread betting Taking a bet on the movement of the spread. A spread is the difference between the buying and selling prices quoted by a stock exchange dealer. The dealer buys at the lower price and sells at the higher.

Spread trust An investment trust at Lloyd's that raises money through share issues and joins syndicates, the aim being to boost returns by successful underwriting.

Standard variable rate Typically in relation to a mortgage where the repayments fluctuate in line with the lender's variable rate, which in turn is affected by interest rates set by the Bank of England.

State earnings related pension scheme (SERPS) The additional pension that was earned on top of the basic state pension between 1978 and 2002. From April 2002 the additional pension is the *State second pension*.

State second pension Also known as S2P, currently this is an earnings-related pension that sits on top of the basic flat rate pension. Only applicable to employees who are not contracted out via a group scheme or individual plan.

Statistical distribution of outcomes This shows the potential range of outcomes. See *mean expected outcome*.

Statutory money purchase illustration (SMPI) The annual illustration of the retirement income, in today's prices, that a *defined contribution* pension plan will generate.

Stepped preference shares A type of share offered by *split capital investment trusts* that provides an income that is expected to rise each year at a fixed rate, plus a fixed redemption price for the shares when the trust is wound up. Each trust offers a different yield and annual increase, depending on the nature of the underlying assets.

Stochastic modelling An actuarial model that assesses the impact on the portfolio and returns of random fluctuations in performance and inflation, among other factors. Monte Carlo modelling is the modern version of this process.

Stocks Broadly these are fixed interest securities with a redemption date. See *shares*.

Structured products A wide range of products that offer an income or growth target linked to one or more indices or baskets of currencies. In some cases the total return may be less than the amount invested.

Sub-investment grade debt Bonds issued by companies that have a credit rating of below BBB–.

Syndicate An annual venture at Lloyd's that is owned by its investors

Systematic risk Also known as market risk, this refers to general market influences and movements that affect all or most investments.

Tangible asset/investment Assets that have an intrinsic value – for example paintings, wine, gemstones. Property is also in this category. Tangible assets are not regulated unless individuals invest via a collective fund.

Taper relief A mechanism that reduces the rate of *capital gains tax* according to how long the individual has held the asset.

Tax avoidance Avoiding tax by exploitation of loopholes. Generally, from April 2004, the Inland Revenue regards special avoidance schemes as unacceptable.

Tax-efficient wrappers Products like a *personal pension* and an *individual savings account*, which are not investments in themselves but can hold a range of investments in a tax-favoured environment.

Tax equalisation An employer's pledge to ensure an expatriate employer will be no worse off when seconded overseas with regard to his or her tax position.

Tax evasion Deliberate omission to pay tax that is legally due. This is a criminal offence.

Tax-exempt special savings accounts (TESSAs) A tax-free deposit account launched in 1991 and withdrawn for new investment after 5 April 1999.

Tax mitigation The use of Revenue-approved investments, allowances and exemptions to avoid tax.

Term assurance An insurance policy that provides a tax-free cash lump sum if the policyholder dies within the period insured.

Terminal bonus A discretionary bonus paid at maturity on a *with profits policy*, based on recent performance of the fund.

Tied agent Until late in 2004 the system of regulation demanded that advisers were either tied, where they could only sell the products of one company, or independent, where they could select products from across the entire market. See *polarisation*, *depolarisation*.

TMT Technology, media and telecom shares.

Top down A strategy that first considers the international and national economic factors that might affect economic growth in a country, a geographic area or an economic category, and gradually work down to the individual companies. See *bottom up*.

Top slicing relief Averages the profit in a life assurance *investment bond* or *maximum investment policy* over the number of years the bond has been held and adds this profit slice to an investor's income in the year the bond matures.

Total charge for credit (TCC) The interest and other charges which affect the real cost of borrowing – even if they are not payable under the credit agreement itself.

Total expense ratio (TER) This shows the *annual management charge* for a fund plus any other costs such as audit fees, custody and administration.

Total return A percentage increase of the original investment taking account of both the income (yield) reinvested, plus any capital growth (the rise in the market price).

Traded endowment policy (TEP) A secondhand *with profits* endowment policy. Market makers exploit the discrepancy between the intrinsic value of a with profits policy and its much lower surrender value by matching potential buyers with sellers.

Trail commission The sales commission paid by a product provider to an adviser on the anniversary of the sale and each year thereafter. Commission is calculated as a percentage of the amount invested or the premium/contribution.

Transfer value The cash value of a *Defined benefit* pension that is provided when a scheme member requests a transfer to a new employer's scheme or to a *Defined contribution* plan.

Trust A legal structure that recognises there can be two owners of assets – the *trustees*, of whom there must be at least two and who have legal control of the assets, and the *beneficiaries*, who are entitled to the income and/or capital but only under the terms of the trust.

Trustee One of two types of legal owner of trust assets – the other being the *beneficiaries*. See *trust*.

Underlying inflation The unofficial term given to the inflation rate in an economy measured by the *retail prices index* minus mortgage interest payments (RPIX).

Underwater shares Shares purchased through a company scheme where the value of shares has fallen below the price when the employee took out the option.

Unfunded unapproved retirement benefit scheme (UURBS) A pension arrangement that employers can use for employees restricted by the earnings cap.

Unit trust A collective fund with a specific investment aim. Unit trusts are 'open ended', which means they may create or cancel units on a daily basis depending on demand.

Universal benefit A social security benefit that is paid to all relevant UK residents irrespective of earned and unearned income, plus capital.

Unlimited liability With reference to investors ('*Names*') at Lloyd's, this status meant that in the event of a call on funds due to heavy insurance losses, the individual's assets, including the home, must be sold if necessary to meet the bill.

Unsecured lending A loan that is not secured against an asset. See *secured lending*.

Upper earnings limit See *National insurance contributions*.

Value investing An investment style where the objective is to identify shares that are underpriced by the market.

Venture Capital Trust (VCT) A quoted investment company that invests in unquoted companies and/or companies listed on the *Alternative Investments Market*.

Vesting The process of converting a pension plan into income or an income-generating arrangement such as an annuity. Vesting enables the individual to gain access to the tax-free cash.

Warrant A security that confers a right but not an obligation on the holder to purchase (call warrants) or sell (put warrants) a quantity of a financial asset on a predetermined date at a predetermined price (the 'strike' or 'excise' price). See *covered warrant*.

Whole of life A policy that combines insurance and investment in order to pay a benefit whenever the policyholder dies. There is no specific term.

Wind up The closure of a pension scheme and distribution of the assets in accordance with the trust deed and rules.

With profits annuity An investment-linked annuity that links the investment mainly to the returns achieved by the underlying *with profits fund*.

With profits fund A fund that invests in equities, bonds and property, pays an annual bonus or return and in addition pays a final or terminal bonus. Returns are smoothed to avoid significant fluctuations. In the case of traditional and unitised with profits funds the policyholder is exposed to the profits and losses of the provider's other business areas.

Wrap account An online facility or 'platform' that allows the investor to see in one place and to aggregate the value of their total range of savings and investments.

Zero A name given to the shares of split capital investment trusts that receive no income but entitle the owner to a potential fixed capital return when the trust is wound up.

Appendix 2 ●●●●

A–Z of websites

The following is a list of the websites referred to in this book.

Age Concern: **www.ageconcern.org.uk**
Allenbridge: **www.allenbridge.co.uk**
Annuity Bureau: **www.annuity-bureau.co.uk**
Annuity Direct: **www.annuitydirect.co.uk**
Association for Payment Clearing Services: **www.apacs.org.uk**
Association of Art and Antique Dealers: **www.lapada.co.uk**
Association of British Insurers: **www.abi.org.uk**
Association of Consulting Actuaries: **www.aca.org.uk**
Association of Independent Care Advisers: **www.aica.org.uk**
Association of Independent Financial Advisers: **www.aifa.net**
Association of Investment Trust Companies: **www.aitc.org.uk**
Association of Lloyd's Members: **www.association-lloyds-members.co.uk**
Association of Pension Lawyers: **www.apl.org.uk**
Association of Policy Market Makers: **www.apmm.org**
Association of Private Client Investment Managers and Stockbrokers:
www.apcims.co.uk
Association of Residential Letting Agencies: **www.arla.co.uk**
Association of Solicitor Investment Managers: **www.asim.org.uk**

B&CE: **www.bandce.co.uk**
Bank of England: **www.bankofengland.co.uk**
Barclays Capital Equity Gilt Study: **www.equitygiltstudy.com**
Bestinvest: **www.bestinvest.com**
Bloomsbury Financial Planning: **www.bloomsburyfp.co.uk**
British Bankers' Association: **www.bba.org.uk**
British Venture Capital Association: **www.bvca.co.uk**
Building Societies Association: **www.bsa.org.uk**

Callcredit: **www.callcredit.co.uk**
Care and Repair: **www.careandrepair-england.org.uk**; **www.carerepair-scot.org.uk**;
www.careandrepair.org.uk

Centre for Economic Policy Research: **www.cepr.org**

Chartered Institute of Banking/Institute of Financial Services: **www.ifslearning.com**

Chartered Insurance Institute: **www.cii.co.uk**

Citywire: **www.citywire.co.uk**

Citizens' Advice Bureau: **www.nacab.org.uk**

Companion Website: **www.booksites.net/**

Conservative Party: **www.tory.org.uk**

Consumer Gateway, run by the DTI: **www.consumer.gov.uk/consumer_web/index_v4.htm**

Consumers' Association: **www.which.co.uk**

Council of Mortgage Lenders (CML): **www.cml.org.uk**

Counsel and Care: **www.counselandcare.org.uk**

Debt Management Office: **www.dmo.gov.uk**

Department for Education and Skills (DfES): **www.dfes.gov.uk**

DfES on-line higher education information student service: **www.studentfinance direct.co.uk**

Department for Work and Pensions: **www.dwp.gov.uk**

Department of Trade and Industry (DTI): **www.dti.gov.uk**

Distribution Technology Ltd: **www.distribution-technology.com**

Economic and Social Research Council: **www.esrc.ac.uk**

Equifax: **www.equifax.co.uk**

Ethical Investment Research Service (EIRIS): **www.eiris.org**

Experian: **www.experian.co.uk**

Financial Ombudsman Service: **www.financial-ombudsman.org.uk**

Financial Services Authority: **www.fsa.gov.uk**

Financial Services Compensation Scheme: **www.fscs.org.uk**

Financial Times: **www.ft.com**

FT Cityline: **www.ftcityline.com**

FTfm Fund Ratings: **www.ft.com/fundratings.com**

FT free annual reports service: **http://ft.ar.wilink.com**

Forestry Commission: **www.forestry.gov.uk**

FTSE Hedge index: **www.ftse.com/hedge**

FTSE International: **www.ftse.com**

FundsDirect: **www.fundsdirect.co.uk**

Fundsnetwork: **www.fundsnetwork.co.uk**

Government Actuary's Department: **www.gad.gov.uk**

Hargreaves Lansdown: **www.hargreaveslansdown.co.uk**

Help the Aged: **www.helptheaged.org.uk**

High Premium Group: **www.hpg.demon.co.uk**
HL Vantage: **www.hargreaveslansdown.co.uk**
HMSO: **www.parliament.the-stationery-office.co.uk**
Home Improvement Trust: **www.hitrust.org**
Home improvement agencies: **www.foundations.uk.com; www.foldgroup.uk**

IFACare: **www.ifacare.co.uk**
IFA Promotions: **www.unbiased.co.uk**
Independent Research Services: **www.irs-spi.co.uk**
Independent Schools Council Information Service (ISCIS): **www.iscis.uk.net**
Inland Revenue: **www.inlandrevenue.gov.uk**
Institute for Economic Affairs: **www.iea.org.uk**
Institute of Actuaries: **www.actuaries.org.uk**
Institute of Chartered Accountants for England and Wales: **www.icaew.co.uk**
Institute of Financial Planning: **www.financialplanning.org.uk**
Institute of Financial Services/Chartered Institute of Banking: **www.ifslearning.com**
Institute of Fiscal Studies: **www.ifs.co.uk**
Investdrinks: **www.investdrinks.org**
Investment Management Association: **www.investmentuk.org**
Investors' Chronicle: **www.investorschronicle.ft.com**
Islamic banking: **www.islamic-banking.com**

Labour Party: **www.labour.org.uk**
Liberal Democrat Party: **www.libdems.org.uk**
Lifetime Group: **www.lifetimegroup.co.uk**
Law Society: **www.solicitors-online.com**
Lloyd's of London: **www.lloydsoflondon.com**
London International Financial Futures and Options Exchange (LIFFE): **www.liffe.com**
London Stock Exchange: **www.londonstockex.co.uk**

Mercer Human Resources: **www.mercerHR.co.uk**
Moneyfacts: **www.moneyfacts.co.uk**
Money Management: **www.ftbusiness.com**
Moody's: **www.moodys.com**
Mortgage Code Compliance Board: **www.mortgagecode.org.uk**

National Association of Pension Funds (NAPF): **www.napf.co.uk**
National Audit Office: **www.nao.gov.uk**
National Institute for Economic and Social Research: **www.niesr.ac.uk**
National Savings & Investments: **www.nsandi.com**
National Statistics Online: **www.statistics.gov.uk**
National Union of Students: **www.nus.org.uk**

Occupational Pensions Regulatory Authority: **www.opra.gov.uk**

Office for National Statistics (National Statistics Online): **www.statistics.gov.uk**
Office of Fair Trading (OFT): **www.oft.gov.uk**

Pensionguide (part of DWP): **www.pensionguide.gov.uk**
Pensions Advisory Service: **www.opas.org.uk**
Pension Service (part of the DWP): **www.thepensionservice.gov.uk**
Pensions Institute: **www.pensions-institute.org**
Pensions Management Institute: **www.pensions-pmi.org.uk**
Pensions Ombudsman: **www.pensions-ombudsman.org.uk**
Pensions Policy Institute: **www.pensionspolicyinstitute.org.uk**
Pensions Trust: **www.thepensionstrust.org.uk**
Personal Finance Education Group: **www.pfeg.org**
Policy Studies Institute: **www.psi.org.uk**
ProShare: **www.proshare.org**

Resources for Economists on the Internet: **www.netec.mcc.ac.uk**

Safe Home Income Plans: **www.ship-ltd.org**
Selestia: **www.selestia.co.uk**
Seven IM: **www.7im.co.uk**
SIPP Providers Group: **www.sipp-provider-group.org.uk**
Skandia: **www.skandia.co.uk**
Society of Financial Advisers: **www.sofa.org**
Society of London Theatre: **www.officiallondontheatre.co.uk**
Solicitors for Independent Financial Advice: **www.solicitor-ifa.co.uk**
Stage, The: **www.thestage.co.uk**
Standard and Poor's **www.standardandpoors.com**
Standard and Poor's fund management: **www.standardandpoors-funds-com**
Standard and Poor's Fund Management Rating **www.funds-sp.com**
Stock Exchange: **www.londonstockex.co.uk**
Student Finance Direct: **www.studentfinancedirect.co.uk**

Tax efficient review: **www.taxefficientreview.com**
Theatrenet: **www.theatrenet.co.uk**
Treasury: **www.hm-treasury.gov.uk**

UK Society of Investment Professionals: **www.uksip.org**

Wentworth Rose: **www.wentworthrose.co.uk**
William Burrows Annuities: **www.williamburrows.com**
Wine investment and fraud: **www.investdrinks.org**
WM Company: **www.wmcompany.com**

Appendix 3 ●●●●

How to prepare a financial plan

This section is reproduced with the kind permission of the Institute of Financial Planning and forms part of the *Certified Financial Planner™ Licence: Syllabus and Tuition Manual*, 4th edition, Paul T. Grainger, Institute of Financial Planning, Bristol, 2001.

---

1. IDENTIFY AND EXTRACT INFORMATION

FROM

- Fact find form
- File notes

⬇

2. IDENTIFY GOALS, TIMESCALES & ATTITUDE

⬇

2.1 List the client's precise goals or objectives and their priority ranking. Include monetary values or "by when" dates where they are known.

2.2 List the client's preferences or constraints in terms of attitudes (especially investment risk attitude), values and beliefs.

⬇

3. ASSET & LIABILITY STATEMENT (BALANCE SHEET)

⬇

3.1 Make a list of
ASSETS under columns headed:–

	OWNER ONE	OWNER TWO	JOINT OWNERSHIP
	xxx	xxx	xxx
	xxx	xxx	xxx
Total	**xxx**	**xxx**	**xxx**

⬇

3.2 Deduct from the list of assets, a list of
   LIABILITIES, under the same column headings:–

	OWNER ONE	OWNER TWO	JOINT OWNERSHIP
	(xxx)	(xxx)	(xxx)
	(xxx)	(xxx)	(xxx)
Total	**(xxx)**	**(xxx)**	**(xxx)**

3.3 Subtract liabilities from assets to produce net assets or net liabilities:–

	OWNER ONE	OWNER TWO	JOINT OWNERSHIP
Net Assets/(Liabilities)	(xxx)	(xxx)	(xxx)

3.4 Make a separate rough working note of any assets which produce income and
   identify whether this is paid:–

   Net of tax   (e.g. investor dividends)
   Gross, but taxable   (e.g. Gilts)
   Gross, but tax-free (e.g. Peps or ISAs)

3.5 Make a separate rough working note of any assets which are potentially free
   from Capital Gains Tax on disposal (e.g. principal private residence or
   Gilts/Corporate loans).

3.6 Make a separate rough working note of the potential size of the estate if one
   spouse/partner dies, under the circumstances of any will or lack thereof, as
   described in the case study.

4. INCOME & EXPENDITURE STATEMENT

4.1 Check your rough notes for income producing assets.

4.2 Identify gross income by person and frequency (e.g. per annum) under
columns headed:–

	PERSON ONE	PERSON TWO	JOINT INCOME
	(xxx)	(xxx)	(xxx)
	(xxx)	(xxx)	(xxx)
Total Gross	**(xxx)**	**(xxx)**	**(xxx)**

4.3 Identify net income after taxation.

4.4 Add in any irregular capital receipts.

4.5 Deduct expenditure per person based upon the same frequency
(e.g. per annum) as income:–

	PERSON ONE	PERSON TWO	JOINT EXPENDITURE
	(xxx)	(xxx)	(xxx)
	(xxx)	(xxx)	(xxx)
Total	**(xxx)**	**(xxx)**	**(xxx)**

4.6 Identify per person **and** total net surplus income after expenditure (or shortfall).

---

5. TAXATION CALCULATIONS (WHERE REQUIRED)

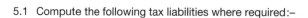

5.1 Compute the following tax liabilities where required:–

- Income Tax   (per person)
- Capital Gains Tax   (per person)
- Inheritance Tax   (per person)

5.2 Identify tax status; i.e.:

- Non-Taxpayer   (per person)
- 10% Tax-Payer   (per person)
- 22% Tax-Payer   (per person)
- Higher Rate Tax Payer   (per person)

6. RESOURCE & SHORTFALL CALCULATIONS

6.1 Calculate any funding projections required for:–

- Retirement Planning   (Pension and Non-Pension)
- Special Projects/Needs   (Long-Term Care, Education Funding)
- Risk Protection   (Life, Health and Medical)
- Loans and/or Debt Management

6.2 Identify and include any:–

- Social Security Benefits
- Other State or Non-State resources (e.g. Maintenance Payments, Child Benefit, Trust income)

7. ADVICE

7.1 Restate/summarise key client goals/objectives, attitude and circumstance.

7.2 Clearly explain the logic behind any assumptions used. Ensure they are in a range of acceptability, or if not, explain why.

7.3 Prepare advice to deal with each specific issue to be dealt with within client's requirements and/or constraints. (Normally three areas of technical advice.)

7.4 Explain why other areas are to be/have been excluded from advice.

7.5 Clearly explain why and state how the recommended course of action solves the problem/meets the objective.

7.6 Ensure any caveats, limitations or implications are explained.

7.7 Ensure that solutions are consistent with client objectives, constraints, attitude etc.

---

8. ACTION PLAN & REVIEW

8.1 Ensure a list of actions is included, stating who is to do what, to whom and by when.

8.2 Ensure it is clear that a review will take place, and why. State who will initiate the review process and by when.

9. APPENDICES

9.1 Write up/tidy up schedules, calculations and working notes as appendices.

9.2 Add any other appendices required.

10. CROSS-CHECK

10.1 Check that all CFP Licence Assessment Standards have been satisfied.

11. SUBMIT PLAN TO THE INSTITUTE FOR ASSESSMENT

CERTIFIED FINANCIAL PLANNER™
Licence
Syllabus and Tuition Manual
Fourth Edition

Appendix 4 ●●●●

Financial planning case study

This appendix sets out a comprehensive case study of Karl and Ulrika Harvey. Your task is to produce a holistic financial plan that comments on the issues identified in the syllabus, with *three* issues being addressed in detail.

Some of the syllabus issues are clearly irrelevant in this case, such as those relating to a business. We would suggest that you select the issues that you would like to address in detail from the six listed below. You should comment on the other three to at least summary level.

- Personal Risk Management & Insurance
- Investments (esp. Ethical Investment)
- Estate Planning (inc. Wills & Trusts)
- Special Needs (e.g. Long Term Care)
- Taxation & National Insurance
- Educational Funding

It is intended that the case study gives you all of the detail that you need in order to complete the report. You should certainly assume that it is complete. However, in the event that you feel that more information is essential to clarify a point or to resolve what you consider to be an inconsistency, please telephone the IFP who will seek clarification from the senior CFP assessor.

You should note that the file note has resulted from meeting(s) that you are deemed to have held. Things that may appear to be inconsistent may be treated as being no more than different people's interpretation of relationships and circumstances.

This exam question is reproduced by permission of the Institute of Financial Planning and is taken from the 'Certified Financial Planning™ Licence Syllabus & Tuition Pack'. The net annual expenditure analysis is provided at the end of this appendix.

Interview Notes: Karl and Ulrika Harvey

Karl and Ulrika have been happily married for 45 years. They met whilst Ulrika was on holiday in the UK. They have one son, James, who was born in the UK. Karl is a retired geologist who regularly used to spend up to six months of each year working outside the UK.

Ulrika did not work until James was 21, but had risen to the post of manager at the local superstore when she retired at 60. Karl has always loved the sea and has paid a regular subscription of £10 per month to the RNLI since 1980, when he was rescued by a lifeboat whilst on holiday on the coast of Cornwall.

Karl's brother, Jim, died in February 2002. His will states that Karl should receive £70,000, made up as follows:-

5284 Lloyds TSB shares, approximate value £40,000
1274 Halifax shares, approximate value £10,000
Cash deposits of £20,000.

Karl expects to receive the bequest within the next few months.

Their son James has had a hard life. He has neither been lucky in love nor life generally. Ulrika says the best thing that has ever happened to him was the birth of his daughter, Susannah, in 1999. Although the mother has since left James for another man, James has successfully won custody of Susannah.

Karl and Ulrika would like to give Susannah a good start and would dearly love to pay for her initial education at a good private school nearby. They are concerned that this might inhibit their future financial security, or if something happened to them, that James might be tempted to use the money for other things and remove her from the school. The couple would like to set aside further money to help Susannah in future years but do not wish to jeopardise their own financial security to achieve this.

Karl and Ulrika regularly pay for all four, including James and Susannah, to go on holidays together. They have seen some fantastic sights since Susannah was born. They wish to continue this for as long as their health allows.

They are concerned they would become a burden to James and Susannah if they needed medical or nursing care. They wish to remain together for as long as possible, preferably in their own home. Karl has had some mobility problems recently and Ulrika has paid to have a stair lift installed to help him.

The couple wish to preserve their estate for James and Susannah but wish to exercise a degree of control on James as he is notoriously bad with money and seems to fritter it away on the strangest things. Karl also wishes to know how best to invest his imminent inheritance to fund their future holidays and unforeseen disasters, to ensure their financial security in the years to come. The couple bought joint life, 5-year guaranteed annuities with their pension arrangements when they retired. Upon death half the pension is paid to the remaining spouse. The pensions escalate each year by 3%.

The couple hold the following investments:-

Person	Investment	Date investment made	Initial investment	Any withdrawals made?
Karl	With profits bond	23/02/98	£20,000	None
Ulrika	Distribution bond	23/02/98	£17,000	None
Karl	National Savings Index-linked cert.	02/01/02	£10,000	23rd issue over 5 years
Ulrika	National Savings Index-linked cert.	02/01/02	£10,000	23rd issue over 5 years
Karl	Treasury 8% 2015	?	£5,000 nominal stock	N/A
Ulrika	Treasury 9% 2012	?	£5,000 nominal stock	N/A

Institute of Financial Planning

CONFIDENTIAL QUESTIONNAIRE
(PERSONAL)

All income and expenditure assumed gross unless specified otherwise

1. GENERAL INFORMATION				Date: 22 May 2002
Full name	Christian names Surname		Status	Date of birth
Self	*Karl Harvey*		*M*	*07/12/24*
Spouse/partner	*Ulrika Harvey*		*M*	*13/06/34*
Child 1	*James Harvey*		*S*	*31/08/62*
Child 2				
Child 3				
Child 4				
Grandchildren	Name			Date of birth
Susannah Harvey				*01/04/00*

Is there anyone else financially reliant upon you?   *No*

Occupation –	*Karl*	*Retired geologist*
Occupation –	*Ulrika*	*Retired shop manager*

Name and title for correspondence   *Karl and Ulrika*

Address for correspondence   *36, Pine Woods, Leeds*

Postcode   *LS2 2NS*   Telephone   *0113 366339*   Fax

Other address (business/home)

Postcode   Telephone   Fax

2. ASSETS (approximate values)	Self	Joint	Sps/ptr	Income
House (main residence)		125,000		
Second house/other property				
Contents/personal effects	8,000		8,000	
Agricultural property				
Woodland/forestry				
Bank accounts	4,000		16,000	0%
Building society deposits		180,000		4%
Tax exempt special savings accs				
National Savings Index-linked savings certificate	10,000		10,000	?
Quoted shares				
Personal equity plans				
Gilts & fixed interest securities	5,000?		5,000?	
Unit trusts				
Insurance bonds	22,000		23,000	
Surrender value of life policies				
Private company shares/VCT				
Business assets – sole trade				
Partnership interest				
Interests under trusts (see 11)				
Anticipated inheritance	70,000			
Other assets (specify)	Cars			
If house owned jointly, as joint tenants or tenants in common? *Joint tenants*				

3. LIABILITIES (approx values)	Self	Joint	Sps/ptr	Income
Mortgage outstanding				
Other qualifying loans				
Overdraft				
Other personal credit: credit card				
Other liabilities (eg guarantees)				
Underwriting member of Lloyds?	No		No	

4. EMPLOYMENT	Self	Spouse/partner
Name of firm		
Director or partner?		
Shareholding		
If a partner or controlling director please complete Corporate Questionnaire also		

5. INCOME	Self	Spouse/partner
Schedule E – pension	14,500	10,000
Bonus/fees/ Other source(s) – Other source(s) state pension	 3,770	 2,256.80
Schedule D – earnings/pension		
Other source(s) earnings		
Total investment income	?	?
Any major change anticipated?	No	No

6. BENEFITS IN KIND	*Self*	*Spouse/partner*
Car (scale charge)		
Medical expenses insurance		
Permanent health insurance		
Share option scheme		
Other		

7. PENSION SCHEME	*Self*	*Spouse/partner*
Final salary or money purchase		
Accrual rate (eg 60ths)		
Normal retirement age		
Scheme contracted in or out?		
Years in scheme to date		
Employer's contribution		
Member's contribution		
Death in service lump sum		
Spouse's pension – in service		
Spouse's pens.– in retirement		
Pension escalation rate		

8. RETIREMENT PLANNING	*Self*	*Spouse/partner*
Pension funds from details in section 7 above		
Preserved pension funds (PPS)		
Contracted out personal pension		
Free standing AVCs		
When would you really like to retire (or be financially independent)? *Already retired*		

9. TAXATION

	Self	Spouse/partner
Country of residence	UK	UK
May this change? If so, when?	No	No
Country of domicile	UK	Norway
Tax district and reference	CT2/3684 P	CP14/2486T
National Insurance No	NS 34 24 08 A	NT 12 46 55 C

10. GIFTS (Chargeable or potentially exempt for inheritance tax)

Date	Nature of Gift	Value £ (gross)	To whom
03/03/02	Cash	6,000	Karl's gift to James
03/03/01	Cash	3,000	Ulrika's gift to James
03/03/00	Cash	3,000	Karl's gift to James

11. INTERESTS UNDER TRUSTS

Beneficiary	Settlor	Nature	Value	Income

12. WILLS (Give main provisions and supply copies if possible)

Self	Spouse/partner

Mirror wills drawn up in 1990. First £20,000 to RNLI then remainder to spouse. If no spouse remainder to James.

13. EDUCATION EXPENSES (Current costs per annum in today's terms)

Child	School cost pa	From	Until
Susannah	4,500	Age 4	Age 11

14. HEALTH

	Self	Spouse/partner
State of health	Failing	Good
Do you smoke cigarettes?	No	No
Hazardous activities	None	None

15. INVESTMENT   See separate sheet

Do you have strong feelings regarding particular investments?	No
Anticipated liabilities or commitments	Details already given

16. PROFESSIONAL ADVISERS

Accountant		
Postcode	Telephone	Fax
Solicitor Small & Co Solicitors, 2 Wrexham Place, Cobham, Surrey		
Postcode	Telephone	Fax
Stockbroker		
Postcode	Telephone	Fax
Bank National	Account No 0456789	Sort Code 20 – 30 – 40
	108 High Street, Leeds	
Postcode LS19 1LY	Telephone 0113 65432	Fax

17. OBJECTIVES *Number in order of importance*

Family security – on your death	1	*Net total income needed in today's money* *£31,000 pa.*
– on spouse's/partner's death	1	*£31,000 pa.*
– on your disability	1	*£31,000 pa.*
– on spouse's/partner's disability	1	*£31,000 pa.*
Retirement planning		*Net income needed in today's money –* *joint total income pa.*
Investment planning & management	3	
Savings from income	5	*Additional commitment unknown*
Education expenses	2	
Estate planning	4	
Business continuation/succession		
Business planning		
Other objectives/desired changes in lifestyle		

Clients' Attitude to Risk

Mortality and morbidity risk

How concerned are you about the risk of financial loss to you/your beneficiaries/ your business caused by:

1. Untimely death?
Karl and Ulrika: Not concerned.

2. Critical illness/disability?
Karl and Ulrika: Very concerned.

3. Medium- to longer-term sickness/disability?
Karl and Ulrika: Very concerned.

4. Needing long-term care in old age?
Karl and Ulrika: Concerned.

Lump sum investment risk

1. Are you prepared to accept that capital/contributions may fall in value and, if so, with how much of your capital can you afford to risk a short-term fall in the value in pursuit of medium- to long-term growth?
Karl and Ulrika: Yes, up to 20%.

2. Of this amount, how much would you wish to invest in higher-risk investments where there may be the prospect of higher returns but also a risk of long-term capital loss?
Karl and Ulrika: As little as possible.

3. To how much of your capital/contributions do you require access and over what timescale?
Karl and Ulrika: Education fees starting in 2004.

4. How much of your capital/contributions do you need to protect against inflation and over what timescale?
Karl and Ulrika: As much as possible to achieve objectives.

5. How much of your capital/contributions do you wish to generate growth and if so what rate(s) and over what timescale?
Karl and Ulrika: Education fees until needed.

6. Does this apply to any special purposes; if not, please explain any differences in approach?
Karl and Ulrika: N/A.

Regular Savings Investment Risk

7. Are you prepared to accept that capital/contributions may fall in value and, if so, with how much of your capital can you afford to risk a short-term fall in the value in pursuit of medium- to long-term growth?
Karl and Ulrika: Yes, up to 20%.

8. Of this amount, how much would you wish to invest in higher-risk investments where there may be the prospect of higher returns but also a risk of long-term capital loss?
Karl and Ulrika: As little as possible.

9. To how much of your capital/contributions do you require access and over what timescale?
Karl and Ulrika: Education fees for Susannah starting in 2004.

10. How much of your capital/contributions do you need to protect against inflation and over what timescale?
Karl and Ulrika: As much as possible to achieve objectives.

11. How much of your capital/contributions do you wish to generate growth and if so what rate(s) and over what timescale?
Karl and Ulrika: Education fees until needed.

12. Does this apply to any special purposes; if not, please explain any differences in approach?
Karl and Ulrika: N/A.

Client Investment Risk Attitude Summary

Refer to definitions below and insert your name in the appropriate box to indicate your risk attitude to investment risk for each objective.

Risk attitude & investment/asset type	Retirement (pension schemes)	Long-term investment over 15 years	Medium-term investment & savings 5–15 years	Short-term savings up to 5 years
No risk to capital	Karl and Ulrika			Karl and Ulrika
Low risk			Karl and Ulrika	
Modest risk		Karl and Ulrika		
Relatively higher risk				
High risk				

No risk to capital – No risk of capital value and accept possible loss of real value due to inflation.

Low risk – Low risk loss of capital but some inflationary risk to real value or return based on fixed rate.

Modest risk – Generally small risk of real or comparative capital loss in pursuit of longer-term capital growth.

Relatively higher risk – Some risk of real or comparative capital loss in pursuit of longer-term capital growth.

High risk – High risk of capital loss in pursuit of growth.

NET ANNUAL EXPENDITURE ANALYSIS

Name: Karl and Ulrika	Date: 22 May 2002

1. HOUSE

1. HOUSE	2001–2002	If you died	If spouse died	On retirement
Mortgage interest / repayment				
Mortgage protection (not endowment)				
Buildings/contents insurance	200			
Council tax	700			
Decorating and maintenance	300			
Garden maintenance	200			
Television licence and rental				
TOTAL	**1,400**			

2. UTILITIES

2. UTILITIES	2001–2002	If you died	If spouse died	On retirement
Electricity	200			
Gas	200			
Water	140			
Telephone	300			
Oil/Solid Fuel				
TOTAL	**840**			

3. HOUSEKEEPING

3. HOUSEKEEPING	2001–2002	If you died	If spouse died	On retirement
Food / general housekeeping	2,000			
Wines and spirits	1,000			
Eating out	500			
TOTAL	**3,500**			

EXPENDITURE ANALYSIS

4. MOTOR	2001–2002	If you died	If spouse died	On retirement
Petrol/diesel/oil				
Allowance towards replacement				
Servicing				
Insurance				
Road fund licence				
AA/RAC membership				
TOTAL				

5. TRAVEL & LEISURE	2001–2002	If you died	If spouse died	On retirement
Rail/bus fares	1,500			
Holidays (average)	4,000			
Club subscriptions	200			
Entertainment				
Cigarettes/tobacco				
Books/magazines/newspapers	180			
Sports/hobbies				
TOTAL	**5,880**			

EXPENDITURE ANALYSIS

6. PERSONAL	*2001–2002*	*If you died*	*If spouse died*	*On retirement*
a. VARIABLE				
Clothing	*600*			
Presents	*3,000*			
Allowances to children/relatives				
Credit card repayments				
TOTAL VARIABLE	*3,600*			
b. FIXED				
Education expenses				
Maintenance/alimony				
Charitable donations/covenants	*K = 120*			
TOTAL FIXED	*120*			

7. SAVINGS & PERSONAL INSURANCE	*2001–2002*	*If you died*	*If spouse died*	*On retirement*
Investments				
Deposit with bank or building society				
Life assurance				
Income replacement insurance				
Medical expenses insurance				
Pension contributions (as paid)				
TOTAL				

TOTAL	15,340			

Mr and Mrs Harvey Tax Calculations **1st December 2003**

Appendix D – Tax Calculations

Breakdown of Income Tax Calculation for Tax year Ending 5 April 2004

INCOME	Karl (£)	Ulrika (£)	Total (£)	Tax Deducted at Source (%)
Earned Income				
Karl's Pension Income	£ 14,500.00	£ –	£ 14,500.00	
Karl's State Pension Income	£ 3,770.00	£ –	£ 3,770.00	
Ulrika's Pension Income	£ –	£ 10,000.00	£ 10,000.00	
Ulrika's State Pension Income	£ –	£ 2,256.80	£ 2,256.80	
Sub Total	**£ 18,270.00**	**£ 12,256.80**	**£ 30,526.80**	
Investment Income				
Joint Building Society Savings Interest (gross)	£ 3,600.00	£ 3,600.00	£ 7,200.00	20%
Gilts – £5,000 Nominal Stock (gross) (8%)	£ 400.00	£ –	£ 400.00	
Gilts – £5,000 Nominal Stock (gross) (9%)	£ –	£ 450.00	£ 450.00	
Sub Total	**£ 4,000.00**	**£ 4,050.00**	**£ 8,050.00**	
Statutory Total Income	**£ 22,270.00**	**£ 16,306.80**	**£ 38,576.80**	

Reduce age allowance by £1 for every £2 over £18,300. Karl is over by £3,970
Therefore, reduce £6,720 by £1,985 = £4,735
Ulrika's income is under £18,300 and therefore gets the additional age allowance (age 65–74)

	Karl	Ulrika	Total
Less Personal Allowance	£ 4,735.00	£ 6,610.00	
Taxable Income	**£ 17,535.00**	**£ 9,696.80**	
Less			
(0–1,960) @10%	£ 196.00	£ 196.00	
tax at 20% on savings income	£ 800.00	£ 810.00	
(17,535–1960–4000) @ 22% on £11,575 for Karl	£ 2,546.50	£ 811.00	
(9,696.80–1960– 4050) @ 22% on £3,686.80 for Ulrika			
Sub Total	**£ 3,542.50**	**£ 1,817.00**	
less Married Couple Allowance £5,635 @ 10%	£ 564.00		
Total Income Tax Payable	**£ 2,978.50**	**£ 1,817.00**	**£ 4,795.50**
Less tax paid / deducted at source	£ 720.00	£ 720.00	
Total tax due	**£ 2,258.50**	**£ 1,097.00**	**£ 3,355.50**
Average Tax Rate	**16.99%**	**18.74%**	

NOTES
You are a basic rate taxpayer at present

Your total net income after taxation is   **£ 33,781.30**

Mr and Mrs Harvey **Estate Planning** **1st December 2003**

Appendix E – Inheritance Tax Calculations

Assumption

1. Karl has predeceased Ulrika and the situation follows Ulrika's death.
2. Karl has received the inheritance of £70,000.
3. All gifts made are within the annual exemption limits and therefore do not form part of the gross estate.
4. Both Wills make a charitable donation of £20,000 to RNLI which is not chargeable.

Assets	Value (£)
House	£ 125,000.00
Contents / Personal Effects	£ 16,000.00
Bank deposits	£ 270,000.00
Investments	£ **76,424.00**
Total Gross Estate Value	£ **487,424.00**
Deduct Liabilities	£ –
Total Value of Estate on Death	£ **487,424.00**
Deduct	
Business Property Relief	£ -
Agricultural Property Relief	£ -
Charitable Donations	£ 40,000.00
Total Taxable Estate	£ **447,424.00**
Less current nil rate band	£ 255,000.00
Net Chargable Estate	£ **192,424.00**
Tax at 40% payable by the estate	£ **76,969.60**

Mr and Mrs Harvey   **Long Term Care / Special Needs**   **1st December 2003**

Appendix F – Long Term Care Cost Shortfall

Assumption

1. Nursing Care costs £400 per week (source Tax Briefs) in a Nursing Home
2. For individual costings I have assumed costs for occasional assistance of 3 days in your home.
   £75 per day or £100 per day if assistance is needed for both of you.
3. Karl will need care assistance first as he is in poorer health.
4. If you both go into a home I have assumed a contingency of £4,000 each for things not provided by
   the home and increases in fees.
5. You will qualify for the higher rate of Attendance Allowance. Currently, £57.20 per week.
6. You both wish to preserve your estate for James and Susannah and do not wish to deplete your estate
   with high care fees.
7. Your applications following medicals will be successful.

Position if Nursing Care is required	Care for Mr Harvey at home (£)	Care for both of you at home (£)	Care for Mr Harvey in Nursing home (£)	Joint Care in Nursing home (£)
Net joint Income (refer to Appendix C)	£ 33,787.00	£ 33,787.00	£ 33,787.00	£ 33,787.00
Attendance Allowance Higher Rate	£ 2,974.40	£ 5,948.80	£ 2,974.40	£ 5,948.80
Total Income	**£ 36,761.40**	**£ 39,735.80**	**£ 36,761.40**	**£ 39,735.80**
deduct current expenditure	£ 20,352.00	£ 20,352.00	£ 20,352.00	£ 8,000.00 (4)
Net surplus income	**£ 16,409.40**	**£ 19,383.80**	**£ 16,409.40**	**£ 31,735.80**
deduct costs for care	£ 11,700.00	£ 15,600.00	£ 20,800.00	£ 41,600.00
Net shortfall in income	£ –	£ –	**– £ 4,390.60**	**– £ 9,864.20**
If no shortfall what is the Surplus	**£ 4,709.40**	£ 3,783.80	**£ 4,709.00**	
Shortfall for each of you				**– £ 4,932.10**

SUMMARY

You only have a shortfall if either of you or both of you need care in a Nursing Home and my
recommendation is that you plan for this eventuality by implementing long-term care cover that will
pay you the benefit directly rather than the carer or nursing home. This way you have the option to stay
in your home or move into a nursing home.

RECOMMENDATION

Therefore, to consider effecting Long Term Care Plans to cover a shortfall of £5,000 each
The estimated monthly costs (source BUPA Care) are:

Karl	£ 89.75	per month	£ 1,077.00
Ulrika	£ 91.58	per month	£ 1,098.96

These figures are affordable and within your budget

BUPA CARE

Couple's discount is available on premiums
Premiums and Benefits can escalate at RPI subject to a maximum of 15%

....

Mr and Mrs Harvey   **Educational Funding**   **1st December 2003**

Appendix G - School Fees Planning for Susannah

School Year Start	Age of Susannah at Start of Year	Tax Year	Fees Required (£)	Discount Back to today's value	Discounted period
		2003/2004	£ –		
September 2004	4 years 5 months	2004/2005	£ 4,725.00	£ 4,590.00	9 months
September 2005	5 years 5 months	2005/2006	£ 4,961.00	£ 4,635.00	21 months
September 2006	6 years 5 months	2006/2007	£ 5,209.00	£ 4,680.00	33 months
September 2007	7 years 5 months	2007/2008	£ 5,470.00	£ 4,785.00	45 months
September 2008	8 years 5 months	2008/2009	£ 5,743.00	£ 4,825.00	57 months
September 2009	9 years 5 months	2009/2010	£ 6,030.00	£ 4,808.00	69 months
September 2010	10 years 5 months	2010/2011	£ 6,332.00	£ 4,940.00	81 months
Total Required			**£ 38,470.00**	£ 33,263.00	

Assumptions

Fees are £1,500 per term starting Autumn 2004 until Summer 2010.
Fees escalate each year by 5%.
As previously mentioned the calculations can be reviewed should reality prove different.

Discount rates applied:

Deposit Rate   4%
3 year certificates 3.65%
5 year certificates 3.75%

Mr and Mrs Harvey   **Revised Income Tax Calculations**   **1st December 2003**

Appendix H – Revised Tax Calculations

Breakdown of Income Tax Calculation for Tax year Ending 5 April 2004

INCOME	Karl (£)	Ulrika (£)	Total (£)	Tax Deducted at Source (%)
Earned Income				
Karl's Pension Income	£ 14,500.00	£ –	£ 14,500.00	
Karl's State Pension Income	£ 3,770.00	£ –	£ 3,770.00	
Ulrika's Pension Income	£ –	£ 10,000.00	£ 10,000.00	
Ulrika's State Pension Income	£ –	£ 2,256.80	£ 2,256.80	
Sub Total	**£ 18,270.00**	**£ 12,256.80**	**£ 30,526.80**	
Investment Income				
Joint Building Society Savings Interest (gross)	£ 280.00	£ 5,560.00	£ 5,840.00	20%
Gilts – £5,000 Nominal Stock (gross) (8%)	£ 400.00	£ –	£ 400.00	
Gilts – £5,000 Nominal Stock (gross) (9%)	£ –	£ 450.00	£ 450.00	
Sub Total	**£ 680.00**	**£ 6,010.00**	**£ 6,690.00**	
Statutory Total Income	**£ 18,950.00**	**£ 18,266.80**	**£ 37,216.80**	

Reduce age allowance by £1 for every £2 over £18,300. Karl is over by £650
Therefore, reduce £6,720 by £325 = £6,395
Ulrika's income is under £18,300 and therefore gets the additional age allowance (age 65–74)

Less Personal Allowance	£ 6,395.00	£ 6,610.00	
Taxable Income	**£ 12,555.00**	**£ 11,656.80**	
Less			
(0–1,960) @10%	£ 196.00	£ 196.00	
tax at 20% on savings income	£ 136.00	£ 1,202.00	
(12,555–1960–680) @ 22% on £9,915 for Karl	£ 2,181.30	£ 811.00	
(11,657–1960–6010) @ 22% on £3,687 for Ulrika			
Sub Total	**£ 2,513.30**	**£ 2,209.00**	
less Married Couple Allowance £5,635 @ 10%	£ 564.00		
Total Income Tax Payable	**£ 1,949.30**	**£ 2,209.00**	**£ 4,158.30**
Less tax paid / deducted at source	£ 56.00	£ 1,112.00	
Total tax due	**£ 1,893.30**	**£ 1,097.00**	**£ 2,990.30**
Average Tax Rate	15.53%	18.95%	

NOTES
You are a basic rate taxpayer at present

Your total net income after taxation is   **£ 33,058.50**

Mr and Mrs Harvey **Estate Planning** **1st December 2003**

Appendix I – Revised Inheritance Tax Calculations

Assumption

1. House is held as tenants in common.
2. Bank deposits are setup as below.
3. Deed of Variation created for the proceeds of Jim's Will.
4. You have made a gift into an A&M trust to fund Susanna's future Education fees.
5. Both Wills make a charitable donation of £20,000 to RNLI which is not chargeable.

Assets	Karl (£)	Ulrika (£)	Total (£)
House	£ 62,500.00	£ 62,500.00	£ 125,000.00
Contents / Personal Effects	£ 8,000.00	£ 8,000.00	£ 16,000.00
Bank deposits	£ 4,000.00	£ 16,000.00	£ 20,000.00
Building Society Deposits	£ 7,000.00	£ 139,000.00	£ 146,000.00
Investments	£ 37,712.00	£ 38,712.00	£ 76,424.00
Total Gross Estate Value	**£ 119,212.00**	**£ 264,212.00**	**£ 383,424.00**
Deduct Liabilities	£ –	£ -	£ –
Total Value of Estate on Death	**£ 119,212.00**	**£ 264,212.00**	**£ 383,424.00**
Deduct			
Business Property Relief	£ –	£ –	£ –
Agricultural Property Relief	£ –	£ –	£ –
Charitable Donations	£ 20,000.00	£ 20,000.00	£ 40,000.00
Total Taxable Estate	**£ 99,212.00**	**£ 244,212.00**	**£ 343,424.00**
Add any Potentially Exempt Transfers	£ 11,000.00	£ 11,000.00	
Less current nil rate band	£ 255,000.00	£ 255,000.00	
Net Chargeable Estate	**£ –**	**£ –**	
Tax at 40% payable by the estate	**£ –**	**£ –**	

Notes

If Karl dies first the value of his estate currently £99,212 will pass into the discretionary trust created under his Will.

If Ulrika dies first the NRB currently £255,000 will pass into the discretionary trust created under her Will.

The monetary value need not be transferred into the trust as the value could be satisfied as an IOU.

Bibliography

Arnott, Robert, and Bernstein, Peter. 'What Risk Premium is Normal?' *Financial Analysts Journal*, March/April 2002.

Blake, David. *Financial System Requirements for Successful Pension Reform*, published on The Pensions Institute website, June 2003 (**www.pensions-institute.org**).

Brett, Michael. *How to Read the Financial Pages*, Random House, London, 2003.

Brinson, Gary, Hood, L. Randolf, and Beebower, Gilbert. 'Determinants of Portfolio Performance', *Financial Analysts Journal*, July/August 1986.

Dimson, Elroy, Marsh, Paul, and Staunton, Mike. London Business School.

Foreman, A. *The Zurich Tax Handbook*, Pearson, Harlow, 2003.

Grainger, Paul T. *Certified Financial Planner™ Licence: Syllabus and Tuition Manual*, 4th edition, Institute of Financial Planning, Bristol, 2001.

National Association of Pension Funds, Annual Survey 2003.

OECD Labour Force Statistics, 1982–2002: 2003 edition, distributed in the UK by Databeuro Limited (**www.databeuro.com**).

Trow, Stuart. *Bluff Your Way in Economics*, Ravette Publishing, 1996.

Vaitilingam, Romesh. *The Financial Times Guide to Using the Financial Pages*, Financial Times Prentice Hall, 2001.

Philips, S. *The Deloitte & Touche Financial Planning for the Individual*, Gee Publishing, London, 2002.

Index

A-Day 269–70, 296–7, 338
absolute return funds 60, 325
absolute return/performance 78, 325
accident, sickness and unemployment (ASU)
    insurance 211
account aggregation 107, 325
accrual 271, 278, 325
accumulation and maintenance trusts 235, 325
acid test 143, 325
active investment management 62–3, 325
    deployment of active management fees 71
activities of daily living (ADL) tests 101
additional pension 25, 258, 261–2, 325
additional voluntary contributions (AVCs)
    273–4, 325
administration platforms 177–83
advisory management 144, 325
affinity (donation) cards 109
ageing population 25
Allied Steel and Wire (ASW) 269
alpha 70, 172, 325
Alternative Investment Market (AIM) 53,
    326
alternative investments 59–60, 69, 170–4,
    326
    ethical investment 190–1
alternatively secured income (ASI) 311–12,
    326
angels 200, 326
annual bonuses 167–8, 326
annual management charge (AMC) 135, 150,
    288, 326
annual percentage rate (APR) 110–11, 207,
    326

annuities 266, 326
    abolition of compulsory purchase at age
        75, 311–13
    DC pension schemes 286, 301, 302–3,
        303, 304–10
    how conventional annuities work 304–6
    long-term care 101
    mortgage annuities 215–16, 335
    purchased life annuities (PLAs) 123–4,
        215–16, 340
    retirement annuity plans 289, 341
annuitisation 301, 326
annuity rate 304, 326
anticipated bonus rate (ABR) 309, 326
antiques 201
APCIMS/FTSE private investor indices 73–4,
    78–9, 81
appeals 262
asset allocation 67–76
asset backing 143, 326
asset classes 50–62
    characteristics 69
asset share 163, 326
assets, and liabilities 12
Association of British Insurers (ABI) 53, 79,
    153
Association of Investment Trust Companies
    (AITC) 79, 80, 152
Association of Residential Letting Agents
    (ARLA) 213
authorisation 172
automated asset allocation strategy for DC
    293, 294
avoidance, tax 230, 344

balanced portfolio 73–4

band earnings 259, 261, 326

Bank of England 44

bank guarantees 222, 335

banking and banks 106–7

   ethical investment 188

   see also debt

bare trusts 235, 241, 326

base rate tracker mortgage 208

basic state pension (BSP) 25, 258, 260–1,
   326

   deferment of claim 260

   eligibility for 259–60

basic sum assured 167–8, 326

bear market 39, 326

bed and breakfast 233, 326

bed and spouse 233, 327

benchmark indices 190, 327

beneficiaries 235, 327

beta 70, 327

Beveridge Plan 22

bid price 85, 327

blue chips 42, 327

boiler room 31–3, 327

bonds 50, 57–8, 69, 121, 128–30, 327

   assessing bond income 131–4

   comparison with equities and cash 60–2

   corporate 9, 57, 58, 134–5, 238

   Eurobonds 58

   traded bonds 58, 130

   UK bonds 57–8

bottom up approach 62, 327

bubbles 40–1, 327

budget deficit 47

bull market 39, 327

buy-out cost 268, 327

buy-to-let 59, 212–14

call options 56, 327

cap and collar mortgages 208–9

capacity 226

capital asset pricing model (CAPM) 70, 327

capital bonds 120

capital erosion 134

capital gains tax (CGT) 232–4, 327

capital gains tax allowance 231, 232, 233, 327

capital risk 9

capital shares 152, 343

career averaged revalued earnings (CARE)
   schemes 271, 328

carry forward 289, 328

cash 59, 69

   comparison with equities and bonds 60–2

   savings 116–17

   tax-free 276

cash flow planning 12, 328

cash individual savings accounts (ISAs) 118,
   121, 179, 180

cash withdrawal cards 110

cashback 208

CAT-marked products 31, 180, 210, 328

cautious managed funds 151, 170

charge cards 109

chargeable gains 232–3, 327

charitable giving 237

Chartered Insurance Institute (CII) 8

chartists 63

cheque guarantee cards 110

Child Trust Fund 242

children

   investing for 241–2

   pensions for 289–90

children's bonus bonds 119

Citizens Advice Bureau 112

civil offences 32, 328

client agreement 13

coherent allocation 68

collective funds 6, 72, 149–75, 337

   commercial property 214

   costs 150

   performance measurement 79–80

   selecting 157

   see also under individual types of fund

commercial property 59, 69, 214

commission 6–7

commission-free structures 7, 328

Common Entrance Examination 250

commutation 276, 328

companies: impact of the economy on 46–7

company share schemes 146–7

completion 205, 328

concurrency 274, 290, 328

constant protection portfolio insurance
   (CPPI) products 169–70, 328

Consumer Credit Act 1974 107, 110
Consumer Credit Counselling Service
       (CCCS) 112–13
consumer education 34
consumer help organisations 112–13
Consumer Prices Index (CPI) 44–6, 116, 328
consumer protection 111–12
contracted in money purchase schemes
       (CIMPS) 287, 328
contracts for difference (CFDs) 145, 328
contracyclical investment strategy 164, 328
contribution holidays 268, 328
conventional annuities *see* annuities
convertible renewal term assurance 93
convertibles 55–6, 328
corporate bond funds 9, 31, 328
corporate bonds 9, 57, 58, 134–5, 328
correlation 50, 328
correlation coefficient 50–2, 329
cost of living increases 275, 276, 319
Council of Mortgage Lenders (CML) 204
coupon 128, 131–2, 329
covered warrants 55–6, 329
credit 107–13
credit cards 108–10, 329
credit ratings 128–30
Crimes of Persuasion website 32
criminal offences 32, 329
crisis planning 15–16
critical illness insurance 97, 329
cumulative performance 80, 329
current account mortgages (CAMs) 209, 329

day trading 145, 329
debit cards 108–10, 329
debt 107–13
debt consolidation 107, 112, 329
debt management 12, 329
Debt Management Office (DMO) 57–8, 121,
       130
decreasing term assurance 93
default 29, 210, 329
default/lifestyle DC investment 292–4, 329
deferment of BSP 260
deferred pensions 275, 320, 329
defined benefit (DB) occupational pension
       schemes 265–83, 329

contributions 272–7
defined contribution (DC) pension schemes
       188, 266, 267, 270, 285–98, 329
    charges and terms for DC arrangements
       291–2
    contributions 288–9
    and retirement income 291, 299–314
definition of disability 96, 329
deflation 115, 329
demographic statistics 23–5
demutualisation 140, 329
depolarisation 27–8, 330
deposit accounts 116–17
deposits 59, 60–2
    see also cash
derivatives 56, 144–5, 330
designated professional bodies 27, 330
direct debit 95
disability, definition of 96, 329
disability pensions 25
discount (trading at) 86, 142, 330
discount brokers 6, 330
discounted rate mortgages 208
discrete performance 80, 330
discretionary management 144, 330
discretionary trusts 235, 330
distribution bonds 156, 338
distribution funds 151, 170, 330
diversification 47, 170
    overseas 69–70
dividend cover 84, 142, 330
dividend yield 55, 83, 141, 330
dividends 141–2
    reinvestment of 61–2
divorce 280
domestic equities 50, 54–7
domicile 236, 330
donation (affinity) cards 109
downside gearing 30, 330
drawdown 30, 275, 286, 303, 310–13, 333

earnings cap 276, 277, 330
easy access savings account 120
econometrics 45, 330
economy 39–48
    economic indicators 44–6, 330
    how to read economic information 42–4

economy (*continued*)
   impact on companies and share prices 46–7
education fee planning 25, 247–55
efficient frontier 71, 330
efficient markets 71, 330
emergency funds 116–17
employee share ownership schemes 146–7
employers
   income protection schemes 95–6
   PMI 98
endowment mortgages 29–30, 331
endowments 153–4, 331
enduring power of attorney 100, 235, 331
enhanced passive management 63
enhanced protection 278–9, 340
enhanced rate annuities 306–8, 331
Enterprise Investments Scheme (EIS) 173, 331
Equitable Life 162, 165–6
equities 50, 69, 137–48, 331
   CGT and 233–4
   comparing with bonds and cash 60–2
   overseas 50, 57
   UK (domestic) 50, 54–7
   yields compared with gilts 134
equity ISAs 179, 180
equity release 214–17, 331
equity release mortgages 31, 215–16
equity risk premium (ERP) 42–4, 331
escalating annuities 306
estate planning 234–5
ethical investment 185–93, 331
Ethical Investment Research Service (EIRIS) 186–7, 331
Eurobonds 58, 331
evasion, tax 230, 344
exchange of contract 205, 331
exchange-traded funds (ETFs) 63, 71, 135, 146, 331
execution-only 27, 144, 331
executive pension plans (EPPs) 279, 331
executors 238

family income benefit (FIB) 93, 331
family protection benefits 276–7, 294
family residence, buying 204–11

Farm Woodland Premium Scheme 197
fees vs commission 7
film financing 200
final results 140, 331
financial advice 5–8
Financial Ombudsman Service (FOS) 28–9
financial pages, guide to reading 81–6
financial plan
   key elements 13–14
   preparation of 351–6
   purpose and construction of plan 11–12
financial planning
   case study 357–78
   efinition 4
   elements of process 4
   and financial advice 5–8
   multi-disciplinary profession 8
   principles of 3–19
Financial Planning Certificate 27, 331
Financial Reporting Standard 17 (FRS17) 266, 332
Financial Services Act 1986 26
Financial Services Authority (FSA) 26–8, 34, 107, 112, 172, 204, 332
Financial Services Compensation Scheme (FSCS) 29, 332
Financial Services and Markets Act 2000 26, 27, 172
Financial Times 81–6
fine art 201
fixed interest savings certificates 118
fixed rate mortgages 208
fixed rate savings bonds 119
flexible annuities 303, 310, 332
flexible mortgages 209
forestry 196–7
formula maturity value 167, 332
fraud 31–3, 201, 332
free asset ratio 332
free standing AVCs (FSAVCs) 274
freehold 204, 332
friendly society policies 156
FTfm funds ratings 82, 86
FTSE indices 52–3, 138–9
   FTSE 100 52, 74, 139, 332
   FTSE 250 52, 74, 139, 332
   FTSE All-Share 52, 53, 74, 78, 139, 186

FTSE All-Small 53, 332
FTSE Fledgling 53, 139, 332
FTSE SmallCap 52, 74, 139, 189, 332
FTSE techMARK 139, 332
FTSE4Good 139, 186, 190–1, 332
private investor indices (with APCIMS)
    73–4, 78–9, 81
fund supermarkets 181, 332
fundamental analysts 63
funded unapproved retirement benefit
    schemes (FURBS) 277–8, 332
funds of funds (FoFs) 151, 170, 332
funds of hedge funds 60, 172
futures 56, 332

gearing (leverage) 141, 143, 152, 332
gemstones 201
gift aid 237, 333
gifts of quoted stocks and shares 237
gilt edged market makers (GEMMs) 131
gilt-equity yield ratio 61, 333
gilts 9, 50, 57–8, 121, 128, 130–1, 333
    assessing gilt income 131–4
    index linked 58–9, 121–2, 130–1, 132–4,
        334
    price fluctuations in traded gilts 130
    yields compared with other investments 134
gross redemption yield 135, 333
group income protection schemes 95–6
group personal pensions (GPPs) 286–7
growth investing 64, 333
growth portfolio 73–4
guaranteed annuity rate (GAR) 165–6, 333
guaranteed income bonds (GIBs) 122–3, 333
guaranteed period 305–6
guaranteed products 168–70, 333, 340

headline inflation 44, 333
hedge funds 59–60, 171–2, 174, 333
high risk investor strategies 144–6
high yield (junk) bonds 128, 333, 335, 343
higher earners 277–9
higher education 250–3
Higher Education Grant 252–3
hire purchase 108, 333
historical context 22–6
HIV/AIDS 94

home income plans (HIPs) 215, 215–16, 333
home reversion 215, 216–17, 333

illegal activities 33–4
impaired life annuities 306–8, 333
income bonds 119
income drawdown 30, 275, 286, 303,
    310–13, 333
income portfolio 73–4
income protection insurance 95–6, 333
income shares 152, 343
income tax allowances 231–2, 333
increasing term assurance 93
independent financial advisers 27, 334
index linked gilts 58–9, 121–2, 130–1,
    132–4, 334
index-linked savings certificates 116, 118–19
index tracking (passive management) 63,
    135, 338
indexation allowance 233, 334
indexed bond funds 71
indices
    comparison with 78
    FTSE indices see FTSE indices
individual savings accounts (ISAs) 134,
    178–81
    cash 118, 121, 179, 180
    contribution rules 179
    self-select 144, 179, 180–1, 342
    taxation 116
industry-wide pension schemes 271–2, 337
inefficient markets 71, 334
inflation 44–6, 117, 334
    comparing performance with 78
inflation risk 9
inflation shock 61, 334
information
    guide to reading financial pages 81–6
    how to read economic information 42–4
    provided by listed companies 140
    real-time market information 145, 340
    sources 5
inheritance tax (IHT) 93, 234–5, 334
inheritance tax allowance 231, 234, 334
initial commission 6, 334
Inland Revenue 230, 240
    see also taxation

insider dealing/trading 34, 334
Institute of Financial Planning (IFP) 4
Institute of Financial Services 8
insurance
  life insurance investment bonds 153–5,
    335
  mortgage related 210–11
  protection insurance 91–104
  school fee planning 248, 249
integrated pension schemes 260–1, 275, 334
interest cover 143, 334
interest free credit 108
interest-only mortgages 207, 215–16, 334
interest in possession trusts 235, 334
interest rates 44, 46, 117, 334
  risk-based 108
interim results 140, 334
intermediaries 5–6, 334
intestacy 237, 238–9, 335
  distribution of an estate under the laws of
    intestacy 239
inverse (negative) correlation 50, 337
investment account 120
investment bonds 153–5, 335
investment grade bonds 128, 130, 335
investment-linked annuities 303, 308–10,
    335
Investment Management Association (IMA)
    54, 79, 151
investment styles 62–4
investment term 10, 61, 335
investment trusts 151–3, 335
  prices in financial pages 86
  split capital see split capital investment
    trusts
Islamic (Shariah) finance 189, 335

joint life annuities 306
joint life policies 93, 335
junk (high yield) bonds 128, 333, 335, 343

labour market 23–5
land registry fees 206
large cap 63, 335
leasehold 204, 335
legacies 237, 335
lending criteria 205–6

letters of credit 222, 335
letting agents 213
level term assurance 92–3
leverage (gearing) 141, 143, 152, 332
leveraged investors 41, 335
liabilities, assets and 12
life assurance 92–5, 210
life assurance ISAs 179, 180
life assurance premium relief (LAPR) 30
life expectancy 23–4, 300
  annuities for shorter life expectancy 306–8
life insurance investment bonds 153–5, 335
life interest trusts 235, 334
lifestyle DC investment 293–4, 329
lifetime allowance 269, 278, 335
lifetime mortgages 215–16, 335
limited liability 225
limited price indexation (LPI) 275, 276, 319
listed companies 55, 172–3
  information provision 140
  Lloyd's quoted companies 225
living costs loans 251–2
Lloyd's of London 221–8
  how it works 222–3
  investment opportunities 225–7
  reform 223–5
Lloyd's vehicles (ILVs) 225–6, 335
loan-to-value ratio 206, 335
local education authorities (LEAs) 251–2, 253
London International Financial Futures
    Exchange (LIFFE) 56, 145
Long Term Capital Management 171
long-term care (LTC) 100–2
long-term care insurance 100–1, 335
long-term care investment plan 102
lower earnings limit 259, 337

Maersk 268
managed care 99
managed funds 151, 170, 336
  FT managed funds service 84–5
managers of managers 151, 336
market capitalisation 52, 63–4, 84, 138, 336
market crashes 40–1
market cycles 41–2, 47
market makers 167, 336
market price 82, 131–2

market risk (systematic risk) 70, 343

market timing 171, 336

market value adjuster (MVA) 163–4, 336

married couple's pension 260

married woman's stamp 259, 336

maturity (redemption date) 128, 336, 340

maxi-ISAs 179

maximum investment plans (MIPs) 153–4, 336

mean expected outcome 68–9, 336

means-tested benefits 23, 24, 336

medical examination 94

mid cap 63–4, 336

mini-ISAs 118, 179

Minimum Funding Requirement (MFR) 267, 268, 336

minimum income guarantee (MIG) 260, 336

mis-selling 26, 29–33, 336
    response to 31–3

Mississippi Bubble 40

mitigation 230, 336, 344

model portfolios 73–4, 78–9, 81

money laundering 33, 336

moratorium clauses 99, 336–7

morbidity 12, 337

mortality 12, 337

mortality cross-subsidy 301, 302, 337

mortgage annuities 215–16, 335

mortgage deed 204–5, 337

mortgage indemnity insurance 210, 337

mortgage interest relief at source (MIRAS) 218, 337

mortgages 204–11, 213, 337

multi-employer pension schemes 271–2, 337

multi-manager funds 170, 293, 337

mutual (collective) funds *see* collective funds

mutual status 140, 337

Namecos 225, 227, 337

Names 222, 223–4, 225, 337

National Association of Pension Funds (NAPF) 54

National Debtline 112–13

National Health Service (NHS) 98

national insurance contributions (NICs) 22–3, 258, 337
    contribution record 258–9

National Savings & Investments (NS&I) 116, 117–20, 337

negative (inverse) correlation 50, 337

negative equity 41, 337

negative ethical screening 187, 337

net asset value (NAV) 86, 141, 142, 152, 337

net relevant earnings 287, 337

net rental income 212–13, 338

net worth statement 13, 14, 338

new issues 140

NHS and Community Care Act 1993 100

nominal 128, 131–2, 338

non-correlation 50, 60, 338

non-distribution bonds 156, 338

non-qualifying policies 155, 340

non-systematic risk 70, 338

non-tangible assets 27, 338

nursing/care homes 100–2

occupational pension schemes 302
    'crisis' 266–8
    defined benefit 265–83, 329
    integrated pension schemes 260–1, 275, 334
    retiring abroad 319–20
    see also defined contribution schemes

October 1987 crash 40–1, 42

offer price 85, 338

Office of Fair Trading (OFT) 107

offset mortgages 209, 338

offshore 156, 338

offshore investment bonds 156, 338

open architecture 157, 338

open-ended investment companies (OEICs) 150–1, 153, 338

open market option (OMO) 300, 305, 338

options 56–7, 338

ordinary shares 55

overseas assignments 316–18, 320

overseas equities 50, 57

overseas markets 69–70, 73

overseas property 212

passive management (index tracking) 63, 135, 338

pay-as-you-go (PAYG) 23, 338

payment of pensions abroad 319

payment protection insurance (PPI) 111–12, 210–11

payroll giving 237

peer group 78

pension ages 258

pension forecasts 262

pension fund surpluses 267

Pension Protection Fund (PPF) 268

pension statements 294–5

pension tax simplification (A-Day) 269–70, 296–7, 338

pension transfers 274–5, 320

pension unlocking 275, 339

pensionable pay 287, 338

pensioners' guaranteed income bonds 116, 119

pensions 25

  DB pension schemes 265–83, 329

  DC pension schemes 188, 266, 267, 270, 285–98, 329

  ethical investment and pension schemes 188

  overseas assignments 316–17

  retirement income and DC schemes 291, 299–314

  retiring abroad 318–21

  state pensions 257–63

Pensions Act 1995 267

Pensions Act 2004 268–9

Pensions Advisory Service 29

Pensions Management Institute (PMI) 8

Pensions Regulator 269

pensions tax credit 260, 338

performance

  impact of ethical screening on 189–90

  measurement and monitoring 77–88

permanent income bearing shares (PIBs) 123, 339

personal equity plans (PEPs) 178, 339

Personal Finance Education Group (pfeg) 34

personal lifetime allowances 269, 278, 335

personal pension term assurance 93

personal pensions 30, 287–8, 302, 339

  choosing a personal pension 290–1

  contributions to 288–9

  leaving the fund in 303–4

retiring abroad 319–20

personal tax allowances and exemptions 230–5

phased drawdown 310–13, 339

phased retirement 286, 310–13, 339

polarisation 27, 339

political context 22–6

portfolio measurement 73–4, 78–9

positive correlation 50, 339

positive ethical screening 187, 339

potentially exempt transfers (PETs) 93, 234, 339

pound-cost averaging 157, 339

precipice bonds 30, 339

preference shares 55, 339

pre-funded LTC insurance 100–1

premium (trading at) 86, 142, 339

premium bonds 118, 339

pre-tax profit margin 143, 339

price/earnings (P/E) ratio 62, 83, 142, 340

price fluctuations 130

primary protection 278, 340

private education 248–50

primary threshold 259, 340

private equity 59–60, 172–4, 340

private income protection insurance 96

private investor indices 73–4, 78–9, 81

private medical insurance (PMI) 97–9, 340

professional indemnity insurance 29, 340

property 59, 69, 203–20

protected products 168–70, 333, 340

protected rights 291, 340

protection insurance 91–104

public sector borrowing requirement (PSBR) 46–7, 340

purchased life annuities (PLAs) 123–4, 215–16, 340

put options 56, 340

qualifying policies 155, 340

quantitative management 63

quoted stocks and shares, gifts of 237

real return 9, 340

real-time market information 145, 340

recommendations 14

recoupment schedule 200, 340

recovery charge 270, 340
redemption date (maturity) 128, 336, 340
reduction in yield (RIY) 150, 340–1
regular premium 7, 341
regulated products 31–3
regulation 26–34
  current regulatory regime 26–9
  property 212
  tangible assets 196
Regulatory Intelligence Agency (RIA) 33
relative return/performance 78, 341
remortgaging 209–10
remuneration 6–8
repayment mortgages 206–7, 341
residence 236, 341
Retail Prices Index/Inflation (RPI) 44, 45,
  46, 116, 341
retirement annuity plans (RAPs) 289, 341
retirement income 291, 299–314
  objectives 300–1
  options for DC investors 291, 302–13
retirement pensions see pensions
retiring abroad 318–21
return on capital 144, 341
reversion annuities 216, 333
reversion plans 215, 216–17
reweighting a portfolio 72–3
risk 341
  assessment 10
  individual's risk profile 8–10
risk-based interest rates 108
risk management 12, 341
roll-up mortgages 215–16
rump gilts 131
running off period 223, 341
running yield 135, 341

Safe Home Income Plans Company (SHIP)
  215
salary exchange/sacrifice 272–3, 278, 341
Sandler, Ron 31
save as you earn (SAYE) 147
savings 115–25
  mortgage related 211
scams 31–3, 201
scheme-specific funding requirement 269,
  341

screening, ethical 186–8
  impact on performance 189–90
Scottish Limited Partnerships 225, 227, 341
second homes 211
secondary markets 166–7
sector classifications 139–40, 341
secured loans 204–5, 341
securities 50, 341
Securities and Investments Board (SIB) 26,
  342
self-assessment tax returns 239–41
self-certification mortgages 206, 342
self-invested personal pensions (SIPPs) 275,
  295–6, 304
self-investment 280, 342
self-regulation 26, 342
self-regulatory organisations 26, 342
self-select ISAs 144, 179, 180–1, 342
settlor 235, 342
share option schemes 146–7, 342
share prices
  impact of the economy on 46–7
  information in the *Financial Times* 81–4
share valuation 140–1
  indicators 141–4
shared appreciation mortgages 209, 342
shareholder activism 53–4, 342
shareholder perks 140
shares 50, 342
  buying and selling 144
  CGT and 233–4
  classes of 55
  gifts of quoted stocks and shares 237
  see also equities
Shariah (Islamic) finance 189, 335
short selling 171, 342
single life policies 93, 342
single premium 7, 342
sixtieths schemes 271, 342
small cap 64, 342
small self-administered schemes (SSASs)
  279–80, 342
smoothed managed funds 165, 342
smoothing 162, 163, 164, 342
social context 22–6
social security benefits 22, 23, 24, 25, 95,
  217, 259

socially responsible investment (SRI) 185–93, 331
Society of London Theatre (SOLT) 200
solvency measure 269
Sotheby's 201
South Sea Bubble 40
split capital investment trusts 30, 152–3, 343
  stepped preference shares of 123, 343
spouses, pensions for 289
spread betting 145, 343
spread trusts 225, 343
stakeholder pension schemes 270, 287–9
stamp duty 206
Standard & Poor's credit ratings 128–30
standard variable rate 207, 208, 343
star managers 71–2
state earnings related pension scheme (SERPS) 25, 258, 261–2, 343
  see also state second pension
state incapacity benefit 95
state pensions 257–63
  retiring abroad 318–19
state school admissions 248
state second pension (S2P) 258, 262, 343
  contracting out of 276, 290
  see also state earnings related pension scheme
statistical distribution of outcomes 68–9, 343
statutory money purchase illustration (SMPI) 286, 294–5, 343
statutory sick pay 95
stepped preference shares 123, 343
stochastic modelling 68–9, 343
stock selection 62
stocks 50, 343
  gifts of quoted stocks and shares 237
store cards 110
structured capital-at-risk products (Scarps) 168–70
structured products 9, 343
Student Loans Company (SLC) 250, 252
sub-investment grade bonds 128, 333, 335, 343
surrender value 154, 166–7
syndicates 222–3, 226, 343
systematic risk (market risk) 70, 343

tangible assets 27, 195–202, 343
taper relief 233, 343
tax avoidance 230, 344
tax-efficient wrappers 68, 69, 150, 177–83, 344
tax equalisation 318, 344
tax evasion 230, 344
tax-exempt special savings accounts (TESSAs) 120–1, 178, 344
tax-free cash 276
tax mitigation 230, 336, 344
taxation 72, 229–45
  buy-to-let 212–13
  equity release 217
  life assurance policies 154–5
  pension tax simplification 269–70, 296–7, 338
  personal allowances and exemptions 230–5
  retirement abroad 320–1
  savings 116
  unit and investment trusts 153
  wine 199
technical analysts 63
term assurance 92–3, 344
terminal bonus 168, 344
tertiary education 25, 250–3
TESSA-only ISA (TOISA) 120–1
theatre 199–200
tied agents 27, 344
TMT bubble (technology, media and telecom shares) 40, 344
top down approach 62, 344
top slicing relief 155, 344
total charge for credit (TCC) 110, 111, 344
total expense ratio (TER) 146, 150, 344
total return 9, 168–9, 344
tradable indices 190–1
traded bonds 58, 130
traded endowment policies (TEPs) 154, 166–8, 344
traded gilts 130
trail commission 6, 344
transfer value (TV) 275, 344
trustees 235, 238, 345
trusts 235, 345

UK (domestic) equities 50, 54–7

unapproved company pension schemes 277–8
underlying inflation 44, 345
underwater shares 146, 345
unfunded unapproved retirement benefit schemes (UURBS) 277–8, 345
unit trusts 150–1, 153, 345
universal benefits 23, 345
university fees 25, 251, 252–3
unlimited liability 222, 224, 225, 345
unregulated (tangible) assets 27, 195–202
unsecured lending 107, 345
upper earnings limit 259, 337

value investing 64, 345
venture capital trusts (VCTs) 60, 173–4, 345
vesting 304, 345

waiver of premium insurance 97
Wall Street Crash 1929 40
warrants 55–6, 345

welfare state 22–5
whole of life plans 93–4, 345
wills, making 237–9
wind up 266–7, 345
    priority order on 269
wine 197–9
with profits annuities 309–10, 345
with profits funds 162–6, 309, 345
WM Company, The 78–9
Woodland Grant Scheme 197
working abroad 316–18, 320
wrap accounts 181, 346

yields 85
    comparing equities, bonds and cash 60–2
    corporate bonds 135
    gilts compared with equities 134

zeros (zero dividend preference shares) 152, 346